Advance Praise for
Becoming a Good Relative

"We are living in times that make it ever so obvious that the American legacy has warped our moral compass. In the best of worlds, we would embrace the universal humanity of all people and treat each other with respect, compassion and kindness. Hilary Giovale unpacks the legacies of historical harm that continue to afflict American society and shows us a way forward toward healing. Her lens is informed by indigenous concepts that encourage harmony between one another and the planet we call home. This book is for people who want to be better and do better for the sake of generations to come."

—**Sharon Leslie Morgan**, Founder, Our Black Ancestry,
and Co-Author of *Gather at the Table: The Healing Journey
of a Daughter of Slavery and a Son of the Slave Trade*

"In *Becoming a Good Relative*, with an unflinching gaze Giovale offers her own story as a pathway for settlers to reach into their own stories for the tools they need to become whole. Being a good relative begins with knowing yourself. This book is a beautiful invitation to accept and transform personal and collective settler histories and live alongside Indigenous peoples."

—**Patty Krawec**, Ojibwe Anishinaabe/Ukrainian
Author of *Becoming Kin: An Indigenous Call to
Unforgetting the Past and Reimagining Our Future*

"Colonizers have been dismembering the language and sacred traditions of countless groups of people for millennia. The cynical believe that this has become the status quo; that there is nothing we can do but forget the past and move on. However, there are others who are rising up to challenge these beliefs. They are devoting their lives to re-membrance.

Hilary Giovale is one such person. In her groundbreaking book, *Becoming a Good Relative*, she encourages us to re-member who we have come from; to re-member our ancestral treasures; to honour the elders among us who are breathing new life into the language, songs, and stories of those who came before us.

Hilary's voice is urgently needed, particularly at this time in our history, when innumerable people are struggling to find meaning, connection, and healing."

Sìne McKenna, Scots Gaelic Songs
and Stories Teacher (ancestralfire.ca)

"Through the journey of *Becoming a Good Relative*, Hilary Giovale initiates white people into the spirit and earthly work of stepping into their collective power to dream and to build a different way of living, in harmony with the earth, manifesting their deepest innate wisdom in healing, repairing, and co-creating a new life with our indigenous family, relatives. As an indigenous person, Nahua (Aztec and Toltec), I couldn't put the book down. Drawing on extensive research and the intimate depths of personal exploration, Hilary provides knowledge and hope filled actions that present and future generations of white settlers can use to reclaim their full humanity through processes of truth telling and healing."

—**Dr. Anita Sanchez**, Nahua (Aztec and Toltec),
Award-Winning Author of *The Four Sacred
Gifts: Indigenous Wisdom for Modern Times*

"Hilary earnestly, honestly, and humbly shares her journey of truthfully facing her life of privilege. In the journey shared herein, she uncovers hidden family secrets. To write this book, Hilary literally climbed, fasted, and prayed in sacred places. All the while she was open to mentors, some of whom serendipitously showed up to guide her. She is bold, courageous, and most timely in sharing this work of reconciliation.

Bahozho—feeling both happy and hopeful, knowing the Holy Ones have touched and reanimated the soul of a person, a woman of open mindedness and character."

—**Steven A. Darden**, Diné Traditional Practitioner

"With a voice of intuitive compassion, *Becoming a Good Relative* will open your heart's eyes. This book offers a physical and spiritual prescription for the awakening paradigm shift that is calling all of us into Divine Alignment. Hilary has been welcomed into the ancient ceremonies of Indigenous cultures. She has come to understand the disruption of the sacred natural order of the Universe and its remedy: the principle that everything is related and connected."

—**Basil Brave Heart**, Oglala Lakota Elder, Korean War Combat Veteran, Boarding School Survivor, and Author of *The Spiritual Journey of a Brave Heart*

"In her authentic reflection and assessment of her privilege, Hilary Giovale has done the hard work of taking off her mask. By using raw testimony and honesty, Hilary not only challenges the reader to confront their privilege, choices, and power; but *Becoming a Good Relative* offers an invitation for collective liberation. Hilary has beautifully and carefully crafted an offering—a model of how we can create a just economy."

—**Dr. Aisha Nyandoro**, CEO, Springboard to Opportunities

"*Becoming a Good Relative* is a profound exploration. With a fearless spirit and authentic boldness, Giovale embarks on an introspective journey, unraveling the intricate layers of her ancestral past to forge a path illuminated by truth. She meticulously unveils layers of her family's past, exposing the complexities, pain, and deliberate lies that have shaped generations.

What distinguishes this book is the author's unwavering commitment to honesty and authenticity. She artfully intertwines personal anecdotes, historical insights, and reflections, weaving a rich tapestry that illuminates the importance of acknowledging the pain caused by deception—pain that reverberates through generations, leaving an indelible impact on our collective ancestry.

This book invites readers to participate in a profound healing process. Giovale eloquently emphasizes the significance of love, intention, and responsible action as pivotal forces in this transformative journey towards healing. Her narrative not only confronts the past but also advocates for a future where these values take precedence.

Becoming a Good Relative is a masterpiece of storytelling and introspection. This book is an essential read for anyone seeking a deeper understanding of ancestral legacies and the transformative power of embracing truth for healing."

—**Beatrice A. Woody**, Global Philanthropic Strategist

"Many ancestral journeys start with genealogy and finish with a trip to ancestral lands, yet Hilary didn't stop there. She kept digging, in the land under her feet. While navigating much-needed, difficult questions and conversations, her journey is supported by deep community, ancestral figures, and liminal experiences. This is the meaningful and transformational work the world needs, rooted in action while engaging the head, heart, and hand."

—**Jude Lally**, Scottish Cultural Activist and Artist (pathoftheancestralmothers.com)

"This is a profoundly brave book. In sharing her journey, in all its pain and revelation and imperfectness, Hilary has woven both a reckoning and a calling-home. May her offering embolden many more of us with white settler lineages to do the work of becoming good relatives—work that is essential for a shared future of wellbeing and liberation."

—**Joanna Levitt Cea**, Co-Author of *Beloved Economies: Transforming How We Work*

"Hilary Giovale models courageous exploration of truth telling, healing, and repair. She boldly amplifies voices and wisdom from sources that are often marginalized. Her humility and courage are refreshing and inspirational. *Becoming a Good Relative* is a must read for anyone grappling with their own relationship with cultural identity, race, and colonization. Giovale reaches those of us who are desperate for new paradigms of living rooted in right-relationship."

—**Kevin Eppler**, Co-Founder, White Men for Racial Justice

"Audre Lorde said the master's tools will never dismantle the master's house. *Becoming a Good Relative* is an invitation for those of us born and raised in the master's house to walk out the door, take a long, slow breath, humbly listen to the people and lands outside, and let our hearts break open with their stories of what we and our ancestors have done. As we unravel the untruths we've been taught about our nation's history, we will find tools of liberation we never could have imagined from inside. For Hilary Giovale these have included learning, "wit(h)nessing" and then truth-telling about racial and colonial violence; building a ceremonial relationship with the natural world; reclaiming European ancestral songs and languages; feeding and forgiving the ancestors; and giving generously of her love, labor and money in the spirit of gratitude and repair. Her story is an invitation to join her. She's holding the door open for all of us."

—**Morgan Curtis**, Ancestors and Money Coach
and Author of *Decolonial Dames of America*

"This book resonates with healing and pragmatic, usable counsel on all octaves—from individual to societal, across cultures and ethnicities, from human to Mother Earth and whatever land we're each Indigenous to, and from ancestral to present time to future generations.

Hilary's four-year journey describes in detail how she faced—grappled with—and ultimately integrated and embodied nuanced and painful learnings around white supremacy, privilege, guilt, the impacts of colonization and intergenerational trauma, having slaveholding ancestors, awakening to power differentials, and more. Her story benefits tremendously from the power of her dedicated and devotional listening—to guidance from dreams, the land, her body's wisdom, and her many mentors. And from her consistent cultural humility and generosity of spirit. With unflinching dedication, perseverance, and compassion, and accompanied by terrific resources to deepen readers' learnings, this book humanizes Turtle Island's and Giovale's own brutal historical legacies, resulting in a journey that's been blessed by many relatives and alchemized by love."

—**Nina Simons**, Author of *Nature, Culture & the Sacred* and Co-Founder, Bioneers

"Hilary Giovale's book, *Becoming a Good Relative*, comes from a place of individual and collective blood memories of acknowledging, healing, and honoring. It is a manifestation of one woman's ongoing journey to align heart and spirit. It offers a guide to first steps in committing to living in Right Relation with our past, present, and future generations."

—**Tia Oros Peters**, CEO, Seventh
Generation Fund for Indigenous Peoples

"As an Indigenous Tewa Elder, I identify with Hilary's lived experiences and share her unconditional love for all our relatives. Her open and honest sharing about who she is and her search for meaning is an act of kindness. *Becoming a Good*

Relative offers a pathway for settler-colonial peoples to comprehend other ways of seeing and feeling the world, and to unlearn the deeply misguided values inherited from a culture of violence. I highly recommend Hilary's book and the practices within it as a tool to help reclaim soulfulness and grow a culture of peace and caring love for self and others."

—**Elder Kathy WanPovi Sanchez**, Sayain Circle of
Grandmothers Coordinator, Tewa Women United

"*Becoming a Good Relative* is a call for all people to come together and honor each other as humans. The author bravely examines her positionality within the cultural and racial divides created to maintain the White supremacy that hurts us all. This beautifully written book shares Hilary's personal journey to wholeness starting from examining early cross-cultural connections to the long-term impacts of ancestors, and how she came to become a true friend, sister, and ally through the lessons learned. A page-turner, I love the honesty and humility expressed in the stories she shares."

—**Alexis Bunten**, Award-Winning Author of "*So, How
Long Have You Been Native?*" *Life as an Alaska Native
Tour Guide, Keepunumuk: Weeâchumun's Thanksgiving
Story, What Your Ribbon Skirt Means to Me: Deb Haaland's
Historic Inauguration*, and several other publications.

"Everyone who considers themselves white, and those who have or work with wealth should read this book. Hilary's journey to tap into her own vocation through spirituality is awe inspiring. In a world built on and still profiting from slavery of our past and present, historical and ongoing genocide, as well as other forms of incomprehensible settler violence, Hilary offers the most sane advice—to lean into that which gives life: community, our planet, and the ways of being interconnected. The sharing of Hilary's journey is beautiful and sorely overdue. The world needs, now more than ever, to know what it means to be a good relative."

—**Dr. David Ragland**, Co-Founder and Co-ED,
The Truth Telling Project; Director, Grassroots
Reparations Campaign; Lecturer on Reparations
as Spiritual Practice, Harvard Divinity School

"Hilary Giovale and her writing are a breath of fresh air and a clarion call to white folks committed to justice and solidarity. Rather than seeking to become anti-racist in thought, she has done the hard, deeper, alchemic work of what truly lies ahead of us—an undoing of spiritual and mental conditioning that will lead to true liberation. We have all been subjected to living a reality created by white manufactured imagination born from millennia of trauma....It is a dingy and grim dream when we pull back the veil. But if we want to live in a different world and create new futures, we must first return to our ancestors, to our memories, to our truths and confront them as they are. The ancestors have returned in us and through us, and as we reclaim their stories, we free our lineages to heal and move through the world from wellness rather than pain and trauma. Hilary's writing is a potent reminder and call to action for us all to return."

—**Brittíni Gray-Chiquillo**, Founder
and ED, Mama Scrap's Incorporated

"Hilary Giovale's stunning book *Becoming a Good Relative: Calling White Settlers toward Truth, Healing, and Repair* exposes the illusory lines that settler colonialism has drawn between countless cultures and civilizations, and between humans and the rest of the natural world. The heartfelt stories, raw vulnerability, and hard truths contained in these pages move the reader to a breaking point, where instead of being knocked down they find themselves breaking open and moving toward a more balanced possibility of relationship with the entire living world. This is the story of a woman's journey into the devastating peril and privilege of whiteness. Though these stories do not shy from the truth, there is more here than the typical polemic that one might expect. There is also a purposeful reaching back that connects her contemporary reality to the Earth-based wisdom that her ancestors held before experiencing their own colonized histories. At the end, we are delivered into the galvanizing hands of Lyla June Johnston, who invites us back into the One Great Circle and asks us to stand together at a crossroads where deeply rooted ancestral wisdom is translated into tangible living knowledge that can guide us into the future."

—**Sherri Mitchell** (Weh'na Ha'mu' Kwasset—She
Who Brings the Light), Author of *Sacred Instructions:
Indigenous Wisdom for Living Spirit-Based Change*

"It is very timely that in this historical moment, when the horrors of settler colonialism are on full display, Hilary is sharing with us her very personal story of what healing and decolonial action look like from the perspective of being a settler. Any settler's story begins with a disconnection from their own ancestors, their own belonging. Hilary's story helps other settlers imagine what reconnection can look like for us in the context of forging alliances across the settler-Indigenous divide, and really showing up—moving resources, taking action, and being a dependable ally—for decolonization in the world."

—**Eleanor Hancock**, Director and Founder, White Awake

"While there are other books that explore the fraught history of the United States and the impacts of colonization on the continent's original inhabitants, *Becoming a Good Relative* is unique for its brutal honesty. Few Anglo authors are willing to turn the mirror on themselves and face how centuries of settler colonialism has benefitted them personally in the way Hilary has done with this heartfelt, courageous memoir. A topic that could be overwhelming is made thoroughly enjoyable as she takes us on her healing journey where she is mentored by Indigenous knowledge keepers and shares wisdom about how European colonizers can take actions to heal the harms caused by their ancestors. Ultimately, this book teaches us something hopeful and beautiful—that true happiness is not about having it all, but about giving it all away."

—**Annette McGivney**, Author of *Pure Land: A True Story of Three Lives, Three Cultures, and the Search for Heaven on Earth*, Winner of the National Outdoor Book Award

"Sometimes it seems that all the problems in our history are coming back to haunt us and it's hard to see how to change our course. Besides being a pleasure to read, *Becoming a Good Relative* will be a resource for many settler-Americans who are ready to look back for answers. I have been on much of this journey in my own way, and I know its challenges, discouragement, and temptations to hide, bypass, or give up. I'm full of admiration for how Hilary handles these challenges, gradually peeling away the social conditioning that came with her upbringing. This brave and honest book brought me a lightness of spirit I wasn't expecting."

—**Louise Dunlap**, Active Elder and Author of *Inherited Silence: Listening to the Land, Healing the Colonizer Mind* (www.louisedunlap.net)

"How does a white person acknowledge the participation of one's ancestors in enslaving black peoples; in being complicit in land-taking and other imperial and colonial projects, without being stuck in guilt and shame? What is beautiful about Hilary's book is her transparency in writing about the challenges of being on this path - the embodied aspects of the emotional, psychological, spiritual, physical, cognitive aspects of unlearning whiteness. She joins a growing decolonial movement of folks who are courageously facing the historical wrongs that their ancestors have participated in and making sure that the unearned privileges that have accrued from their actions will not be passed on to future generations."

—**Leny Mendoza Strobel**, Founding Elder, The
Center for Babaylan Studies, and Editor of *Babaylan:*
Filipinos and the Call of the Indigenous

"Giovale's insights into the interplay between philanthropy and social change offer a compelling approach to building community. By highlighting the inherent power dynamics embedded within philanthropy, she encourages readers to reimagine more equitable and sustainable models of community engagement and solidarity. *Becoming a Good Relative* is a timely invitation to embark on a journey of self-discovery, accountability, and collective healing."

—**Erika Danina Williams**, Philanthropic
Advisor, RSF Social Finance

"From the vantage point of the Earth and its sacred waters, Giovale's work clearly explains that challenging the assumptions of hierarchy, extractive logic, and White supremacy is in the interest of every one of us: all of humanity, and all of creation. At a moment when ecological overshoot evidenced by climate change makes it clear that we all bear the consequences of colonial logic and the fallacy of perpetual growth, *Becoming a Good Relative* signals a way to change course."

—**Sarah Augustine**, ED, The Coalition to Dismantle
the Doctrine of Discovery, and Author of *The Land is*
Not Empty and *So We and Our Children May Live*

"Readers of this book will embark on an unlearning and learning adventure—unlearning the status quo created by the harm inflicted upon Indigenous peoples by colonial systems, and learning to heal the wounds of colonialism through relationality, respect, and personal reparations."

—**Edgar Villanueva**, Author of *Decolonizing Wealth* and Founder and CEO, Decolonizing Wealth Project and Liberated Capital

"*Becoming a Good Relative* is a prayer and manual for societal change, urging us to reexamine our relationships with history, culture, and each other. Hilary's exploration serves as a blueprint for engaging in the world with reverence, love, and a deep sense of responsibility towards fostering equitable relationships across differences."

—**Taij Kumarie Moteelall**, Intersectional Feminist Writer, Director, and Producer

Becoming a Good Relative

Calling White Settlers toward
Truth, Healing, and Repair

Becoming a Good Relative

Calling White Settlers toward Truth, Healing, and Repair

Hilary Giovale

GREEN WRITERS PRESS | *Brattleboro, Vermont*

Printed in Canada.

10 9 8 7 6 5 4 3 2 1

Green Writers Press is a Vermont-based publisher whose mission is to spread a message of hope and renewal through the words and images we publish. Throughout we will adhere to our commitment to preserving and protecting the natural resources of the earth. To that end, a percentage of our proceeds will be donated to environmental and social-activist groups. Green Writers Press gratefully acknowledges support from individual donors, friends, and readers to help support the environment and our publishing initiative.

GReen
wRiTers
press

Giving Voice to Writers & Artists Who Will Make the World a Better Place

Green Writers Press | Brattleboro, Vermont

www.greenwriterspress.com

ISBN: 979-8-9876631-7-2

COVER ILLUSTRATION BY ASHLEY MATELSKI

COVER DESIGN BY BRYN KRISTI

PRINTED ON ACID-FREE 100% POSTCONSUMER-WASTE PAPER BY FRIESENS CORPORATION.

Land Acknowledgment

THIS BOOK was written at the foot of a sacred mountain, a female being of kinship, that stands within the traditional homelands of Diné, Hopi, Havasupai, Hualapai, Apache, Yavapai, and Paiute Peoples, as well as several Pueblos. The mountain is known by many names, including *Dokoʼoʼosłííd* (Diné), *Nuvaʼtukyaʼovi* (Hopi), and *Wiihaagynpacha* (Havasupai).

My relationships with this Land and her Peoples are foundational to these pages. As a ninth-generation settler, I am committed to disrupting settler colonialism by acting in solidarity with Indigenous sovereignty. I seek to support Indigenous Peoples' well-being and the vitality of this land, with my time, skills, and resources.*

With gratitude and respect for this Land and her Peoples—past, present, and future:

Ahxéheeʼ (Diné), Askwali (Hopi), Haangyo (Havasupai)

---

* I recommend the booklet *Land Acknowledgements: Historical Context and Contemporary Inquiries*, a collaboration by Sequoia Samanvaya (https://www.sequoiasamanvaya.com/) and Collective Wisdoms (https://www.collectivewisdoms.org/).

Dedication

*This book is dedicated to all who have been injured by
settler colonialism.
It is for European-descended settlers who wish to
become good relatives.
This book is an offering to our collective liberation
and the nourishment of Mother Earth.*

———

*I return the income I receive from sales of this book to
the Decolonizing Wealth Project and Liberated Capital,
"a donor community and funding vehicle aimed at
moving untethered resources to Black, Indigenous,
and other people-of-color communities for liberation
and racial healing," and Jubilee Justice, whose mission
is to "heal and transform the wounds suffered by the
people and the land through reparative genealogy and
regenerative agriculture."* [1]

Contents

PART THREE ~ THE FABRIC

APPENDICES

Foreword

BY YEYE LUISAH TEISH
Chief/Iyanifa (Initiated Elder) in the Ifa/Orisha tradition
of the West African Diaspora, Author of *Jambalaya: The
Natural Woman's Book of Personal Charms and Practical
Rituals* and *A Calabash of Cowries: Ancient Wisdom for
Modern Times*

I'M SITTING here looking at the page before me, marveling at the journey Hilary has taken to write this book.

I forget the year but remember when we sat on the side of a building in New Mexico under a great tree. We'd both attended a women's spirituality conference. The keynote spoke of the importance of Sisterhood; the power inherent in Women, and our responsibility to heal our ancestral wounds.

The words fell on our ears as we looked around the room, searching for signs of Sisterhood. I remember the look of recognition in the eyes of this woman as she looked at me. We shared a smile and a nod that bridged the gap of race and class, and then introduced ourselves to each other.

During the lunch break, we sat on the edge of a concrete embankment under a majestic tree. The conversation revealed who we are and what we have in common. We share a pride in Womanhood, a relationship to Spirit, and a commitment to healing the racial wounds so embedded in our history and experience.

A few months later, while taking a walk in the woods, Hilary heard the ancestors whisper. Shortly after, she called me and asked for a *diloggún* reading. The Yorùbá tradition has preserved a system of divination using cowrie shells to reveal the requests and directions of the seeker's ancestors. It names those things we are born to do and reveals what we must do now and the impact of that doing on the future. During Hilary's divination her ancestors whispered in my ear. I asked her, "What about your book?"

"I haven't written a book," she answered.

I delivered the message as clearly as I could. "The book is already written," I said matter-of-factly.

Reluctantly, she confessed that she'd been thinking about writing something that would address the relationship between "settler descendants" and the descendants of the original people of the lands where she lived and walked. She expressed some uncertainty about her right and her ability to write such a book.

But the voice of the ancestors spoke loudly. So, I told her, "You are the perfect person to write this book. Let go of your resistance and let the ancestors speak." I gave her a ritual, a writing prompt, and a deadline. I assure you that the ancestors insisted that she write this book. Now it is in your hands.

Many years of work went into the birthing of this book. She did extensive research to uncover the facts and the figures, the history of these lands, and the stories of the people. The content of this book is historically accurate. Another kind of "research" also informed this work. It's the "knowing" that comes when you feel the Earth beneath your feet and listen to the whispers of the wind. It is the creativity that reveals itself in dreams and manifests in ritual.

Over the years, I have been a spiritual counselor, a ritual advisor, and a friend with Hilary. I've watched her grow through emotional changes and even physical transformations while working on this book. Hilary has done the internal work of careful self-examination, unpacking colonization, and humbly seeking Indigenous Elders for guidance.

We spent days and sometimes nights laughing at ourselves and crying over the injustice in our history. We've attended spiritual events and taken a detour through the cemetery to utter ancestral chants and to recognize as kindred people we've never met before.

Becoming a better relative is what this book is all about. We two women, fair and dark, spent days, and sometimes nights researching and writing, looking for the best words, laughing, and dreaming, asking for the right prayers to make us better relatives.

As you turn the pages of this book, I ask *you* to hear the whispers of the ancestors, to feel the heart of Hilary, and to embrace all the people of our Earth. Turn the page and see yourself here. Let us hold your hand as you go through the transformation to become a better relative.

I watched Hilary grow pregnant with the ancestors' message. She nurtured it as it grew inside of her, and now she has birthed it into the world. Hold this baby in your hands, take her into your heart. Remember the power of Sisterhood.

To all my relations.

Author's Preface

THIS BOOK was written on land that is now called the United States of America. I love this land's waters, rocks, mountains, oceans, butterflies, trees, birds, and flowers. In some ways, my relationship with this land is simple: I was born here, and this land has been taking care of me all my life. I have distant ancestors among the Original Peoples of this land. In other ways, my relationship with this land is complex: I am also descended from European settlers, removed in time and space from *their* ancestors' ancient lands and lifeways.

This land was soaked with blood and tears through a genocide that has been largely unacknowledged and willfully forgotten by many of us. Over the past decade, becoming more aware of the historical context into which I was born awakened a calling to find a path to right relationship with this land, a path to belonging.

My European ancestors migrated to this land beginning twelve to nine generations ago. Some must have chosen to come here in search of new opportunities, while others were desperate to survive. After a long, difficult voyage by sea, they arrived on these shores. I can imagine the complex emotions they must have carried with them on their journeys. Perhaps a mixture of relief, optimism, grief, and dread? They probably tried to leave painful memories behind, keep their divided families alive in their hearts, and embrace new beginnings.

For centuries before their migration, various forms of war, colonization, famine, and displacement had been taking place throughout Europe. The earlier Paleolithic and Mesolithic European cultures, which were likely more egalitarian and peaceful, had long been forgotten. By the time my ancestors emigrated, some of them had been stripped of their lands and languages. In their process of re-settling, they became part of systems that inflicted incalculable harm. For example, the third generation of immigrants on at least one side of my family received land grants and enslaved people.

After many generations of ancestral amnesia and denial about this history, I received an invitation to wake up and re-member that *we are all related*: waters, rocks, mountains, oceans, butterflies, trees, birds, flowers, and *all* people.

This book was seeded by my relationships with Indigenous Peoples, places, movements, knowledge, and worldviews of the continents that are now called North and South America. In his book *Sand Talk: How Indigenous Thinking Can Save the World*, Australian Aboriginal scholar Tyson Yunkaporta writes: "An Indigenous person is a member of a community retaining memories of life lived sustainably on a land base, as part of that land base." He describes Indigenous Knowledge as "any application of those memories as living knowledge to improve present and future circumstances."[2]

Some Indigenous cultures have inhabited their respective places for thousands of years. Profound, long-standing relationships with a place foster place-based worldviews. Over the last five centuries, Eurocentric colonial dominance has spread throughout the world like a disease. On every continent inhabited by humans, colonial violence has stolen the lives of Indigenous Peoples. In many cases, the survivors and their descendants have been forcibly removed from their lands. This pattern is devastating because relationships with land are inherent to Indigenous cultures.

As keepers of complex legacies and cultural identities, not all Aboriginal, Native American, Indian, Tribal, and First Nations identify themselves as "Indigenous."[3] According to my research and experience, at the time of this book's publication, "Indigenous" can be capitalized to respectfully identify diverse cultures throughout the world.[4] I've used it accordingly in this book, for clarity. I also acknowledge that there are imitations to this term and that there can be issues associated with it. In my personal interactions, I defer to the identifiers that communities and individuals choose for themselves.

"Turtle Island" is a widely used name for the continent that is also known as North America.[5] It originates from oral histories of Algonquian- and Iroquoian-speaking peoples.[6] I've used this term to honor an Indigenous creation story of this continent and subvert the colonial names that have been imposed here. I wrote this book on Turtle Island, whose land, waters, and Peoples have taught me. This land has nourished the last several generations and the current generations of my family in countless ways.

An Already Written Book

One morning in the spring of 2016, I went for my usual walk in the woods near my home in Flagstaff, Arizona. On this particular day, something unusual happened. This time, among the Ponderosa pine trees, I heard an insistent whisper: *you need to write a book.* I had only the faintest glimmer of what the book was about, and I was afraid to write it.

As the days passed, this unwritten book kept nudging me. Wondering what to make of this persistent message, I contacted someone I'd recently met at a conference. Yeye Luisah Teish is a respected Black Elder and priestess of the Ifa/Orisha tradition of West Africa.[*] I'd been moved by her session on ancestor reverence, storytelling, and ritual. Without mentioning the unwritten book that was nudging me, I simply asked if she'd be willing to offer me some spiritual guidance. Yeye Teish agreed, suggesting a *diloggún* reading, which is a system of divination in her Yorùbá tradition.

We both dressed in white for the reading. She instructed me to breathe deeply as she cast the cowrie shells. Right away, she announced in a tone of authority that my ancestors were busily whispering in her ear about a book that I had written. Shocked, I cautioned, "But I haven't written a book."

At this, the ancestors said through Teish, "The book is already written." Cold fear flooded the pit of my stomach, and I

---

[*] Yeye Teish teaches wonderful classes and leads spiritual work on reparations with Jubilee Justice. Please see her website (http://www.yeyeluisahteish.com/).

immediately started protesting. Yeye Teish generously helped me find the courage to begin writing this book by patiently listening to all of my excuses. Then she (gently) informed me that my reasons for not writing this book were bullshit. She gave me a writing prompt with a deadline.

Following dreams, intuitions, and synchronicities like a trail of breadcrumbs, years of writing ensued. From this auspiciously unplanned beginning, this "already written" book became an emergent way of being. Using elements of ancestry, place, nature, history, spirituality, religion, dreams, myth, ritual, gender, and community, I began developing stories that were new to me.[7] Along the way, writing this book awakened my creativity and filled me with joy. Through inquiries on race, colonization, and reparations,[*] the ancestors helped me to imagine a different world.[†]

———

This book is a humble offering to the complex process of healing the wounds of colonialism. In these pages, I've made my best effort to examine the contents of the inheritance that was bestowed upon me at birth: white American settler[‡] privilege. This book shares the wounds I discovered in myself and offers stories of healing. It considers how people of privilege can wake up, do our work, and learn to become good relatives from the inside out.

An astute Diné scholar, artist, community organizer, and beloved

———

[*] The harms that African-American and Indigenous communities have experienced are distinct. Reparations to these communities must address different needs. I've discussed this more toward the end of the book.

[†] When I read Kremer and Jackson-Paton's *Ethnoautobiography*, I discovered that I was immersed in a process the authors refer to as "ethnoautobiography." On page 183, they write:

> By withdrawing our consent from the racial contract, we are able to view the realities of privilege as well as the great social costs to *all* individuals and societies....Only then can we begin to reimagine another world, a different world.

[‡] For a fascinating discussion of the term *settler*, please see pages 31–37 of *Living in Indigenous Sovereignty* by white Canadian settler and scholar Elizabeth Carlson-Manathara, with Swampy Cree scholar Gladys Rowe.

sister named Lyla June Johnston* (who wrote the closing words), once shared a story from her visit to Palestine. A Palestinian man told her that when we share money, we should offer it on top of outstretched hands, with open palms. In this way, we are not *giving* someone money. Rather, we are asking them to take it back. This story illustrates why, on outstretched, open palms and with an open heart, I offer all the income I receive from sales of this book to the communities whose resources, land, lives, and labor were stolen to generate the privilege from which I benefit. I humbly ask them to take it back.

———

This book has been informed by my participation in activist, spiritual, Indigenous, academic, and philanthropic communities. It was written with consultation from these communities. Between 2019 and 2023, I sought feedback and guidance on this work from more than sixty readers of diverse backgrounds and expertise. All of them are dedicated, caring, brilliant people. Unsurprisingly, they did not always agree with each other. I've done my best to embrace complexity by listening, learning, and synthesizing an understanding that feels authentic for me.

While some of the experiences in this book are shared in chronological order, the insights produced by living this book are nonlinear. They go in circles and waves, fold back on themselves, make loops and delve into other dimensions. They take turns that lead off into the bushes, where a lost treasure is rediscovered and explored.

This book is a re-membering. (Please see the Glossary for a definition). During the years of writing this book, mountains, trees, and oceans invited me to sit with them. Eventually, I sensed the mountain holding me as a grandmother cradles a grandchild, heard the trees breathing, and perceived the ocean waves moving in sync

———

* To learn more about Lyla June's inspiring poetry, music, organizing, and scholarship, please see her website (https://www.lylajune.com/).

with my own blood. The land taught me that, long ago, all humans were Earth-honoring people.

Our Earth-honoring ancestors knew how to adapt to all kinds of weather. They designed beautiful, sustainable homes, respected water, and harvested their own medicine. The patient work of their hands yielded bowls, thread, shoes, tools, and musical instruments. The land gave them their languages, dances, songs, and foods. Throughout the world, our ancestors built their resilience based on interdependent kinship. When circumstances required it, they migrated and began anew. They learned how to become relatives with new plants, animals, lands, and waters. They ensured the continuation of their people, ultimately giving life to the bodies we inhabit today. Our blood and bones still hold their tenacity.

In the United States, white settlers have lived within Eurocentric cultural narratives that depict humanity moving forward on an ever-improving road to progress. This book takes the time to question what we left behind and discover what we might redeem. Prior to several thousand years ago, the world's human population practiced Indigenous lifeways, in interdependent relationships with places all over the planet. Today, only 6 percent of the world's population is Indigenous. That 6 percent has been socially, politically, culturally, and economically marginalized throughout the world. Even so, Indigenous Peoples steward 80 percent of the world's remaining biodiversity.[8] Over centuries and millennia, Indigenous communities have developed sophisticated traditional ecological knowledge to ensure future generations' ability to thrive.

I have Celtic ancestors, who lived for centuries or even millennia in the lands now called Scotland, Ireland, England, Spain, and France. In their honor, I have told my story in the three parts of this book (three being a sacred number in Celtic cosmology). In memory of my ancient Germanic and Nordic grandmothers, each of the three parts is titled to evoke one of the Norns. The Norns are archetypal maidens who weave the webs of destiny in Norse mythology.[9]

This book includes poetry and quotations by Indigenous, Black, Latinx, Asian, and Jewish authors who have inspired me. It also contains quotations and poems by European and Euro-descended authors who have helped me understand myself and my ancestors. It includes some Scottish Gaelic proverbs and a contemporary chant written in a 4,000-year-old language that is being reconstructed by the University of Wales.*

Throughout the process of writing this book, I received mentorship from Indigenous Elders, scholars, and communities who taught me to listen to my heart and trust my intuition. Along the way, I also learned from a wide variety of books, classes, and experiences. These resources can be found in notes at the bottom of some pages, as well as in the Appendices and Endnotes.

The sources that initially attracted me are widely accessible to a general audience. I'm not a scholar, but as my interest in certain historical topics deepened, I also delved into some academic sources. Some of the sources that spoke to me tell a particular story that revealed my healing path. On this path, I explored *my perceptions* of how historical events interact with our present time. This book was propelled by curiosity, intuitively guided research, and deep concern for the future of life on our planet. It tells my story, rather than a singular truth. My story is only one among billions.

———

Part One ~ Spinning the Thread illuminates the seismic shift of my white settler worldview. Through a series of experiences in Ecuador, Scotland, and Democratic Republic of Congo, I began seeing things differently. Suddenly, I could perceive realities that had been there all along: colonialism, patriarchy, the social construct of whiteness, ancestral memory, and intuitive ways of knowing. Part One also touches on the healing I experienced while building bridges across cultures.

In some of these stories, Black, Indigenous, and People of Color

---

* Please see the University of Wales's *Celtic Lexicon* website, a work in progress (https://www.wales.ac.uk/en/CentreforAdvancedWelshCelticStudies/ResearchProjects/CompletedProjects/TheCelticLanguagesandCulturalIdentity/CelticLexicon.aspx). Carolyn Hillyer brings this reconstructed language to life in the book *Her Bone Bundle / si knâmi grendyo.*

(BIPOC) as well as Indigenous, Black, and People of Color (IBPOC) generously shared reflections that guided me. I've capitalized the words "Black," "Indigenous," and "Color" to honor these identities. In his work, Black therapist, trauma specialist, and best-selling author Resmaa Menakem uses the term "bodies of culture" to describe all "human bodies not considered white."[10] Inspired by his insight, I embed "culture" in the BIPOC acronym as well, to emphasize that racialized identities involve culture as well as skin color. The acronyms "IBPOC" and "BIPOC" are used interchangeably throughout this book. (For definitions of these acronyms and why I've used both, please refer to the Glossary.)

These acronyms encompass diverse identities and cultures, including multiracial and multicultural relatives. Acronyms cannot begin to express the complex lived experiences of individuals and communities.* They are not a substitute for relational understanding between peoples over time. I've used these acronyms to call attention to systemic racial hierarchy, which exists throughout the world.[11]

To be accountable to my ancestors' colonial legacies, I've focused specifically on the United States. This book inquires how we might undo hierarchies, end segregation, and work toward equity. Because this book focuses on divesting from the social construct of whiteness, I've kept "white" in lower case. As I write, the conditions that necessitate racial labels and acronyms are evolving. My own understanding will continue to develop after this book is published.

Part Two ~ Weaving shares stories from a four-year process of contemplation. On the last day of 2015, I learned that some of my settler ancestors received grants of stolen land from the U.S. government. Some of them also enslaved people. The next day, I began a process of learning to be accountable to this history. Seven key elements guided this process, which I've woven together throughout the book:

---

* The BIPOC acronym encompasses diverse communities that have experienced colonization and racial oppression differently. I recommend reading books and watching films from a variety of perspectives to begin understanding these nuances.

- Land
- Ancestors
- Water
- Dreams
- Philanthropy
- Fasting Ceremony
- Indigenous Solidarity Work

These years of contemplation were like traversing a labyrinth. Labyrinths are meandering paths that twist and turn, eventually leading the walker back to the starting place, changed by the experience.[12] I continually discerned the path, doubled back, and passed the same seven landmarks. The weaving grew deeper and more profound with each passing year.

I was given tremendous homework. Eventually, I started taking practical steps toward becoming a good relative. I couldn't have predicted or imagined the realities that would take shape over the coming years. For example, after years of transmuting my own amnesia, denial, and shame, I sat with Indigenous grandmothers in truth and reconciliation circles. They held my hand, called me "sister," and said that I was forgiven for the role my ancestors played on this continent. I participated in Indigenous-led ceremonies, including the Ceremonies for Human Reunion in Europe, and an International Ceremony of Repentance and Forgiveness. Within the same region in which my ancestors once received a grant of stolen land and bought and sold human beings, I began building relationships and returning resources.

Part Three ~ The Fabric shares experiences of rekindling ancestral memory. After the four years of contemplation described in Part Two, I began to access a comforting, innate knowing of my ancient ancestors' presence. Reweaving the fabric of memory has helped me to identify with some of their traditional worldviews and practices. This allows me to embrace my ancestors' complexity and brings me joy, inspiration, and strength for the work ahead. Part Three is an invitation to re-member your own ancestral blueprints.

The Appendices include questions for reflection, historical notes on the invention of whiteness and the European witch-hunts, suggested practices, and a glossary. As you read, please turn to the Appendices at any time.

———

This journey is about re-membering to connect rather than divide, relate rather than control, and belong rather than exploit.[13] Though this book works with stories from my own life, it is not only about my particular life and personality. It is also about the Interconnected Us, and our collective healing. Each of us is carrying pieces of the puzzle that may eventually be fitted together to bring our world back to balance. Living this book has been an experiment. I invite you to read it in the spirit of curiosity, listening between the lines for your own re-membering.

This book is not an appropriation of Indigenous identity, medicines, languages, songs, foods, ceremonies, or religious symbols. Nor does it imply that Indigenous cultures *should* share their teachings with settlers. As psychologist and counselor Robyn Ward writes, "Part of understanding the boundaries that exist today is sitting with the heartbreaking discomfort of the boundaries disrespected in the past."[14]

Most Indigenous communities are not inclined to open their cultural practices to outsiders. I respect this choice, particularly in light of the invasive behavior, disrespect, and projection that Indigenous Peoples often receive from outsiders. Even within Indigenous communities, cultural practices are shared according to well-considered protocols. I have made the choice to leave out certain details of Indigenous ceremonies and practices I have observed or participated in, out of respect for these boundaries.

This book is not a claim that I've got it all figured out. I am just an imperfect human being who is dedicated to a process of relationality, respect, healing, and personal reparations, one step at a time. I wrote this book as an act of love. You are invited to join this adventure in the ways that call to your heart.

The First Paradox

Within the parts of the world that have been harmed by colonialism over the last several centuries, white experiences and people have been normalized and prioritized, while non-white experiences and people have been othered and marginalized. This is true of Canada,* Australia, New Zealand, Africa, Central America, South America, Pacific Nations, and India. In this book, I've focused on the United States. This is where I live, and I want to be accountable to my ancestors' presence as early settlers here. In the United States, many relatives of Color and Culture are struggling to survive racial oppression and terror. The struggle takes different forms, depending on unique identities, histories, and circumstances.

Due to this pattern, reading this book may not feel relevant or safe for everyone, because this book focuses on stories that are embedded in white experience. In my relationships with Filipinx, Latinx, Black, and Turtle Island Indigenous Peoples, I have heard the need for white settlers to break our silence, tell our stories, and do the work of coming together to face our past with honesty and integrity. I have received encouragement and support to begin this process myself, and to share my process transparently with others. That is the focus of this book.

Many of the topics I've shared in this book were new for me because I was acculturated into whiteness since birth, which limited my perception. For others, these topics are far from new. IBPOC have been sharing and talking about these topics through their scholarship, advocacy, art, writing, and films for generations. I encourage you to listen to the truths, histories, and visions they express. Some are quoted throughout this book, and more recommendations are available on my website, www.goodrelative.com.

This book was written by repeatedly choosing discomfort. Black therapist, trauma specialist, and best-selling author Resmaa

---

* To read Indigenous and settler perspectives on settler colonialism in Canada, please see *Living in Indigenous Sovereignty* by white Canadian settler and scholar Elizabeth Carlson-Manathara, with Swampy Cree scholar Gladys Rowe.

Menakem[15] shares that white bodies need to build the capacity for discomfort, in order to interrupt white-body supremacy.[16] Noticing our discomfort, sitting with our discomfort, and not acting impulsively from our discomfort helps us become sensitized and appropriately responsive to Black bodies and "bodies of culture."[17] Embracing physical, emotional, and racial discomfort gestated my commitment to dismantling white supremacy, an ideology of domination, from the inside out. I hope to support thriving, sovereign, and joyful BIPOC communities. Becoming a good relative is helping me work toward our mutual liberation.

For many, discomfort is a reality of daily life—not an option. But being uncomfortable *was a choice* for me. I benefit from layers of intersecting privileges, such as socioeconomic status, fair skin, cisgender heterosexual identity, an able body, a supportive family, education, and health care. While writing this book, I had access to international travel, conferences, workshops, nutritious food, supportive relationships, free time, undisturbed sleep, running water, electricity, and nature.

These privileges create filters in my perception. Some of these filters have already been revealed by generous and wise IBPOC readers. More will be revealed after this book is published. Having the capacity to write about historic and current inequities is an outgrowth of that inequity. How can one who has so many advantages write about dismantling privilege? Within this question lies a humbling paradox, the first of many paradoxes in this book. Within these pages, I've done my best to navigate seemingly divergent truths. I've tried to expand my perception and accept complex realities.

Many marginalized peoples do not have access to the resources and free time that enabled me to write this book. And yet, their voices and perspectives are essential to understanding these topics. My sacred charge has been to listen, learn, and integrate those perspectives along with my own.

PART ONE

Spinning the Thread

I am living a life I don't regret
A life that will resonate with my ancestors,
and with as many generations forward as I can imagine.
I am attending to the crises of my time with my best self,
I am of communities that are doing our collective best
To honor our ancestors and all humans to come.[18]
~ADRIENNE MAREE BROWN~
(Black Author, Facilitator, and Doula)

Bubbles of Denial

WELL INTO my thirties, I lived in a socially approved trance. I did not understand that I was white; I just thought of myself as being normal. I didn't blink in spaces where white people were overwhelmingly represented as authorities; I just thought they were the experts. I did not think that I grew up privileged; I just knew that my family had descended from poor, hard-working, devout people. I had never heard of settler colonialism; I just thought that America was a nation of immigrants. There was no point in learning about my ancestors; I was an individual, and they were uninteresting people from a long time ago. I thought that white supremacy was no longer relevant. In my mind, white supremacists were only found on the fringes of society, like Neo-Nazis and the Ku Klux Klan.

Things that had happened in the past had no bearing on the present. Since childhood, I had been immersed in the idea that everyone had equal opportunities in this land of freedom. I thought that dreams, intuition, and feelings were just noise, but intellectual analysis was legitimate. I didn't listen to the Earth. Earth was a thing to be managed, controlled, bought, and sold. I never thought about water. Water was something that came out of the tap for me to use whenever I wanted to.

Let me assure you, this worldview did not develop because I had chosen it. It did not result from being purposely deceived by someone I loved or because I wanted to participate in ecocide and racism. This worldview was the expected outcome for a middle-class, white American woman with a loving family, good education, and plenty of enriching experiences. But as I would begin learning in my late thirties, the people, places, and ideas that were absent from my early experiences conveyed powerful messages about what mattered and what didn't, who was important and who wasn't. In the years of writing this book, many of the bubbles that made up my white settler worldview popped. As each bubble popped, pain surfaced. Working through my pain instigated a process of healing.

———

When I discuss whiteness, I'm talking about more than just a skin color. I'm referring to a social identity that developed during the founding of the United States. Over centuries, European settlers of diverse languages, cultures, and identities were gradually lumped together into an undifferentiated group called "white." (Along the way, as I learned more about the history of this country, I compiled my understanding of the historical creation of whiteness. You can find these notes in the Appendices.)

As an adult, when I began building relationships with communities of Color and Culture, suddenly I could perceive my own whiteness for the first time.* I found it surprising and uncomfortable to see realities that had been invisible to me all along, even as they were obvious to others. The process of learning to consciously navigate my own white settler identity continues to this day. Over the years, I've realized that whiteness affects how I've always been treated by the world around me. It has shaped how I think about myself. Much of that began changing as I wrote this book.

Along the way, I learned that the social identity of whiteness benefits all white people. It advantages us unequally, depending on class, gender, sexuality, and various other characteristics. White privilege is a force that shapes reality in powerful ways. To varying degrees, white privilege confers systemic financial, educational, social, and medical advantages upon white people.

I've explored my whiteness through stories of "White Peril," a phrase I learned from an insightful, warm, and funny friend. Calvin Terrell is a Black speaker, trainer, and consultant.† I first heard him

---

* On page 36 of her book *Liberated to the Bone: Histories, Bodies, Futures*, white cultural worker and bodyworker Susan Raffo writes, "The only people who get to move into adulthood and experience life without awareness of being raced are white people, even as white people are as raced as everyone else."

† To learn about Calvin's speaking, coaching, and facilitation, please see his website (https://www.calvinterrell.com/).

share about White Peril during a workshop he was teaching. His concept resonated strongly, and I've worked with it for several years. I understand White Peril as an outcome of historic trauma generated by intra-European violence. More than two millennia of slave trading,[19] the Roman Expansion, and centuries of witch-hunts offer examples of profound violence perpetrated by Europeans, against Europeans.* (For Calvin's thoughts on White Peril, please see the Glossary.)

White Peril may originate with historical events, but it has affected me during my own lifetime. The stories in this book share how whiteness has imperiled me *and* the world surrounding me. For example, I've often been ignorant about the past and unaware of the big picture. My resilience has been impaired, and I've sometimes been oblivious to my impact. For most of my life I was deprived of meaningful connection with my ancestors, isolated, and overly identified with individualism. My sense of belonging to Mother Earth and my ability to practice an Earth-honoring culture have been impeded. Being locked into rigid either/or thinking has limited my capacity to take responsibility, forgive, and imagine different ways of being. White Peril does more than endanger those who identify as white. It also puts the land, water, and communities around us at risk. Like a child with a loaded gun, my unexamined White Peril made me dangerous to myself and others.

With Calvin's permission and consultation, I've used his phrase "White Peril" in this book, along with "white privilege."† White privilege bestows unearned advantages on us. At the same time, White Peril hurts us. I've explored this paradox throughout these pages.

---

* I recommend:
  - "European Trauma and the Invention of Whiteness," chap. 4 of *My Grandmother's Hands: Racialized Trauma and the Pathway to Mending our Hearts and Bodies*, by trauma specialist Resmaa Menakem.
  - The *Reparations 4 Slavery* website includes an extensive list of resources about traumatic events that took place in various part of Europe throughout different historical eras. See: https://reparations4slavery.com/white_trauma_white_supremacy/.

† White scholar Peggy McIntosh wrote about white privilege in the 1980s. Since then, this phenomenon has become widely known. See: https://www.newyorker.com/books/page-turner/the-origins-of-privilege.

My experience of whiteness has included various forms of suffering, such as amnesia, denial, ignorance, perfectionism, exceptionalism, entitlement, grief, shame, rage, insecurity, self-delusion, and despair. In exchange for maintaining my comfort and security, whiteness has diminished the full expression of my humanity.

Unpacking my White Peril instigated healing and helped me find the work that is uniquely mine to do in support of humanity's mutual liberation. This is an ongoing endeavor. As you read, I invite you to consider: has White Peril affected you? If so, how will you heal and find the work that is uniquely yours?

Whiteness was written into law in the colony of Virginia nearly four centuries ago.[20] These centuries have offered advantages to those of us who are considered white. The privileges we enjoy stem from a system of racial hierarchy that causes tremendous harm. Along the way, white silence has become an insidious force that upholds white dominance.* I've chosen to break my own silence in this book and share how popping bubbles of denial can feel.

But First, Let Me Introduce Myself

Before we begin popping these bubbles, I'd like you to know a little more about me. I was raised in a middle-class family by loving parents who are still married. My father is a retired music professor, and my mother is a retired teacher and actress. During the last few generations, our family has moved often. I was born in Tennessee, on Chickasaw land, and spent the second half of my childhood in Southern California, on Yuhaviatam and Cahuilla land. I attended college in northern Arizona and have lived here since then, on land that is sacred to at least thirteen Nations.

Now forty-nine years old, I've been married to a funny, insightful, supportive white man for over twenty years. When we met, we

---

* Read about the violence of white silence in chap. 3 of *White Women: Everything You Already Know about Your Own Racism and How to Do Better*, by Regina Jackson and Saira Rao.

were surprised to discover that neither of us owned a television. We've been happily living television-free lives ever since. We have two children who intrigue us as they grow up and become more of themselves. My husband's extended family runs a multigenerational business. With the income we receive from this business, we can give money away, a practice that is sometimes known as philanthropy. We met when we were both working for the company, and he currently works there.

For fifteen years, I performed and taught improvisational group dance. I also facilitated women's groups, including groups for adolescent girls and survivors of sexual and domestic violence. This book was written in time carved out between raising children, community organizing, cooking, walking in the woods, folding laundry, taking care of pets, tending relationships, attending board meetings, volunteer work, dabbling in filmmaking, reading books, and becoming a good relative.

Our family lives in an old house that holds the memories of the more than a century of families who lived here before us. If you were to visit our home where this book was written, you might notice the pear, apple, plum, and cherry trees outside. You'd see a pile of firewood on the front porch and be greeted by our goofy dog at the front door. I'd invite you into the kitchen, offer you a cup of tea, and listen to your story while fixing you something to eat. You might smell bone broth simmering on the stove and enjoy a bowl of homemade soup. Our house is full of beeswax candles, unfinished projects, dark chocolate, and love.

Stacks of books fill our house. Paintings of Mountain, Ocean, Buffalo, Elk, Forest, and Goddess hang on the walls. My children, mother, aunt, grandmother, and great-grandmothers made quilts, pillows, and textiles that hold our stories in their threads. A simple, well-loved altar rests in a corner of the dining room. There, you'd be welcome to sit in the rocking chair where my mother nursed me as a baby and where I rocked my little ones to sleep. This altar is one of the places where my heart slowly mended over the eight years of writing this book.

Philanthropic Alchemy, v 1.0

When I was growing up, my family valued frugality and didn't have much extra money. During my early childhood, my parents often had to stretch to make ends meet between paychecks. But we never went hungry, and we always had running water and electricity. I grew up in a supportive environment with access to ballet classes, health care, and dental care. I was part of an extended family who valued giving what we could and caring about hunger, poverty, and racism.

On Thanksgiving, my parents, brother, and I would often deliver meals to people who were elderly or disabled, and alone. I remember the visceral sensation of going into their apartments or nursing homes with a warm tray of food, stepping into other worlds. We would often stay and visit for a long time with people we had never met before. Even though they were invisible to us most of the year, I knew then that these people were always present. I wondered how they got by on the days when nobody came to visit. Their loneliness carved a tender space in my heart. I often thought about them long after November had passed.

A supportive community surrounded our family to offer help with my brother, who was born with multiple disabilities that require him to use a wheelchair. From the time I was a toddler, I watched my parents tirelessly advocate for his education and health care. Sometimes I hated that we were not as "self-sufficient" and "normal" as other families. I didn't know anyone else who had a sibling with disabilities. But looking back, I see that it was a gift to receive support with responsibilities that were too much for any nuclear family to handle alone. Because of the support of our extended family and community, my brother grew into a unique and engaging man whose presence blesses the lives of many.

Though we lived in predominantly white neighborhoods and socialized mostly with middle-class white people, my parents, grandparents, and I were able to cultivate a few relationships with Black and Latinx people. In our family, nobody talked about being white. Whiteness was just "normal" for us, a state of being we didn't question. Sometimes the things we *don't* discuss shape our identity even more than the things we *do* talk about. A vast spectrum of class privilege exists among white people, which means we all experience whiteness differently. Because of this, I have lifelong blind spots to the experiences of white people who live with food insecurity, intergenerational poverty, and homelessness. Class differences equate to vastly different life experiences.

In my mid-twenties, I married into a family that had more financial means.* Some of them were engaged in philanthropic giving, often in support of education and the environment. Suddenly, I was immersed in narratives that contrasted from those of my own family. On one hand, being in proximity to wealth was a relief. I no longer worried about paying my bills and I had opportunities to travel. On the other hand, my middle-class upbringing had instilled a confusing mixture of mistrust and envy regarding wealth. I felt responsible for integrating into another family culture. As I tried to adapt to different class norms, I often felt a disturbing dissonance.

After my husband and I were married in 2000, I began an interdisciplinary graduate program in Liberal Studies on "Good and Sustainable Communities."[21] In these university classrooms, Christians, white men, corporations, and the wealthy were often blamed for everything that was going wrong. Through observation, I became aware that wealth was something I should not identify with or discuss if I wanted to stay comfortable. My proximity to wealth would make me a pariah in my job of organizing guest lecturers for the university department, at dinner parties, in classes, and mother/baby playgroups. It seemed best to avoid ostentatious jewelry and fancy cars, and just keep a low profile. This behavior is often considered "tasteful discretion" in wealthy families. But as the years passed, I understood that our silence about class, wealth, and race tends to combine with White Peril in ways that can generate profound harm.

Before I started doing philanthropic work, I imagined that when I was a matronly older woman and my children were grown, I would

---

* My husband's family has taught me a great deal. To respect their privacy, I've focused on sharing my own story rather than theirs.

finally have the energy and expertise to spend my time evaluating grant proposals and making weighty decisions. It seemed that philanthropy was the realm of sophisticated people. I was intimidated by these resources that weren't really mine. I feared I'd never understand how to do philanthropy the "right" way. Besides, I was ashamed that we had access to more than we needed when others did not have enough. To become a philanthropist, I would be forced to acknowledge the overabundance permeating our lives.

As the years passed, my husband's parents invited me to take part in their family's philanthropic giving. The invitation was permeated with unbelievable generosity, trust, and encouragement. As I considered their offer, gradually, the yearning of my heart became louder than the paralysis of my fears. I felt compelled to do something *now* about poverty, plastic pollution, climate change, gender-based violence, and other issues. I realized that each of us has gifts embedded within our temperaments, spiritual callings, and life situations that allow us to contribute meaningfully. Although I still felt unqualified, philanthropy was inviting me to become an apprentice. This apprenticeship has changed me in ways I couldn't have imagined. I will always be grateful.

———

With the support of my husband, our families, and other mentors, I eventually developed a practice I call Philanthropic Alchemy. I use the word "alchemy" because the practice is based on combining and transmuting various elements to create something life-sustaining. Philanthropic Alchemy includes both interpersonal and institutional philanthropy. It is relational and restorative. Through this process, I learned that material wealth can only be accumulated within societies that have long prioritized economic growth above communal, environmental, and spiritual well-being.* To acknowledge having

---

* Today's billionaires may appear to be "self-made," but the current potential to build enormous wealth rests upon centuries of extractive economic choices that continue today.

wealth is to acknowledge being at the top of a pyramid that advantages a few. This pyramid leaves the majority in multigenerational financial insecurity or poverty.

For those who are opening to this perception, being stationed at the top of this pyramid carries dissonant feelings. In Eurocentric culture, it can be easy to equate economic status with virtue and importance. But when I started considering wealth and poverty in relation to whiteness and settler colonialism, it looked very different. What if economic disparity is the symptom of a sickness that has been infecting humanity for millennia? What if our inequitable economy is working *exactly as it was intended*? Philanthropic Alchemy taught me to no longer accept neat and tidy interpretations of wealth, such as "we are just incredibly blessed," or "we value hard work." Instead, I started sitting with paradoxes and learning from discomfort.

My first foray into Philanthropic Alchemy began a few years after I'd started giving philanthropically. In 2013, I was making an invitation list for a fundraising workshop[22] that I was co-hosting. With shock, I realized that everyone on the invitation list was white. Not only that, but *I didn't know any* Indigenous, Black, Latinx, Asian people *or* BIPOC-led organizations to invite. When this bubble of denial popped, I was surprised. I became consciously aware of the vacuum of racial segregation in which I was operating. I hadn't deliberately intended this, and to my knowledge, I hadn't done anything to create it. Yet here it was staring back at me.

This realization made me deeply embarrassed and uncomfortable. Though I didn't yet understand the racial bias that creates this vacuum, it was clear: I had to do something. I scheduled a meeting with some white friends to ask for introductions to IBPOC farmers, nonprofit leaders, and community organizers. Soon, I began behaving more relationally. I called people on the phone rather than relying on email. I invited them into conversations, listened to their concerns, and held spaces open for them before every RSVP was filled by white guests. Something inside me said that it was important to cultivate these relationships.

When the day of the fundraising workshop arrived, I stood before a packed room and welcomed everyone. My heart blossomed with joy when I saw faces of many different human Colors and Cultures looking back at me. The relationships that began during the two-day workshop seeded a more diverse network over time. Cultivating relationships with BIPOC and learning about Indigenous worldviews soon became an eye-opening practice. This learning grew in tandem with the budding philanthropy my husband and I were practicing, and they are intertwined.

Philanthropic Alchemy opened my eyes to realities that had previously been invisible to me. The socioeconomic class I'd married into offered more access to these relationships than I had previously experienced. I was regularly humbled and inspired by opportunities to build relationships with people from different backgrounds than mine. I enjoyed reaching across the divides and building bridges. At the time, I was not fully cognizant of the power embedded in my position as a philanthropist. But over time, I began understanding power differentials more deeply, and taking steps to shift them. (In Part Two, I've offered some ways that people with various levels of class privilege can join in solidarity with IBPOC communities.)

Philanthropic Alchemy took me on a steep uphill learning curve. It rewired my understanding of the land that is now called the United States of America, the communities here, and the economic systems that determine who has institutional power. In 2019, six years after my realization that I didn't know any BIPOC to invite to the fundraising workshop, my husband and I had changed. We were returning over 90 percent of our annual philanthropic budget to organizations led by and for Black and Indigenous Peoples. We were working with forms of philanthropy that return decision-making power to the communities from which it has been taken through colonization, slavery, genocide, extraction, and gentrification. This book shares my stories about the healing that enabled this dramatic change in a short time.

Parts of this book address institutional philanthropy, which is usually the realm of those who have proximity to wealth. But I've also done my best to speak to our commonalities across class. Writing this book has taught me about another form of philanthropy that is *interpersonal* rather than *institutional*. Interpersonal philanthropy does not require money. I see it as an expression of our shared humanity.

Interpersonal philanthropy takes place when we listen, care, and share with our neighbors, when we take our kids to pick up trash in the riverbed, or when we serve food at a local soup kitchen instead of shopping on Black Friday. Interpersonal philanthropy can manifest in how we interact with someone who is begging. Do we ignore them, or toss some change their way without looking? Or do we make eye contact, say hello, and offer a handshake?

Elders* sharing wisdom over cups of tea offer interpersonal philanthropy. People living in underpasses who share kindness with passersby extend interpersonal philanthropy. It spontaneously arises in stories told around campfires. It is present in gifts of homemade jam, handknit scarves, and extra produce from a friend's garden. Throughout these pages, I've shared stories about some of the interpersonal philanthropists who have generously taught me. I see Mother Earth as the ultimate interpersonal philanthropist, who takes care of us every day by providing water, food, air, and beauty. Interpersonal philanthropy brings joy and richness to my life without giving or receiving even one dollar.

In the aforementioned forms of *institutional* philanthropy, we dramatically changed our giving orientation over a few years. I have found that it's also possible to change the orientation of our

---

* I capitalize *Elders* as an honorific to describe people whose communities acknowledge them in this way. From my perspective, Elders' warmth, compassion, insight, knowledge, kindness, courage, wisdom, and humor serve the well-being of their communities, and even the world.

interpersonal philanthropy. Learning the stories and embracing the humanity of those whose life circumstances are different than our own enables this kind of change.

The Teachings of the Rainforest

When I look back to the person I was in my early thirties, I feel tenderness for her. While mothering my young children, I was often haunted by despair. The mounting social and environmental crises were alarming. Like many parents, I wondered how my children's lives would be impacted. Would there be clean air for them to breathe when they grew up? Clean water for them to drink? At the same time, I was insulated in a bubble of privilege that kept me uncertain how to be part of solutions. Wondering what to do and longing for guidance eventually delivered unexpected answers. I received the first of these answers from an experience with a non-profit organization called The Pachamama* Alliance.[23]

I first read about this organization in *The Soul of Money*, by co-founder and humanitarian Lynne Twist.[24] She shares how she, a white American, came to be in relation with Amazonian peoples, including communities that had long maintained isolation from the outside world. Achuar people belong to an Indigenous warrior culture in the rainforest that spans present-day Ecuador and Peru. Their Elders had received prophetic dreams indicating that they would receive threatening contact from "the modern world," sometime around the year 2000. Oil extraction was poisoning the land and waters all around them. Some of the Achuar people decided to preempt this intrusion by initiating contact with the modern world. To actively protect their self-determination, they requested to meet with a small group of people from the north.

---

* On page 175 of his book *The Time of the Black Jaguar: An Offering of Indigenous Wisdom for the Continuity of Life on Earth*, Peruvian author Arkan Lushwala defines *Pachamama* as "Mother Earth, Mother of Time, Mother of the Universe" in the Runasimi language (also known as Quechua).

In the mid-1990s, through a series of synchronicities, Lynne Twist, her husband Bill, and some of their colleagues responded to the Achuar invitation and brought a group to visit with Achuar people on their land. These people from the industrialized world would eventually become partners in protecting Achuar and other Indigenous Amazonian communities from oil, mining, and logging extraction. Together, they formed The Pachamama Alliance.

As Lynne shares in her book, dreams are central to the Achuar culture. For them, dreams even hold the power to shape reality. The Achuar leaders told their new partners about the "Dream of the Modern World," a dream that is always striving for a future of *more*. It is a dream of unhindered economic growth, the commodification of nature, and spiritual disconnection. As they understood it, this dream was wreaking havoc that could ultimately destroy life on Earth. Over time, Achuar and other Indigenous Peoples asked their partners within The Pachamama Alliance to return home and do the work to "change the Dream of the Modern World." They described this as a task that could be completed within one generation.[25]

Reading this story captured my imagination. As someone who was immersed in the Dream of the Modern World, I wondered what it would take to change it. A few years later, in 2012, my nine-year-old daughter and I joined a journey to Ecuador with The Pachamama Alliance. I was curious if we would receive any guidance about how a different dream might feel. For several days, our group drove through twisting, mountainous roads in a big bus. Then we boarded small planes and flew through clouds over a vast canopy of green, into the rainforest. We spent happy days traversing the river by canoe and hiking through the rainforest to observe plants and animals. One afternoon we visited a village and spent several hours with an Achuar family in their home.

In their oval-shaped hut, there were no walls. The thatched roof was upheld by sturdy pillars. A wooden bench circled half of the hut, the space for receiving visitors. All the family's belongings were visible from this vantage point. They slept on a mosquito net-draped wooden platform, on which were laid a few clothes and blankets. Their shelves held bowls handmade with clay from the riverbanks and painted with plant dyes. I was fascinated and humbled. I also felt out of place with my fair skin, blue eyes, and tourist clothing in the equatorial heat. We were a long way from home.

As we visited with the man of the house, he wove a basket from long, slender grasses. His pregnant wife was across the hut from us, and their baby slept in a tiny hammock. The woman prepared *chicha*, a fermented manioc beverage and a staple of their diet. Manioc is a starchy root vegetable that grows in the tropics. Children played around the outside of the hut. Chickens wandered in and out, shooed often by her "ccht, cchht!!" Everyone appeared to me to be happy, clean, and well-fed.

After spending several hours together, I was inspired by this glimpse into this family's world, simultaneously simpler and more sophisticated than my own. The community grew their own food by singing to the spirits of the garden. Their children played with clay, sticks, flowers, and water rather than plastic toys. They required no electricity to meet their basic needs.

I will never forget returning home after this journey. I was overwhelmed by how much stuff we had, as well as the complexity of managing our "modern world" lifestyle. During the following weeks, my daughter and I worked together to release some of her stuffed animals, knick-knacks, and extra clothes. We bundled them up together and delivered them to local shelters, and to younger cousins and friends. Our visit with the Achuar family began shaping a sense of "enough-ness" within our family. It gave us a visceral experience of how little we really needed. In the years since, we've been proud when our children have embodied sufficiency from within.

During our time in the rainforest, we were invited to spend a night in a nearby Achuar village. Partway through our hike to the village, we stopped to meditate in the rainforest. Our guide cleared a private space for each of us with a machete, laying a banana leaf down and checking for snakes and spiders. Sitting on my banana leaf, a prayer began forming in my heart: how could I contribute to changing the Dream of the Modern World? In the coming years, this became a guiding inquiry. Eventually, my husband and I recognized that modernity tends to be cast as inherently superior. But we are striving to understand the nuances and problems with modernity as well.

That night in the rainforest, our group camped on the grounds of the village. Gigantic trees danced with the wind, gentle rain fell, and millions of monkeys, birds, and insects called to each other. It was the darkest night I had ever experienced. Still feeling far from home, but surprisingly comfortable on the ground, I drifted off to sleep. Slipping into a dream state, I felt like a giant corkscrew was opening the crown of my head. Stars poured in, filling my whole being with light. After some time, a harsh voice interrupted my reverie:

"You are a colonizer. You are a privileged American woman lying on the ground in the Amazon rainforest. You came here with your silly curiosity, and you are exploiting these people."

In anguish, I listened to the voice rage. Eventually, the dream changed:

An Achuar man lies down on the outskirts our camp. Gradually, our group of women is surrounded by kind men from the village. The voice fades away. I feel better. We are all together.

Rising the next morning in the rainforest, it was hard to discern if this had been a dream or reality. After talking with our group, I learned that there hadn't been any men encircling our camp. I shrugged it off as "nothing but a dream." Later, I had experiences that taught me how dream messages can combine with waking events over time, to offer teachings.

When I recalled this episode several years later, I realized that my dream in the rainforest made me consciously aware of the legacies of colonization that were weighing on me. I did not understand how to approach them during our visit to Ecuador. In the coming years, I would begin learning.

Liminality

We are children of broken clans and cultural desolation.[26]
~ DOUGLAS STEWART ~
(Scottish-Canadian Poet)

A few months later, my husband and I traveled with our two children and my parents to Scotland. We went as a celebration of my parents' fortieth wedding anniversary, in honor of our Scottish ancestry. But I'd never really felt drawn toward this part of the world. My perception had always been that Scotland was gray, rainy, and uninteresting. I thought of it as being without much in the way of culture, except for bagpipes, dreary churches, and plaid.

The first place we visited was a satellite of the Findhorn ecovillage, on a tiny Inner Hebridean Isle called Erraid.[27] For a week, we lived with the residents and other visitors who had come from around the world. We chopped wood, weeded the garden, cleaned the kitchen, collected eggs, and dodged attacks from an aggressive rooster. On the summer solstice, when the sun set dimly for only a couple of hours, we attended a community bonfire. It was a joy to watch our little ones running along the beaches, jumping in the springy grass, and discovering the treasures of a place that was new to them.

Erraid could only be reached when the tides were right. As we loaded our luggage onto the small boat that would carry us there, seals had silently watched us from the shore with their big, dark eyes. Inhabited by more sheep than people, Erraid was a quiet place. Despite its beauty, I felt restless and disoriented. What were we doing here, where we had to light a fire to stay warm in mid-summer? Where the darkness never really arrived?

One evening I walked to the top of the highest hill on Erraid. I saw the curving shoreline below interspersed with moss-covered islets. The waves rolled in and out, intermingling along these circular channels woven by the land. Everything was impossibly green. The sunlight sparkled on the water. I was suddenly overcome by a familiar childhood sensation, like when my grandparents would read enchanting bedtime stories. Behind me, the ruins of old stone cottages stood below. An awareness floated in: *You know this place. You have been here before.* As soon as my mind began arguing with this, my body started to hum, drowning out further mental chatter. There was nothing to rationalize. My body simply knew this place.

On the next leg of the trip, we traveled to Balquhidder, located inland in the southern region of the Highlands. One of my father's ancestors had hailed from this area a long time ago. We arrived at a small, stone church whose cemetery held the bones of Saint Angus. He was thought to be the first person who brought Christianity to Balquhidder. Rob Roy, who had a reputation as a sort of Scottish Robin Hood, was also buried there. Uneasily, I went inside.

An entire wall had been dedicated to listing the clans of the area. Some of the powerful clans adopted other families and clans, creating kinship bonds. To my surprise, there was our name—the surname I had grown up with, on the wall! This name was one I had been teased about as a child because of its similarity to menu items at McDonald's. I was eager to shed it for what I considered the more aesthetically pleasing Italian name "Giovale" when I married. The name on the wall offered evidence of our connection to this land, inter-clan relationships, and deep history: McFatter. I would later learn that this was an anglicized version of the Gaelic name *mac Gille Pheadair*, meaning "servant of St. Peter."[28]

Next to the clan names, a small sign noted the history of the land on which it was built. It said the church was located at the base of a hill that the early inhabitants of the region considered sacred. I immediately found myself making excuses to my family. I exited the church and headed up the muddy trail outside the church to the hill behind it. Walking rapidly through the rain, tears sprang up in my eyes.

Reaching the top of the hill, my perception shifted. I heard a distant drumbeat. In my peripheral vision, I saw several figures dancing in a circle around flickering firelight in a dark night, although it was physically a drizzly afternoon. This moment felt both eternally long and over in a second.

As if startling awake, I felt that I had been standing on the hilltop for a long time. Worried that my family would be looking for me, I scurried downhill, where the sound of rushing water guided me to a waterfall cascading over giant rocks. Overwhelmed again, I felt something pulling me to the river, and I stood beside it for a while, staring into its depths.

Taking a deep breath to shake off these haunting sensations, I rejoined the rest of my family. I was quite sure that I had been gone too long, but they had barely noticed my absence. My cells longed to return to the hilltop and the river, but I did not know how to explain this. It was time to move on, so we resumed our afternoon. The bubble of denial that said I had no connection to my ancestors' lands had popped.

Years later, the Gaelic word "*dùthchas*" (pronounced "DOO-chuss," with a soft "ch"[29]), gave my longing a name. The word *dùthchas* derives from ancient cultural and linguistic roots and it has developed complex layers of meaning over time in both Scotland and Ireland.[30] "*Dùthchas*" can be used to describe a feeling of connection with ancestral land, and the hereditary characteristics passed down through families in relation to place.[31]

During our trip to Scotland, I could not foresee how these experiences would gradually change me. Our family knew nothing of our ancient ancestors at the time of our visit. However, years later, I realized that we were intuitively drawn to places of significance. For example, the seals we encountered in the Hebrides pointed us toward selkie folklore. In Scottish tradition, selkies are shapeshifting seal spirits who can become human for a time and return to seal form. They are creatures of the ocean, islands, and remote coastlines. Ten years after this trip, I honored the selkie archetype by learning to sing selkie songs in Gaelic.

In the Highlands, our visit to Balquhidder drew us to *Tom nan Aingeal*, the "Hill of Fire." This may have been where our people practiced a sacred relationship with fire, ceremonially renewing their hearth fires twice a year during the festivals of *Beltane* and *Samhain*.[32] Local people considered it a fairy mound, a portal between this world and the Otherworld.[33]

Mysteriously propelled to the top of the hill and the river below,* I would later understand this as an ancestral impulse toward a place of the *Sìdh* (pronounced "shee" in Modern Gaelic).[34] "*Sìdh*" derives from an Old Irish/Old Gaelic word that refers to the divine beings of the Celtic Otherworld. It also refers to the "earthly portals that connected that world with our own."[35] Some *Sìdh* mounds are pre-Celtic, Indigenous burial sites, while others are naturally occurring glacial formations. Respectfully, people often refer to the *Sìdh* indirectly, by names such as "The Good People."[36]

As I would later learn, in Celtic cosmology, the Otherworld of the *Sìdh* has parallels with our world. Peace is manifested in our world by maintaining good relations with the Otherworld. Sometimes, when "The Good People" decide to interact with human beings, the worlds meet. Other times, humans cross invisible boundaries at certain places or times, inadvertently encountering the *Sìdh*.[37] These interactions are embedded with codes for ethical behavior and reciprocity. For example, the *Sìdh* sometimes give magical gifts to humans, which must be shared generously in return. In her book *Celtic Myth and Religion*,† Celticist Sharon Paice MacLeod writes:

> The path to developing right relationship with the inhabitants of the Celtic Otherworld is based upon truth and honor. It is filled with potential blessings and teachings, as well as obstacles and challenges.[38]

I still wonder: did The Good People invite us into a relationship with generosity, truth, and honor during our visit to Scotland? Surprising blessings, teachings, obstacles, and challenges began arriving after our visit to *Tom nan Aingeal*.

---

* I was blessed to return to this place with Gaelic song teacher Sine McKenna in 2023.
† Celtic peoples once inhabited vast territories, spreading from as far east as today's Turkey, throughout the European continent, to as far west as today's Ireland. On page 18 of her book *Celtic Myth and Religion*, Celticist Sharon Paice MacLeod writes, "The standard definition of *Celtic* refers to both language and culture. The Celtic peoples spoke Celtic languages, which were part of the larger Indo-European family of languages."

White Peril: Colonizers' Guilt

Not long after the harsh voice in the rainforest accused me of being a colonizer, it faded into a vague memory. I had no framework to process those words, and my denial was still largely intact. A couple of years later, in 2014, another bubble was ready to pop. I was about to learn a practice that I refer to as "wit(h)nessing." Wit(h)nessing is a relational, compassionate, and intuitive form of listening and observation. While wit(h)nessing, I perceive another's story empathically, from my heart.* (For a definition, please see the Glossary.)

Wearing my philanthropist hat, I traveled to eastern Democratic Republic of Congo (DRC) with the Nobel Women's Initiative,[39] as part of a delegation on sexual violence in conflict. I felt intuitively drawn to this trip, even though it was riskier than my usual activities. Driven by deep concern for the ways in which war harms women, I went with an intention to listen. I did not realize that I was about to wit(h)ness, from an outsider's perspective, what colonization does to communities long after those in power consider it to be over. We took small planes from Kigali, Rwanda into a remote area in North Kivu province, where we were to meet with one of the grassroots leaders who started a clinic for survivors of sexual violence.

As soon as we landed, we were whisked into a meeting with the United Nations. The Congolese women wore vibrant, gorgeous clothing and the Congolese men were serious in their Western clothing. After being welcomed in Swahili and French with friendly handshakes and warm smiles, we were ushered to our seats. A ceiling fan turned lazily overhead, and blinds were drawn over the barred windows. The humidity settled over us like a blanket. In the small, crowded room, I was seated on a bench in the second row around a long table. The man who was running the meeting put a map of the province on an overhead projector. A point on the map indicated the village in which we were currently sitting. Red shading showed

---

* I first learned this term from Nigerian author Báyò Akómoláfé in his course "We Will Dance with Mountains" (https://www.dancingwithmountains.com/). I've used it here with his permission.

all the areas of armed conflict nearby. We were surrounded by war on all sides.

The map indicated the distance to the nearest conflict zone. I sat on the bench and let it sink in. I began trying to calculate the number of kilometers into miles to understand how close it was. Soon, I was sweating, nauseous, and dizzy. I started to wonder if I would return home from this place unscathed. Would I see my husband and children again? Prior to the trip, I had been told that we would be visiting regions in which armed conflict *might* be taking place. But sitting this close to it was a different matter. At the same time, I was flabbergasted by the realization that there are people around the world who live every day surrounded by armed conflict, and who have no means of escape.

As we traveled through different parts of the country, we met with NGOs and individuals working to denounce sexual violence, change the patriarchal culture that values girls and women similarly to livestock, and heal survivors' souls and bodies. Patriarchy is a historical development that is fueled by war and enforces male domination. (For a definition, please see the Glossary.)

Many of the people we met had been attacked, received death threats, or have had people close to them murdered. I met a courageous woman who was running a center for survivors with limited supplies and uncertain funding. She bore a deep scar across her forehead from being attacked with a machete. Stunningly, she survived and continued the work. Her presence beamed love and compassion, and her smile felt like sunshine. I wondered: how did she find the strength to continue?

Since the Rwandan genocide in 1994, the adjacent country of DRC has been embroiled in complex political upheaval. Being one of the most resource-rich nations on Earth has not helped its citizens. International corporate interests contribute to power struggles for control of natural resources and profits. This leads to armed conflict among various militias. They strategically use sexualized violence against families and villages. This destabilizes the entire population.

In Bukavu, South Kivu province, clusters of joyfully trilling women greeted us at the airport. They all wore matching tailored dresses and headwraps. Their warm welcome and the lush beauty of the land offered a stark contrast to the stories we were about to hear. That evening, we sat with about thirty women who were all survivors of sexualized violence. They wanted to share their stories with our delegation of mostly white Canadians and American women. The room was hot, the doors and windows closed to protect their anonymity. Speaking about these types of crimes is extremely dangerous in eastern DRC.

That night, I glimpsed the devastation of war. The suffering in the room was tangible. I was stunned by the women's perseverance and survival. While listening, I found myself wit(h)nessing: breathing slowly and deeply, with precise focus on each storyteller. My heartbeat echoed like a drum. Each breath became a prayer for their safety. I was immersed in an overwhelming longing for peace now that I was wit(h)nessing the reality of war.

There were common threads woven throughout their stories. They told us about entire villages that had been raped and massacred. We heard about kidnapping, enslavement, mothers being sexually tortured while their children were forced to watch, women left with fistulas, HIV, young women having babies after gang rape and being too traumatized to care for them. After these horrors, survivors were often rejected by their families and villages. And the perpetrators walked away with impunity.

—

After hearing more survivors share their stories in the coming days, I came home from eastern DRC with a traumatic stress disorder. I suffered nightmares, sleeplessness, poor appetite, and an unfamiliar energy that buzzed incessantly around my head. I found myself getting into futile arguments, trying to assert the urgency of the situation in DRC. I was soon referred to a trauma therapist, and he informed me this condition could deteriorate into PTSD. I was aware that many Congolese women never receive access to trauma therapy. I also felt an urgency to *do something right away* to support them. But I had no idea where to start.* So, I began my own process of treatment.

In the coming pages, you may notice that this book frequently mentions my tears. As Robin DiAngelo explains in her book *White Fragility*, we white women often weaponize our tears to derail challenging conversations within cross-racial settings.[40] Historically, white women's weaponized tears have had deadly consequences.[41] However, in my experience, "healing tears" are different. To be clear, the stories I've shared in this book focus on healing tears. They took place primarily while crying *alone,* often on the land or beside the water. A few stories include crying in the context of relational or spiritual healing.

During the trauma-informed treatment process I began soon after traveling to eastern DRC, I learned to dance, stomp, shake, wail, and roll on the floor. Eventually, I learned to sing, play percussion instruments, and enact ritual. In addition to these embodied forms of expression, healing tears helped me process my shock, grief, and rage. Allowing my raw emotions to move (in settings that would not cause harm to others) rather than denying my emotions and getting stuck, was a valuable part of my process. I learned that treating my own trauma was an important step that could mitigate my potential to traumatize others. Untreated trauma can spark endless cycles of violence.

Along the way, an indelible truth was delivered to my doorstep. The horrors I had wit(h)nessed came from the impacts of colonization. In a swift insight, I understood that the men who commit these crimes are not born evil. They are caught in intergenerational cycles of trauma that are difficult to transform. The ongoing circumstances in their country present complex challenges. Today, insatiable Western appetites for new laptops, phones, and electronics drive competition for minerals that are mined in DRC. I heard

---

* In the years that followed, my husband and I built a relationship with Congolese visionary Neema Namadamu. We follow her leadership in support of Congolese-led solutions with her U.S.-based nonprofit, Hero Women Rising (https://www.herowomenrising.org/).

Congolese women share how mines destabilize their communities with dangerous working conditions, increased poverty, and gender-based violence.

It has been hundreds of years since Europeans began exploring Africa and taking the land and the people as their own. Now, in eastern DRC, militias roam the countryside using sexualized violence as a weapon of war. These militias replicate the models that were employed by Belgian King Leopold's colonial security forces.[42] Today, women, men, children, babies, and entire communities still bear the brunt of this historic trauma.

———

During my own healing process, a local organization that provides services for survivors of domestic and sexual violence invited me to facilitate a dance and embodiment-based support group. One evening, a survivor's story struck a chord. She was an Indigenous woman who had been gang raped by many men outside a mini mart in her community. All of them were still walking free and continuing to harass her. She described going to a clinic after domestic violence, where her skull fractures were dismissed as "minor abrasions." She related how, just a few nights before, her young son was almost strangled to death when his father wrapped a chain around his neck in a drunken rage. She and her son escaped in their bare feet. They went to their family who refused to help for fear of retribution.

Listening to her story, my face burned and my stomach churned. In a flash, I understood—the nearby reservation where she lived bore similarities to a war zone. The circumstances she described were nearly identical to eastern DRC. A house of cards came tumbling down inside my mind. Though my comprehension was still tentative, I suddenly became acutely aware that in the United States, European-descended people like me are descended from colonizers. Our ancestors came to this land many generations ago and began systematically stripping people of their human rights, land, and resources. Our ancestors brought illnesses and state-sanctioned genocide that reduced the Indigenous population to 2 percent of its original size. The impacts of our history were evident in her painful story. Seeing this sinister truth made me feel broken. I longed to fix the brokenness right away. My mind began frantically grasping for solutions that all seemed impossibly out of reach.*

The outcomes of colonization were becoming clear on a personal level: I lived in a warm house with a supportive husband. Our family had access to nutritious food, education, health care, and safety. We were residing at the foot of a mountain that is sacred to her people. Meanwhile, the woman who'd shared her story was a refugee. She was running from a slice of land that was doled out to her people by the United States government and later polluted by corporate interests. Estranged from her community, she was recovering from gang rape and escaping an abusive alcoholic who tried to kill their child. For her, every day was an attempt to survive these circumstances. At the time, I was unaware of how long my ancestors had been in the United States. But I began to see that we were connected. Our stories were entangled in ways that filled me with regret.

When people of privilege stir from their slumber and awaken from the Dream of the Modern World, our bubbles of denial pop. We make connections like these, and it hurts. The shame of it is monstrous. Too often, we turn away. But this time, I chose not to.

Grandmother Moon Speaks

A few weeks later, our family went camping in the desert on an evening in early spring. Sitting on a rock, blanket-wrapped in the chilly air, I gazed at the full moon shining over the silent land. The moon was low and so bright that it illuminated all the shadows of the sharp, arid landscape.

---

* When white settlers start becoming aware, we sometimes feel an urgent impulse to "fix" and "help." Herein lies another paradox. Restorative action is urgently needed. At the same time, slowing down, reeducating ourselves, doing our inner work, and building relationships is critical. Discerning which steps to take sometimes requires slowing down.

The other delegates with whom I'd traveled to DRC were now busy generating social media campaigns, publishing articles, doing speaking engagements with Nobel Peace Prize Laureates, organizing a global summit on sexual violence in conflict, making documentaries, and giving keynotes to raise hundreds of thousands of dollars for the ongoing work against sexual violence in DRC. Meanwhile, I had been going to therapy multiple times a week and dissolving into puddles of grief on the floor.

I did not know what to do next, and I felt like a failure. The experience had eclipsed the well-oiled life I lived only a few months before. In quiet despair, I turned my face to the biggest, brightest presence I could see that night, and I asked the moon: After all I wit(h)nessed, what is my work?

I had never spoken with the moon before, but to my surprise she spoke back in one succinct word: *Relationship.* I did not hear the moon's answer with my ears. I heard it with my heart. Though I did not yet understand what she meant and was surprised to receive a message from the moon, I could sense that she had spoken truth to me.

———

My friendship with Chicana community organizer Clarissa Durán was a particularly supportive relationship after my trip to DRC. Clarissa and I first met in 2013, during a women's leadership gathering that was hosted by the nonprofit organization Bioneers.[43] On the first day of the training, I noticed how she stood like a mountain: solid, grounded, and strong. Her warm, funny presence was magnetic, and her laugh was a welcoming invitation. I felt safe with her, and I hoped to know her better. After returning home from the training, Clarissa and I became friends.

In the coming years, Clarissa opened my mind to many ideas that were new to me. When we first met, she was focused on cultural revitalization and intergenerational community health programs within her traditional agrarian culture of northern New Mexico. Clarissa's class, race, and cultural experiences as a Chicana woman differed dramatically from mine. We began a series of frank conversations.

One day we were talking about the depraved acts that white people have committed against the Indigenous Peoples of this continent throughout American history. Many of them were incidents I had only remotely heard of, such as the 1890 Wounded Knee massacre in South Dakota, when the United States Seventh Cavalry killed hundreds of unarmed Lakota grandparents, women, and children.

Clarissa said, "The challenges Indigenous communities are facing today come from historical trauma like this."

"I feel awful. What should I do?" I asked.*

Clarissa replied, "Your people were colonized too. You should learn about what happened to your ancestors in Europe. Our ancestors brought the two of us together. When we ask for their help, they connect us with people who can help us."

This stumped me—it was the first time I had heard anyone speaking about ancestors as entities who can still influence our lives.

When I shared with Clarissa about the taboos against discussing wealth that I'd noticed in graduate school classrooms, among white friends, and within my community she said,

"What if you were open about it, and shared honestly about the complexity you're dealing with?"

I gulped. The thought was terrifying.

Clarissa continued, "Telling the truth about your situation is what really allows people to trust you."

I often felt uncomfortable during our conversations. But I could also feel that Clarissa loved me as a sister. My denial was still too deep to fully integrate what Clarissa shared with me during our first conversations. I had to be exposed to these concepts in different ways over the years before her seeds sprouted. Looking back, I am

---

* I am grateful that Clarissa was willing to teach me. Later, I learned that asking this question of BIPOC friends can sometimes generate unwanted emotional labor. White settlers can engage this inquiry by seeking out some of the many resources and classes that are available. We can also discuss these topics with our white friends and family.

grateful for friends like Clarissa who had the patience to discuss these topics with me, even though I was still in the thralls of a delusional worldview.

Throughout our friendship, Clarissa often spoke of her warm relationship with her ancestors and how she would someday help humanity when she became an ancestor. In 2022, she suddenly crossed into the spirit world. I hope to honor her legacy by sharing what she taught me.

Water's Wisdom

In 2014, a few months after I returned from Africa, the moon's teaching about relationship led me to some human teachers. Clarissa invited me to join her for a special training with Tewa Women United,[44] a nonprofit organization in northern New Mexico that works to create peace by ending violence against Mother Earth, women, and girls.* We gathered for an experiential session with some relational trauma healing methodologies, facilitated by Elder Kathy Sanchez and several other women. They shared some unexpected guidance.

At the beginning of our session, one of our teachers showed us the clay pots that had come from her Pueblo. They lined the room, in various shapes and sizes, decorated with geometric patterns. Each one contained water. She explained that objectification of water is built into the English language, in the ways we discuss water as an "it," a resource, something to be sold or managed. In her culture (and in many other traditional cultures) water is a Being. Water hears what we say, carries our prayers, is capable of healing trauma, and must be respected. This teaching was turning everything I thought I knew upside down. I was being introduced to Water as Life. (Based

---

* In personal correspondence with Elder Kathy Sanchez and Corrine Sanchez, March 2023, they said, "Tewa-speaking homelands include the pueblos of Nambé, Pojoaque, San Ildefonso, Ohkay Owingeh, Santa Clara, and Tesuque. These pueblos can be found along the Rio Grande in what is now called northern New Mexico."

on this teaching, I've capitalized "Water" throughout the remainder of this book.)

Elder Kathy Sanchez placed piles of small rocks in our laps, so we could physically experience how the heavy burdens of trauma are passed from one generation to the next. Sometimes our ancestors carried trauma silently, as a means of survival. But silence can also compound trauma intergenerationally. She said the generation that begins talking about the trauma starts healing the family—backward into the previous generations, and forward into the future generations.

Next, she explained that change happens from the inside out. We are like caterpillars who metamorphose into butterflies within the darkness of their cocoons. Transformation must happen on the inside before we can emerge as healed people on the outside. At the end of our session, Elder Kathy gave me a small bottle of Water. Women all over the world had prayed ceremonially with this Water. She shared that Water carries the memories of our ancestors, and she encouraged me to try to listen for them. In the coming days, she gave me permission to share my understanding of these teachings. I've offered my understanding here.

I doubted I'd ever experience something as mystical as ancestral memory. Several years later, though, after praying with Water in intentional ways, Water-oriented ancestral memories began to find me. For example, Celtic peoples maintained reciprocal relationships with springs, wells, and other bodies of Water. They honored Water by offering objects made of finely wrought gold and silver to lakes.[45] Some European folk traditions once included reverent practices near springs and wells, such as making offerings, lighting candles, praying, collecting sacred Water, and healing children.[46]

Tewa Women United altered my worldview in ways that are still unfolding. They were the first to teach me about the importance of unpacking intergenerational trauma. They helped me commit to meaningful change, from the inside out. They catalyzed a profound shift in perception—the substance coming out of the tap, that I had taken for granted my entire life, is actually a Sacred Power.

—

I'd been spinning threads from the experiences I had in Ecuador, Scotland, and DRC. Interacting with Indigenous Peoples and Grandmother Moon offered insights that were new to me. Increasingly, I was noticing the wounds of whiteness in myself and the world around me. In the next part of my journey, I would begin learning more about settler colonialism.

White Peril: Settler Ignorance

One summer day in 2014, I sat on the floor of my living room with a new friend named Marie Gladue. Marie's loving heart is seasoned with a spicy dash of temper and her sharp intellect is mixed with a generous portion of humor. She is a Diné grandmother, scholar, and community organizer who raises sheep in the tradition of her grandmothers. A warm breeze blew through the open windows, caressing us with aromas of the nearby Ponderosa pine forest and an approaching monsoon rainstorm.

Marie and I had recently bonded over our shared interest in historical trauma,* and we were developing a curriculum that combined her cultural knowledge with my background in movement and embodiment. Over the next couple years, we facilitated our Healing with Earth and Sky workshop series for survivors of sexual and domestic violence, Indigenous groups, visitors from African nations, and Euro-American settlers. In the process, our relationship deepened as we learned more about how colonization has impacted each of these groups in different ways.

My interest in historical trauma was provoked by my experiences in eastern DRC. In contrast, Marie's interest in historical trauma had been a long-standing part of her life. Marie is descended from people

---

* For an explanation of historical trauma, please see pages 168–72 of *Unsettling Truths: The Ongoing, Dehumanizing Legacy of the Doctrine of Discovery*, by Mark Charles and Soong-Chan Rah.

who survived the Navajo Long Walk.* In 1864, under President Abraham Lincoln's administration, Kit Carson led a campaign to destroy the homes and foods of Diné people.[47] The United States Government used these brutal techniques to push Diné communities off their land at gunpoint, in today's Arizona and New Mexico. The survivors were held captive for four years and were not allowed to return home until 1868.†

On this sweet, warm summer day, as Marie and I brainstormed, made lists, experimented with movement, and talked about how to care for the people who attended our workshops, a story bubbled up out of her. This story was passed down through her community's oral history of the Long Walk.

"The Diné people were force-marched for three hundred miles. Along the way, the Elders, pregnant women, sick people, and children who could not keep up were either shot or left to die. They were freezing and starving. When the survivors of the walk finally made it to the Bosque Redondo at Fort Sumner, New Mexico, they were held there for four years in a concentration camp. They were forced to assimilate to the American way of life. Many more died. Soldiers raped the women, and so a lot of the people who came back from the Long Walk were mixed-blood. Nothing would grow in the soil, and the people were starving.

"In 1868 our leaders negotiated a treaty, and the people were allowed to return to some parts of our homeland. Our land was now called the Navajo Reservation. Before they could leave, they were made to stand in a courtyard, where the soldiers had tied a goat to a post. The people were told: 'You must follow the laws of the United

---

* Prior to colonial contact, the people referred to themselves as *Diné*. *Navajo* is a name that was imposed by Spanish colonizers. It was later adopted by the United States government.

† To learn about the Navajo Long Walk, I recommend:
  - The young readers' book *Navajo Long Walk: The Tragic Story of a Proud People's Forced March from Their Homeland* by Joseph Bruchac; illustrated by Shonto Begay.
  - *The Long Walk: The Forced Navajo Exile*, by Jennifer Denetdale.
  - *Navajo Stories of the Long Walk Period*, edited by Broderick H. Johnson; illustrated by Raymond Johnson and Teddy Draper Jr.

States government. You must send your children to school. If you don't, you will be breaking the law. This is what we will do to you if you break the law.'

"And then," continued Marie, "They beat that goat to death."

Silence filled the room and ice gripped my heart. Although I had been living for over twenty years on the same lands from which her Diné ancestors were forcibly removed, I hadn't fully grasped that they were *her* ancestral lands. I had a vague memory of learning about the Long Walk during graduate school, but my perception was that it had happened "a long time ago" and that it was "in the past." In an academic setting with my settler denial intact, its cruelty didn't register. Because I didn't have any relationships with Diné people at that time, I had no idea how much the displacement was still impacting them. Now, I could feel that the Long Walk was still haunting my dear friend Marie, sitting next to me there on the floor.

Over time, I would learn about the impact of colonialism on Marie's family—the shaming of their identity as Diné people; the stealing of their language as generations of children were punished for speaking *Diné Bizaad* in boarding schools; the pressure to abandon traditional lifeways in order to survive within a capitalist economy; the collusion by corporate and government interests to once again relocate Diné people from their homelands in 1974;* the racial capitalism that would desecrate one of their holy mountains as a repository for snow manufactured from treated sewage Water, enabling settler recreation. (I've shared more about this mountain in Part Two.)

Sitting on the living room floor, I did not yet understand these far-reaching impacts. But I could viscerally sense Marie's pain. With healing tears in my eyes, I said, "Marie, I didn't know. I am so sorry."

---

* To learn more about the so-called Navajo-Hopi land dispute:
- Marie recommends the film *Broken Rainbow* (https://www.youtube.com/watch?v=W5z8OgMfXXc) and the book *Unreal City: Las Vegas, Black Mesa, and the Fate of the West*, by Judith Nies.
- Diné Elder Viki Blackgoat recommends *The Wind Won't Know Me: A History of the Navajo-Hopi Dispute*, by Emily Benedek.

With a prayer, Marie quickly lit a single leaf of dry sage. She held the smoking leaf between her fingertips as we bent our heads toward each other. She shared the importance of cleansing ourselves when we speak of such difficult things. She said, "This is why we need healing for our people."

———

Years later, I understood that my ignorance about this history has roots within heroic American mythology that was engineered for the descendants of colonizers to believe and uphold. I learned it by osmosis as a child while watching cartoons that depicted "Indian savages" as a form of comedy. In our elementary school textbooks, the 1872 painting "American Progress" showed an angelic lady in a white dress floating through the sky. She was the idealized embodiment of Manifest Destiny and westward expansion.[48] At school, church, and home, the underlying assumption was that this is "our" land. We did not read the books or watch the films that could have educated us about what really happened. In our segregated neighborhoods, Indigenous histories were invisible to us. We didn't have any relationships with those communities, so there was no one to contradict our heroic mythology.

A few generations after the Long Walk, the descendants of the government officials and soldiers who enacted the atrocities would gradually forget what transpired. Or, if they chose to remember, they would sometimes pass these horrific stories down to future generations as a point of misguided family pride. In the coming generations, the settlers who claimed the stolen Diné homelands as their own would tell themselves that they were just buying "private property" at a fair market price.

As children, we would be immersed in stories that normalized our perceived superiority. We would be told that such historical events were unfortunate, but that they had happened a long time ago...so long, in fact, that they may as well be forgotten. Our ancestors' inherent "innocence" would become the air we breathed, generation after generation. Our unquestioned belief in the innocence of our people keeps us in a perpetual childlike state that prevents us from becoming the good relatives who are needed now.

European colonizers obliterated many of the Indigenous inhabitants of this continent with disease, massacres, sterilization, and displacement. Subsequent generations of white settlers would be raised to perceive that (so-called) Indians lived on (so-called) reservations and that was just how life had always been. Our European ancestors intentionally impoverished the Original Peoples of Turtle Island by destroying their foods and homes, and then passed down a lie depicting "Native Americans" as poor, homeless people. In some parts of the United States, particularly in the east, Indigenous presence and identities were almost entirely erased. Our settler ancestors enacted profound physical, sexual, and emotional harm upon the First Peoples of this land, and then taught us to think of their descendants as alcoholics and drug addicts.

In my experience, settler colonialism tends to make white settlers ignorant of our people's history on this continent and thereby, complicit in its ongoing perpetration. However, by making sustained efforts to educate ourselves, we can pop our bubbles of ignorance. This is a critical step toward becoming a good relative.

This book has been largely informed by my relationships with generous interpersonal philanthropists like Clarissa and Marie, who have kindly shared their stories, hearts, and homes with me. These relationships allowed me to begin understanding the impact of genocide that has been undermining Indigenous populations on Turtle Island for over 500 years. I share these stories to underscore the healing that can emerge from cross-cultural relationships.

White Peril: Spiritual Orphanhood

I was raised in Evangelical Christian churches. Christianity was the religion practiced on both sides of my family for as many generations as we can remember. Throughout my childhood, I loved hearing stories about Jesus, especially his teachings about unconditional love for the poor and disenfranchised, and the times he multiplied food to feed the hungry.

When I was growing up, my family attended church every Sunday. As a young child, I enjoyed going to Sunday school. But church started feeling dissonant to me as a teenager. Anxiously, I sat on the pew each week in my pearls, pantyhose, and modest dresses, desperately longing to escape. Male ministers stood above the congregation, preaching authoritatively. I had a hard time connecting with what they were saying. Even though I had been brought up with the concept of "original sin" and the assertion that non-Christian people were destined for hell, these ideas suddenly felt repugnant. I didn't resonate with most of the hymns and felt phony singing them. So, I refused to sing. To manage my discomfort and keep the peace with my family, I went numb and silently endured church each week.

When I was fifteen, all the teens in our youth group were asked to sit together in a circle. We were given a chart outlining human sexuality on a linear continuum. Eye contact and holding hands were at the beginning and heterosexual intercourse was at the end. The youth pastor discussed each item on the chart. Then he asked us to publicly confess which activities we had done, and with whom. Although I was innocent of almost everything on the chart, this activity disgusted me. It felt like public shaming and an invasion of our privacy. I was also disturbed when pastors encouraged us to proselytize and convert others. They said it was our responsibility to save their souls from hell. But I felt it was disrespectful to assume we knew best and push our beliefs on others.

Even though it hurt my grandparents, parents, and extended family, I eventually parted ways with the church. At the time I didn't understand my act of resistance. When I look back at my adolescent self, struggling on the pew and longing to escape, I honor the emergent intuition that pushed me toward something unknown. I now understand that I was following an impulse to cultivate ways of understanding the world that predate institutional Christianity.*

For years afterward, I thought that there was nothing left for me

---

* I recommend *Buffalo Shout, Salmon Cry: Conversations on Creation, Land Justice, and Life Together*, edited by Steve Heinrichs. This book includes robust dialogues among white Christian settler, Indigenous Christian, and non-Christian Indigenous perspectives.

in the spiritual realm. But as a young mother, I sensed that spirituality had something to do with the environmental and social crises of our time. I wondered if I would ever find a spiritual path to resonate with my desire to care for Earth and humanity.

———

In my late thirties, when I began learning about Indigenous cultures and building relationships with Indigenous Peoples, something clicked. Their cultural techniques for living in harmony with land, animals, and Water were magnetic. Their ceremonies for life events, seasons, and planting engaged my imagination. Hearing that ceremony could heal trauma felt like a forgotten memory.

I was beginning to see that there might be a few Indigenous gatherings I'd be invited to attend, in the context of the new relationships I was developing. But mostly, these cultural practices were closed to people like me. As soon as my eyes were opened to the beauty of these lifeways it was clear that I was not part of those communities. I didn't have the skills or opportunities to fully immerse myself in Indigenous ways of being. Over time, I developed the humility and compassion to accept this reality. There are valid reasons for the protection of Indigenous cultural practices within each culture *and* in relation to outside cultures. Centuries of painful events created the need for Indigenous Peoples to protect their cultural privacy.*

In the fall of 2014, Marie and I took a road trip. While we drove, Marie shared stories of her *Kiinaaldá* (pronounced "kee-nahl-DAH"),[49] the coming-of-age ceremony Diné girls have at the onset of their menstruation. When Marie told her mother she had started her first period, her mother immediately went around the neighborhood calling out to everyone that there was about to be a *Kiinaaldá*. This ceremony takes place over four days of a girl's first period, in an intergenerational community setting.

———

* Cultural privacy is a concept I learned from Cara Romero (Chemehuevi) and Alexis Bunten (Aleut/Yup'ik) in a Bioneers Indigeneity webinar (https://bioneers. org/indigeneity-program/). I've used it here with their permission.

Smiling, Marie described how, on the last morning of the ceremony, before dawn, her mother ceremonially washed her hair.
Instead of pouring cold Water over Marie's head, her mother made
the extra effort to heat the Water over the fire. This was a sweet
surprise that has stayed with her to this day. Marie also described
her annoyance, after grinding corn by hand for four days, to learn
that she was not going to eat a piece of the big cake she was making.
Her labor was solely to benefit the community.

Marie reminisced and we laughed together. I thought it was exquisite that this traditional ceremony was still being practiced by Diné
families close to my home. Raised within mainstream American culture, I couldn't fathom a whole community coming together for four
days of a girl's first period, to teach her, honor her, and receive her
blessings. Listening to Marie, I was enchanted and saddened at the
same time. Her story was showing me a contrast that made my heart
ache: Marie's matriarchal, matrilineal, matrifocal, and matrilocal
Indigenous culture* openly honors menstruation in community. My
patriarchal settler culture cloaks menstruation in secrecy and shame.

My daughter was approaching adolescence. I wanted to mark the
occasion ceremonially, but I had no idea how to do this in a way that
was authentic for us. I wondered about our ancestors. Surely, there
was a time when European girls were initiated as they came of age?
I had spoken with my daughter about creating our own ceremony
when her time came, but she was opposed to having our friends or
relatives participate. People don't typically do things like that in our
community, and she would have been mortified. I was beginning to
grasp how these menstrual taboos have been replicating one generation after the next, shaping Eurocentric culture in insidious ways.

---

* In personal correspondence with Diné Elders Viki Blackgoat and Marie Gladue,
January 2023, they shared that, historically, Diné culture is matrilineal (meaning that
kinship is passed primarily through the mother's line), matriarchal (meaning that
women lead Diné communities), and matrilocal (meaning that families live on the
woman's family land). In personal correspondence with Lyla June Johnston (July 2023),
she also referred to Diné culture as matrifocal (meaning that it centers women). She
conveyed that even though women are centered and honored as life-givers, male and
female energies are equal and complementary, and each is uniquely essential.

That night after the road trip, I sat alone in a dark, quiet room. Suddenly, it felt like my heart was being pulled out of my chest. The words "spiritual orphan" popped into my mind, and I started sobbing. I realized that's what I was. No matter how many stories I heard about Indigenous ceremonies, for me, these stories could not restore belonging to a culture that was connected to the Earth and honored the feminine.

I did not know anyone who could show me the way back to my own roots. At that time, I believed that I would never know the ceremonies practiced by my ancestors long ago in Europe. I could learn about the Indigenous cultures of Turtle Island, but only to a point. I did not want to engage in cultural appropriation* that would cause further harm to the First Peoples of this land. I did not want to perpetrate any more harm.

Several years later, dreams began guiding me back to my own ancestral European roots. (I've shared more about this in Parts Two and Three.)

Pray for Your Teacher to Find You

After becoming conscious of my spiritual orphanhood, I grieved throughout the following winter. I was becoming aware of the colonial dynamics that made me feel as though learning Indigenous practices of Turtle Island was prohibited. White people had shown time and again that we were not trustworthy. At the same time, I was experiencing something that I now understand as a sacred longing for reconnection. But I did not know how to begin.

During the spring of 2015, I attended a workshop with a Q'ero Elder from the Andes of Peru that was hosted by a local organization. The topic of the day was Indigenous Wisdom and Sustainability. When it came time for questions, I asked, "How can I connect with

---

* I recommend pages 111–28 of *Rites and Responsibilities: A Guide to Growing Up*, by Hungarian-descended anti-racist educator Darcy Ottey. She discusses the nuances of cultural appropriation, exchange, and recovery within the colonization-damaged cultural landscape surrounding us.

Indigenous wisdom, when my Indigenous European roots were severed long ago? I have no way to find them." I felt desperate asking this question, and my voice shook.

Through translation from Quechua, the Elder answered, "We are going to do a ceremony today, and you must pray for your teacher to find you. Breathe your prayer onto a petal. We will place it in the bundle." He carefully assembled cotton, seashells, candies, cookies, gold, silver, and other offerings. Finally, a basket of red flower petals was passed around the room. We were instructed to hold the delicate petals in our fingers and exhale our prayers into them. The petals went into a bundle for burning that afternoon.

On the way home, I felt better. I was grateful that my mood had finally lifted on that beautiful spring day. That night, something unusual happened—a Diné friend invited me to a ceremony the following day on the nearby mountain, known as *Dokoʼoosłííd* (pronounced "doh-koh-oh-STHLEED")[50] in the Diné language. I was surprised and honored. The next morning, I headed to the designated meeting spot outside of town. I pulled up just as the group was about to depart. When I arrived, I found myself in a gathering of about forty Indigenous People from different Nations. There were one or two other white people present. We kept our heads down and looked unsure of ourselves.

I didn't understand the plan for the day, and my friend had disappeared into the group. So, I silently watched everyone and followed their lead up a trail to the inner basin of the volcanic mountain. I had heard that it was important for women to wear long skirts to ceremonies. That small piece of cultural competence made me feel a little better about my participation in this adventure. I hadn't brought any food or Water, but I was dressed comfortably for the day and my shoes were functional. Mostly I walked alone, in silence. But an older Diné man joined me for a while. We chatted briefly and then he said, "When we get to the place to make our offerings, the Holy People are going to be watching you. Talk to them and ask them for exactly what you need."

After walking for several miles, we arrived at the location for the ceremony. Cradled in the belly of a volcano, spring had made a soft, green nest for us. We sat together in an opening surrounded by tall aspen and pine trees. Tender blades of grass, moist soil, sunny skies, and fresh breezes accompanied us. After many prayers and songs I didn't understand, each person was invited to come forward and make an offering and a prayer. Feeling awkward that I didn't know about, much less have, an appropriate offering, I quietly offered a little tobacco I'd brought. With the kind advice of the two men in my heart, I silently prayed for my teacher to find me.

———

Years later, I would taste the fruits from the seeds that were planted that day. Gradually, I would understand that I had brought my yearning for reconnection and a prayer for my teacher to find me to a powerful being of kinship: this million-year-old volcano has been revered by Indigenous Peoples of the region and woven into their cosmologies for countless generations. She is a primordial grandmother: mysterious, powerful, and delicate. When I visited her as a spiritual orphan and asked for her help, she embraced me as her own grandchild. There was no human being who would teach me what I needed to know. Instead, *this teacher*, a sacred mountain, would begin weaving webs of connection. She began showing me how to change the Dream of the Modern World.

White Peril: Cultural Sampling

> *Cha bhi fios air math an tobair gus an tràigh e.*[51]
> (The worth of the well is not known until it dries up.)
> ~ SCOTTISH GAELIC PROVERB ~

In 2003, when my daughter was a baby, I saw a flier advertising a "Tribal Style Bellydance" class close to my home. The first time I attended the class, I was captivated by the dance's sinuous movements and elaborate costuming. I began taking classes every week. For the next fifteen years, I learned, taught, and performed this dance. I even wrote a master's thesis about how "Tribal Style Bellydance" benefits young women's body image. Today, I no longer use the term "Tribal Style Bellydance." Over time, I saw that belly dance emerged from decades of cultural appropriation. Also, non-tribal people carelessly using the word "tribe" in their marketing can be painful for Indigenous Peoples.[52]

This fusion-based art form was developed in the 1990s by Americans who incorporated music, movements, and costuming from various cultures throughout the Middle East, Africa, central Asia, eastern Europe, and India. They designed methods of group improvisation on which the dance was based. The style became popular throughout North America, Australia, and Europe. About thirty years after it was first developed, its originators began trademarking the dance as their intellectual property and selling it in certification programs. This made me uneasy because I could perceive the power differentials in the situation. Those who were repackaging and consuming "tribal" held exponentially more social, political, and economic power than the actual tribal cultures that had inspired this new art form. I ceased participating in the community and eventually stopped performing and teaching altogether.

In 2018, fifteen years into my bellydance journey, my friend Alexis Bunten generously read an early draft of this book. Alexis is an Aleut/Yup'ik cultural anthropologist, media-maker, author, and researcher.* She has a brilliant mind, brimming with fascinating nuances. Over the years of our friendship, I have come to cherish her astute insights. In her review, Alexis mentioned the concept of "cultural sampling." She didn't define it precisely, but she asked me to think about it.

I was already somewhat familiar with the concept of cultural appropriation—when a person or group in a powerful social position takes another culture's dance, dress, music, language, or name without permission. By introducing the concept of "cultural sampling," Alexis launched a process of self-reflection. Eventually, I started to see my interest in "Tribal Style Bellydance" as a form of cultural

---

* Alexis works with Alaska Native Resilience Circles (https://www.wejumpscale. com/resilience-circles) and Indigenous-led tourism.

sampling. Over time, cultural sampling became a framework that helped me understand some important nuances.

For example, "Tribal Style Bellydance" takes cultural aspects out of context, combines them, and markets them to Westerners. Typically, as dancers, we did not know which culture a specific movement, song, or costuming piece came from. We did not cultivate relationships with dancers from the cultures we were sampling or learn their histories. We were not in reciprocity with their communities. Without explicit permission from culture-bearers, we mixed things together and then sold them to other Western women. This is cultural sampling. As Alexis later shared with me, another form of cultural sampling happens when Westerners become interested in a particular culture or place for a short time, and then move on to other cultures and places in rapid succession.[53] In this pattern, we *consume* culture rather than becoming good relatives to cultural practitioners and communities over time.

Similarly, some Western spiritual seekers culturally sample elements of Hinduism, Buddhism, "Native American Spirituality," or "Shamanism." Sometimes, in New Age contexts, various aspects of different cultures are mixed together, marketed and sold. Over time, I learned that commodifying and selling sacred objects and practices are particularly egregious forms of cultural sampling and appropriation.

My process of healing from White Peril popped a bubble of denial about cultural sampling. Looking back to 2003, I feel compassion for how I was enraptured by "Tribal Style Bellydance." I was primed to take part in cultural sampling because my white identity had felt bland, empty, and meaningless for a long time. Disenchanted with my Eurocentric Protestant Evangelical upbringing, I was also fed up with our patriarchal culture that seeks to control women's bodies, appearance, and body image. With aversion to my own roots, I perceived my ancestors as irrelevant. In hindsight, I can see how these wounds made me hungry for a dynamic and liberatory cultural experience.

My first bellydance class in 2003 was a delicious experience. I felt welcome to participate in an earthy, feminine, artistic aesthetic. The dance embraced women of all shapes, sizes, and ages. After being immersed in a body-shaming, youth-glorifying culture my whole life, this first experience of body acceptance felt revolutionary. Most of all, as the years passed, dance classes and performing troupes gave me a sense of belonging. But it took me fifteen years, and Alexis's insight, to realize that my perceived liberation and belonging had come at the expense of other cultures, without permission, acknowledgment, or reciprocity.*

———

Most of the ancient Indigenous cultures of Europe were interrupted by various forms of colonization. Some of our European ancestors were violently dispossessed of their land, land-based lifeways, and languages. Industrialization has been spreading throughout the world since the 1700s, razing cultural and biological diversity. Today, because of these histories, many white people feel culturally impoverished. We are aching for cultural vitality and connection with Mother Earth.

After years of reflection and conversation with white friends, I realized that some of us still carry aversion to our ancestors' cultural practices that were vehemently prohibited and purposely erased. Other cultures sometimes seem more appealing or accessible to us. As privileged outsiders, we can easily feel entitled to take things out of context, mix them together, and jump from sampling one marginalized culture to another. The interplay of hungry Westerners, cultural commodification, and capitalism can further endanger marginalized cultures.

After centuries of hegemony, cultures that still have some or all their traditional knowledge are rare. At the same time, the insights they offer are critical, especially considering the urgency of the

---

* Episode 3, "Music," of The 1619 Project docuseries explores a similar (and widespread) phenomenon. Most "American" music has roots within African-American culture. These origins have been largely disregarded and unreciprocated by white culture. See: https://1619education.org/builder/lesson/1619-project -docuseries-viewing-guide.

climate crisis. In some cases, traditional cultural practitioners and Elders willingly share their wisdom with those who are immersed in the Dream of the Modern World, to help us learn to protect Earth and all living beings by reclaiming our full humanity.

As you know, I started writing this book after a Yorùbá *diloggún* reading with Yeye Luisah Teish. My participation in Q'ero teachings and a Diné ceremony catalyzed my relationship with a mountain of kinship. And, as you will soon read, I was about to begin an immersion into a traditional ceremony of another culture. I was intuitively drawn to the Earth-based relational worldviews that are woven throughout Indigenous cultures. I had never experienced that kind of expertise anywhere else. At first, I did not understand the complexities of cultural appreciation, appropriation, and sampling. (For definitions of these terms, please see the Glossary.)

During my ongoing inquiry into White Peril and cultural sampling, I have done my best to examine my own assumptions and seek accountability. Not everyone would agree with the path I took, but I want to be transparent. The teachings I received from a variety of Indigenous cultures restored my capacity to be in sacred communication with Mother Earth. Without being prescriptive, they showed me how to begin making personal reparations to both African-American communities *and* Indigenous communities. They also led me on twisting, turning routes to ancestral memory.* This taught me that both intact and severed Earth-based cultures are connected by a common root system, still thriving underground.

In her book *Sacred Instructions*, Penawahpskek author Sherri Mitchell writes about some traditional prophecies that have been shared by Wabanaki, Hopi, Mohawk, Anishinaabe, and Lakota peoples.[54] Passed down through generations, these prophecies foretold the environmental damage that European colonialism has wrought on Turtle Island. They predicted a time in seven generations, when

---

* On page 19 of *Living in Indigenous Sovereignty*, Elizabeth Carlson-Manathara shares a perspective that resonates with my own experience: "By attending Indigenous ceremonies, non-Indigenous people can learn the spiritual skills necessary to connect with their own ancestors and ancestral traditions."

people of all identities would come together to bring healing to this land.* They speak of our present time as a crossroads, when white people will at last *humbly* seek guidance from Indigenous relatives to re-member their balanced roles within the human family. Mitchell notes our responsibility not only to observe these prophecies, but to "actively participate in their unfolding."[55]

How we do this is critically important.

After centuries of gorging on the poverty and power of hegemony, sometimes, we white settlers are starving for connection. When we seek connection by bypassing our inner work or denying our White Peril, our presence can easily have unintended consequences. It is possible to harm the cultures we so admire by consciously or unconsciously co-opting their identity.

Indigenous ceremonies have been shamed and suppressed by religious institutions since Europeans first arrived on Turtle Island. They were criminalized by the United States government until the American Indian Religious Freedom Act in 1978. Many Indigenous communities are just now beginning the arduous process of reclaiming their land, identity, ceremonies, and languages. I support their cultural recovery by respecting their privacy.

At the same time, some communities have invited outsiders into their ceremonies and shared them freely. I have often wondered how these families and communities developed the will to include white settlers.† Because of their generosity, I experienced sophisticated and advanced spiritual technologies that have the capacity to turn even the oppressor into a relative.

---

* On pages 226–27 Mitchell writes:
  We are not placeholders in time but guardians of the future. As such, we have the responsibility of dreaming the next seven generations into being. This dreaming is the work of our lives. It is what we were born to do. In order to complete this task, we must join our hearts and minds in a unified prayer.
† Please see *Living in Indigenous Sovereignty*, by Elizabeth Carlson-Manathara with Gladys Rowe, for a variety of well-considered perspectives on white settlers' participation in Indigenous ceremonies.

As you build relationships, please know that settlers are not *entitled* to participate in Indigenous cultural practices or ceremonies. This can be uncomfortable for us to feel, and it is a reality we need to accept. If we are eventually *invited*, we must embody humility at every turn. Today, with awareness of how cultural sampling perpetuates harm, I avoid it. I've developed these guidelines to follow while learning from other cultures:

Ten Guidelines for White Settlers to Engage in Respectful Cross-Cultural Learning

1. Prioritize relationships and move at the speed of trust. Begin by sharing food. Dedicate yourself to long-term relationships.
2. Know the history of the people who host you. Be in service to healing the history. Take meaningful action in solidarity with their struggles and in support of their well-being.
3. Respect cultural boundaries, even if you do not yet understand them.
4. Be accountable to the communities that host you.
5. Ask, "How (if at all) can I help?"* Respond by sharing time, skills, networks, and resources as requested.
6. Build respectful, reciprocal relationships with communities, including Elders and culture-bearers.
7. Learn to speak a few words (or more) of the language.
8. Rather than teaching or selling their practices, develop your own understanding about what other cultures are teaching you.
9. Become grounded in who you really are instead of copying, appropriating, or over-identifying with other cultures.†
10. Consider reconnecting with the practices of your own Earth-honoring ancestors.

---

* This is a guiding question I learned from Lyla June Johnston in a Medicine Theory webinar (https://lylajune.wixsite.com/medicinetheory).

† In some cases, white settlers respectfully follow and practice an Indigenous culture's ways with such commitment that they are accepted and "made a relative" in that culture.

My arc of learning to respectfully receive teachings from other cultures has been rewarding. At times, it has also been fraught. When challenges arise, I check myself, slow down, and return to this list. After centuries of exploitation and division, building bridges takes humility and commitment over time. I will always be grateful to those who took a leap of faith to include me.

Support

In the spring of 2015, I made an offering and prayed on the sacred mountain for my teacher to find me. Later that afternoon, I was invited to support an Indigenous fasting ceremony that was to take place a month later. With respect for the people and community that invited me, I have chosen not to reveal their names or location. I *can* tell you that they are dedicated to healing human relationships with Earth. They have given permission, input, and encouragement for this book to be written. To protect the well-being of the traditional culture, I've omitted details about the fasting ceremony. I made these choices to respect cultural privacy.[56]

Before I arrived at the ceremony, I wasn't told much. But I was told that I would need to wear a long skirt, help out in the camp, and pray for the people who would be fasting. While supporting the ceremony, I watched people being placed, one by one, to sit alone in the high desert for several days. During this time, they stayed in the same place with two wool blankets and no food or Water. The ceremony required sobriety. No plant medicine or other substances were used. They were there to pray, listen, and receive instructions.

While they prayed, I cooked, cleaned, and sat in the dusty soil underneath juniper trees in the sweltering heat. Previously, I had endured car camping for only a day or two, with mixed results. And I'd camped for one night in the Achuar village. Now, I camped for six days with no running Water and no electricity. This was the longest I had ever gone without a shower and my cell phone was dead. As requested, I tried to stay focused on the people who were fasting by drinking Water on their behalf and praying for them. But it was as though I was wrestling with a rambunctious monkey inside myself throughout the entire ceremony. He bounced around the walls of my mind, arguing with everything he saw, trying to figure it out, and telling me how ludicrous it is for people to fast alone in the wilderness for multiple days.

When I first wit(h)nessed this ceremony, I saw people being left alone in what I thought of as "wilderness." Years later, Diné Indigenous food systems scholar Lyla June Johnston explained how the word "wilderness" reinforces the concept that humans are separate from nature. Before Europeans arrived, there was no "wilderness" here—there were vast landscapes with diverse climates and geography that were highly managed by their Indigenous inhabitants. Using culturally advanced techniques, they cultivated food forests for millennia before the arrival of Europeans. As Lyla shared, portions of this land have now become "wilderness" because the extensive land management of the Original Peoples was and still is prohibited or encumbered by colonial settlement.*

—

One night during the fasting ceremony, a lightning storm lit the sky with tremendous power. Heavy rain deluged our camp. Cold winds rattled my tent, and I shivered in my sleeping bag. Jolted awake with a racing heart, I felt terrified for the people who were praying all alone. How could they endure this? None of them had tents. They were sitting alone in a lightning storm, soaked by cold rain. Tossing, turning, and worrying, I feared for their lives.

In the morning, I was still alarmed. Surely, I thought, it was

---

* In a personal conversation with Lyla June Johnston, April of 2020, she said:
    The human and natural worlds are now separate from each other, but they used to be enmeshed. The colonial mind deemed our cultures primitive, but in fact, they were incredibly advanced. We understood and leveraged complex ecological systems, and yet we never enslaved or overruled nature. To be humble with Creation does not mean being uncomfortable or dirty.
  To learn more about Lyla's doctoral research, please see her TEDx Talk, "3,000-Year-Old Solutions to Modern Problems" (https://www.youtube.com/watch?v=eH5zJxQETl4).

time for us to go retrieve the people who had suffered all night. But the ceremony continued. The hot sun was already rising in the sky, evaporating the cold rain of the night before. I took a deep breath and resolved to pray even more.

After a couple more days, the people who had been fasting returned to camp. Silence permeated their presence. Their humanness shone in a way I had never seen people shine before. It was like watching a silent river moving regally across the land. They were sunburned, but not blistered. They were dusty, but radiant. They were full of palpable gratitude and love. Washing dishes, I observed them as they sat down to eat their first meal. The monkey stopped bouncing in my head and everything was quiet in my mind. A door was opening to something I didn't know how to name.

When it was time to go, I stared at the bumpy dirt road ahead, and tears welled up in my eyes. In my blood and bones, I could sense that I had just been given a life-altering assignment.

The Language of Symbols: Falling

After leaving the fasting ceremony, I received an important dream:

> I am standing on top of an old stone tower. It looks like a medieval fortress in the Scottish countryside. Standing with me is a father figure, but not my own father. We look over the side of the tower together. I am horrified when he falls over the edge. In a panic, I run down the spiral staircase inside the fortress. Turn after turn, it feels like forever until I reach the bottom. Outside the fortress, I see this shape on the ground:

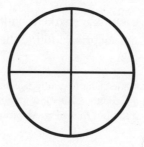

The man's body is nowhere to be seen. In the center of the circle,
embers glow. Their presence conveys that his heart is still alive,
even though he is no longer here physically. A part of him will
continue living. His fire can be rekindled.

Baffled by this dream, I followed the breadcrumbs that were
laid out before me. Six weeks later I asked if I could participate in
the fasting ceremony I'd supported. With a handshake, my four-
year commitment was sealed. (It is customary to make a four-year
commitment to the fasting ceremony in which I participated.) As
the years passed, I would understand that this teaching dream foretold the healing of my ancestral lineages and the rekindling of my
ancestral memory.

The fasting ceremony was freely offered—there was not a fee for
anyone to participate.* Instead, everyone was encouraged to be in
reciprocity from their heart. I reciprocated by donating food and
labor in the community. Throughout and since my four-year commitment, I've contributed to Indigenous organizations that are leading economic development, cultural revitalization, food sovereignty,
and land rights throughout Turtle Island. I've also supported (and
will continue to support) Indigenous relatives having access to their
ceremonies. Over time, I developed and practiced *Ten Guidelines*
for White Settlers to Engage in Respectful Cross-Cultural Learning.

Once a year for the next four years, I would sit alone, amidst
sandy soil, dry grasses, piñon pine and juniper, to fast, pray, and
listen for instructions. (I've shared what I heard and experienced
in Part Two.)

This four-year process eventually sparked an interest in my ancestors'
cultural practices. To my surprise, I found that some of them bore

---

* The appropriation and commercialization of Indigenous ceremonies is harmful.
To learn more and take action, visit the Center for Support and Protection of Indian
Religions and Indigenous Traditions (https://www.spiritprotection.org/).

similarities to my experiences within the context of the four-year fasting ceremony. For example, among early Celtic societies, seers performed divination based on natural phenomena such as the flight of birds.[57] In addition, sacred sleep and trance states were part of rituals in Ireland and Wales.[58] In her book *Celtic Myth and Religion,* Celticist Sharon Paice MacLeod writes, "From rising up in the morning to smooring the fire at night, all of existence was imbued with awareness and ceremony."[59]

Within eighteenth-century poetic schools in Scotland, students would spend all day alone in complete darkness.* Lying down with a plaid wrapped around their heads and a stone on their bellies, they would compose poetry.[60] In another example, the *taghairm* ritual was practiced in Scotland even into the nineteenth century. Here, MacLeod describes it:

> ...a person was specially selected from the community to undertake the ritual. Ritually wrapped in a bull's hide, they were taken to a secluded place (sometimes near a waterfall) where they were left alone to receive wisdom and guidance from the supernatural world.[61]

Eventually, developing an interest in my ancestors' Earth-honoring, traditional ways brought me wholeness and peace. (I've shared more about this in Part Three.)

Becoming a Different Person

I like hot showers. I also like clean sheets, comfy beds, cool glasses of Water, hot cups of tea, two delicious meals a day, and snacks. I did not grow up camping, and once had a fit when I tried to camp as an adult. The ice and food melted in the cooler because I hadn't

---

* Please see page 69 of *Soil and Soul: People Versus Corporate Power,* by Scottish author Alastair McIntosh, for a fascinating description of this practice, which was recorded in 1695.

packed it properly. Before I took part in the fasting ceremony, snakes, spiders, rats, and bugs gave me the willies. Sitting in the rain felt dangerous, like I might become hypothermic. I was unapologetically averse to getting dirty. I did not like feeling out of control. So why did I decide to fast alone outdoors for multiple days without Water or shelter?

My former self, who grew up believing that her mind was separate from her body and from nature, was about to become someone else. In the summer of 2015, I started to viscerally understand that Mother Earth was the foundation for all life, and that she was being endangered by human delusion. I was being given an assignment to learn directly from Her, by building a relationship with Her.

The way it was explained to me, through sacrifice, commitment, and resilience, surviving Indigenous communities preserved and protected their cultural practices for generations, despite oppressive conditions. Guided by their ancestors and Elders, some families and communities made the remarkable choice to invite non-Native people into their ceremonies, to unite the human family. As the years passed, I was increasingly awed by the generosity and forgiveness embedded in this choice. It continues to be the most humbling gift I have ever received.

My commitment to the fasting ceremony led me into a labyrinth of deep contemplation. I soon discovered that my teachers would mostly be other-than-human beings. Over the next four years, I would spend a great deal of time alone, learning to watch, pray, and listen. My extended family and white friends were, by turns, shocked, worried, curious, baffled, annoyed, and supportive of my sudden immersion into these other ways of being.

During the first part of this journey, some of my bubbles of denial popped. I was starting to see whiteness, philanthropy, colonialism, historical trauma, Water, culture, and land through different eyes.

PART TWO

Weaving

Women are spinners and weavers; we are the ones
who spin the threads and weave them into meaning
and pattern. Like silkworms, we create those threads
out of our own substance, pulling the strong, fine
fibres out of our own hearts and wombs. It's time
to make some new threads; time to strengthen the
frayed wild edges of our own being and then weave
ourselves back into the fabric of our culture.[62]
~ SHARON BLACKIE ~
(British Psychologist, Author, and Jungian Mythologist)

PART TWO is a weaving that took place over four years of contemplation from 2015 to 2019, guided by seven landmarks:

- Land
- Ancestors
- Water
- Dreams
- Philanthropy
- Fasting Ceremony
- Indigenous Solidarity Work

During these four years, I began recording my dreams every morning, and my dream journal became a source of important information. Sometimes, for several weeks in a row, I would have only a few dreams. At other times, my dreams would be disjointed and jumbled—the typical mental chatter of daily life. I had annoying anxiety dreams in which I showed up for a final exam, unprepared, with no pants on. But I also began having another type of dream that offered teachings.

The teaching dreams were distinct, and they came with intriguing story lines. Symbols, such as stone towers, snakes, geometric shapes, Water, and the repeated phrase "a long time ago," got my attention. They often felt like they carried messages from my ancestors. Today, teaching dreams still spark my curiosity and carry a strong emotional impact. I awaken from them enchanted or captivated by a new insight. I'm immersed in their spell for hours or days afterward, and they continue revealing their meanings over the coming months and years.

My teaching dreams offered insights that I couldn't have accessed in waking life. Parts Two and Three were written by following them to find out where they would lead. Later, I discovered that some of the dreams were pointing to ancestral archetypes, mythologies, and symbols of which I had no prior knowledge. Other teaching dreams predicted events that would take place in the coming days or years.

Additionally, I learned to treat my menstrual cycle as sacred. This time is called "moontime" in some traditional cultures because of its relationship to the monthly phases of the moon. Rather than seeing moontime as shameful, inconvenient, and dirty, (as it tends to be portrayed in Western culture) I began to perceive moontime as a teacher. I adopted a practice of taking time off from normal activities and spending time on the land or by the Water to rest during my moontime. My family supported this. Powerful teaching dreams sometimes arrived during these days. For me, honoring moontime also honors grandmothers, whose experiences encompass decades of moontime teachings.

The Dream of the Modern World tends to value intellect and rationality more than intuition and felt sense. But my four years of contemplation taught me that accessing and trusting other ways of knowing is a valuable skill. I reclaimed dreams, waking visions, intuitions, and gut feelings as reliable forms of knowledge. I wit(h)nessed prayer and ritual creating change, and moontime as a ceremony. These ways of knowing can combine with events in daily life, connect us with people, and communicate powerful messages about our life assignments.* Welcome to the labyrinth.

The First Year

Grandmother Anaya's Gift

In the late summer of 2015, friends and family led me to a remote spot surrounded by pinion pine and juniper trees. I hadn't spent much time mentally processing my participation in this fasting

---

*To hear how dreams, intuition, visions, and ritual have informed humankind for most of our history, listen to "For the Intuitives" (Parts 1 and 2) of *The Emerald* podcast (https://www.buzzsprout.com/317042).

ceremony. It was entirely driven by instinct. Now that the moment was here, I watched, anxious and speechless, as they walked
away and left me alone among the trees with two wool blankets.
Immediately, a hummingbird flew up and hovered for a moment as
if to say, "Welcome." Soon after, a mother turkey and her adolescent
chicks walked by in a stately, silent parade.

During the previous couple of years, my Diné friend Marie and I
had been co-facilitating our Healing with Earth and Sky workshops.
I was certain I would receive useful instructions on our work. What
I didn't understand is that I had just entered the realm of the spirits,
and whatever was shared with me would be their decision, not mine.

For the first time, I spent several nights outdoors with no tent.
Distant lightning silently illuminated the black night sky. The days
felt eternally long as I sat, petrified, lonely, and uncomfortable on
my wool blankets. One afternoon, in desperation, hunger, and
thirst, I spoke to the trees surrounding me and asked for their help.
Exhausted, I lay down and closed my eyes. In this physically and
emotionally depleted state, I was gifted with a vision.

From behind my eyelids, I saw a rough stairway descending into a
tunnel in the Earth. Slowly, I climbed down the stairs. At the bottom
was a small, wooden door with a rounded top. Tentatively, I turned
the handle. To my surprise, I found myself inside an earthen kitchen
with whitewashed walls. There were little windows peering onto a
sunny meadow outside, and potted herbs sat upon the windowsill.
In the center of the kitchen was a rough, round, wooden table with
two handmade wooden chairs. And at the table sat a grandmother.
At first, all I could see were her hands. They were wizened, gentle,
and dark brown. But eventually as I looked up, I could see her white
hair and her kind blue eyes looking back at me.

Grandmother knew I was hungry and thirsty. She plucked some
leaves from the meadowsweet on her windowsill and made some
tea. She buttered a thick slice of homemade, seeded bread and
handed it to me. I ate and drank, feeling profoundly grateful that
she was looking after me. I asked her name, and she said it was
Anaya. Then, Grandmother Anaya handed me a red cloth covered
in white embroidery. At first, I thought it was a handkerchief, and

I didn't understand why she was giving it to me. But then I had a feeling that the cloth had something to do with moontime.

Through imagery, Grandmother Anaya communicated that the cloth was a talisman for connecting to a vast, underground lake. She explained that women can lie down on the Earth during our bleeding time. We can place this type of cloth between our bellies and the Earth. This can protect us and help us as we connect to the Waters underground. I was shown images of umbilical cords that connect our wombs to these deep Waters. Then, Grandmother said, "When the women re-establish their relationship to the underground lake, the Waters of Earth will be healed. Go, take this, and tell the other women."

———

After my four-year commitment was complete, I realized this experience included images that carry meaning within deep time. These images lay buried in my consciousness for years, gradually revealing their significance. For example, 10,000 to 12,000 years ago, some of the first people who settled for extended periods of time in today's Britain and Ireland had dark skin and blue eyes. When I saw their modern-day facial reconstructions, I recognized Grandmother Anaya's kin.[63]

Grandmother Anaya's teaching included meadowsweet flowers and underground Water. I was moved when I learned that around 4,000 to 5,000 years ago, meadowsweet flowers were strewn on the floor of burial chambers in today's Britain. The body of the deceased person would be placed over the flowers in a position like that of a child in the womb. Remnants of meadowsweet-infused honey mead have been found in clay cups, buried alongside the dead to accompany them.[64] Reading about this, I reflected how Grandmother Anaya's meadowsweet tea encouraged ancestral connections in the years to come. And, as I later learned, in some places, Water emerging from springs and wells* was revered by Celtic peoples, possibly because of its connection to the underworld.[65]

---

* On page 6 of her book *Celtic Myth and Religion*, Celticist Sharon Paice MacLeod notes that within Celtic lands, offerings have been made at springs and wells since the late Bronze and early Iron Ages.

The buttered bread Grandmother Anaya fed me felt physically restorative, even as I continued fasting. I later learned about the importance of bread and butter for my Scandinavian ancestors. For example, in pre-Christian Scandinavia, people ritually prepared and ate sacred breads. They also buried these breads in the earth during planting time.[66] When the light began returning in early spring, Vikings made offerings of butter to honor the sun.[67]

My vision also included a piece of embroidered fabric. I later learned that during the first millennium CE, spinning and weaving fabric were culturally significant skills women cultivated in various parts of Europe. Sometimes, they blessed their cloth with incantations or used it for healing.[68] In the coming years, I would understand that Grandmother Anaya had immersed me in an experience imbued with multiple layers of ancestral memory.

After several days of fasting without Water, I was beyond any level of thirst I'd ever experienced. My mouth was dry, my skin was peeling, and I was dizzy and disoriented. At the completion of the ceremony, a dipper with my first sip of Water was placed in my hands. I shakily held it, looking into the depths of the small cup, as indescribable gratitude and need took over. I communicated wordlessly with the Water about how much I had missed her. Loving familiarity passed between us like between a mother and her child. I cried before drinking the tiny dipper of Water that now looked as big as the whole universe. Fasting without Water allowed me to glimpse Water's infinite blessing.

The following year, in 2016, after making my own red and white embroidered cloth and working with it as Grandmother Anaya instructed, I attended the Ceremonies for Human Reunion in Europe. This was a series of ceremonies organized by Diné Elder Pat McCabe, and I've shared more about them in the coming pages. At the dinner table one evening in northern France, I was drawn to an Italian woman with dark hair and a warm smile. Her name is Silvana Rigobon, and her work takes her all over the world, teaching women to honor their menstrual cycles.[69] Suddenly, I felt as if

Grandmother Anaya was tapping me on the shoulder. So I pulled a chair up next to Silvana and told her about my vision and the embroidered red cloth.

She listened to my story and said, "Come with me. I want to show you something." We went outside, where she unzipped a large suitcase she had brought from one of her recent retreats. It was full of embroidered cloths just like mine. Her workshop participants had sewn some of them. Others she had collected on her travels around the world. She told me that guided by her intuition, she used the cloths to decorate the spaces where she taught and create altars to the feminine.

This was my introduction to the language of the spirit world. If we make the space in our consciousness, we can receive messages that complement and mirror the messages being received by others. I learned that the language of dreams, visions, intuition, and symbols wants to be heard. It has something valuable to share with us.

Nona's Dresser

One autumn evening, a few months after my first fasting ceremony, I was in the kitchen making dinner. I heard a loud *thunk* and my son began screaming in the dining room. With lightning-fast maternal panic, I discovered that a tall wooden dresser had come crashing down, narrowly missing him. All the items on top had somehow flown far across the room and landed on the wooden floor unbroken. They included a tall glass vase and a framed photo of my husband's late Italian grandmother, Nona.

After visualizing the horrible injuries he could have sustained had the dresser landed on top of him, I began asking my son questions: "Did you pull all the drawers out? Did you stand on an open drawer?" He had only opened a small drawer to locate a pencil. There had been no shenanigans to precipitate this bizarre incident. It was puzzling. How does a large piece of furniture that has been sitting there uneventfully for years suddenly fall over and project items across the room?

I had recently met Yeye Teish, a warm, wise, intuitive expert in ancestor reverence, who wrote the foreword to this book. I asked her opinion about this incident. She prescribed an ancestor ritual to be carried out over the next week. I was to create an altar and sit with it for some time every day, talking to Nona.

As the week progressed, I sat before the altar every day. At first, I felt foolish staring at an inanimate piece of furniture covered with fruits, flowers, and other offerings. But as the days passed, I started to sense a quiet presence permeating the room. Suddenly, I could *feel* how much we had unintentionally neglected Nona. She'd scrupulously saved money throughout her lifetime and left an inheritance for her grandchildren when she had died five years earlier. Nona's money had enabled me to travel to Ecuador and DRC. We had always expressed gratitude to our living relatives for Nona's gift. But as I sat with Nona that week, I realized that I had been remiss in thanking the dead. By devoting time and attention to Nona, I learned that she was sad to be forgotten and neglected, as anyone would be.

This opened my mind enough to create an ancestor altar near the dresser. Following instructions in Yeye Teish's book *Jambalaya,** over the next few weeks I did a spiritual cleansing of my house and dedicated a special corner to the people in our family who have passed on. I began sitting at this altar, trying to fathom who my ancestors were.

Some of them I had known well, such as my beloved maternal grandparents, Nana and Poppop. Others I had heard stories about, like my eccentric great-grandmothers. One of them was well-mannered, elegant, and had a "problem with men." Another left her home in a sod house in Nebraska, moved to the West Coast under mysterious circumstances, and came home with flapper-style beaded jewelry. Some ancestors I had photos of, like my maternal great-grandparents whose parents emigrated from Northern Ireland to Canada. In photographs of them from the 1800s, the women wore corsets and had their hair tightly pulled back. The men wore

---

* Please see pages 19 and 83–87 of Luisah Teish's book *Jambalaya: The Natural Woman's Book of Personal Charms and Practical Rituals.*

suits and long beards. Most of them looked uncomfortable, stiff, and bewildered.

For the first time, I began to wonder: who had they been in life? And what about those from the time before cameras? Sitting at my ancestor altar, a blank space yawned back at me from the doorway of these questions. Over time, working with this altar, I would discover much about my ancestors.

A few weeks after creating the ancestor altar, the following teaching dream arrived one night as I slept:

> *From inside a small apartment, I hear a crash and a heart wrenching wail. Someone has violently thrown my beloved childhood cat against the wall outside. Her injuries are so serious she will probably die. Peeking out the doorway, I see relatives walking down the hallway toward me. Some wear raging expressions that silently scream, "It had to be done." With a finger over their lips, others silently caution, "Shhhh…don't talk about it."*

> *Horrified, I turn back inside, where my deceased paternal grandmother awaits. She leans forward, and I assume she is going to embrace me. Instead, to my surprise, she drapes a long, green snake around my neck. Reaching up to touch the snake, I find that my normally short hair is long and curly.*

> *Whose snake is this? Whose hair is this?*

The dream woke me up and carried me to the ancestor altar in predawn darkness, shaking. A few hours later, my daughter and I went to a restaurant we'd never visited before. We were seated beneath a painting[70] depicting the curly haired woman from my dream, with a long, green snake draped around her shoulders. She was pregnant. When I saw the painting, my jaw dropped. An unfamiliar sensation shimmered around my body. The language of symbols was telling me something.

Eventually, I would understand the dream and the painting as initiatory experiences. The dream depicted family patterns of alternately justifying colonial violence and keeping quiet about it. My grandmother offered a blessing that transformed me into someone else. The snake, a symbol of the underworld and Water in Celtic tradition, is associated with healing and fertility.[71] The color green is associated with the Celtic Otherworld.[72] I was about to find out that I was metaphorically pregnant with a developing ancestral assignment.

Synchronicities like this have guided the process of writing this book. Over time, I began to view them as evidence of magic. I am not special, and I cannot take credit. These forms of communication are available to all people. They are gifts to be cherished, savored, and understood over time.

When it first started happening to me, I felt awed. I often wondered if I was just "making it up." Eventually, I learned to trust these episodes as evidence of a vast, loving Intelligence who speaks to us: humorously, metaphorically, and yes—magically. Many of us come from lineages who were told over centuries that magic does not exist, that magic is "crazy," and that magic is evil, punishable by torture, exile, or death. In my opinion, reclaiming our human relationship with magic is an important step toward restoring our power as whole and complete human beings.

White Peril: Amnesia, Grief, and Rage

It is one thing to do something, and another to deny it.[73]
~ JAMES BALDWIN ~
(African-American Author and Activist)

Though I did not yet know it, my ancestor altar was doing its work. Soon, an important encounter would begin to answer some of my questions. Several weeks after creating the altar, I met a new friend one winter morning at a roadside diner. Sunny Dooley is a Diné storyteller, and we didn't yet know each other very well. The night before, I had listened to Sunny tell a story that made me feel like I was a little child wrapped snugly in a blanket. Afterward, intuitively, I felt there was something Sunny and I were meant to discuss, so I invited her to breakfast the next day.

After coffee was poured and pancakes were served, I told her about my yearning to work collaboratively with Indigenous Peoples. Without missing a beat, Sunny replied, "Well, that is because you carry the epigenetics of the oppressor. You carry their DNA. We're told at this time, that DNA is turning back on itself, and coming to help us. It's turning back to make things right again."*

Her statement, made matter-of-factly over breakfast, seemed blunt. It had a ring of truth to it, even though in my understanding, I didn't feel it was true. You see, I had always understood my ancestors to be poor, devout, humble people who immigrated to Canada four generations ago, and later to the United States. I thought Sunny's statement was interesting, if not accurate. I was immersed in a white settler myth that had always allowed me to perceive them as innocent bystanders rather than oppressors.

A few weeks later, I visited my parents. My mother has a wonderful memory for family connections and stories, and we were looking at old photos together. At the end of the night, she gave me a book of family genealogy that was written by a great-uncle and his wife. In the book, I was surprised to discover that on my father's side, we had an ancestor who immigrated to Turtle Island in 1739 from Argyllshire, Scotland. Remarkably, nearly all of his descendants had been traced. He was my sixth-great-grandfather. Having access to genealogy records like this is one of the many advantages of white privilege.

Deeper in the book, I read that one of his grandsons, my fourth-great-grandfather, had inherited a plantation in North Carolina and an enslaved man from a family friend. This fact entered my consciousness with a sickening thud. For the first time, I realized that I carried the DNA of someone who had actively taken part in the colonial land grab and slavery. In 1833, shortly after the Trail of Tears began, my fourth-great-grandfather was living in Mississippi.

---

* I recommend Mark Wollyn's book *It Didn't Start with You: How Inherited Family Trauma Shapes Who We Are and How to End the Cycle*. He writes about "transgenerational epigenetic inheritance" and how the traumatic experiences of perpetrators and victims can be handed down for resolution in subsequent generations.

There, he received a grant of land that was likely stolen from Choctaw*
people, signed by President Andrew Jackson. He enslaved more people in Mississippi. After his death, his children fell into a dispute over
the estate, and they went to court. Records of these enslaved people
survived on a ledger of his so-called "property":

1 boy Trace	$700
1 boy Ben	$300
1 boy Willis	$350
1 boy John	$700
1 woman Elvira	$100

These people's names were followed by oxen, cattle, horses, guns,
meat hogs, beehives, spinning wheels, furniture, "bookes," etc. One
of his sons later sold people:

Boy John	$1005
Boy Isaac	$935
Eliza Negro	$592

Seeing their names with prices, lumped together with livestock,
farm equipment, and furniture, made me nauseous. Sunny was right
about my carrying the epigenetics of the oppressor. Shakily, I lay down.
I stared at the ceiling for hours before broken sleep finally claimed me.

After a restless night, the next morning I sat down to breakfast
with my parents and children. Gathered around a table at a diner,
we drank coffee and waited for our eggs and potatoes to arrive.

"I started reading that book of family genealogy last night. Did
you know that there was an ancestor who came to North Carolina in
1739? His grandson received a land grant. He and his descendants
enslaved people in Mississippi." I was sure that this revelation would
render my parents and children as stunned as I was.

---

* Eight years later, I attended the Choctaw Indian Fair (https://www.choctawindianfair.
com/) and visited the sacred *Nanih Waiya* Mound in Mississippi. *Yakoke Fehna Hoke*
(thank you very much), Dan Isaac and family.

My mother looked questioningly at my father: "I can't remember, did we know about that?"

My father shrugged and replied, "Well, that's what was expected at that time, of anyone who owned land. That was just what people did."

Now I was even more stunned: this had been known in our family for some time, but conveniently "forgotten." Our family had fallen into a culturally approved amnesia about how long we'd been in the country, and the fact that our ancestors had been landowners and enslavers. Over time, I understood this as a phenomenon stemming from unprocessed shame about our white settler history on this land. It is not limited to my family. Rather, it is a *deeply ingrained*, insidious pattern.

Learning about my ancestors' long-standing presence on this land was going to take some time to process. I had recently finished reading journalist Ta-Nehisi Coates's memoir *Between the World and Me*, in which he explains what I was seeing: the problems in America today are founded in a Dream. He describes the Dream as one that turned Catholic, Corsican, Welsh, Mennonite, and Jewish[74] immigrants into those who believe they are white. The Dream turned Indigenous Africans of diverse cultures into bodily commodities for forced labor. The Indigenous Peoples of Turtle Island aren't even on the radar within the Dream. Coates's Dream underpins the social, economic, political, and educational systems of the United States. It is maintained today by amnesia and denial. He writes:

> The forgetting is a habit, yet another necessary component of the Dream. They have forgotten the scale of theft that enriched them in slavery; the terror that allowed them, for a century, to pilfer the vote; the segregationist policy that gave them their suburbs. They have forgotten, because to remember would tumble them down out of the beautiful Dream and force them to live down here with us, down here in the world.[75]

Interestingly, Coates's "Dream" is the same word used by the Achuar people to describe the phenomenon creating the conditions of the "Modern World."

Having this history specified among my own ancestors helped me understand that the Dream is actually a Nightmare. I decided to do everything in my power to awaken from it. As I would soon find out, for those who identify as white, almost everything in our experience conspires to keep us asleep in this Nightmare. In the airport on the way home, I found that I was too ashamed to look Black people in the eye. I wanted to crawl out of my skin. Horrified, I wondered how they would react if they knew I was the descendant of colonizers and enslavers. At home, I was compelled to either obsess or forget, my mind chattering, "It's too late! What can be done now? If you told people about this, you would be ostracized!"

In the following weeks, I began to process the fact that the freedom, comfort, and privileges I enjoy today were built on the backs of Trace, Ben, Willis, John, Elvira, John, Isaac, and Eliza as well as the Indigenous Peoples of North Carolina, Mississippi, Louisiana, and all the other states our family later occupied. This made me ache with shame and remorse.

Other times, I was overtaken by rage. With shock, I woke up to the possibility of other descendants in our family tree, unacknowledged in the genealogy book. Did my great-grandfathers rape Eliza and Elvira and disown or sell their mixed-race offspring? Years later, with the help of professional genealogist Sharon Leslie Morgan,[76] I would learn about a mixed-race Black woman who was likely a descendant of one of my ancestors. Tragically, she lived in a mental institution for many years until her death in the 1960s. She had no surviving descendants.

Sometimes I yearned to find the descendants of the people my ancestors enslaved, look into their eyes, and apologize. At the same time, I understood that in the unlikely chance of finding them, such an apology might be unwelcome or cause further suffering. And what about the Indigenous Peoples my family displaced? I had recently begun to understand land dispossession as contributing to genocide. I woke up and realized that my family helped perpetrate their displacement. We forgot these things over time, as if they were just necessary evils on our road to "progress." As I continued waking up from this Nightmare, I finally understood that throughout my life, I have been an unconscious beneficiary of this legacy. I wondered: even with my good intentions, how could I possibly provide a remedy?

Intellectually, I understood that this sordid tale is only part of my ancestry, not its totality. I vaguely understood that there were events in Europe preceding these that had probably influenced my ancestors' behavior. But I didn't want to turn away from unpacking it any longer, and unpacking it hurt like hell.

The best guidance I received came from the forest. There, I allowed my tears of grief, shame, rage, and remorse to fall freely. The forest encouraged me to open, and let it move all the way through, rather than shrinking away from it. Years later, I understood this as an ancestral impulse. The presence of sacred trees is woven throughout ancient European cosmologies. During the winter of 2016, I didn't know about that yet, but I followed my intuition. Within the trees' embrace, I was overtaken by spontaneous wailing and sobbing that racked my body and left me empty as a shell. My healing tears poured into the snow, soaking into the underground Waters that nourish the trees. Often, I was not sure if these tears even belonged to me.

Were these the tears of my ancestors, who struggled to adapt to new lives far from their families and their peoples' bones? Or could they be the tears of enslaved peoples, haunted by memories of the vile ships that carried them far from home? Who agonized over their families being divided for sale, and who were forced to work to death? Could they be the tears of Indigenous Peoples who cared for their children and Elders as they perished from illnesses imported from Europe? Who were forced to abandon beloved homes, streams, and forests, and relinquish them to the European invaders?

After the years of work described throughout Part Two, I understood that I was indeed crying the tears of ancestors who were impacted by colonization and enslavement. Some of the tears expressed the grief of my own ancestors—people who had lived through events so extreme, they had forgotten their past identities as Earth-honoring people. When they came to this continent, they participated in stripping others of *their* ancestral lands and cultural identities. The tears of my ancestors taught me that grief is necessary for healing.* Saltwater cleansed my eyes and my heart, over and over again.

One evening during this process, I received an intuitive nudge: I would write a letter to transparently share about these experiences with people I trusted. Since the Nightmare is held in place by amnesia and denial, re-membering and openness would become the antidote. While writing the letter, I was taken into grief, remorse, shame, anger, blame, dread, and despair. But as the process continued, I caught glimpses of compassion, love, and curiosity. I was starting to learn how to make peace with two identities that seemed divergent: the one carrying the epigenetics of the oppressor, and the one carrying a prayer for unity.

Just as I was finishing the letter, the phone rang. It was a friend who is a Hopi farmer. He asked what I was doing. With trepidation, I told him the whole story. He said:

Remember to love yourself. That is the most important thing. You are the one who can stop the cycle. You must learn how to talk about this in a good way and still, not everybody will want to hear it.

The first person who read my letter was Yeye Teish. When we discussed it, I couldn't believe I was admitting my ancestors' part in this history out loud. How would she react? With her big heart, she received my news compassionately. She wanted me to know that sisterhood can be greater than the stain of slavery. She encouraged me to keep working with my ancestral material.

Ensuing conversations with other friends were also humbling and tender. One letter recipient shared her joy that seven generations after the assault upon her ancestors, a descendant of the perpetrators would come forward to acknowledge and mourn the assault.

---

* The poem "Obligations 2" by Oglala Lakota poet Layli Long Soldier helped me process my grief. You can find it in *New Poets of Native Nations*, edited by Heid E. Erdrich.

Through this process, the hairline fracture in my shell of denial, amnesia, and rage became a fissure. Despite all odds, descendants of survivors *and* perpetrators of America's atrocities met each other in recognition of our people's shared past.

Colonized by Vikings

One evening during these challenging weeks, my son asked me to read him a children's book* called *Scotland's Vikings*,[77] which had been buried unread on our bookshelf for years. On that cold winter night, we snuggled together under the covers. As we read, I felt a shock of recognition. Through illustrations, photographs, and stories, the book tells of the Vikings' colonization of Scotland over the course of more than 700 years. On a map, I saw an area from which my sixth-great-grandfather emigrated nine generations before, highlighted as a Viking stronghold. He was the first known immigrant on that side of my family. His grandson later received land grants and enslaved people.

Page after page, the book conveyed the Vikings' ferocity, their bloodthirsty attacks on monasteries, their lust for gold and treasure, and their complex navigation techniques. They sailed the open oceans and the rivers to carry out trade far from home and launch deadly surprise attacks. After occupying parts of Scotland for years, decades, and then centuries, it describes how they intermarried with local people, and how their names, language, customs, and culture became interwoven with Scottish society.

---

* In addition to history books for adults, I recommend history books for young readers. They help me access a sense of history that is emotionally connected and imaginative, rather than just intellectual. A few examples include:
  - *Keepunumuk: Weeâchumun's Thanksgiving Story*, a Wampanoag story about the origins of Thanksgiving, written by Danielle Hill (Wampee Washpanoag), Alexis Bunten (Unangan/Yup'ik), Anthony Perry (Chickasaw); illustrated by Gary Meeches Sr. (Anishinaabe).
  - *Crazy Horse and Custer: Born Enemies*, by author and illustrator S.D. Nelson (Lakota).
  - *Navajo Long Walk: The Tragic Story of a Proud People's Forced March from Their Homeland*, by Joseph Bruchac (Abenaki) and illustrated by Shonto Begay (Diné).

That night, a veil of oblivion was pulled off my head. For the second time I was introduced to the idea my own ancestors had been colonized. They endured 700 years of settler colonization on their land, to the point where who was Viking and who was Scottish was probably indistinguishable. I started to grasp that the blood of Viking colonizers and the blood of colonized Gaels ran intermingled through our veins. I pondered what might have happened to our Viking ancestors that enabled their cruel treatment of our Gael ancestors. I wondered whether the imprints of this violence are still circulating within our family, and among the Scottish diaspora. If so, how long will it take to end?

Some of us believe that violence is inherently part of human nature and therefore, impossible to stop. Given the violent histories that have been noted since the beginning of recorded history, this is an understandable view. Yet, I feel that changing our human relationship to violence is both possible and necessary for the continuation of life on Earth. We can do the work to understand how history impacted our ancestors and how it shapes us today. Each of us has the capacity to *choose* forgiveness and peace. Each of us can contribute to ending the cycles of violence.

As we read on, my son said, "This is about *us*, Mom!" By asking me to read him the Viking book, he offered an invitation to make peace with our complexity. The ancient cycles of victim and perpetrator have made impressions within our DNA. And the longing to become a good relative was beginning to reverberate in my cells.

Why Amnesia?

> White America could not perpetrate five hundred years
> of dehumanizing injustice without traumatizing itself.[78]
> ~ MARK CHARLES AND SOONG-CHAN RAH ~
> (Diné Author and Korean-American Author)

Whiteness has been the subject of much writing, teaching, and scholarship. Public discourse on the topic became widespread during the racial justice uprisings after George Floyd's murder in the summer of 2020. But I find that we white people still tend to have amnesia about our own history of settler colonialism. Among ourselves, many consider it inappropriate, distasteful, or even rude to discuss such things.

As I began sharing my ancestral discoveries with my white friends and family, I encountered blank stares and shrugging shoulders, accompanied by a quick change of subject to something more timely, relevant, or entertaining. I was often told reassuringly, "Well, that was a long time ago. Everyone thought differently then. You shouldn't feel guilty about that."* Far from being placated, I wanted to scream. People literally could not hear what I was saying. I felt isolated in a process that was rewiring my core identity.

What I had discovered in my own family history posed a threat to the person I thought I was, and to the person I was taught to be. Looking back now, it felt like I was receiving an ancestral push toward truth and healing after many generations of silence. The process went far beyond a tidy phrase like "white guilt." I was rapidly becoming someone I did not recognize.

What was now glaringly obvious and "in my face" all the time was being actively ignored by well-meaning white people all around me. Overwhelmingly, I felt pressured to calm down, behave, and just stop talking about it. Why? Talking about the shadows of colonialism and enslavement contradicts the heroic American mythology that we learned as children. Within the Euro-American diaspora, our capacity to deal with our ancestral legacies is compromised. We are part of a culture that is more invested in maintaining a narrative of innocence and denial than in embracing truth and healing.

On the night of December 31, 2015, I learned about my ancestors' long-standing history on this land. The next day, January 1, 2016, the process of unraveling our family's amnesia began. I imagine this work will continue for the rest of my life. I hope it will persist into future generations as well. Over the years, I came to see our amnesia as a complex response to wounding that happened long ago.†

---

* Over time, I began distinguishing guilt from accountability. Staying stuck in guilt is not helpful. Moving into accountability catalyzes necessary change.
† Please see:

When our European ancestors carried their diseases, poverty, disrupted communities and families, severed cultures, and violence to Turtle Island, it did not expunge their own historical trauma. Establishing dominance over the unique civilizations that were already thriving on this continent did not make us whole again. Kidnapping African leaders, healers, holy people, Elders, mothers, fathers, and children to build us a wealth-accumulating economy did not bring us peace. In her book *Inherited Silence,** Euro-descended Elder Louise Dunlap shares how she perceives the suffering of our settler ancestors:

> ...a nightmarish, button-your-lips suffering that warped the mind, closing it to compassion for other humans and encouraging brutality against perceived enemies and the Earth itself. These ancestors struggled with a punishing legacy that still afflicts us.[79]

Our ancestors' punishing legacy went into the underbelly of our society. Today, it hides out behind a polite mask of denial. Almost everything in Eurocentric culture conspires to keep us asleep. Amnesia is the path of least resistance. The ancestors were showing me an unpopular truth: unleashing their tears and reviving their memory might just be the messy, raw, healing balm for the wounds our people sustained and perpetrated so long ago. If we muster the courage to traverse these shadows, who might we become on the other side of all that pain? Who *are* we underneath the denial, amnesia, grief, guilt, and shame? Let's find out.

- *Healing the Soul Wound: Trauma-Informed Counseling for Indigenous Communities,* by Apache/Tewa/Lakota psychologist Eduardo Duran, for his insights on the "soul wound" of colonization.
- Chaps. 11 and 12 of *Unsettling Truths* by Mark Charles and Soong-Chan Rah, on the perpetration-induced trauma of white America.

* I recommend pages 199–219 of Louise Dunlap's *Inherited Silence: Listening to the Land, Healing the Colonizer Mind,* about our European settler ancestors' unmetabolized grief, shame, and perpetration-induced suffering.

Ceremonies for Human Reunion

> Remember you are water. Of course you leave
> salt trails. Of course you are crying. Flow.[80]
> ~ ADRIENNE MAREE BROWN ~
> (Black Author, Facilitator, and Doula)

One Spring morning in 2016, I awoke to a quiet conversation. Visolela Namises, Sunny Dooley, and I were rooming together during the Ceremonies for Human Reunion. Our friend Pat McCabe, a Diné Elder, had invited us to be part of these ceremonies. We were traveling with women Elders and grandmothers from the Mapuche Nation of Chile, Arhuaco Nation of Columbia, Nahuatl Nation of Mexico, Aboriginal Australia, Malaysia, Namibia, and the Diné Nation. The ceremonies were meant to address the times in which men, women, and children were persecuted as witches in parts of Europe. In Pat's understanding, this trauma played a role in European imperialism.

During the previous week, Visolela, Sunny, and I had been sharing a corner room in a dusty attic in northern France. Visolela, a Namibian grandmother with a warm laugh and dreadlocks piled upon her head murmured:

"Sometimes the old people back home ask me, what is the meaning of this word 'land'? That word does not exist in our language, and they have a hard time understanding what it means. So I try to explain it to them. But we have always called ourselves 'People Who Walk upon the Sand,' because where we live it is just sand, everywhere. And everywhere we go, we are upon the sand. We do not have an idea about land, because that would be dividing up the sand."

Our Diné roommate, Sunny Dooley, was dressed in green clothing and turquoise jewelry with her hair tied in a *tsiiyééł*, a Diné hair bun. She replied in a sparkling voice, "Yes! It is the same for us. We call ourselves the 'Earth Surface Divine People' because wherever we go in this human body, that is all we are doing, just walking upon the surface of this sacred being, Mother Earth, with her permission. We do not use the word 'land' either."

Sleepily, I thanked Visolela and Sunny for this enlightening conversation. They shared their stories with me through relational generosity, which I think of as interpersonal philanthropy. (For a definition of this term, please see the Glossary.) Because I come from white American culture, I was trained to think of Earth's surfaces as land, property, and parcels. From birth, and perhaps even from ancestral memory of feudalism in the Middle Ages, I've been immersed in the construct of "private property." I was taught to perceive land as a resource to buy, sell, and rent. For my entire life, I had only experienced land as a *thing*, divided up according to utility, borders, and ownership.*

———

A year earlier, when Pat had first told me about the vision she'd received for the Ceremonies for Human Reunion, my heart immediately resonated with it. Though I didn't know much about the European witch-hunts at the time, I gratefully accepted her invitation to travel to the ceremonies. In the coming years, I would learn more about the historical events that had brought Sunny, Visolela, and I together as roommates in a dusty attic in northern France. (I've shared my detailed notes about the history of the witch-hunts in the Appendices.)

The most concentrated episodes of witch-hunting took place between the sixteenth and eighteenth centuries. The German-speaking lands of west-central Europe and Scotland saw the highest number of executions.[81] In various places and times, complex economic, political, religious, social, and cultural conditions combined to generate this terrifying phenomenon. In the process, some of the practices and beliefs that had long been part of traditional cultural worldviews were viewed with suspicion, demonized, and severely

---

* To hear more about the construct of private property as it relates to the European witch-hunts, please listen to the BBC Radio 4 podcast series *Witch* (https://www.bbc.co.uk/programmes/m001mc4p).

punished. Many tight-knit agrarian communities were deeply impacted by witch-hunting accusations, trials, and executions.

One afternoon in 2023, as I was reading about the witch-hunts, the book fell open to a page with an illustration.[82] My hands began trembling. The illustration was made in 1577, in a German-speaking part of Switzerland. In it, a daughter is suspended by her arms in a torture chamber. Her mother weeps nearby, awaiting her turn to be tortured. A working man turns a crank to intensify the daughter's suffering, while an elite man looks on authoritatively.

This illustration gave me a visceral feeling for the witch-hunts. Peasant families and communities were dehumanized in order to advance elite agendas. Even centuries later, my heart could sense the cruelty of the time. Generations of children grew up in a climate of mistrust, knowing that people around them were being accused of witchcraft, tortured, strangled, and burned alive. People of all genders who were exposed to any aspect of witch persecution (including those who did the accusing and the torturing) must have suffered deeply. Perhaps they internalized their suffering and shame for so long, it eventually seemed normal.*

Witch prosecutions in German-speaking areas were at their most frightening and deadly in the eight years between 1626 and 1634.[83] I thought of my German ancestors, who began immigrating to Turtle Island in the following decades. Throughout my life, my family's German heritage has been shrouded in amnesia. None of the identity, language, culture, stories, or history have been passed down.† I

---

* Please see:
  - *My Grandmother's Hands*, by Resmaa Menakem. He describes how victim/perpetrator trauma can pass from one generation to the next and how internalized trauma responses can work their way into cultural norms.
  - *Gather at the Table: The Healing Journey of a Daughter of Slavery and a Son of the Slave Trade*, by Thomas Norman DeWolf and Sharon Leslie Morgan. They discuss how perpetrators are impacted by the harm they inflict, how victimized people can become aggressors, and how these cycles are passed through generations.

† German American immigrant communities maintained strong cultural identities for centuries. After the First World War and continuing after the Second World War,

wondered what horrors my German ancestors experienced before their grandchildren made the long voyage across the sea.

———

During the Ceremonies for Human Reunion in 2016, Pat shared her perceptions of how the so-called "witch" hunts impacted European communities over many generations.[*] She told us that much of the Earth-based and traditional knowledge that had been passed down through previous generations was interrupted and severed. She described the complex, intergenerational trauma of these events as an "archetypal wounding of humanity." In her understanding, this wound contributed to European imperialism.[†]

For four days each, gatherings took place in England, Spain, France, and Italy. They were offered freely for anyone to attend. The guidance for the ceremonies emerged from counsel Pat had received in ceremony. The Elders and grandmothers retold old stories from their traditions regarding "the Truth of who the Woman is to Creation and who Creation is to the Woman." Local European Elders were also invited to tell stories.[84] We heard the types of stories that have been told to young women during initiation ceremonies in cultures throughout the world.

During the Ceremonies for Human Reunion, songs, seeds, and dances were offered. Water blessings were administered with flowers, feathers, and a broom. Percussion instruments and rituals brought us healing. We took part in a ceremony to honor moontime. A

German Americans increasingly assimilated into whiteness. See: https://www.loc.gov/classroom-materials/immigration/german/shadows-of-war/.

[*] Episode 13 of the BBC Radio 4 podcast series *Witch* (https://www.bbc.co.uk/programmes/m001mc4p) includes an interview with Pat McCabe in which she shares some of her reflections about the Ceremonies for Human Reunion.

[†] European immigrants also brought witch-hunting with them to the land that would eventually be called New England. In 1692 and 1693, more than 200 people were accused of witchcraft in the Salem, Massachusetts, witch trials. Twenty were executed. See: https://www.smithsonianmag.com/history/a-brief-history-of-the-salem-witch-trials-175162489/.

miniature coracle, which is a small, round boat, was filled with prayer cloths and offerings and sent down the river.*

While attending the ceremonies in France and Italy, I sat quietly on the ground with our European hosts and other guests. We listened to the Elders' and grandmothers' perspectives on the archetypal wounding of humanity. I heard that the wound had originated among our European ancestors, and that it traveled around the world, impacting Indigenous Peoples everywhere. They emphasized that the wound has hurt all of us, and they asked us to come back together as one family by realigning with the vibration of Truth.

During our lunch breaks, some of the Europeans began sharing their feelings and questions with me:

- How can we accept these teachings when some of them belong to other cultures and not our own?
- We feel grief and shame about our ancestral legacies of imperialism.
- We are sad that we can't remember our ancestral traditions.

I felt both unsettled and relieved during these conversations. They were imbued with a kind of kinship I had never experienced before. For the first time, I realized that some Europeans felt as bereft as I did, from the events that occurred among our ancestors long ago.

———

On the last day, the Ceremonies for Human Reunion took a different turn. It was a sunny spring day in the northern Italian countryside. We were being hosted by a warm, tight-knit rural Italian community. Our group gathered on the grounds of a rustic villa, surrounded by vineyards and charming stone buildings.

---

* This coracle ritual was facilitated by Elder Carolyn Hillyer (https://thebraidedriver. co.uk/) and her community at a stone circle in Devon, England. A *coracle* is a small, lightweight, bowl-shaped wicker boat covered in waterproof material, suitable for fishing. Coracles have been made in Wales for thousands of years. Today, they are still used in parts of Wales and beyond. See: https://www.visitwales.com/inspire-me/days-out/magic-coracle.

That morning, to my surprise, Pat invited me to join the grand-mothers and Elders during the ceremony. She asked each of them to stand. She prayed with each one individually, addressing the harm that had come to her people through European conquest. At the very end of the row, I was uncertain. Should I sit or stand? How could I stand with dignity, considering the violence our European ancestors have inflicted throughout the world?

Finally, our Aboriginal Australian friend Dinnawhan White, who is on her path to becoming an Elder, was standing next to me. Dinnawhan sobbed as she heard Pat's acknowledgment of the colo-nization of Australia. In that moment, it became clear. My heart was moved by Dinnawhan's pain and the harm that had come to her people. Solidarity and compassion overruled my insecurities. I rose to my feet to stand with Dinnawhan, wrapping my arm around her shoulders.

At the end of the row, Pat and I now stood alone. I wondered what could she possibly say to me, a child of broken European lin-eages? With tears in her eyes, Pat addressed the suffering of my ancestors who had immigrated to Turtle Island. She acknowledged that they took land and enslaved people. Out loud, she prayed about something that was just beginning to form in my consciousness: a commitment to heal their legacy. Holding a feather and a bowl of Water, she lovingly wiped the tears from my face. Time stood still.

Re-Membering the Sacred

> Reconnecting is one route to wholeness, to
> reassembling our missing parts. The method
> employed does not lie outside; instead, it is a
> journey inwards, deep into our bones, our cells, our
> DNA, where remnants of ancient memory have
> been passed down through the generations.[85]
> ~ Jude Lally ~
> (Scottish Cultural Activist and Artist)

The Ceremonies for Human Reunion made impressions that changed me in the coming years. Four years later, in 2020, I began exploring archaeology, archetypes, and mythologies from my ancestors' ancient cultures. Some aspects of their cosmologies bore similarities with the Indigenous ways from which I had been learning.

Reading *Before Scotland: The Story of Scotland Before History* by Scottish historian and journalist Alistair Moffat, I learned that the prehistoric peoples of today's northwestern Europe left behind evocative clues about what was important to them. For example, in what today is called England, twenty sets of 11,000-year-old deer antlers were found. The ancestors had drilled holes in them so they could be worn as headdresses.[86] In today's Denmark, within a 6,000-year-old burial of a woman and her premature baby, the mother wore a necklace containing teeth from forty-three different stags. The baby was cradled beside her, placed on a swan's wing. Nearby, also in Denmark, a child was buried with a piece of local stone in his or her mouth. The stone had been carved in the shape of a tongue.[87]

In today's Hebridean Islands, beginning around 3,500 years ago, bereaved relatives mummified the bodies of two ancestors in a peat bog. The bodies were later exhumed and kept by the community for centuries, before eventually being buried under a house around 3,000 years ago. I don't know the intentions behind these practices. But learning about these sites allowed me to viscerally *feel* how important deer must have been to the ancestors. I sensed how they might have practiced their nature-based spirituality, how they cherished their children, and how they demonstrated devotion to their ancestors. Even centuries after their living memory had passed, the community still treated those two ancestors with reverence, by including their bodies among the living.[88]

Exploring the folk tales and mythology of my ancestors, I learned that Europeans once revered female as well as male deities. Their deities were associated with the land, birds, and animals that sustained the people, as well as healing, death, prophecy, and crafts.[89] One example is the *Cailleach*, (pronounced "KAHL-yakh")[90] whose name literally means "veiled one."[91] This "Old Woman," as she is sometimes called, is a primordial creatrix of what is now called Scotland and Ireland. She is ancient, sometimes large in stature, and strong. She forms Scotland by dropping boulders out of her apron as she strides boldly across the land. In *Cailleach* mythology, she often interacts with the landscape. One of her stories takes place on Néifinn Mountain in County Mayo, Ireland,[92] where some of my ancestors lived. In another, she lives on the Hebridean Isle of Erraid, where my family visited in 2012.[93]

I came to perceive the *Cailleach* as a crone who formed features of the landscape where my Scottish and Irish ancestors lived. In one tale, she washes her shawl white in her enormous cauldron* and lays it out to dry on the mountains. In other tales, she brings winter to their land. She cares for her own herds of wild deer and cattle, the same animals that nourished my ancestors. Perhaps some of her stones formed the walls of their cottages. Her tales were told while their peat fires smoldered, babies cried, stews bubbled, and their home-spun threads became warm woolen blankets. The *Cailleach* evolved through layers of time and history, adapting as the people changed.

Another example is the pre-Christian Celtic deity *Bríg* (pro-nounced "BREEG" in early Ireland).[94] *Bríg* embodies the sacred number three of Indo-European tradition. She is described as three sisters all named *Bríg* or Brigid. Each is known for her unique gift of healing, smithcraft, and poetry.[95] Celticist Sharon Paice MacLeod writes, "*Bríg's* name comes from an Indo-European root word mean-ing 'High or Exalted One.'"[96] She is still revered in Ireland, likely evolving into the figure of Saint Brigid, who is associated with "fer-tility, abundance, and protection."[97]

Every new year, as the sun rises perceptibly earlier each day, Imbolc (pronounced "IM-blk")[98] is upon us. For the Irish and Scottish Celts, early February was a season that emphasized wom-en's concerns. The people celebrated the birth of new animals and the return of fresh milk among the mother cows and ewes.[99] Imbolc is a time to welcome *Bríg* and ask for her blessing and protection upon the family, the household, and all our relatives. During this time of year, my dreams of sunrise, birth, and milk announced the presence of *Bríg*, even before I knew anything about her.

---

* Her cauldron is embodied by the Corryvreckan Whirlpool off the west coast of Scotland. See: https://whirlpool-scotland.co.uk/180-2/.

In 2020, three generations of my family celebrated Imbolc together and honored *Bríg* for the first time. We baked buttery oat bannocks* as an offering to *Bríg* and as a delicious treat for us. Some of us placed pieces of cloth known as *Brat Bhride* (pronounced "BRAHT-vreeja")[100] outside on the eve of Imbolc so that they could absorb *Bríg's* healing dew before sunrise. We also made strips of this fabric into prayer cloths called *clooties* (pronounced "CLUE-tees")[101] to tie to the cherry tree in our backyard, carrying prayers for healing in our community and the world. Similar practices took place throughout the year in Scottish and Irish communities, especially within trees near healing wells.

I felt relieved when these burials, archetypes, and folk tales showed me that within the historical layers, our ancestors' lifeways had once included more balanced ways of being. Some ancient European communities ritually honored their dead. They respected the Old Woman who created features of the landscape and cared for wild creatures. They celebrated mother's milk, the elixir of new life. They conducted fire rituals to protect their homes and animals. They sought poetic instructions from the Otherworld. Just like some of the Elders who were guiding me, they used prayer cloths and relied on divination. Once upon a time, they knew that the well-being of the land and the people depended upon thoughtful consideration. I began to dream of the European diaspora re-membering, after centuries of disconnection.

Scottish cultural activist and artist Jude Lally was the first person to introduce me to the *Cailleach* and *Bríg*. They came to life in my consciousness through Jude's online school, Path of the Ancestral Mothers.† Jude eventually made felted wool dolls of the *Cailleach* and *Bríg* that grace my ancestor altar. In the following years, we began a cross-cultural collaboration. Jude would donate her artwork and classes, our Diné Elder friend Andy Dann would donate his

---

* Each year on Imbolc, I prepare rosemary oat bannock. For the recipe, see: https://gathervictoria.com/2018/01/15/rosemary-oat-bannock-for-imbolc/.
† Sign up for Jude's mailing list to receive notifications of her classes (https://www.pathoftheancestralmothers.com/).

handmade silver jewelry and craftsmanship, and I would donate my time. Together, the three of us raised funds to support a school Andy's community built for Diné cultural survival and intergenerational healing. Partnering with Andy and Jude helped me revitalize my own ancestral teachings while building cross-cultural relationships.

———

During the first year, I embarked on a path toward understanding the disease of colonialism. In the second year, the lessons of suffering, grief, greed, and paradox would deepen. An Indigenous-led movement would offer me insight, and ancient ancestors would reveal themselves through an opening the size of a keyhole.

The Second Year

The Gift of Suffering

During my second fasting ceremony, I learned a lot from suffering. After only two days, I felt extremely dehydrated and uncomfortable. Lying in anguish under the blistering sun, I desperately stared at the clouds while gnats dive-bombed my ears. Although I had done this once before, I had forgotten how challenging it was. I spent hours feeling annoyed and discouraged. How could I have thought that this was going to help anything? Unable to focus, I fantasized about root beer floats, cool cotton sheets on plush beds, and air conditioning. The story in my head went like this: I am meant for comfort. I am not made for fasting without Water in the high desert, but for hotel rooms, room service, and ice-cold lemonade. I am simply not cut out for this!

After prayers for rain and hail, heavy rain clouds finally converged. Coyotes, clowns, rain goddesses, and witches danced in the clouds, taunting my parched body and confused mind. A powerful storm began dumping rain. It felt like the lightning was striking inches away. Within a few minutes I was shivering, cowering under my wool blanket, and trying to drink rain by holding out a cupped hand. As I licked my cold, damp hand covered in dirt and rabbit poop, I found out that it's virtually impossible to drink Water this way. I was convinced that my time on the land had been useless.

In the following days and weeks, I started to perceive the lesson: I'd been shown the part of me that is a brat. In the coming years, I understood that my white conditioning confronted me with a particular set of characteristics. For example, I felt victimized despite my choice to be there, doubted my resilience, and was certain that I wasn't strong enough. I felt entitled to abundant Water, food, and comfort. Mother Earth gave me some tough love to show me that these things are precious gifts not to be taken for granted.

During my days and nights alone on the land, I spent hours staring into space. I tried to surrender to the discomfort, fear, and loneliness. I looked as carefully as I could, but often saw nothing except the slow progress of the sun across the sky from sunrise to sunset. I listened to my relentless doubts dismissing all my reasons for being there.

But after returning to the company of other people, back to communion with Water and food, I could tell that I had been immersed in a different dimension. Deprivation from comfort allowed me to experience something extraordinary—an experience of unconditional love. Despite my tantrums, Mother Earth loved me. Even though I came empty-handed, with nothing but prayers, she had graciously held me and taught me.

I began perceiving her generosity and nourishment within a day or two after the ceremony. It was present in my perceptions: colors were brighter, hugs were warmer, fruit was sweeter, and peace filled my heart. My belly had been completely empty, but she filled my heart with contentment that I would return to in the coming months and years. Usually most of us are too busy, too distracted, and too comfortable to perceive this precious state. But it exists, nonetheless. I was learning that an entirely different kind of nourishment is accessible by showing up thirsty, hungry, and committed.

A month later, I *did* visit a hotel. All the elements of my fantasy were there: abundant fluffy towels, a hot shower, a plush bed with clean sheets, plastic bottles of ice-cold Water, air conditioning, and long buffet tables of food. The lawns were manicured. The sand on the beach was raked daily. The helpful staff met our every wish. But compared to the nourishment I had received while fasting on the land, this felt like cardboard, a poor imitation of the real thing. On the faces of the other guests and in my own heart, I could sense that we were being lulled to sleep in the arms of a Nightmare.

Before my second fasting ceremony, I had shared my prayer with some Black friends: to be in service to healing my ancestors' legacy of enslaving people. They encouraged me to stay with the discomfort and not look away. For two days during the ceremony, with difficulty, I tried to focus on my prayer. Years later, I realized that my internal tantrums and delusional hotel fantasies were forms of resistance. It was hard to sit with the legacy of chattel slavery that had been perpetrated and then forgotten by my own people. There is nothing like fasting alone on the land to reveal the parts of yourself you'd rather not see.

One night, while dozing in and out of sleep, I was awakened bolt upright, my eyes magnetized to the stars above. Like my dream in the rainforest, I felt stars pouring into an opening in the crown of my head from the depths of the night sky. For a time, I perceived nothing but Stars above, within, and around me. It was an extraordinary feeling. My whole being was permeated with a sublime sensation of belonging. During this experience, I said to the Stars, "What about my ancestors who enslaved people? How am I going to make this right? What should I do to work toward racial justice?"

In my mind's eye, the Stars showed me a giant reel of film for a lengthy movie. On each frame were moments that had been captured to tell the overarching story of humanity. I saw that my intergenerational tale of enslavement was only one frame on the reel of film. As the reel unwound, I saw that it went on in perpetuity, and that the frame showing this portion had already long disappeared. Trying to focus on it was like trying to climb up a sandy hill, only to have the sand slip through your fingers and toes, replaced by ever more sand. No matter how hard I tried, I could not get a grip on it. The Stars attuned me to their light, presence, and vibration. They sang of how we humans ourselves are made of Stars. They infused my being with light for quite some time on that dark, lonely night, and then continued to interact with me for weeks afterward.

This experience was a tremendous blessing. But I was also concerned about spiritual bypassing, the habit of easing discomfort by focusing exclusively on the spiritual aspects of life that make us feel good. It can take various forms, such as insisting that historic harm has nothing to do with the present, or that we are "all one." Spiritual bypassing keeps us stuck, unable to do the deep work required for real healing. (For a definition, see the Glossary). At that time, I was already aware of the ongoing, violent oppression that is the living legacy of slavery in the United States. My heart was yearning to support Black relatives' safety and well-being. Part of me wanted to resist spiritual bypassing by arguing with the Stars. I have unwittingly forgotten their message many times.

Eventually, I would understand that the Stars' image of the giant reel of film is about sacred movement. Everything is moving and everything always has been moving. Getting stuck blocks the flow of sacred movement. In the coming years, my experience with the Stars gave me the will to keep moving through the guilt, shame, and grief I felt about my ancestors enslaving people. Over time, I developed enough strength to face the horror of slavery more fully. Three generations of my family began working with the painful ancestral legacies we carry. This opened my capacity to begin making personal reparations to Black communities. I've shared about this in The Fourth Year.

Today, I am still learning to make room for seemingly divergent dimensions of reality and accept their coexistence. How to sit with the unspeakable and not look away? How to use guilt and shame as catalysts for healing? How to accept divine love and belonging at the same time? I am weaving a basket inside my heart that is big enough to carry these questions.

Sacred Mountain

> To claim our descent from the perpetrators is a renewal
> of faith in human beings. If slavers, invaders, committers
> of genocide, and inquisitors can beget abolitionists,
> resistance fighters, healers, and community builders,
> then anyone can transform an inheritance of privilege or
> victimization into something more fertile than either.[102]
> ~ AURORA LEVINS MORALES ~
> (Puerto Rican/Ashkenazi Author)

I am blessed to live at the base of the sacred mountain known as *Dokoʼoosłííd* (pronounced "doh-koh-oh-STHLEED")[103] in the Diné language, the western mountain of Dinétah. This mountain stands within the ancestral cultural territory of Diné, Hopi, Havasupai, Hualapai, Apache, Yavapai, Paiute, and several Pueblo peoples. This is the mountain to whom I made an offering and a prayer for my teacher to find me in the spring of 2015.

I moved to this community as a college freshman. In my white settler ignorance, I had never heard of sacred landscape. I had no framework to understand this mountain's long-standing relationships with the region's Indigenous Peoples. But, as my mentors later taught me, the mountain's intelligence, power, and blessings work on the people who live nearby, whether they are aware or not.

Diné friends shared the context that, in their cosmology, this mountain is an anchor of *Kʼé* (pronounced "k-EH"),[104] meaning kinship. Its sacred orientation is the heart, community, and gathering with family at sunset. It is a place for prayer and the reverent gathering of medicinal plants. However, after Euro-descended settlers claimed this land as their own, the mountain has been perceived differently. Viewed through the lens of racial capitalism, the mountain represents settlers' "right" to outdoor recreation. It is seen as a profitable resource. In an example of the Dream of the Modern World manifesting physically, a ski resort was built on the slopes of the holy mountain in 1938.[105]

Several decades later, a changing climate made the ski resort's business model less viable, so the ski resort proposed to clear cut old growth alpine forest and build a pipeline. The pipeline would carry reclaimed waste Water to the top of the mountain. This reclaimed Water would be manufactured into artificial snow by the ski resort. Despite years of organized resistance by Indigenous communities and their allies, the proposal was approved by the United States Forest Service. Old growth trees were cut, and snowmaking infra-structure was built. Over the last decade, each year, our city has been leasing the ski resort 1.5 million gallons of treated sewage Water for manufacturing snow.[106]

In our community, discussion about the ski resort is polarized. Some describe it as a necessary evil in which they participate for employment or recreation. Others speak of it as a travesty, some-thing they actively boycott. Still others insist that we can't let "the minority" curtail recreation or people's rights to economic devel-opment. Indigenous friends speak of it as a desecration. Using this sacred site for recreation disrespects their Mother, their existence, and future generations. They also describe it as a profound error for which we will *all* someday pay the consequences.

One sunny fall weekend in 2016, I joined a group who came together at the base of *Dokoʼoosłííd* for conversation. White guests who ski or have worked at the resort were present. Our group also included several Diné guests. Among them were artists, activists, and culture-bearers, as well as business and climate leaders. I had a feeling that something meaningful was about to happen.

A delicate conversation began. Our Indigenous friends ap-proached the situation with equanimity. Each of their perspectives gave an opportunity for the group to see *Dokoʼoosłííd* as a sacred being. We heard teachings about her relationships with the other sacred mountains throughout the world. We heard about the Holy People, the deities, who live within and around her. We heard about her significance as a female, a bringer of life. We heard their cultural imperatives to honor her as a grandmother. Later, several white friends said to me, "I will never see this mountain in the same way again."

Beyond a debate about artificial snowmaking, these Indigenous perspectives encouraged us to see every being present as part of one family. *Doko'o'osłííd*, the shimmering ice on the mountain's peak, the pine trees, the spider, the elk, and the humans sitting there in the room all became relatives. With amazement, I realized that we white settlers were being guided by Indigenous sisters and brothers about how to be in the presence of a sacred mountain of their homeland. People generously stepped forward to wash dishes, cook food, keep the fire, offer prayers and songs, and share meals and music with each other.

Over the weekend, many of us perceived that the mountain was suffering from years of neglect and abuse. Long ago, the white settler nation had claimed this mountain as the property of its federal government. Since then, her traditional caregivers have been prohibited from freely interacting with her. In many places, access to the mountain is restricted by private property laws. The Forest Service requires permits for certain ceremonies and the gathering of medicinal plants. Law enforcement has been known to harass Indigenous Peoples when they go to the mountain to pray. I longed to support the mountain's First Peoples in taking care of her again. I also longed to care for her myself. Years later, when I began studying the songs of my Scottish Gael ancestors, I would recognize this affinity to the mountain as part of my ancestral blueprints. Some of my ancestors' songs honor the mountains of Scotland.*

The morning after our gathering ended, I stood alone and greeted the sun as it rose over the peak of *Doko'o'osłííd*. As the light shone on my face, I dissolved into healing tears that soaked into the ground: the first of the Water offerings I would make to the mountain every day for the next year. Then I understood that a dream I've carried for a long time had begun to manifest. This dream invites us to listen to our Indigenous neighbors with humility and respect. Over time, listening can enable those of us who have lost touch with our ancestral teachings to re-member.

---

* "*Chì mi na Mòr-bheanna*" ("The Mist-Covered Mountains") is one of these songs. Brian Ó hEadhra includes a recording on his album *Òrain Cèilidh Teaghlaich*.

Ancestral Convergence

On a rainy autumn evening in 2016, I took my husband out for dinner for his birthday. We went to a charming local teahouse after dinner and ordered hot drinks to go. As we walked through the freezing rain to find our car and drive home, I saw a pair of legs sticking out from behind one of the buildings. The legs were shivering. Without a thought, the tea in my hand propelled my arm and then the rest of my body toward the person who was sitting on the sidewalk in the rain.

Eye to eye, I saw that he was an Indigenous man, and that he was cold and wet. I folded the warm drink into his hand and asked his name. "Auggie," was his reply, in a forlorn, shivering voice. I asked Auggie if I could help him. He looked into my eyes. In the same tone of voice, inflection, and language of my nine-year-old son, he said "Huggie."

Again, with no thought, Auggie put the drink down and we grasped each other in a bear hug so tight that it cracked my upper back. This was a relief since my back had been out for weeks. I don't know whether Auggie realized, but he had become a sidewalk chiropractor. As the bear hug continued, Auggie and I both started quietly sobbing, and we continued to hold each other.

After the hug, Auggie and I started talking. He was an unsheltered person, and he had probably been drinking alone for a long time. He was from somewhere on the reservation. He kept saying that he wanted to get home, and I asked again if I could help. His response was vague. After a while I could see that he didn't really want my help.

During our conversation, again Auggie asked for a "huggie." After our second hug, I looked at him and said, "I see you." He asked me to think about him sometimes and pray for him. Then he told me a third grade-style joke about a turtle, and we laughed together.

My husband was waiting patiently nearby. He has accompanied me in interactions like this many times, offering to buy dinner, drive people where they need to go, and listen to their stories. These are some of the ways he supports our relatives who have become invisibilized, in dark alleys and deserted underpasses. Standing up and holding hands, we walked back to our car and drove the few blocks back to our house through the freezing rain.

——

My heart was heavy as I climbed the stairs. I felt terrible that we were here in this warm house while Auggie was shivering in the rain. I crawled into bed with our son to say goodnight before he went to sleep. Cuddling under the covers, I told him about Auggie, his request for "huggies," his longing to get home, and his wish that I think about him sometimes and pray for him. My child was transfixed by this story. He wanted to hear it over and over. He worried about whether Auggie would be OK on that cold night and wondered if he would eventually make it home.

My son wanted assurance that *he* could find his way home if he were ever lost, that *he* would be comforted and loved no matter what. That night, I was being asked to serve as a conduit for the Mother Love all people need sometimes, whether they are unsheltered adults on the street or children at bedtime. We prayed for Auggie together and my son drifted off to sleep.

As I lay there under the warm covers listening to the rain on the roof, I could sense that I was changing. When I was still entranced by the Dream of the Modern World, I would have felt detached pity about the unknown circumstances that left Auggie shivering on the street, drunk and alone. I would have perhaps given him five dollars and gone on my way without much more thought, oblivious to how his life was inextricably linked with my own.

But at this point in the process of waking up from the Nightmare, there was no choice but to grieve. I was beginning to understand that we are all related. Auggie's people belong to a sophisticated culture that is based upon a complex clan structure. Not so long ago, intact, sustainable food systems nourished their communities. They lived in elegant earthen houses embedded with cultural teachings.[*]

---

[*] These homes, called *hoghans*, are still being designed, built, and used within Diné communities today.

Homelessness was not part of their cosmology. As long as they were within the four sacred mountains, they were always home.

Meeting Auggie gave me another painful glimpse into the ongoing consequences of colonization. Kit Carson's 1863 campaign to burn Diné crops, destroy livestock, and push people off their land was a starting point.[107] The Navajo Long Walk and forced assimilation in boarding schools compounded these traumas in the coming generations. These may have been some of the circumstances that left Auggie freezing in the rain that night.

We white folk were just a few blocks away from Auggie in a historic home that had been built by European settlers. I had a belly full of locally raised, artisanal foods. We were warm, dry, and safe. No one would disturb our sleep tonight. I could finally see the trajectory that had landed us here, beginning with my ancestors who came to this continent as settlers nine generations before. I wondered what had started that trajectory for *them*?

My mind buzzed like a bug caught in a jar. I wondered, "What could I have done differently? Should we have given him a ride somewhere and helped him get a hotel room? Should I have invited him to our house? Maybe I should have given him money or bought him food?" Finally, after bashing against the side of the jar repeatedly, the bug landed, deflated, at this point. I don't know what to do. The situation is complex, and I don't know what to do about it. And perhaps that is the point. There was no "white savioring" my way out of this. I couldn't make it neat and tidy. Seeing the current impacts of these historic realities is messy and heartbreaking.

I never saw Auggie again, but our encounter has continued to teach me. In the years since then, I have been humbled when I remember our conversation. When he comes to mind, I often realize that I've been taking my warm house, full belly, intact family, and privileged settler life for granted. The memory of Auggie nudges me back into awareness and gratitude. For years afterward, my son brought Auggie up in conversation. Together, we wondered if he made it home, if he is well, and if he has enough to eat. I am grateful for his generosity as a sidewalk chiropractor and interpersonal philanthropist who generously taught me.

We white settlers can educate ourselves about the impacts of European invasion, settlement, and Indigenous displacement. Reading the work of Indigenous authors helps us understand the historic and current struggles of the people on whose land we are living. However, my encounter with Auggie was one of many that taught me that reading is no replacement for emotional, spiritual, and relational experiences. These experiences help us viscerally re-member how we are all related.

How can we white settlers learn to become good relatives to those who bear the most painful burdens of our presence? In my opinion, making the effort to understand the complex historical trauma impacting IBPOC communities is important. Cultivating compassion is another essential step. Love is our guide.

A Time of Prophecy

> Upon suffering beyond suffering, the Red Nation shall
> rise again and it shall be a blessing for a sick world. A
> world filled with broken promises, selfishness, and
> separations, a world longing for light again. I see
> a time of seven generations when all the colors of
> mankind will gather under the sacred Tree of Life and
> the whole Earth will become one circle again. In that
> day, there will be those among the Lakota who will
> carry knowledge and understanding of unity among
> all living things, and the young white ones will come
> to those of my people and ask for this wisdom.
> I salute the light within your eyes where the whole
> universe dwells. For when you are at that center within
> you and I am at that place within me, we shall be as one.[108]
> ~ *Tȟašúŋke Witkó* (Crazy Horse) ~
> (Oglala Lakota Ancestor)

In the fall of 2016, a peaceful, Indigenous-led movement captivated attention throughout the world. Energy Transfer Partners

Corporation was building a Tar Sands pipeline destined to carry oil through Standing Rock Sioux land in North Dakota. In violation[109] of the 1868 Fort Laramie treaty, the Dakota Access Pipeline (DAPL) was slated to tunnel underneath the Missouri River, destroying burial sites and ceremonial grounds. Members of many Indigenous Nations gathered in camps to protect the Waters, accompanied by friends from around the world.

I began organizing solidarity gatherings and fundraising to support the movement. From home, I avidly followed developments between the Indigenous frontline organizers, the police, the Army Corps of Engineers, and the corporation. During this time, a teaching dream came:

> *My children and I arrive at a camp in Standing Rock. After wandering distractedly for some time, we find ourselves at the bank of a river flowing with black Water. Women are praying there. They invite us to join them. One of the women says if we cross the river while the Water is low, we'll arrive at the other side. I hold my children's hands and we cross the black river together. We are going to a ceremony on the other side.*

A few days later, I listened to a presentation by Dallas Goldtooth, a Mdewakanton Dakota/Diné speaker at the National Bioneers Conference. During his talk, Dallas shared about the Black Snake prophecy, in relation to the DAPL and other pipelines. He described the Black Snake as "a manifestation of the sickness of society," and a being whose "purpose…was to bring sickness and destruction."[110] Dallas's description offered insight into my dream of a few days before. For some of us, the Black Snake has been "normalized" for a long time. In 2016, it was finally becoming visible to us, and we were questioning our relationship to it. My dream spoke of the need to take future generations by the hand and safely cross to the other side of the greedy Black Snake worldview. The dream indicated that women will show us how to cross.

Several days later, militarized police from seven states and the Army National Guard began violently arresting the peaceful Water protectors at Standing Rock. Afterward, as I learned from friends who were at Standing Rock, people were pulled out of a sweat lodge* nearly naked, handcuffed with zip ties, and detained in the cold for hours before being taken to jail.[111] Indigenous Peoples were singled out and beaten by police. Pepper spray was used against the Water protectors and sound canons deafened them.[112] In jail, some women were strip-searched while male guards watched, and some were held captive in dog kennels.[113] Some of the Water protectors had numbers written on their arms, reminiscent of the Nazi Holocaust.[114]

Though I was not physically present in North Dakota, I was outraged. I realized that somehow, authorities defiling the sacred, the state-sanctioned appropriation of ancestral lands for profit, and watching people being beaten into submission† all felt familiar to me. My blood remembered similar feelings of terror, even though I hadn't experienced those things in my own lifetime.

A few days later, Diné Water protector Lyla June Johnston organized a forgiveness walk surrounding the jail where many of the Water protectors were being detained. I was astonished when I read that 700 people came, even as these injustices continued. Watching from afar, my heart aligned with their improbable choice to forgive. I wondered—could I have found the will to forgive in similar circumstances?

It was becoming clear that peaceful people who love life and Water could not defeat military tanks defending corporate interests. Nor could they overcome hundreds of police in riot gear armed with

---

* Sweat lodge ceremonies are part of some Turtle Island Indigenous cultures. To read about a similar practice in Ireland, see page 69 of *Soil and Soul: People Versus Corporate Power*, by Scottish author Alastair McIntosh. He mentions the sweat lodges (*tigh n'alluis*) that were once used in parts of Ireland to prepare for peace-seeking meditation practices.

† Similar human rights violations took place before, during, and after the civil rights movement in the South.

pepper spray and guns. I was wit(h)nessing relatives who chose to embody radical love and forgiveness in the face of brutality. I imagined their courageous choice creating profoundly different outcomes over time.

Several weeks later, another teaching dream arrived:

> *My husband and I are sitting on dilapidated truck seats on desert sand. Beneath us, I glimpse a gigantic black serpent weaving in and around the benches. Time is suspended. If we move quickly to escape, the snake will see us and strangle us to death. If we wait, our risk of being enveloped by the snake grows.*

Shortly after this dream, the Army Corps of Engineers rescinded their commitment to undertake a full environmental impact survey at Standing Rock with Tribal consultation. Under the new administration of President Donald Trump, the Army Corps of Engineers granted an easement for Energy Transfer Partners to drill under Lake Oahe.

During the Standing Rock movement, throughout the world, Water protectors offered prayers, made phone calls, sent emails, gathered donations, and signed petitions. Law enforcement sprayed hundreds of peaceful Water protectors with fire hoses for six hours in below freezing temperatures. Peaceful protectors sustained traumatic injuries from concussion grenades, rubber bullets, hypothermia, and humiliation.[115] Unlicensed security guards terrorized Water protectors with attack dogs and pepper spray.[116] A group of veterans apologized to Lakota Elders for the atrocities that our country has inflicted on Indigenous Peoples. On their knees, with bowed heads, they wept and begged for forgiveness.*

Despite all of this, our government chose to uphold the Black Snake worldview. It was yet another betrayal of Indigenous Peoples

---

* I recommend watching the recording of this apology: "Forgiveness Ceremony: Veterans Kneel at Standing Rock" (https://www.youtube.com/watch?v=OjotlPIlRqw). How does it affect you?

by the United States. It was also a willful endangerment of Water, upon which all our lives depend. Years later, even after the pipeline had leaked several times, President Joe Biden enabled the Dakota Access Pipeline to continue transporting oil.[117]

———

Six years later, in 2022, when I recalled my dreams during the Standing Rock movement, I understood them more fully. The Black Snake mentality influences many aspects of our lives as white settlers. It has been growing amongst us, as a sickness in our society, for generations. Over time, for some, greed has been rewarded, and it has become a way of life. Trying to escape it or simply doing nothing will both imperil us further.

With inspiration from *Tȟašúŋke Witkó's* (Crazy Horse's) prophecy about the "young white ones" who seek Indigenous wisdom, I dream a third option. We can learn how to belong to this place. We can tend to our history and humbly follow Indigenous leadership. We can support our Indigenous relatives protecting and caring for this land once again. Let us cross over the Black Snake mentality and go to the ceremony on the other side.

The Picts

While preparing for my third fasting ceremony in the spring of 2017, I began reading about some of my ancient ancestors. Up until that point, I'd been afraid that I'd find millennia of warfare, generations of patriarchy, and legions of hungry ghosts in their stories. Yet, several of the BIPOC friends in my life had encouraged me to learn about my ancestors. It was important for me to follow their advice and find out where it would lead.

Five years before, I'd seen a reference to Picts on the church wall next to my paternal clan name in Balquhidder, Scotland. Though I'd never heard of the Picts before, their name sparked my curiosity.

As I would later discover in my family's genealogy book, one of my fifth-great-grandmothers came from a family in northern Scotland, whose name was thought to be of Pictish origin.[118]

The Picts were Celtic peoples who lived during the first millennium CE. The first written accounts of them emerged from their contact with Romans. Most of the surviving information recorded about them came from outside their culture.[119] In her book *Picts, Gaels and Scots*, Scottish archaeologist Sally Foster describes the Picts as "the descendants of the native Iron Age tribes of Scotland."[120]

———

When I first started reading about the Picts, I was overcome by a visceral sensation of peering at an intricately decorated room through a keyhole. In my imagination, I saw their tattoos, made with sharpened bone tools and plant resins that permeated small holes in their skin. Their tattoo designs may have communicated about their genealogy or served as talismans.[121] I began to taste the flavor of their existence and hear echoes of their extinct language. The Picts revered Water deities with names such as *Buadhnat* (The Virtuous or Healing One) and *Nectona* (Pure One).[122] Hundreds of evocative Pictish stone carvings have been found placed throughout their territories. They include mirrors, combs, crescents, flowers, deer, and serpents.[123] Their carvings of boars, horses, dogs, and bulls depict the most prominent animals in Celtic religion.[124]

Peering through my imaginary keyhole at the Pictish ancestors, curious sensations flowered in my belly and chest. What I was sensing of their early lifeways somehow felt familiar. I recognized the Picts as relatives. Years later, I would understand that I was beginning to cultivate ancestral memory. In my experience, feelings of comfort, curiosity, and affinity are indications of ancestral memory waiting to be rekindled. These feelings eventually encouraged me to learn a bit more about Pictish history.

I learned that Roman troops invaded southern England in the year 43 CE and began spreading north to Scotland in 79 CE, subjugating tribal peoples with a variety of military and economic strategies.[125] However, the people in the north, whom the Romans called "*Picti*" in 297 CE, fiercely resisted Roman invasion. This term, meaning "painted people," may have initially been used by the Romans to identify "'barbaric" people outside of the Roman cultural sphere." Eventually, in the seventh century, they began using the term "Picts" to describe themselves.[126] They started as geographically separate groups. But these diverse groups unified to resist the Roman invaders.[127]

The Picts were exposed to Christianity when an Irish nobleman turned missionary, Columba, came to the island of Iona in the sixth century.[128] In his book *Warriors of the Word*, Celtic Studies scholar Michael Newton writes, "Christianity deliberately sought to disenfranchise druids and defeat paganism, collaborating with political leaders to do so."[129] I was beginning to perceive combined political and religious force as a pattern that started early among my people. Later, this pattern became instrumental in European imperialism throughout the world.

Pictish and Gaelic peoples had probably been intermingling for some time before Viking raids began in the late 700s.[130] Complex political upheaval finally brought the Picts into alliance with Gaels when they joined forces to battle Vikings.[131] The Picts were eventually absorbed into the political entity of Alba, which later became Scotland. Newton writes, "the Picts were Gaelicized and receded into

* I recommend these reflections on the lasting impacts of the Roman Empire:
  - On page 22 of her book *The History of White People*, historian Nell Irvin Painter shares a central theme established by Julius Caesar: the "tension between barbarism and civilization" that has "reverberated for two thousand years."
  - On pages 213–21 of *Come of Age: The Case for Elderhood in a Time of Trouble*, culture activist Stephen Jenkinson discusses how the ethos of the Roman Empire impacted those it conquered and how this imprint continues in our present time.

the historical horizon."[132] In the following centuries, legends associated with assimilation and disappearance were attached to them.[133]

The Picts probably referred to themselves as "Priteni" in their own language, which was a P-Celtic, or Brythonic, language.[134] But in the process of assimilation, their language was lost.[135] After the middle of the ninth century, their stone carvings were no longer made.[136] In the coming centuries, a lack of interest in Pictish texts ensured that their writings were not preserved.[137] Pictish identity had been erased.[138]

Learning even this small amount of the Picts' complex history helped me understand *why* the IBPOC people in my life had been asking me to learn about my ancestors. My heart blossomed when I glimpsed the faded remnants of the Earth- and Water-honoring Pictish culture. After their land was invaded by Roman troops, the Picts responded with militarization. Their religious conversion, assimilation, and eventual erasure were all part of a familiar pattern I was learning to recognize.

———

In my life as a white settler, the first time I heard the word "decolonization" was in the spring of 2014 during a healing camp I attended on Diné lands. Along with the other participants, my twelve-year-old daughter and I shaped pottery out of clay. We mixed blue corn meal with juniper ash and formed the mixture into traditional corn cakes that we cooked over the fire. We moved our bodies with the seven directions in a dance workshop. I remember thinking it was inspiring that our Diné neighbors were undertaking this process of decolonization, which was necessary after the colonization that had happened to *them*.

It would take me several years to begin understanding the nuances of decolonization. Eventually, I learned that Indigenous Peoples have been developing decolonial theory and practice ever since Europeans began invading and colonizing this continent.[139] Today, decolonization can sometimes refer to healing processes such as those we were invited to experience at the Diné camp. These types of settings and activities can begin healing internalized colonization.

After listening to a Bioneers keynote address by Hupa, Yurok and Karuk professor and author Cutcha Risling Baldy,* I later understood that the purpose of decolonization is returning Indigenous land and life. To avoid centering decolonization on white settlers, I use this term sparingly. (For a definition, please see the Glossary.)

When I read about the Picts, it was as though a small light had suddenly been turned on within a dark room. I remembered (again) that my European ancestors had also experienced various forms of colonialism, such as the Roman Expansion, Viking raids, military and economic subjugation, religious oppression, transitions from tribal societies to nation-states, and erasure of their language and identity. Trauma specialist and author of *My Grandmother's Hands* Resmaa Menakem writes:

> Throughout the United States' history as a nation, white bodies have colonized, oppressed, brutalized, and murdered Black and Native ones. But well before the United States began, powerful white bodies colonized, oppressed, brutalized, and murdered other, less powerful white ones.[140]

Though I had been introduced to this concept before, dense layers of denial had kept my amnesia intact. The seeds my friend Clarissa planted when she said, "All peoples have been colonized," had sprouted. I could sense them developing roots and growing a different identity. The binary of "us" and "them" began to dissolve.

———

We are deep within the labyrinth now. In the second year, I sat with my resistance and was blessed by the Stars' unconditional love and belonging. An Indigenous-led movement and awareness of settler colonialism began shaping different perceptions of reality for me. During the third year of this contemplative journey, I would

---

* I recommend Cutcha Risling Baldy's 2020 Bioneers keynote speech, "Indigenous Voices for Decolonized Futures" (https://bioneers.org/cutcha-risling-baldy -indigenous-voices-decolonized-futures-zstf2101/).

increasingly be invited to face history's wounds. My internalized racism and challenging truths about money and power would become visible to me. Eventually, I would be soothed by ancestral apology and song. Welcome to the third year.

The Third Year

Decolonization

During my third fasting ceremony in the summer of 2017, I was immersed in the sun's intensity, the light of a full moon and sparkling stars, magnificent monsoon lightning and hailstorms. I felt the desert of thirst in my throat and the emptiness of hunger in my belly for many days. This book whispered instructions to me: listen, observe, and record my process of decolonization to share with others.

As I shared in the previous pages, decolonization returns Indigenous land and life.[141] In my opinion, decolonization is not a buzzword, marketing strategy, or a means to assuage settler guilt.[142] At the same time, I learned to support the return of Indigenous land and life by undertaking a process of *settler* decolonization[*] that I've shared with you in this book. This process rewired my identity, perception, and comprehension of history. I was immersed in a mysterious nonlinear transformation that continues today.[†]

———

One afternoon during the late summer of 2017, I visited the foothills of the sacred mountain near my home. Several weeks before, I had completed my third fasting ceremony. Light rain kissed my face

———

[*] For Canadian stories of settler decolonization, I recommend *Living in Indigenous Sovereignty*, by Elizabeth Carlson-Manathara with Gladys Rowe.

[†] I recommend Nayyirah Waheed's poem "the.release" on page 85 of her book *Salt*.

like a gentle sister. The mountain was a solidly seated Grandmother looking over my shoulder. Millions of pine needles transmitted information like antennas between the cosmos and the mountain. Their cleansing, aromatic oils permeated the air. I breathed deeply and walked slowly, surrounded by sunny yellow, brilliant violet, and deep orange wildflowers. My heartbeat was just one of the many heartbeats of this land. I was wildly in love with the beauty of this place, cradled in its loving embrace like a baby in the arms of her mother.

At the same time, I felt unsettled. My consciousness was expanding to hold beauty and harm at the same time. Joyously communing with the colors, scents, and textures of this place, I also felt the cognitive dissonance of my presence as a white settler on stolen land and as a descendant of enslavers. Rather than just thinking about it, I could viscerally feel the need for reparations.* I was afraid that our colonial government would never develop the will to make reparations. I was also worried that *I* wouldn't know how to begin making reparations.† With a mixture of despair and cautious optimism, I sank down on my knees in the shade of an ancient Ponderosa pine and asked for help. My tears fell on the ground under the tree and the land held me.

———

Two years later, I listened to a presentation by Mandan, Hidatsa, and Arikara professor and author Michael Yellow Bird.[143] I felt a shock of

---

* The United Nations outlines five conditions that must be met for full reparations:
    1. Cessation, assurances, and guarantees of non-repetition
    2. Restitution and repatriation
    3. Compensation
    4. Satisfaction
    5. Rehabilitation
The Movement for Black Lives includes this and other important information in the paper "What Are Reparations?" See: https://m4bl.org/wp-content/uploads/2020/11/defining-reparations.pdf.
† Indigenous and Black communities are each calling for distinct forms of reparations. I see these as being mutually beneficial rather than mutually exclusive.

recognition when I heard him explain how the physical extremes of fasting ceremonies, prolonged meditation, and spending time in nature can increase neuroplasticity. In *For Indigenous Minds Only*, he shares about a process he calls "neurodecolonization":

> Neuroscience research shows that deep reflective prayer and sacred ceremonies and practices…are just a few on a long list of practices that can create positive changes in our brains…

> The goal of neurodecolonization is to delete old, ineffective brain networks that support destructive thoughts, feelings, memories and behaviors—not only those that occur for most people, but also those that are intimately connected to the past and contemporary oppressions associated with colonialism.[144]

Yellow Bird's work is primarily oriented to Indigenous Peoples' well-being, and I respect that.* Astonished, I realized that I had been taking part in practices that can also rewire the brains of settlers. The fasting ceremony was beginning to heal my mind from the disease of colonialism. During the third and fourth year of this journey, the ceremony taught me how to begin making personal reparations. I imagine that the Indigenous Elders who first included white settlers in their ceremonies must have known that these kinds of outcomes were possible.

I was beginning to perceive that within white settler culture, our minds are colonized from our earliest consciousness. My culture of origin colonized my mind by teaching me to:

- Rely exclusively on rational thought
- Disregard somatic, intuitive, and spiritual ways of knowing
- Prioritize individual security over the well-being of the collective

---

* Gratitude to Michael Yellow Bird, who gave permission to cite this work, August 2022.

- Think in either/or binaries
- Suppress my emotions and "behave"
- Seek approval from patriarchal, hierarchical institutions
- Disregard the past, be industrious, and make "progress"
- Uphold white economic dominance
- Perceive myself and others as "sinful"

Decolonizing our minds can help us to change these destructive thoughts and patterns from the inside out. Choosing this path is unsettling. Throughout my journey, I repeatedly felt perplexed, broken, and disoriented. Over time, I began feeling more clear, whole, and empowered.

During the years of writing this book, neurodecolonization rewired me from the inside out. It eventually helped me feel secure enough to embrace returning this land to the care of her Original Peoples. For example, I began advocating for tribal management of federal land, supporting Indigenous youth-led work to rename one of the peaks on the sacred mountain at the federal level,* following Indigenous leadership to protect sacred sites, and investing in LandBack initiatives. White settlers can re-member old/new realities based on the Indigenous values of mutuality and care.

———

When I devote myself to perceiving things as they really are, the sovereign beauty of Mother Earth leaves me speechless. I enter silent interdependence with her. The rain beckons me outside, lulling me with her voice. My heart lights up as I watch birds flitting among the quaking aspen leaves. I greet spiders in many sizes, shapes, and colors. I honor the handprints left by ancient relatives on canyon walls. The river is a primordial being who remembers all the creatures who

---

* In my community, a group of Hopi and Diné youth led an initiative to officially rename the peak *Öomawki*, a Hopi name meaning "House of the Clouds." Previously, the mountain had been named after Louis Agassiz, a naturalist who conducted inhumane research at Harvard University in the 1800s to advance white supremacist ideologies.

have tasted her Waters since the beginning of time. Life becomes sweeter, deeper, and much quieter. Unconditional love is present in every moment.

When I don't allow sufficient time and space, all these wonders slip beneath my radar. I become numb: mindlessly scrolling on my phone, snapping at my children, angrily reacting, feeling victimized, and indulging in endless mental gossip. I am afraid of not having enough. I forget the privileges I enjoy every moment and the miracle of being alive. I try to be right by making others wrong, all in the privacy of my own head. This is my colonized mind. It still wants to assert itself. Bit by bit, I am rewiring my mind and embracing other ways of being.

The Catalyst of Shame

Marie came to visit, toting an old pillowcase loaded with four legs of her Navajo Churro mutton. She had recently butchered one of her sheep. Marie announced that he was fat and delicious from eating the summer grasses sustained by abundant rain. With smiling eyes, she told me how this sheep went calmly and quietly. She spoke to him in *Diné Bizaad* to explain that she has taken care of him all his life and now it was his time to take care of her, the family, and the rest of the flock. He seemed to understand. She prayed with him before she ended his life. I listened as I wrapped the mutton legs for storage in the freezer. The sheep's story was comforting to me. His legs would feed our friends and family in the months to come.

I had bought mutton from Marie at every opportunity over the last several years. Each sheep Marie raised represented her commitment to her ancestral land and cultural lifeways. This commitment means that she lives without running Water and a paying job in the city. She juggles the continuation of her culture with the need for money that has been imposed by capitalism.

Marie and I sat down to a familiar conversation over a cup of tea. Sharing her family stories, she educated me about the so-called Navajo-Hopi land dispute. This conflict was manufactured beginning in the 1970s. The United States government and Peabody Coal colluded to create friction between Hopi and Diné communities, pushing Diné people off the land where they had lived for generations. This garnered resources for corporate profit and "progress." Subsequent mining severely reduced ground Water and polluted the land with tons of radioactive waste.

The matriarchs of Marie's community actively resisted the forces that pressured them to move from their homes and relocate to cities. Proudly, Marie told me about her mother, Katherine Smith. Katherine was a notorious resister who fought with police and once fired a shotgun in the air to protect her land from federal agents. But even as federal policies were actively oppressing Marie's community, she was taught a whitewashed version of history. Like many Indigenous children of the nineteenth and twentieth centuries, she left her parents and her home at a young age to attend boarding school.

My friendship with Marie inspired me to learn more about boarding schools in the coming years. The understanding I've shared here emerged from listening to the personal and intergenerational stories of Diné, Havasupai, Hopi, Choctaw, and Lakota Elders over the course of a decade.[*] I also read books and watched films that were recommended.[†]

---

[*] Gratitude to Marie Gladue, Andy Dann, Viki Blackgoat, Dianna Sue WhiteDove Uqualla, Mona Polacca, Pat McCabe, Dan Isaac, and Basil Brave Heart for sharing your stories.

[†] Recommended resources:
- *In Search of April Raintree*, by Beatrice Mosionier.
- The film *Indian Horse*, directed by Stephen S. Campanelli (https://www.indianhorse.ca/en/film).
- Interview with Basil Brave Heart (https://bioneers.org/conversation-with-oglala-lakota-elder-basil-brave-heart-part-1-zmbz2108/).
- The curriculum guide "American Indian Boarding Schools: An Exploration of Global Ethnic and Cultural Cleansing" (http://www.sagchip.org/ziibiwing/planyourvisit/pdf/aibscurrguide.pdf).
- The *New York Times* 2023 multimedia article, "The Native American Boarding School System" (https://www.nytimes.com/interactive/2023/08/30/us/native-american-boarding-schools.html).
- Michael Jacobs's *Wellbriety Journey to Forgiveness* film (https://www.youtube.com/watch?v=RYU8CSxieaA).

The boarding schools originated with Manifest Destiny, a nineteenth-century delusion. Under Manifest Destiny, European settlers acted as though they had received a divine mandate to spread westward through the "promised land" of Turtle Island, claiming it as their own.[145] Government policies enforced Manifest Destiny by relocating Indigenous Peoples, coercing them onto reservations, making their cultural practices illegal, and sending their children to boarding schools. These policies ensured the domination of European settler society and its control over the land. Between 1830 and 1933, twenty-four American presidents condoned these genocidal policies.[146] At least 523 boarding schools existed in the United States, and at least 408 of these institutions received federal funding.[147]

The objective of the boarding schools was to assimilate Indigenous children into white American culture. Colonel Richard H. Pratt spearheaded the Carlisle Indian Industrial School in Pennsylvania, "the first government-run school for Native Americans." He was known for the phrase "Kill the Indian, Save the Man."* The United States government populated boarding schools by hunting down, kidnapping, and coercing young children to leave their families. Trying to adapt to the pressures they were facing, some parents made the heartbreaking choice to send their children away to school. Often, the schools were administered by religious institutions.

In the schools, children were forced to violate cultural taboos by having their hair cut. They were often severely punished for speaking their languages. Many were forcibly renamed with English names.[148] They were obligated to convert to Christianity and required to wear Western-style clothing. Their cultural ways were disparaged as being sinful. Many suffered emotional, physical, and sexual abuse, including torture. Many were expected to submit to forced labor and military-style living conditions.[149] Thousands of children died from abuse and neglect and were buried in unmarked graves. All of this was to ensure their assimilation to American identity.

---

* Please see the Carlisle Indian School Project website for stories and reflections on the history of the school (https://carlisleindianschoolproject.com/past/).

In the years following my kitchen conversation with Marie, I spent more time with Indigenous friends of various ages, within their spaces. I learned that the history of boarding schools is still achingly active, impacting their lives on a regular basis. The trauma is palpable in their whispered stories, passionate public speeches, trembling hands, and tears. Wit(h)nessing them, I came to perceive boarding school trauma as one of the deepest wounds imaginable.* The original assault of forced assimilation is still present, and it has compounded intergenerationally.

In conversations with other white settlers, I've realized that many of us know little or nothing about this history. Personally, I was only taught a glorified version of Manifest Destiny in elementary school. I did not know about the existence of the boarding schools until I took a course in graduate school at age twenty-five. In the kitchen, when I confessed my ignorance to Marie, she said:

"It was a silencing. The schools made it so many of us, both settlers *and* Indigenous, wouldn't know the true history."

I wondered aloud: "Why does our settler denial continue?"

Marie said: "If white people were confronted with the truth, they would feel overwhelming shame. The threat of shame keeps them brainwashed."

———

Ugly specters were sitting with us on the barstools in the kitchen. Buying four legs of mutton wasn't going to fix it. Nearly 300 years after an ancestor of mine first set foot on this continent, I am a ninth-generation beneficiary. One hundred fifty years after her ancestors were forced on the Navajo Long Walk and survived the concentration camp of Fort Sumner, Marie deals with complex historical trauma and ongoing oppression.

---

* To support some of the work to heal boarding school trauma, please visit the National Native American Boarding School Healing Coalition (https:// boardingschoolhealing.org/).

Increasingly, I found myself in conversations that made my heart constrict. Layers of denial and amnesia were being pulled away to reveal unvarnished, brutal truths. Once I saw these truths, there was no unseeing them: they became my constant, uncomfortable companions. I floundered, desperately searching for a way to make sense of it all. Always, the first thing I found was blame: of myself, other white people, and the European immigrants who brought their ignorance and entitlement to this land. Blaming seemed like a way to avoid complicity.

But when I went to a level deeper than blame, when I let my heart open, I felt something dark, heavy, and silent: shame.

———

After Marie left my house that day, I put my head on the counter and wailed in shame. I could sense the tremendous debt of this history; a debt so overwhelming it is impossible to repay. After my healing tears dried, slowly I understood: Shame feels terrible to me, but not as terrible as being a target of genocide must feel. Not as terrible as the families of missing and murdered mothers, daughters, sisters, and relatives must feel. And not as terrible as those who witness their sacred ancestral sites being desecrated for corporate profit must feel.

We live in a nation that has expressed almost no acknowledgment or remorse for its history. Our society has stuffed its shame down into the underbelly. When I was brought up to be white, I was indoctrinated into social norms that insisted upon my complicity. Although it was uncomfortable, shame was offering me a wakeup call. It was a useful signal to indicate the presence of harm. This shame made me want to reposition myself, reconsider lifelong assumptions, and come into integrity by learning how to do things differently. Instead of being debilitated or deflated by shame, I would use it to undo my own brainwashing.[150]

White researcher-storyteller Brené Brown's work on vulnerability and shame[151] motivated me to use shame as a catalyst in the coming years. Shame naturally arises when we become aware of participating in something that is out of integrity with our values. In my experience, vulnerability can neutralize the debilitating effects of shame. I've written this book with the hope that present and future generations of white settlers will develop the courage to vulnerably acknowledge the brutality of our peoples' past and initiate intergenerational processes of truth-telling and healing.

The film *Dawnland* documents an example of one such process. It tells the story of the first government-endorsed Truth and Reconciliation Commission that took place within the five Wabanaki communities still present on the land now called Maine. This commission formed between 2012 and 2015, gathering testimony from 200 people. The participants had been impacted by state and federal policies that removed Indigenous children from their families and placed them in foster care with white families. Nationally, Indigenous children are three times more likely to be placed in foster care than settler children. In some communities, they are nine times or even twenty times more likely. This is an ongoing, present-day iteration of cultural genocide.

At the end of this truth and reconciliation process, the commission issued a report with fourteen recommendations[152] that began creating transformation for both settler and Indigenous communities, including:

- Cultural techniques like longhouses, language centers, healing circles, economic sovereignty, and ceremonies
- More Indigenous foster homes for children in need of care
- Better training and support for non-Indigenous foster care families[153]

It is not easy for people who have experienced profound trauma to share their stories. In community truth and healing circles, I have wit(h)nessed that it can be difficult for white settlers to hear these

---

* I recommend the 2018 film *Dawnland: A Documentary about Survival and Stolen Children* (directed by Adam Mazo and Bender-Cudlip). See: https://upstanderproject.org/films/dawnland.

stories, as well. Building bridges after 500 years of genocidal policies is a slow, delicate process.

In 2021, Laguna Pueblo Secretary of the Interior Deb Haaland commissioned the Federal Indian Boarding School Initiative to investigate the impacts of boarding schools in the United States.[154] This was an important step toward addressing the need for truth, healing, and restoration. This initiative and the Maine Wabanaki-State Child Welfare Truth and Reconciliation Commission* offer glimmers of hope that we will increasingly work together to face the shame of the past and co-create solutions for healthy futures. The unconditional love of Mother Earth can give us the strength that we need.

White Peril: Ancestral Avoidance

> The past has a future we never expect.[155]
> ~ RAOUL PECK~
> (Haitian Filmmaker)

Continuing to wrestle with my family's legacies of colonization and enslavement made me averse to spending time at my ancestors' altar in the dining room. I was angry. How could they have done those things and left us swimming in an ocean of White Peril? I only knew about the misdeeds of a few among multitudes, but those few loomed large in my mind. Sometimes I slipped into the habit of mentally labeling my people "perpetrators." It was so painful to imagine the harm they inflicted during their lifetimes. To avoid the pain, I indulged in rigid thinking and ignored my ancestors.

In hindsight, I understood my aversion as a symptom of per-petrator trauma† that was passed down from my ancestors who

---

* Another example is taking place as this book is being written: the California Truth & Healing Council is listening to the experiences and oral histories of Indigenous Peoples on the land that became known as California. They will issue a final report with their findings in 2025. See: https://tribalaffairs.ca.gov/cthc/.
† I recommend:

had engaged in land theft and slavery. In his book *It Didn't Start with You,* director of The Family Constellation Institute[156] Mark Wollyn describes how sometimes, even the forgotten or repressed transgressions of previous generations resonate in the lives of their descendants until they are unearthed and faced honestly. He writes, "Traumas do not sleep, even with death, but, rather, continue to look for the fertile ground of resolution in the children of the following generations."[157]

One night a teaching dream arrived, and it helped me take steps to recalibrate my relationship with my ancestors:

My beloved grandparents are grocery shopping, late at night. Under dim, fluorescent lighting, they slowly push a big grocery cart with a loaf of bread inside. Later, I see them sitting off to the side, eating sliced bread alone. They gaze at me longingly, but I am too preoccupied to go sit with them, cook for them, or take care of them.

This dream reminded me of the beloved dead among my ancestors. There were many who imbued future generations with inspiration and kindness. For example, my maternal grandparents built respectful relationships with Black communities in the segregated South. During my childhood, I saw my grandparents love unconditionally, feed the lonely, and befriend the disenfranchised.

Among earlier generations, one great-great-grandfather took to his bed and died of depression after he lost his job in an Irish linen factory. After a great-great-grandmother immigrated to America, she missed Ireland so much that she took the long voyage back

---

- On pages 97–109 of *My Grandmother's Hands*, Resmaa Menakem describes the vicarious trauma perpetrators experience, how trauma can pass through generations and ultimately manifest as cultural norms, and the suffering that comes from moral injury.
- On pages 164–95 of *Unsettling Truths*, Mark Charles and Soong-Chan Rah share their thoughts on the perpetration-induced trauma of white America.
- In *Perpetration-Induced Traumatic Stress* by Rachel M. MacNair, she shares her research on how this phenomenon afflicts various groups of people.

home. She never saw her relatives in America again. As I'd learned from Nona's ritual, neglect hurts our ancestors. Perceiving my people exclusively through the lens of "perpetrator" was to see them myopically.

The dream of my grandparents eating alone made me long to reconnect with them. One evening, my husband and I carried out a ritual. We built a fire, laid a blanket on the floor, and covered it with flowers, fruit, and photographs to make an altar for all of our grandparents. We spent several hours cooking soup over the fire. We honored our grandparents by sharing happy memories of them, acknowledging all they taught us, and giving thanks for lives they gave us.

Then we told our grandparents about the complex legacies they left. We shared what their great-grandchildren are facing: climate change, political instability, and unearned advantages. We told them about the terror and inequity our BIPOC relatives experience. We spoke about the present-day impacts of the previous generations and asked for their help creating balance for the future generations. On a chilly autumn evening, we ate hot soup by the fire. Facing the past honestly, we rekindled our ancestors' memory.

Ancestral Acceptance

> It was almost as if the ships bringing the good
> people of Europe to America brought also the
> predators they were trying to escape.[158]
> ~ THOMAS GALLAGHER ~
> (Irish-American Author)

A few years later, in 2020, my white friend Elyshia Holliday and I began co-facilitating circles of European-descended settlers. Together, we unpacked our peoples' legacies, rekindled our ancestral memory, and made personal reparations plans.[159] In these circles, I heard that ancestral aversion is a common experience for many white people. We tend to sever the parts of ourselves that relate to painful histories. Learning about the historical contexts that impacted our ancestors can help us embrace their complexity and build empathy. Wit(h)nessing our ancestors' stories in community settings can transform aversion to acceptance.*

For example, in 2021, I read about The Great Hunger in Ireland. The sources I found helpful include *Paddy's Lament, Ireland 1846–1847: Prelude to Hatred,* by Irish-American author Thomas Gallagher, *The Great Hunger: Ireland 1845–1849,* by Irish author Cecil Woodham-Smith, and *An Indigenous Peoples' History of the United States,* by American historian Roxane Dunbar-Ortiz. These sources gave me a visceral sense of how this tragic time may have impacted my ancestors.

Potato blight and colonial politics combined during the Great Hunger, leading to a humanitarian crisis and waves of migration.† Between 1845 and 1851, 1 million Irish perished because of starvation, eviction, and famine-related diseases. During these years, 1 million survivors left Ireland to settle in the United States and elsewhere. Many emigrated against their will, or as a last-ditch effort to survive. Some of my ancestors were among these refugees. Within the long-term aftermath of the Great Hunger, by 1900, the population of Ireland had reduced to half of what it was before the famine began.[160]

More than two centuries before the famine, during the early 1600s, England had "conquered Ireland and declared a half-million acres of land in the north open to settlement."[161] The British government recruited mostly poor Scottish Protestants to settle on the agricultural land in Northern Ireland which had been stolen from Irish Catholics. In his book *Soil and Soul,* Scottish author Alastair McIntosh describes this as "breaking the unity of Gaelic-speaking peoples."[162] These settlers became known as "Scots-Irish."

To displace the Irish, the British government attacked ancient

---

* Gratitude to Tita Leny Strobel for encouraging us to tell our stories. See: https://www.lenystrobel.com/.

† *Go raibh maith agat* ("Thank you" in Irish) to the Choctaw Nation for the humanitarian relief they gathered and sent to the Irish people during this time. See: https://www.choctawnation.com/about/history/irish-connection/.

systems of culture and governance. Bounties were offered for the heads, scalps, and ears of Irish people, a sinister tactic which would later be used against Indigenous Peoples on Turtle Island.[163] In the last five years of the seventeenth century, an additional 40,000 Scottish Protestants immigrated to Northern Ireland as famine refugees.[164] In the coming centuries, many Scots-Irish descendants went on to play prominent roles in the United States, including seventeen American presidents of Scots-Irish descent.[165]

Through British rule, including land dispossession and settler colonialism, many Irish Catholics were blamed for their own impoverishment. When potato crops failed in 1845, they began living a nightmare. They were still producing enough wheat, oats, barley, butter, beef, eggs, pork, and lamb to sustain four times the Irish population for a year.[166] But these nutritious foods were forcibly exported. The British government resisted delivering digestible emergency relief foods. Entire communities were evicted from their homes, endured famine-related diseases, and died agonizing deaths. Reading about this, for the first time, I could sense the despair my Irish ancestors must have felt, and my heart ached for them.

Masses of the famine survivors began making the dangerous journey across the Atlantic Ocean to Turtle Island. Due to overcrowded, unsanitary conditions and insufficient Water and food on some of the ships, many perished. Those who survived were often treated with contempt. In American newspapers, periodicals, best-selling books, and schoolbooks of the time, the Irish were stereotyped with words such as "dirty," "incurable," "leprous," "ragged," "disorderly," "brutish," "dark," "ugly," "savage," and "vicious."[167] Nevertheless, after only a few generations, most Irish immigrants had assimilated into whiteness and American identity.[168] Their descendants would be blessed by opportunities to live increasingly stable, fulfilled lives on Turtle Island.*

Learning this history helped me understand *why* some of my

---

* For an account of how the Irish eventually came to benefit from white settler privilege, please see pages 129–32 of *Not a Nation of Immigrants: Settler Colonialism, White Supremacy, and a History of Erasure and Exclusion*, by historian Roxanne Dunbar-Ortiz.

people accepted whiteness as a viable alternative to their Irish identity. In their desperation and trauma, they probably saw whiteness as
a means to earn their livelihoods and ensure their children's survival.
I was learning to see them with empathy rather than judgment.*

———

In 2022, my husband, children, parents, and I traveled to Ireland.
A decade had passed since our trip to Scotland, where I'd felt my
first inklings of connection to this part of the world. We visited
some of the places where our people had lived. My maternal
great-grandfather once made a pilgrimage to Slemish Mountain in
Northern Ireland before he emigrated to Canada as a young man.
In his honor, I walked partway up Slemish Mountain and sat next
to a tree that was bedecked in ribbon and cloth offerings for the
fairies, or *Sìdh*. Surrounded by sheep, gazing on the landscape with
his eyes, I took in the beloved country he had left behind.

In County Mayo, where some of my father's people lived, we
visited the "Lost Valley of Uggool," a famine village.[169] There, we
walked among ruined stone cottages and trees our ancestors once
considered sacred.† From a descendant of a survivor, we learned that
half of the villagers had died of starvation during the Great Hunger.
The other half were evicted shortly thereafter. In the Museum of
Country Life,[170] we glimpsed some of the sophisticated livelihood
skills our ancestors once practiced, such as spinning, weaving, agriculture, blacksmithing, animal husbandry, butter and cheese making,
thatching, basket-making, and boat construction.

In Dublin, the National Museum displayed exquisite gold torques
designed by ancient Irish artisans. And at the pre-Celtic Neolithic

———

* Cecil Woodham-Smith's book, *The Great Hunger: Ireland 1845–1849*, was recommended by an Irish woman who said that her family still experiences historical
trauma in the aftermath of the Great Hunger.
† That day, we walked among hazel, oak, and hawthorn trees. These are some of the
sacred trees that inspired Ogham script, the "first alphabet of Europe," as detailed
by Irish botanist and medical biochemist Diana Beresford-Kroeger in her book *To
Speak for the Trees: My Life's Journey from Ancient Celtic Wisdom to a Healing Vision
of the Forest*, pages 189–282.

tomb of Newgrange, we walked down a narrow passage, mysteriously aligned with the sunrise on winter solstice. We stood silently in the inner chamber, a place of reverence. I felt the wonder of our Irish ancestors' existence before they were colonized, oppressed, and shamed for existing. I admired their genius, perseverance, and hard-earned skills for living sustainably. Learning their histories and visiting their land allowed me to fall in love with them.

These experiences helped me accept that my ancestors are woven throughout the historical cast of characters in Irish history. The ancient ones may have included builders of stone monoliths and creators of gold torques, as well as blacksmiths, craftspeople, and farmers. The last several generations included Irish, English, Scots-Irish, and those who became white settlers on Turtle Island. I embraced the reality that my people have experienced complex roles as victims, perpetrators, and survivors through the generations.

The Birthing Treehouse

I am walking in a vast forest of tall trees. Overhead is a treehouse meant for birthing. I look down at my belly and see that I am pregnant. I ascend the ladder to the treehouse to give birth.

The treehouse is full of women all gathered around a dead baby. With horror, I take in the appearance of the baby. It is tiny, small enough to fit in a shoebox. It resembles a broken-down 1950s baby doll that belonged to my mother as a child. The blond hair is matted, and the skin is hard plastic. Yet, I know this is a real baby who was stillborn in the treehouse.

Overwhelmed with grief, I sit down at a round table. It is full of women whose faces I can't see. I fold my arms on the table, put my head down, and cry—until I feel someone grasp my hand. When I lift my face to look at her, I see that it is Nana, my beloved, late, maternal grandmother. Nana looks at me lovingly and squeezes my hand. She says, "It's going to be alright."

Waking from this teaching dream in the spring of 2018, I could still feel Nana's hand in mine, warm and comforting. A few days later, I co-hosted a women's circle. Two hours into the circle, we had only begun to address our first topic: how are you? When I listened to those from Jewish, Indigenous, and Latinx backgrounds, it was like being in another country. I had to stretch my hearing to catch the meaning between their words. Fears of holocaust, genocide, and displacement were more tangible for them than they were for me. Their ancestors and relatives had suffered those things in recent memory.

Across our differences, we shared similar concerns about the social and environmental violence that seemed to be growing exponentially all around us. We compassionately wit(h)nessed each other. I shared my dream of the birthing treehouse. In the presence of our circle, the dream revealed its meaning:

We are here to give birth. In the process of birthing, we are side by side with death. Diseased colonial thinking has been spreading throughout the world for a long time. Now, our illusions of stability are dying. Our climate is rapidly changing. Extinction is escalating. Poverty, inequity, and social unrest are growing. The Dream of the Modern World now looks as lifeless as a broken, plastic doll. Yet, it is not separate from us: it is our own baby whom we created collectively. Looking at this baby is frightening, but its death must be mourned.

I recalled how I felt before giving birth. In the last weeks of pregnancy, I remember looking down at my enormous belly and thinking, "there is no way this will happen." My mind refused to accept that I could accomplish this superhuman feat of delivering what appeared to be a gigantic baby.

Yet when the moment arrived, my mind ceased its anxious chatter. There was no choice but to surrender to instinct. My second child was born at home in a birthing pool. Labor took a little over an hour from beginning to end. Throughout, a relentless feral beast twisted and burned my spine with fire. My back felt as though it would break in half. I was certain that my body could not withstand that much pressure.

A replica of a statue I call the "Grandmother of Willendorf" caught my eye from across the room.* This figurine was carved approximately 30,000 years ago, and she was discovered in Austria in 1908. I like to imagine her cradling the memory of her Indigenous European sculptors in the Earth for tens of thousands of years, bringing the echoes of their presence forth in our present time. While giving birth to my son, I saw her heavy breasts and belly, her grounded posture. I viscerally re-membered that many ancient grandmothers survived birthing, as did generations of mothers who came afterward. With my eyes focused on her, I felt her assurance that I would survive this birth. Moments later, my son was born, and the family rejoiced.

While sharing my dream in the circle, the warmth of Nana's hand, the glimpse of her face, and her soothing words returned to me. She hadn't appeared with such clarity since she had died more than a decade before. Her presence conveyed that the beloved ancestors are with us in our endeavor of birthing a New Dream for the Modern World, even as we face death and destruction. The Grandmothers are awaiting us in their birthing treehouse. They sit at a round table amidst the treetops in another realm. They are holding our hands here on Earth and encouraging us to follow our instincts: breathe, push, and live.

White Peril: Poisoning Ants

For me, one insidious aspect of whiteness is how it manufactures blind spots in my perception. During the third year of this contemplative journey, I began wondering about my unconscious racist conditioning. One night, I sat before my altar with a bowl of Water

---

* More than 250 female statuettes, sometimes referred to as "Venus" figurines, have been found in today's southern France, northern Italy, the Danube-Rhine region, Russia, and Siberia. For a discussion of these figures' characteristics, uses, and possible meanings, please see pages 23–27 of *The Divine Feminine in Ancient Europe: Goddesses, Sacred Women, and the Origins of Western Culture*, by Celticist Sharon Paice MacLeod.

held close to my belly. Setting an intention without thought,* I asked for a teaching dream to show me what I needed to see:

I am preparing for my child's birthday party. A long time ago, I was told to sprinkle poison on everything; otherwise, ants would ruin the party. I have a big can of poison that looks like a saltshaker, and it's filled with white powder. I vigorously sprinkle it in the cracks between the sidewalk and all over the ground. But suddenly, I remember that I must put it around the tables, so the ants won't eat the food! I must remember to keep washing my hands, because I am dealing with poison. And I must remember to re-apply the poison right before the party begins.

With a start, I realize three things: 1) I am almost out of poison and there will not be enough to cover all these spaces, 2) I am killing ants, and 3) This poison will go into the ground and pollute the Water.

Horror-stricken, I realize that I am poisoning families of ants. I'm killing complex societies in which each ant is critical to the group's survival. With heartache, I remember what an Elder recently said: humanity needs to learn to become like ants, working together cooperatively for the good of the whole.

Why am I killing ants? I'm filled with despair when I understand that I have been contaminating the ground Waters with poison. But I've come this far. The damage is done. The party must go on, and I don't know how to stop. I find myself spreading huge piles of poison. I sprinkle it under the guests' cars and in every imaginable place. I willingly "forget" my sadness about the ants and the Water, stuffing it down deep inside.

---

* Inspired by a teaching from Unangan Elder Kuuyux Ilarion Merculieff and shared here with his permission.

The symbolism of this dream struck me first. Tiny black and brown ants, working cooperatively underground, were being destroyed by a white woman thousands of times their size. I was wielding an endless supply of white poison. This imagery evoked desperate sorrow that made me want to ignore the dream. And yet, I had invited this dream through the sacred medium of Water. It was important to listen.

I wondered: how am I continuing to poison the ants? How am I obeying voices that quietly conveyed who was important, what was necessary, how to exert control and manage outcomes? These questions raised the despair of being an unwitting tool of white supremacy, which was devised long before my birth and had been invisible to me for most of my life.* I was starting to understand that if I do nothing to dismantle it, I am complicit in upholding it.

The dream illustrated how whiteness and racism have shaped my psyche, how I've unconsciously complied with instructions from "a long time ago" to subjugate others and keep them out. It exposed my assumed dominant position. It showed how I can get stuck in habitual, harmful behaviors. It also uncovered an unconscious fear of admitting that I don't know what else to do. Even when I felt remorse in the dream, I rationalized my behavior and kept going. The moment I stuffed my feelings down, endless supplies of poison appeared so the party could go on. In her book *Waking Up White*, white racial justice educator Debby Irving writes:

> I think of how I stifled my feelings as a child, how I pressed them down. Then I turned around and did it to other people. Isn't this what "oppression" is? Pressing down and invalidating feelings and pressing down and invalidating people?[171]

The dream showed me other possibilities as well. I sensed how the ants are interdependent with the land and the Waters. I recognized

---

* On page 36 of her book *Liberated to the Bone: Histories, Bodies, Futures*, cultural worker and bodyworker Susan Raffo writes, "White supremacy...is a system of coddling European-descended people so that they, so that we, don't have to feel the impact of the wounds our people brought with us over the ocean and then transplanted directly into this land and into people's bodies."

their networks thriving underneath the pavement, the grass, the tables, and the cars. The dream made me want to become an ant-sized relative within these interdependent networks. It galvanized a desire to unlearn my racist patterns. I want to set aside the poison. I want to learn to be like an ant, cooperating with others for the good of the whole.

How (if at all) Can I Help?

> I'm starting to think that real spirituality…manifests
> as people rolling up their sleeves and serving the
> visions crafted by Indigenous Peoples themselves.
> Asking, "How can I help? If at all?" And moving in
> service of whatever the answer to that question is. It
> looks like not just leveraging privilege but working to
> create a world where you no longer have privilege…[172]
> ~ Lyla June Johnston ~
> (Diné Artist, Scholar, and Community Organizer)

In 2016, the messages of the Standing Rock movement made me feel hopeful, included, loved, and fully human. Being welcomed into a movement of Indigenous creation, with their permission, inspired me. At the end of 2016, I began supporting Indigenous-led grassroots work in my own community. Later, I would come to understand this commitment as a sacred yearning. I was developing a longing to be part of making things right again by supporting the visions and solutions crafted by Indigenous Peoples themselves.

Indigenous spaces felt different from the white feminist community organizing I had previously been part of. I had always wondered why it was so hard to get Indigenous, Asian, Black, and Latinx people involved in "our" feminist movement.* Then I began noticing white feminists not listening to the realities expressed by

---

* Please read about white feminism in chap. 4 of *White Women: Everything You Already Know about Your Own Racism and How to Do Better*, by Regina Jackson and Saira Rao.

these communities, and not taking steps to prioritize their voices. I eventually decided to focus my energy in support of Indigenous relatives. This felt resonant with my desire to contribute to changing the Dream of the Modern World.

Over the years, I learned that entering Indigenous spaces as a white person requires humility. There is a long history of our being oblivious, thinking we know best, trying to take over, and getting exasperated when our techniques don't work. We are not entitled to enter these spaces as *self-appointed* allies.* Becoming a good relative is something that may (or may not) be recognized in us over time *by the community.* For me, this is an ever-evolving practice.

In Indigenous spaces, I try to listen more than I talk. What I am listening for is, "How (if at all) can I help?" This inquiry sometimes leads to tasks such as taking meeting notes, fundraising, scheduling and hosting meetings, cooking meals, networking, and washing dishes. Occasionally I am invited to speak publicly with the group or assist with a writing project. Observation is important. This means not asking too many questions, believing what I hear, and allowing myself to be quietly impacted. It means that sometimes, stepping back is needed more than stepping forward.

After we gather, I mentally review our interactions. Sometimes I realize that I've been asserting my opinions even when I don't know what I'm talking about. Other times I find myself panicking inside my head, yearning to steer us toward a plan or timeline that seems "logical" from my point of view. I become aware of how my conditioning guides me toward behaviors that are habitual but also don't feel right anymore.

One time I found myself blabbing uncontrollably, with what I thought was advocacy for the tireless community work of three

---

* I recommend:
  - *How to Be an Ally to Indigenous Peoples: A White Paper in the Spirit of a Red Paper*, by Alice Woodworth and Joe Parker (https://static1. squarespace.com/static/5e02559d2a11646407b253a3/t/5f89aa2c0ccf92609a8 be266/1602857519575/Allies7GenFundFinal11-2017-3.pdf).
  - "Being an Ally in Indian Country," a training by the Native Wellness Institute (https://www.nativewellness.com/).

friends. Like a white savior, I insisted that they should be paid for their work. Afterward, I had a nagging, uncomfortable feeling. Eventually, I saw that I had projected my ideas onto a situation that I hadn't taken the time to understand, also known as "whitesplaining." When I realized my mistake, I picked up the phone to apologize. Exposing and taking responsibility for my white settler conditioning can feel intimidating. But it is the right thing to do. That conversation helped build more trusting relationships over time.

In my experience, Indigenous community organizing feels different than organizing that is rooted within Eurocentric culture. By observing, I noticed that the matriarchs listened deeply, and that they were often invited to speak first and last. We often began community gatherings with prayers, offerings, acknowledgment of the sacred Mountain and Water. We grounded our community dialogues in these and other Indigenous practices. If conflict arose, we paused what we were doing to listen, understand each other, and affirm our interrelation.

This methodology is not always focused on a linear timeline. Perhaps, through a Western lens, it could be perceived as inefficient. There was circularity in how we operated. When we reached a turning point in our projects, we gathered in a circle, where we hugged, ate, and talked. The group naturally affirmed the wisdom of Elders, elevated the voices of youth, and honored Mother Earth. My task was simple: I just kept showing up, generous with my energy and honest about my limitations.

My previously unconscious ways of operating were being rewired. During these years of contemplation, I'd visited other dimensions and experienced oneness with the cosmos. But after these spiritual experiences, I returned to the physical dimension. Deep wounds and inequities have been manufactured in physical reality for centuries. I was grateful for opportunities to integrate these realities and become a more complete human being.

Often, we white settlers are living in segregation from Indigenous Peoples. In some cases, we have absorbed the colonial lie that Indigenous Peoples no longer exist or are no longer relevant. Many of us are afraid of making mistakes or feeling unwelcome. These fears are understandable, and they originate with our history on this land. If you are not yet in relationship with Indigenous Peoples in your area, I encourage you to learn who they are, research their history, and find out what issues are currently impacting them. Look for opportunities to attend Indigenous-led educational events, assist with Indigenous-led projects, and support Indigenous-led organizations.

The crises that disproportionately harm these communities offer white settlers an invitation to re-member and reenact "a social norm of nurturing and being nurtured."[173] Showing up in service to the visions and needs of Indigenous individuals and communities can become a long overdue form of nurturing from white settlers. In turn, *we* are nurtured by restoring the honor of our own humanity.

Philanthropic Alchemy, v 2.0: Wealth on Stolen Land

I'm at the drive-thru ATM to withdraw some money. When I put in my PIN, gold coins and a desiccated goat leg fall out of the slot. Mortified, I quickly run outside to stuff the items into my trunk. I hope I can hide them and drive away before anyone finds out.

This teaching dream came during my second fasting ceremony in 2016. I knew that it was an assignment to work on my relationship with money. The assignment felt daunting. I tucked the dream (and the assignment) away, until they returned with clarity one evening in the spring of 2018. That night, I met five Indigenous friends at the local university. We had been invited to speak to a class about our social and environmental justice work in the community.

We began with introductions. One by one, each of them spoke their languages, describing their intergenerational relationships to ancestors, clans, Water, land, and plants. This introduction style had become familiar to me over the previous few years. Listening to the soothing sounds of their languages wash over the room, I felt a recurring anxiety: how should I introduce myself? The Western norm of identifying ourselves by profession seemed hollow to me now. When the time came for my introduction, I was surprised by what came out of my mouth:

> My name is Hilary Giovale, and I am a ninth-generation American settler of Scottish, Irish, German, and Scandinavian descent. For all the generations that my family has been living on this continent, we have been living on stolen land.

Sitting back, somewhat shocked, I glanced at my Diné friend Darrell Marks.* Smiling, he placed his hand over his chest and inclined his head slightly. To me, this gesture conveyed that my words had landed well with him.

Until this moment, I had been processing this newfound identity in the privacy of my own mind and heart. But as soon as these words were spoken to a room full of people, their truth rang like a gong. The land we call America is *all* occupied territory. Every inch of this land was enmeshed in relationships with Indigenous Peoples before European settlers arrived. The connections between the land and her Original Peoples have been altered, obscured, or ended by settler colonialism. The white settlers who now occupy this land have largely forgotten or denied that this land had sophisticated, sustainable relationships with her Original Peoples for millennia *before* our people arrived. It seems we have come to believe that this land is rightfully *ours*.

With this truth ringing, my role as a philanthropist suddenly appeared far more complex than it had before. With newfound clarity, I saw that in the United States, wealth is built on stolen land. Our nation's founding economy relied on stolen lives and labor. It

---

* Darrell is committed to supporting unsheltered relatives and Indigenous youth in our community. He is also a recipient of the JFK Profile in Courage Award. See: https://www.jfklibrary.org/events-and-awards/profile-in-courage-award/award-recipients/covid-courage-2021/darrell-r-marks.

still manufactures gross inequity. This wealth-producing economy commodifies trees, Waters, mountains, bees, and human bodies. What does that mean for the beneficiaries, the few who decide how philanthropic money moves? How do my implicit biases impact my philanthropic giving? (I've offered some answers to these questions in The Fourth Year.)

For now, these questions sat in my lap awkwardly, like an overgrown, obnoxious child. My ATM dream revealed a disconcerting impulse to hide the loot and run away in embarrassment. But now, the time for transparency had arrived. Instead of hiding, I would embrace the discomfort of unpacking my unconscious narratives about power, money, and philanthropy. Though it's often been a bumpy ride, this is the road I decided to take.

White Peril: Self-Delusion

I consider my friend Edgar Villanueva to be an exemplary philanthropic alchemist. With his warm presence, charming Southern accent, and astute analysis, he transmutes pain into healing, deprivation into abundance, and ignorance into insight. Edgar is a member of the Lumbee tribe of North Carolina, in the region where my sixth-great-grandfather settled after his migration from Scotland in 1739. His grandson, my fourth-great-grandfather, later inherited a North Carolina plantation and an enslaved man in the will of a family friend. When Edgar and I first met in 2016, I took note of our ancestral entanglement and immediately silenced it with a nervous gulp. I did not know how to be in integrity with it yet.

In the spring of 2018, Edgar was preparing for the publication of his book, *Decolonizing Wealth*. He sent me portions of the manuscript pertaining to grief and apology.[174] This was an opportunity to review a conversation we'd had a year earlier, which he'd quoted in his book. After reading the passages, I could sense that something more was needed from me. That night, before going to sleep, I asked for clarity. Emerging from sleep early the next morning, a small voice whispered: "You know, you could apologize to Edgar."

Another, argumentative voice replied: "Oh no, there's no need for that. That would be overkill. It's just too much."

I was learning to distinguish between the voice of my heart and the voice of my mind. My heart usually asks for the thing that is most challenging, vulnerable, and risky. My mind wants to protect my ego, uphold the status quo, and keep me complicit. It was the voice of my heart that suggested this apology, and I chose to listen. By inviting me into a conversation about his book, Edgar had opened a door. I felt that it was time for me to walk through that door and apologize directly to a descendant of those who had been displaced by my family's settlement.

From the moment I first learned about my ancestors' presence in North Carolina, I felt an impulse to apologize. But my fear impulse was stronger. I tied myself up in a tangle of knots. How could I authentically apologize when I enjoy the comforts of settler privilege? How could I apologize when it could pour salt on old wounds? How could I apologize when I might be ostracized? How could I apologize when I have no clue how to fix it? How could I apologize when I don't know any descendants of the people my ancestors displaced?

Yet, here was Edgar's and my ancestral entanglement in North Carolina. Here was his book, conveying *how* to apologize. He writes:

Apologizing turns us from the inward focus of grief, outward to the Others who were harmed. . . . Apologizing requires that white people of wealth snap out of their paralyzing white fragility and guilt, and just step up.[175]

Over the next week, the apology wrote me. I passed through many gateways labeled "Your Apology Will Never Be Enough: Why Bother?" Once again, I began weaving a bigger basket in my heart: one that could hold divergent realities. Into the basket I placed my sorrow and regret, the fact that I didn't personally displace Edgar's ancestors but still feel remorse, the fact that it was a long time ago and that the echoes still reverberate. I had to embrace my futility to make it better, and my ability *to try*.

I revised my apology many times. Layers of deflection arose, still trying to excuse, deny, or analyze. Finally, I remembered the apologies I have received in my life that have both hurt and helped. I realized that a true apology is simple. It comes from the heart and acknowledges the feelings of the one who has been harmed. It does not justify the harmful behavior. It allows the pain to exist in plain sight.

During this process, more of my White Peril was unearthed. I saw my self-delusions: the compulsive need to have it figured out, do it right, fix it, and maintain control (or at least look like I'm in control). Once, a white mentor shared the adage: "Don't let the perfect be the enemy of the good." Peeling back these layers to create a good apology to Edgar and his family took brutal self-honesty and time. Below is an excerpt from my letter:

> *I apologize for the guns, alcohol, land theft, displacement, star-vation, disease, heteropatriarchy, death, rape, cultural genocide, Manifest Destiny, capitalism, boarding schools, segregation, dehumanization, greed, kidnapping, religion, slavery, sexual abuse, lies, racism and white supremacy that descended upon your Lumbee ancestors and other Indigenous Nations when my European ancestors settled on this continent. I am deeply sorry for the terror, loss, trauma, betrayal, humiliation, pov-erty, invisibility, and confusion you and your family must have experienced through the generations.*

Courageous Love

With my apology to Edgar sealed in its envelope, I placed it on my ancestor altar late one night. Lighting candles and filling a bowl with Water, I spoke to my ancestors. I told them about the letter and asked for their guidance. Leaving the letter on the altar overnight, I asked them to send me a message. This teaching dream came in response:

> *I am standing in an old stone building. Outside, meadows and forests expand over the land. I'm given an assignment to put thirteen items in order.*

A Voice says: 'There are Black Jaguars here. You must calm your mind, have courage, and open your heart. If a Jaguar approaches you slowly, you may live. But if a Jaguar runs toward you, you will die.'

As I sort the items, a Black Jaguar approaches stealthily on my left. Registering its powerful jaws and body, I feel terrified. But at that moment I remember the instructions.

Willing myself to be calm, I summon courage and breathe slowly into my heart. The jaguar stalks around me in a circle. Another jaguar approaches from the right, stalking around me in a circle. The jaguars' paths intersect, and they leave. I am alive.

The ancestors relayed an important message with this dream. My interpretation of it was informed by Peruvian author Arkan Lushwala's book *The Time of the Black Jaguar*:

For Indigenous People of South America, the black jaguar is a much-respected spirit…it gives us what we really need, even when it hurts. When a power like the black jaguar shows up, it is time to change, and there is no possible negotiation.[176]

The morning after this dream, I returned to my altar. I thanked the ancestors for their message and held the letter close to my heart before placing it on the mailbox. Facing generations of harm, denial, and silence was changing me from the inside out. I was learning to wake up and do my own work. Making this ancestral apology required a courageous kind of love, and it helped move me into restorative action.

In the coming years, I began supporting fellow white settlers with their ancestral apologies. I learned that offering an ancestral apology directly to a *person* can have unintended consequences. These kinds of apologies can sometimes re-traumatize the recipient, put them in an awkward position, or compel them to do emotional labor. To avoid these pitfalls, when making an ancestral apology directly to a person, it is important to be clear about our motivations, so as not to cause further harm. Rather than apologizing in person or in front of a group, I recommend sending these types of apologies as letters, within the context of a trusting relationship. This respects the recipient's dignity and allows ample time and space for them to process.

From my perspective, ancestral apologies are most effective when they carry no expectation of forgiveness, or of any other response. In the coming pages and the Appendices, I've shared how to ritualize ancestral apology as a prayer. This can often be a more accessible way to start.

Edgar's book was published in October of 2018, and he brought my apology letter on his book tour. When he spoke at conferences, universities, and professional gatherings throughout the United States and Europe, he read excerpts of the letter aloud. This was unexpected and humbling for me. In the following years, as our paths continued to unfold, Edgar and I both expressed our gratitude for how the ancestors have brought us together. Our relationship has made mutual healing possible.

Song to Forgotten Ancestors

Whatever you sing to them…
Is only your heart answering their love.
And the words you sing are not your own
Though you sounded them they are older than you
They rise from the soul of your people
Music of your emigrant ancestors
Whose hard history left a long soul scar.[177]
~ DOUGLAS STEWART ~
(Scottish-Canadian Poet)

I had purposely shut down my singing voice as a teenager, when singing hymns in church made me feel phony. Now rusty, my singing voice appalled me in the rare moments when I used it. But something told me that learning to sing some ancestral songs was important. I began with an old Hebridean song of the selkies, shapeshifting seal spirits.* The song transported me back to the midsummer evening on the Isle of Erraid, when I stood on a hilltop overlooking the sea. My ancestral memory began stirring with the message *"You know this place. You have been here before."*

One afternoon, while listening to Irish songs, a rush of longing swept through me. I heard something familiar to my DNA: something once dear, but long forgotten. An Irish keening song sounded like grief for a long-lost home. Tears of relief bubbled up from inside me. When I tried to extinguish my candle after listening to the songs, the flame continued burning brightly. Taking deep breaths, I tried again three more times, yet the flame burned steadily. I suddenly understood this as a sign from the ancestors. Perhaps an ember of what had been repressed was waiting for the opportunity to be rekindled.

————

Due to colonialism, Indigenous children of Turtle Island were required to exclusively speak English in boarding schools. This was a means to enforce their assimilation to American identity. Generations later, this repression of language and culture continues to impact their communities. I'd often heard Indigenous friends express the importance of their languages, saying, "English cannot adequately express the layers of meaning within our languages." Today, across Turtle Island, many Indigenous relatives are reclaiming their ancestral languages.

My mentors had encouraged me to learn my own ancestral

---

* Gratitude to Madi Sato for sharing this song with me. Listen to Irish singer and songwriter Mary McLaughlin's recording of "Sealwoman/Yundah" on her album *Daughter of Lir.*

languages, which I resisted for some time. Eventually, I learned about the pressures my Scottish Highlander ancestors faced. The British crown outlawed the Gaelic language in 1616.[178] Subsequently, a "policy of cultural genocide" required the children of traditional Highland leaders to be sent away to English-language schools at age nine.[179]

Highlanders were stereotyped as "rebellious, bloodthirsty savages" who needed proper religion and education to counteract their ignorance.[180] Eventually, some Highland tenants were even required to fund English-language schools in their own communities, to enforce their assimilation into Anglophone (English-speaking) culture.[181]

This pattern continued in the following centuries. For example, even into the twentieth century, some Scottish children were still being shamed and beaten for speaking Gaelic on the playground at school. Alastair McIntosh writes:

> In some schools they had to hang a spoon round their neck. This could only be got rid of by informing on some other poor kid, who in turn inherited it. Whoever had the spoon at the end of the day got sent home with a thrashing.[182]

At the beginning of my ancestral journey in 2016, 400 years after King James I outlawed the Gaelic language, I wasn't even aware that my Scottish ancestors had once spoken Gaelic. Now, I finally understood why I didn't know.

Colonialism also contributed to the erosion of Highland clan and kinship-based systems of governance. During the Highland Clearances of the 1700s and 1800s, small farming communities were evicted or relocated to make room for profitable sheep pasturage or hunting estates.[183] Lands that had been commonly held for centuries were subdivided to maximize "productivity."[184] With the loss of their land, waves of Highlanders migrated to Turtle Island and elsewhere. By this time, their traditional lifeways and culture had been interrupted and disparaged for a long time. It hurt me to realize how my people had been dehumanized.[185]

This understanding gave me the nudge I needed to learn some of my ancestral songs. Beginning in 2020, I eventually connected with Elders who graciously guided me. In my understanding, "Elders" are not self-identified, and the term does not apply to everyone who has reached old age. Rather, the community surrounding a person bestows this honorific title. Different cultures and communities have different ways of identifying Elders. From my relationships with Elder-honoring communities, I now perceive "Elder" as a term that identifies those whose warmth, compassion, insight, knowledge, kindness, courage, wisdom, and humor serve the well-being of their communities, and even the world.

· In my perception, one of the many harms of whiteness is its dismissal of elderhood. In white culture, old age tends to be seen as a time of diminished relevance, rather than a phase of life to be honored and respected. We white settlers sometimes seek guidance from Black and Brown Elders. I feel that we *also* need Elders of our own lineages to guide us. I started noticing when white communities around me identify someone whose warmth, compassion, insight, knowledge, kindness, courage, wisdom, and humor serve the well-being of their community, and even the world. I began learning from these European-descended Elders as well.

One of these Elders is Sìne McKenna.* Sìne is generous, sensitive, loving, and creative, and she has beautiful snowy hair. She descends from Gaels of Scotland and Ireland who immigrated to Montreal, Canada several generations ago. This was similar to the migration path that some of my ancestors followed. Sìne's great-great-grandfather, a survivor of the Irish Famine of 1847, was so traumatized by his experiences that he refused to speak about Ireland until the day he died. Fortunately, his son made the choice to revitalize the family's ancestral memory. Subsequent generations of Sìne's family were blessed by his decision. Inspired by her parents' devotion for their ancestral heritage, Sìne grew up with a passion for the language,

---

* Sìne McKenna teaches Scottish Gaelic songs and stories online (https://ancestralfire. ca/). I also recommend Mary McLaughlin's Irish singing and story classes (https:// www.marymclaughlin.com/).

music, and stories of our people. As an adult, she spent time in Scotland learning to speak and sing in Gaelic.

In her class, Sìne graciously conveys stories about various aspects of our ancestors' lives. Her teachings are gathered from poems, family stories, academic sources, and her long-standing relationships with culture-bearers in both Scotland and Canada. Here I've shared some of Sìne's depictions that resonated with me. Before immigration, our ancestors' lives revolved around agricultural cycles. They reverently cared for their animals and the land, practiced unique community rituals of blessing and protection, and cultivated vibrant relationships with the Otherworld. I came to see our immigrant ancestors as people who experienced deep emotion, but whose emotion wasn't always readily expressed. Some longed for their homeland decades and generations after they'd left. In Sìne's class, while reflecting on the past, we explore what it means to be part of the Gaelic diaspora today.

Some of Sìne's lyrics come from *Carmina Gadelica*, a six-volume anthology of prayers, hymns, incantations, work songs, charms, and cures. Scottish folklorist Alexander Carmichael devoted much of his life to collecting verses from Scottish Gaels, mostly in remote parts of the Highlands, between 1860 and his death in 1912. He published some of the volumes of *Carmina Gadelica* himself. Others were published posthumously by his family. Carmichael's work made an immense contribution to the preservation of Gaelic culture, which had been disparaged by Anglocentric hegemony for a long time.* Unfortunately, the original melodies of the songs have been lost to time, but Sìne creates new melodies to accompany the lyrics Carmichael collected.

---

* An essay titled "The Kilted Exciseman: Alexander Carmichael (1832–1912)," by Professor Andrew Wiseman, describes a controversy that surrounded *Carmina Gadelica* decades after its publication. During Carmichael's time, editorial methods often involved "polishing" source material to cast it in a more flattering light according to the tastes of Victorian English-speaking culture. In the 1970s, Carmichael was critiqued for having employed this practice. Wiseman speculates that, perhaps in a desire to revitalize his culture that had been so harshly disparaged, Carmichael took steps to ensure that these cultural materials would appeal to readers. Despite this controversy, I remain grateful for *Carmina Gadelica* because it preserved some elements of Gaelic culture that would have otherwise been lost.

Some of the verses within *Carmina Gadelica* had been part of *cé-ilidh* (pronounced "KAY-lee") gatherings.[186] *Céilidhean* (pronounced "KAY-lee-un," plural of *céilidh*)[187] took place in Highland homes during winter evenings. Friends, family, and neighbors would gather to sing and dance, sharing stories, poems, and traditions with each other. Beginning in the 1600s, as Anglophone influence increasingly repressed the Gaelic language, *céilidhean* may also have served as a form of resistance to cultural assimilation.[188]

Many layers of history had passed between the eras when Celts lived in kinship-based tribes and when *Carmina Gadelica* was published. It did not offer an intact cosmology by any means.[*] Nevertheless, after a year of practicing these songs, I could sense ancestral memory reweaving within my blood and bones. I felt that some of the Gaels' ancient cosmology was still imprinted within these old songs, blessings, and cures.

For example, *Togail An Teine*[189] (pronounced "toe-kell-an-CHenuh")[190] is a blessing to sing while kindling one's fire for the day (or lighting a candle). This song and ritual allowed me to viscerally experience how my ancestors might have related with fire. It conveys the importance of tending the hearth in family life by invoking the presence of *Brìg*. It asks her to bless the fire, the floor, and the household. *Smooring* (smothering) the fire for the evening and preserving embers for the following morning involves a similar blessing. In Celtic cultures, a variety of rituals involving fire were used to bless and protect newborn babies and mothers, livestock, crops, land, and souls transitioning to the spirit world.[191]

Urnaigh Maidne (pronounced "OOR-nee MAT-nuh"),[192] a morning prayer, illustrates how the Gaels might have prayed at the beginning of each day.[193] It enfolds the singer in a *caim* (pronounced "KIME"),[194] a circle of protection. I had wit(h)nessed similar practices in the prayers of Diné friends. *Urnaigh Maidne* invokes sacred speech, thinking, sleeping, waking, watching, hoping, life, lips, soul,

---

* I recommend the Cailleach's Herbarium post, "Scottish Cultural Appropriation—Revisited" (https://cailleachs-herbarium.com/2023/03/scottish-cultural-appropriation -revisited/).

and heart. This is a song I like to ritually sing as a blessing of protection for myself and others.

Some of the other Gaelic songs Sìne taught me carry blueprints for reverent relationships with New Moon,[195] Sun,[196] Ocean,[197] Mountains,[198] Mist,[199] Apple Trees,* Stars,[200] and the Divine Feminine (in the form of *Brìg*).[201] In addition, she taught me songs of grief, longing, and sorrow that express the challenging aspects of life. Some of these lyrics came from *Carmina Gadelica*, while others were passed down through oral history. Some were based on historical events and written more recently. For me, these songs began to shape a sense of the worldviews that brought my ancestors peace, joy, and resilience.

In online *céilidh* gatherings with Michael Newton,[†] I learned that some Gaelic work songs were imbued with sympathetic magic. The ancestors used kindness and praise to coax butter from milk and flour from grinding stones as they labored.[202] Learning about these traditions of my Highland ancestors allowed me to experience some of the techniques they used for relating to the world around them. I found that the faintest threads of our ancestors' lifeways are still visible, waiting for us to reweave them.

> How does it happen that the lore
> And ancient power of a people withers
> Isn't worth remembering?
> How does the change occur
> When the secret knowledge, the potent words
> Spells, medicines, chants
> Things passed on from age to age

---

* Carmichael, *Carmina Gadelica*, vol. 5, pp. 483–84: "*Craobh nan Ubhal*" (The Apple Tree). Sìne McKenna's class materials share:

> The apple tree is the supreme symbol of wisdom in old Celtic lore: apple trees bearing both flowers and fruit appear in the Celtic Otherworld, and an apple branch is handed to Gaelic leaders and heroes by the Sìth—fairies—as an invitation to a spiritual calling, journey, or quest.

† Michael Newton is a Celtic Studies Scholar who has done extensive research and writing about the traditions, culture, and history of the Scottish Highlands. You can connect with his work through the Hidden Glen Folk School (https://www.hiddenglenfolk.org/).

Are abandoned or written down on paper
That gets put away for safekeeping
But no longer used?[203]
~ DOUGLAS STEWART ~
(Scottish-Canadian Poet)

Some of the surviving Gaelic lyrics I learned were collected during the nineteenth century. At this time, remnants of old poems, spells, and songs were kept in memory by people in remote parts of Scotland. *Their* ancestors, the earlier Celtic peoples, did not rely upon written language. Historical accounts of poetic recitation, oral history, recitation, bardic praise, and satire indicate that the spoken word was regarded as a source of honor and power.[204] The Celtic ancestors share this trait with some traditional peoples today. Many times, I've sat in Indigenous circles, wit(h)nessing their *knowing* that spoken words can create reality. I felt empowered speaking and singing ancestral words that were passed down and remembered. In my experience, the memory that is transmitted through ancestral languages can help us realign with Earth and reclaim the sacred power of the word. (Please see the Appendices for ideas on how to start learning an ancestral language and ideas for building relationships with Elders who can teach you.)

―――

The third year took me further into the twists and turns of the labyrinth. Honoring my loving ancestors, using shame as a catalyst for transformation, and embracing other ways of knowing gave me a sense of purpose. Publicly acknowledging and privately accepting my presence as a settler on stolen land began rewiring my mind. My ancestral apology to Edgar brought clarity.

We are now in the center of the labyrinth, where the way forward is challenging to discern. All we can do is place one foot in front of the other, trusting that the process will lead to emergence. Sometimes walking a labyrinth means retracing the same steps that brought us to the center. We return to the starting point, changed by the experience. My fourth year of contemplation would highlight the Doctrine of Discovery, gentrification, and support for IBPOC community-led work through reparative philanthropy. Water, stars, relationships, ritual, and forgiveness would illuminate the path. Welcome to the fourth year.

The Fourth Year

Women, Water, and Stars

We give thanks to all the Waters of the world for
quenching our thirst and providing us with strength.
Water is life. We know its power in many forms—water-
falls, and rain, mists and streams, rivers and oceans.
With one mind, we send greetings and thanks to
the spirit of Water. *Now our minds are one.*[205]
~ OHÉN:TON KARIHWATÉHKWEN—WORDS
BEFORE ALL ELSE ~
(Haudenosaunee Thanksgiving Address)

A forest of cholla cactus formed a spiky gateway. Their magenta blossoms would bless the desert with color for only a few summer days. During the cool early morning or evening hours, I wandered among the cacti, staring into the depths of each blossom and inhaling its scent. The petals' silky texture seemed out of place in the desert. How could such a fine fabric emerge from this dry, sandy soil? The cholla blossoms smelled like rain. They indicated the presence of a precious element, scarce in this environment: Water.

Within each blossom, a microcosm thrived. Several ants, a spider, and other intricately detailed insects coexisted. One evening, a tiny green spider grasped a dead fly twice her size, managing her prey with delicate translucent forelegs. The next morning when I returned to the same flower, the spider had doubled her size and the fly was nowhere to be seen. I pondered her ability to eat a creature twice her size.

I was alone on the land, honoring my moontime as a ceremony by fasting and praying with Water. At dusk, I laid a wool blanket upon the ground, cradled by an old juniper tree. In the gaps left by the branches overhead, stars twinkled, lulling me to sleep. A vivid teaching dream arrived:

> *The iridescent Andromeda galaxy appears in a black night sky. The galaxy is surrounded by a ring turning counterclockwise, right to left.*

This dream woke me briefly, and then I plunged into another:

> *Women come from all directions to form a circle in a meadow. They hold hands. From the outside, an Elder approaches them. White hair cascades down her back in a long braid. The Elder joins the circle with an unformed question. It is important that the women find the right question to ask.*

Awakening at dawn, I walked to the dry riverbed nearby and sat on the sand wrapped in my wool blanket. I pondered the two dreams. Suddenly, the Elder's unformed question appeared in my mind: How will we restore our human relationship with the cycles of Water?

As the day heated up, ants crawled all over me. Sometimes, I felt a small pinch when one of them bit my hand, foot, or elbow. My first instinct was to brush them off, but then I remembered the ants I'd ruthlessly poisoned with white powder in a dream. Perhaps these embodied ants would teach me another lesson now. I watched them scurry all over the trees and the dry soil. They were full of purpose. I asked one of the ants if it had something to say and I heard, "You humans have not explored all your options yet."

My body curved and adapted to the contours of the sandy soil and the plants. I had no roof over my head, no food to cook or eat, no emails to answer, no meetings to attend, and no dishes to wash. Instead, I listened to the roar of the thunders, the pulse of the rain, and the breath of the wind, singing back to them in response. In this state of attunement, I could sense how my songs interacted with the elements and created subtle changes.

The question was: how will we restore our human relationship to the cycles of Water? During these days of moontime ceremony, I received knowings that seemed ancient. At the same time, they felt relevant to our current realities of climate change and ecological loss. Sitting with a simple bowl of Water under the hot, blue sky, pieces of information landed within me. The information was not linear or logical, but it was sound. It did not originate in my mind, but it resonated with the Waters of my body.

I was shown images of the underground lake and the red cloth Grandmother Anaya gave me during my first year. I remembered her instructions: "When the women re-establish their relationship to the underground lake, the Waters of Earth will be healed. Go, take this, and tell the other women." Receiving the next layer of insight, I now understood the underground lake to be the womb of Mother Earth. During our bleeding time, we can connect. This is a time of subtle communication between people who have wombs and the underground Waters. Eventually, the underground Waters emerge and travel throughout the world. They nourish all life.

In vision, I saw an ancestor on the shore of a windswept island somewhere in northwestern Europe. With her arms outstretched, she called to the winds, the waves, and the sea birds. Her hut was nearby. It was a simple, rounded structure that would eventually return to Earth without a trace. She was attuned to this place. She knew how to call the rain and calm the sea. Years later, when I saw images of modern reconstructions of wattle and daub Celtic round-houses, I recognized my ancestor's hut. Although I had no prior knowledge of the roundhouses, this was an experience of ancestral memory appearing in waking vision.

During my moontime ceremony, I received a knowing that the relationship between the humans and the Waters has been inter-rupted by war, conquest, and other devastating events that have emerged from ideologies of "progress." I came to understand that climate change is not only a result of rising carbon emissions. It is also about damaged human relationships with Earth and the natural cycles of the Waters. Our human disrespect has been wreaking havoc on Water. When these knowings surfaced, healing tears fell into the Water bowl. Grief for all that has been lost became the remedy for re-membering. Each evening, I offered Water imbued with my tears to the plants around me. We restored each other.

———

As Havasupai/Hopi/Tewa Grandmother Mona Polacca says, "We are in the eleventh hour."[206] Correcting our course is urgent. At this time, I was made to understand, women and people with wombs will be the first to remember. Our remembrance will offer a warm invitation that embraces and includes our human relatives of all genders. Water moves in cycles: from underground lakes to springs, rivers, oceans, mist, clouds, rain, snow, and hail, which eventually return to the underground lakes. Because women's lives also include continual cycles of transformation, we have a unique capacity to restore human communication with Water. Now is the time for all peoples to re-member our balanced human relationships with the Waters.

Water Speaks, I Listen

When you have me all the time, you
forget how much you need me.

July Fourth

It was the Fourth of July in 2018, my forty-third birthday. What I wanted for my birthday was not a party, presents, or cake. I wanted time with the sacred mountain and the forest. I packed some Water and other treasures, to spend the day in reflection.

As I passed through our historic downtown in the land now called Flagstaff, Arizona, the holiday was underway. Decorated fire trucks adorned the town. Neighbors donned their red, white, and blue glittery hats, T-shirts, and other Independence Day regalia. One woman cheerfully waved her American Flag, wearing an Uncle Sam hat and cowgirl boots. They were making their way to the Fourth of July parade. Later, they would enjoy barbecues, drink beer, and eat ice cream. They would celebrate the day the United States claimed independence from the British Empire.

I used to enjoy celebrating this holiday in conjunction with my birthday. Before climate change robbed the land of much of its moisture, fireworks were a regular feature of the Fourth of July. As a child, I cherished the treat of lying outside on blankets with our extended family. We stayed up late watching colorful starbursts against the night sky, the "boom" following a few seconds later. When one of my uncles joked that the fireworks were for my birthday, I believed him. It felt special that my birthday was also the birthday of our nation!

These memories now felt like a fairytale. Everything looked different, once again. As I drove through streets abuzz with holiday energy, I saw oblivion. All the celebrants were people of European descent. As innocent children, we were told stories of our nation's honorable founding fathers. Our trusting ears were filled with mythologies of a heroic nation. We believed in its ideals of freedom, liberty, and the pursuit of happiness. In the minds of our nation's children, who later became adults, these stories became belief systems and worldviews.

I was one of those children who stood in classrooms every morning with her hand over her heart to recite the Pledge of Allegiance. Now I understand its final words, "liberty and justice for all," as part of a myth. This myth used pretty words to enlist children in upholding a brutal system. The system ensured superiority for some and terror and erasure for others. It has never delivered "liberty and justice for all." As a child, I didn't feel right putting my hand over my heart and saying those words. But I also didn't know why.

Not until my forties did I understand the realities underpinning our settler heroic American mythology. Popping my bubbles of denial and building bridges across cultures changed me. It gave me the will to see things differently. Now I understand: the words I recited as a child are incongruent with the past *and* incongruent with present reality.

Each year, my community enthusiastically celebrates July Fourth. Even into adulthood, many of us have never realized that our parents, teachers, and community leaders taught us to recite lies about this nation. We learned to do this in exchange for being considered good students and upstanding citizens. Today, many of us still do not understand that this land was home to thousands of diverse Indigenous communities. Our ancestors occupied and stole their land to ensure *our* freedom and independence. From 1778 to 1871, the United States signed approximately 368 treaties with Indigenous Nations.[207] Since then, as Western Shoshone professor Ned Blackhawk notes in his book *The Rediscovery of America*, the treaties have consistently been disregarded and broken, by both land-hungry white settlers *and* Congress.[208] It is not our fault that we were deceived as children. But it is our responsibility to wake up and learn the truth of what really happened.*

———

One example of a movement that challenges heroic American mythology is Indigenous Peoples' Day. Beginning in 1989, this movement has worked its way through municipalities and states across Turtle Island. Indigenous Peoples' Day, the second Monday in October, reclaims and renames Columbus Day, a holiday that was established nationwide in 1937. Touted as an explorer who "discovered the New World," Christopher Columbus actually just got lost on his way to the East Indies. Along with other explorers, he imported a delusional worldview of Eurocentric superiority.

———

* Recommended reading:
  - "Trail of Broken Treaties," a twenty-point position paper issued by the American Indian Movement in 1972 (https://cwis.org/wp-content/uploads/documents/premium/293wb10017.pdf).
  - Some of the treaties can be viewed online (https://americanindian.si.edu/nationtonation/treaty-of-fort-harmar-with-the-six-nations.html).

Columbus enslaved, raped, kidnapped, and tortured Taíno[209] and other Indigenous Caribbean peoples.* Rather than being celebrated, I think that Columbus's actions should be openly discussed and grieved. Indigenous Peoples' Day challenges the myth that Europeans were chosen people with a divine destiny to colonize this land. In my experience, it cultivates respect for those who were thriving here long before Columbus's arrival.

———

Driving through the quintessential July Fourth scene in 2018, I thought of the Indigenous relatives in my life. For them, this holiday is yet another painful reminder of settler culture occupying their homelands. Among a subset of Americans (most of us think of ourselves as "Americans" now, rather than "settlers") there might be some awareness of the broken treaties, horror of boarding schools, trauma of relocation, or the ongoing crises of missing and murdered Indigenous People largely ignored by authorities. But these realities raise uncomfortable feelings. Mostly, they are forgotten, relinquished to "the past" as though they have nothing to do with us.

I'd met a Hopi man a few days before who shared with me how he and his family were confounded by the lack of rain. They were faithfully doing their ceremonies as always, but now the rain did not come as it used to. They dug deeper and deeper holes in the sandy soil to plant the kernels of corn their ancestors had cultivated without irrigation for over 1,200 years. In just a few years' time, the size and vitality of their corn plants had deteriorated.

His story made me want to squirm in shame and anxiety. But I listened quietly while holding my son's hand. He said that many of the Hopi men were on the verge of giving up their ancient tradition of planting and caring for corn. The crop yields no longer justified the hard work of planting, tending, and harvesting.

Each Fourth of July, I now seek independence from heroic

---

* Listen to "Blood of My People" by Taíno-descended artist Brother Mikey, from his album *Happiness*.

American mythology, and *interdependence* with All My Relations. I can no longer celebrate this day with patriotic pride. Instead, I listen for its complexity: layers of pain, history, gifts, challenges, and potential. I want to be accountable for my privileged settler existence. I long to be part of the healing.

Berry Picking

We once hired a permaculture landscape company to design our backyard. Sleep deprived after months of nursing our baby, I requested a simple design as close as possible to zero maintenance. The company used many plants with edible fruits. Our children would enjoy eating from the bushes and trees.

Ten years later, in 2018, our baby, who had grown up a lot, welcomed me home one spring evening.

"Mom, Mom, come out to the backyard—I want to show you something!"

Grabbing my hand, he pulled me excitedly toward the trees. With a grin, he pointed to clusters of tiny cherries hanging like delicious little promises. Turning around to face the tree behind us, we glimpsed small green plums. In the trees across the yard, baby apples and pears were taking shape. With the setting sun glowing on our faces, we hugged each other in joy: we would have fruit this summer! We had seen blossoms on the trees, but in this high altitude they often freeze late in the spring. This year, the unseasonably warm winter and spring would allow us to harvest sweetness.

As spring turned to summer, we were delighted to see currants and berries ripening all over the bushes in our yard. There were so many we couldn't eat them all. We made cobblers to temper their tartness and invited friends to pick as many as they could. Living with this bounty, I could sense the changes the previous decade had brought.

Originally, we designed our backyard from a perspective of white, progressive sustainability. For example, we grew edible plants so our children could experience picking and eating fruits in the backyard.

We limited our use of potable Water for irrigation. We asked the landscaping company to design a gray-Water system and beds that would catch and retain rain. We composted and made sure everything was organic. We made use of all the microclimates in our yard to plant a variety of trees and bushes. But we did not yet perceive ourselves as settlers on stolen land. We still thought of the land and Water as "things" rather than beings.

Now, as I picked these currants, berries, and cherries day after day, I could sense how my years of contemplation were guiding me toward a relationship with this place. In the backyard, I greet the sun every morning. I give thanks for the sacred gift of my breath. I pray with a glass of Water and offer some to the land before I take my first sip. Each morning, I marvel at the ice of winter, the buds of spring, the bounty of summer, and the rusty hues of fall. In the evenings when our family eats together, we make a plate with small portions of our food. With a prayer, we offer this plate to the spirits of this land.

In the backyard, a family of skunks lives under the deck. We eat our dinners there in the summertime, laughing at the sounds of the skunk babies playing with each other underneath our table. In the evenings, Mama Skunk leads her children to our compost pile. Food scraps from our kitchen go into the compost pile, which became the skunks' dinner. Our compost eventually nourishes the flowers I pick to honor the ancestors, the herbs that flavor our food, and the fruits that I bake into cobblers.

Our house was constructed at the beginning of the twentieth century, some thirty years after the town was founded. In an early photo, white women in high-necked blouses, corsets, and long bustled skirts stand together on the front porch. I used to think of this place as "our house," a place we paid a fair market price to own. I used to consider the backyard a property that we were responsible for maintaining. But now, this place has become a Relative: a mother who feeds us; a brother who amuses us; a father who protects us; a sister who holds our hand when we are grieving.

In my friendship with a Diné man named Darrell Marks, he sometimes offers guidance as a generous interpersonal philanthropist. Darrell had recently asked me to define "gentrification" for his teenage son, Makaius. I explained that gentrification happens when the lower-income inhabitants of a neighborhood are displaced by higher-income people moving in and driving property values up. Darrell turned to Makaius and stated: "Gentrification is how this town was made, by pushing the Indigenous People out."

His words hit their mark. I gulped as another bubble of denial popped in my mind. I wondered about the Original Peoples of this land: the children, farmers, medicine people, and grandparents. They were pushed out so white settlers could claim this land as their own and build the house in which we live. It was a painful realization.

I was becoming acutely aware of our presence as settlers. We are transplants here. "Owning" a backyard at the foot of a sacred mountain is one of the advantages of gentrification. Being able to hire a permaculture landscaping company is another. Harvesting the fruits of the land is another. These advantages are built upon centuries of choices and structures that have been built through settler colonialism. They have culminated in our participating in gentrification without even realizing it.

In 2018, our backyard offered a bounty of apples, pears, plums, cherries, currants, and berries. They grew on plants that have developed the intelligence to thrive with little Water at high altitude. These plants know how to coexist as part of an integrated ecosystem in which each one has enough. They support each other through symbiotic relationships. Can we learn from these plants and become integrated members of this ecosystem, rather than an invasive species?

Considering these questions awakened my heart's wish to become a better tenant. Asking "How (if at all) can I help?" and moving in response to what I hear is teaching me how. White settlers can begin transforming gentrification by committing to right relations and supporting reparations.

As I've mentioned earlier, our community lives together at the foot of a sacred mountain, a being of kinship. In her presence, we enjoy coming together when the sun sets in the west every evening. This land loves to share sweetness with her grandchildren. Clouds rolling in over the mountain bring monsoon rains to nourish forests, prairies, and fruits. After harvesting currants, I noticed the symbiotic relationship between currants and pine trees on the slopes of the mountain. Backyard currants introduced me to mountain currants.

On a gorgeous late August day, as the sun warmed the backyard in the morning, I sang gratitude while picking cherries and currants in their juiciest, sweetest moment. I raised my face to the monsoon rainstorm that afternoon, to welcome Water. That evening, I placed all the cherries and currants into a basket decorated with the wild sunflowers that grow here. I took the basket to a gathering of Indigenous relatives and shared it. As we ate from the basket, a Mohawk friend offered a Haudenosaunee prayer naming the plants as relatives who teach us how to live rooted in place.

Autumn was coming. The pears, apples, and plums would soon ripen with the changing season. I would continue listening for how we can work together to nourish all the children of this land.

Discovering the Doctrine of Discovery

These insights about heroic American mythology, patriotism, and gentrification were new to me. But many communities have been confronted by these realities for centuries. Learning about the Doctrine of Discovery offered me more context. In her book *The Land is Not Empty*, Tewa-descended author Sarah Augustine defines the Doctrine of Discovery:

> ...a system of laws and policies meant to permanently remove Indigenous Peoples from the birthright of their lands and wealth by force: genocide, relocation, urbanization, and forced assimilation.[210]

Three decrees issued by two fifteenth-century Popes underpin the Doctrine of Discovery. In the minds of some, these decrees, known as papal bulls, formally justified European imperialism.

In 2015, my husband and I co-created two short films to support the Long March to Rome.[211] This was an intertribal effort to rescind two of the papal bulls, an act that would have formally acknowledged the impacts they have had throughout the world. Our films began with words from the *Romanus Pontifex* Papal Bull, issued by Pope Nicolas V on January 8, 1455:

Invade, search out, capture, vanquish and subdue
All Saracens and pagans whatsoever,
And other enemies of Christ wheresoever placed...
And reduce their persons to perpetual slavery...[212]

Three years later, the books *Unsettling Truths* by Diné author Mark Charles and Korean-American author Soong-Chan Rah, *Pagans in the Promised Land*, by scholar Steven Newcomb, and *Sacred Instructions*, by Penawahpskek attorney Sherri Mitchell offered me more insight. I've shared my understanding here.

In 312 CE, the Roman emperor Constantine converted to Christianity. He had seen a cross in the sky, "inscribed with the words, 'In This Sign, Conquer.'"[213] He became the first Roman Emperor to appropriate Christianity for political purposes. The Roman Empire then adopted Christianity as its official state religion in 380. Also in the fourth century CE, the Roman Catholic Bishop Augustine of Hippo promoted the "just war" theory. This is the idea that war is inherently noble, and that killing can be justified when it is in service to God.[214] In the coming centuries, religious and government institutions began colluding in devastating ways. The Roman Catholic Church would increasingly be linked with wealth, oppression, and war.

In the fifteenth century, the Catholic Church issued three papal bulls as "divine law," assuming the authority to dehumanize all non-Christian peoples. These documents provided false justification for the transatlantic slave trade. They underpinned the Doctrine of Discovery, a legal framework that European monarchies used to justify their "discovery" of lands that had already been inhabited for millennia.[215] Centuries later, in 1823, the papal bulls informed a United States Supreme Court decision that dispossessed Indigenous Peoples of their land.[216] Mitchell writes, "This ruling was later adopted by Canada and Australia, and became the foundation for nearly all subsequent land-takings from Indigenous Peoples around the world."[217]

The Doctrine of Discovery inspired "Manifest Destiny," a term that was first used in the United States in 1845.[218] As I shared previously, this was the delusion that European Christians were God's "chosen people" who were fulfilling their divine destiny by expanding westward, occupying the entire continent, and cultivating the "promised land" of Turtle Island.[219] Proponents of Manifest Destiny believed in their divine right to spread democracy and capitalism.[220] Boarding schools were designed to cruelly dispossess and assimilate Indigenous Peoples who stood in the way of Manifest Destiny.

———

While editing interviews for our films in 2015, I heard our friends sharing the current ramifications of this ideology. Their stories cracked my heart open. Afro-Indigenous farmer Bill Edwards related: by emboldening the minds of the conquerors, the papal bulls created one of the most powerful weapons the world has ever seen.*

Their words helped me understand the papal bulls, Doctrine of Discovery, and Manifest Destiny as the basis for institutionalized private property rights in the United States. Although many of us have never heard of them, they influence our lives every day. They have nothing to do with the humble, loving teachings of Jesus, and everything to do with taking land and consolidating wealth.† Sherri Mitchell writes, "Our dance with illusion has been a long one. It is millennia deep and is therefore deeply embedded into the mass consciousness."[221]

---

* Gratitude for Bill Edwards, who became an ancestor during the COVID-19 pandemic. Listen to his words: https://vimeo.com/148686345.

† Christian congregations are actively participating in dismantling the Doctrine of Discovery. Please see *The Land Is Not Empty: Following Jesus in Dismantling the Doctrine of Discovery*, by Tewa-descended author Sarah Augustine, and join the Coalition to Dismantle the Doctrine of Discovery (https://dismantlediscovery.org/).

When the Long March to Rome delegation visited Pope Francis I in 2016, they became one of many groups who have petitioned the Vatican to rescind the fifteenth-century papal bulls. Six years later, an Indigenous Canadian delegation visited the Vatican, in the spring of 2022. They also called on the Pope to revoke the papal bulls. The delegation pressed him to acknowledge the harm of the Doctrine of Discovery and the subsequent abuse perpetrated by Catholic residential schools.

In response, on April 1, 2022, Pope Francis offered a historic apology for the "deplorable conduct" of some Catholics within Canada's residential schools.[222] A few months later, he visited Canada, where he stood before hundreds of boarding school survivors and begged forgiveness for the "evil committed by so many Christians" in Catholic residential schools.[223] To me, the Pope's apology felt like a good starting place. Yet, it largely neglected the institutional nature of the harm. Pope Francis took another good step on March 30, 2023, when he made a statement to formally reject the Doctrine of Discovery.[224]

From my perspective, a next step would be for the Catholic Church and colonial nation-states to acknowledge the profound harm that the Doctrine of Discovery has inflicted upon humanity and Mother Earth. Imagine what could unfold if religious institutions and colonial governments worked together on policy changes, reparations, and returning stolen lands to their Original Peoples. The institutions that have conspired to enact colonialism must undertake a deep, collective reckoning. I imagine such a movement completely rewriting the Dream of the Modern World.

White Peril: Forgive(n)

I walk in a golden valley between two hills, strolling companionably with a bear. Our paths weave together. Sometimes we are close together and sometimes further apart, but we are always aware of each other. I carry a watermelon to feed the bear when he gets hungry.

In the summer of 2018, my son and I visited South Dakota. I had forgotten about this dream from several months earlier. Now, I recognized the same hills and the valley we were driving through. The land brought my dream back with its original clarity. We had a watermelon in the trunk, and we were bringing it to the Bear. My son and I were on our way to Pine Ridge to visit an eighty-five-year-old Oglala Lakota Elder named Basil Brave Heart, whom I would soon come to know as a generous and loving interpersonal philanthropist. Years later, Basil would share that his grandfather gave him the name *Mato Wakeya* (meaning "Bear Who Looks After His People from the Top of a Hill") when he was born.[225]

In the weeks before our visit, I'd been reading the words of Nicholas Black Elk, Wallace Black Elk, Frank Fools Crow, Mary Crow Dog, Joseph M. Marshall III, and other Lakota authors.[*] Immersing myself in their stories and histories, I delved into a world that was unfamiliar to me.[†] Here, I've shared an understanding that these sources, as well as subsequent conversations with Basil Brave Heart, helped me develop.

First, I read about the Lakota territories in the 1860s, when the *wasichu*[‡] (pronounced "wa-SEE-choo")[226] culture was beginning to impact people's lives, but the Black Hills remained largely untouched

---

[*] *Walking in the Sacred Manner* by Mark St. Pierre and Tilda Long Soldier; *The Day the World Ended at Little Bighorn: A Lakota History* by Joseph M. Marshall III; *Black Elk: The Sacred Ways of a Lakota* by Wallace Black Elk and William S. Lyon; *Lakota Woman* by Mary Crow Dog and Richard Erdoes; *Black Elk Speaks* by Black Elk with John Neihardt; *Fools Crow: Wisdom and Power* by Thomas E. Mails.

[†] I recommend the film *Lakota Nation vs. United States* (directed by Jesse Short Bull and Laura Tomaselli), in which Lakota people define their own history in relation to the settler nation.

[‡] In a conversation with Basil, he shared that *wasichu* is a Lakota word for "those who steal the fat." *Wasichu* was later used to describe white settlers. Lakota is Basil's first language, and he generously provided all the spellings and pronunciations of Lakota words in this book. During a conversation in March 2023, he said:

> Prior to European settlement on Turtle Island, Lakota was an oral language. It was first put into writing by missionaries. The meaning of the words and the sounds of the words are far more important than how they are spelled. The Lakota language comes from a sacred paradigm. Spelling is part of a linear, secular paradigm.

by encroachment. I read of buffalo hunts and the treat children received when they ate the liver straight out of the buffalo. Little boys
were able to shoot arrows and guns with precision at age nine, and
they became men when they were young teenagers. The people lived
in interdependence with the land. They harvested wild turnips, dried
meat for the long winters, and lived in kinship-based communities
that could quickly mobilize as weather, conflict, or food supplies
required. It also seemed to be a world of challenging conditions, in
which warriors helped to ensure the peoples' survival.

Lakota people increasingly experienced pressures in the land that
was now called the United States of America. An iron horse (the
railroad) bisected the traditional grazing grounds of bison herds
that had long provided food, shelter, and spiritual companionship
for the people. The Great Father (the American President) of the
settler nation was a faraway but omnipotent presence. He easily
made weighty decisions that impacted cherished lifeways and the
future of the people.

In 1874, General George Armstrong Custer alerted Americans
to the presence of gold in the Black Hills. With this announce-
ment, the second Fort Laramie treaty of 1868 that guaranteed *Oceti
Sakowin* (pronounced "oh-CHET-ee sha-KO-weehn")* sovereignty
and ownership of the Black Hills became worthless in the eyes of the
wasichu nation. Under the delusion of Manifest Destiny, an endless
train of wagons soon dominated Indigenous lives. White settlers
sought their fortunes in gold, treating the sacred hills as a commod-
ity. Increasingly, the land's original inhabitants were dehumanized as
so-called "savages." As these pressures mounted, conflict escalated
between and among the tribes, the cavalry, and the settlers. Even
150 years later, I could imagine the heartbreak and anger Lakota
people must have felt, as the United States government disregarded
its treaties in order to appropriate their land.

As Diné Indigenous Food Systems scholar Lyla June Johnston
later explained to me, the Plains people were not nomads who

* Basil shared that *Oceti Sakowin* means "The Seven Campfires," which includes
present-day Lakota, Dakota, and Nakota Nations.

aimlessly roamed the land, living hand to mouth. They had per-
fected techniques to maintain biodiversity and create habitat for
the cherished buffalo.* I can imagine the anguished grief the people
must have felt when the United States government "funded the
wholesale destruction of the once vast buffalo herds of the Plains."[227]
The Original Peoples' highly developed practices of tending and
managing the land were coerced into a lifestyle of Eurocentric agriculture, government commodities, and square houses. Violence
enforced their conformity to this way of life.

Pressure mounted throughout the so-called Indian Wars.
Visionary Lakota leaders, including Crazy Horse and Sitting Bull,
were killed. This period of conflict culminated in a massacre at
Wounded Knee. On December 29, 1890, a group of people was
disarmed and attacked by the United States 7th Cavalry. The 200
to 300 victims were mostly women, children and grandparents who
had been terrorized by relocation, starvation, and the grief of seeing
their way of life pressured to the verge of extinction.[228] The cavalry
used Hotchkiss Mountain Guns and hunted people down up to
a mile away. Twenty Congressional Medals of Honor were later
awarded to soldiers who carried out this massacre.[229]

In 1889, the Pine Ridge reservation was established as Prisoner
of War camp #334.[230] In the following decades, *wasichu* domination coerced the people of Pine Ridge into poverty and dependency
upon the United States government. I continued reading about the
American Indian Movement and Wounded Knee occupation of
1973, when Indigenous Peoples from across Turtle Island raised
a powerful voice to resist the federal government's disregard for
treaties. Learning about the current staggering levels of poverty,
inadequate housing, low life expectancy, infant mortality, unemploy-
ment, alcoholism, and suicide on the Pine Ridge reservation made

---

* To learn more about Lyla's doctoral research, please see her TEDx Talk,
"3,000-Year-Old Solutions to Modern Problems" (https://www.youtube.com/
watch?v=eH5zJxQETl4).

my heart ache.* As I became more aware of the founding realities of our country, I wondered: as a child of the *wasichu* nation, how could I walk in integrity with these heavy burdens?

———

I walked into Basil's home subdued. In the midst of a summer heat wave, we sat together in his air-conditioned living room. The cozy space held his Korean War memorabilia, photos of his ancestors, art, and thriving houseplants. A devoted puppy nestled on Basil's lap. Near the beginning of our visit, Basil asked: "Why have you *really* come here?" We did not know each other very well, but I could see that he always had a funny story and a chuckle close at hand. His warmth and genuine curiosity encouraged me to share the heavy questions I'd been carrying. I figured since he'd asked directly, I might as well reply frankly. With a nervous gulp, I said:

"I found out a few years ago that some of my ancestors received grants of stolen land and enslaved people in Mississippi. I have been struggling with this ever since. Indigenous Peoples have shown me unbelievable compassion. Just being with them has taught me a lot. I've heard about the Lakota teaching that we are all related. Why do you extend compassion even to the descendants of colonizers? I don't understand."

As it often is with Indigenous Elders, Basil did not answer my question directly. He smiled, continued petting his dog, and said, "So you are here to find out about your life's purpose."

"Well, yes, I guess I am." He had clarified a great deal already.

———

In the coming days, my son and I spent sweet time together in

———

* To imagine this transforming, please listen to the "Liberation" episode of *The Light Ahead* podcast (https://www.belovedeconomies.org/about-the-light-ahead-podcast).

silence on Basil's land. The expansive landscape, fields of sage, and sunflowers nourished our eyes. As my son whistled on a blade of grass to the cows all around us, I listened to the land and to Basil. An astonishing picture began to emerge. Born in 1933, Basil was raised by his grandparents, who were alive at the time of the Wounded Knee Massacre. In 1938, when he was five years old, his Grandmother Lucy taught him about the massacre. She explained that he mustn't be angry with the people who had committed the atrocity. She said, "They did not know what they were doing. You need to forgive them. Pray for their ancestors and their descendants."

On the night of the massacre, some of Basil's relatives had camped on the grounds of the Catholic Church to protect the "black robes" (priests and nuns) from potential retaliation. Immediately following a massacre, Lakota compassion for white settlers within their community went *that* deep.

When Basil first told me these stories, I recognized their similarity with the messages of Jesus. But as Basil shared in the coming years, his Grandmother Lucy did not speak English, had no exposure to Christianity, and had never been to church. The principles of *waunshila* (meaning "compassion," pronounced "wa-OON-shee-la")[231] and *wokintunze* (meaning "forgiveness," pronounced "wo-keehn-TOON-za")[232] are Lakota values. As Basil explained, forgiveness and compassion are Original Instructions* that were encoded into the Lakota language. "Original Instructions" is a term used by some Indigenous cultures to describe the natural laws that have been transmitted through oral tradition.[233] (For a definition, please see the Glossary.)

Basil's stories opened my heart in wonder: I was visiting someone whose family had embraced radical compassion and forgiveness in the face of atrocity. My son and I carried these stories with us to Wounded Knee. Basil taught us how to offer tobacco during our visit, quietly and humbly. Prior to our trip, my son had said he would be bored. But he was very attentive as we entered the grounds of the

---

* I recommend *Original Instructions: Indigenous Teachings for a Sustainable Future*, edited by Anishinaabe, Cree, Métis, and Norwegian scholar Melissa K. Nelson.

Wounded Knee cemetery. Following his lead, we visited every grave and read every headstone. Finally, we reached the mass grave and memorial at the center. Sensing the sorrow of that place, we held hands and placed our offerings on the ground together.

———

Several weeks later, Basil asked about my experiences during our visit.

I said, "One morning at sunrise, I lay down with my face on the ground. I felt the bloodshed of your people, and I cried. My tears soaked into the ground."

He replied, "I think that the trauma is surfacing through the land as a way to move us toward forgiveness."

Then Basil shared some words spoken by one of his Elders, Frank Fools Crow, during a ceremony long ago. After vocalizing the words in Lakota, he translated them into English, saying: "My relatives, what we are doing in these sacred ways needs to go out into the world and make ripples like a stone being dropped into the Water."

Basil continued, "My grandma and my Elders all taught me to forgive and include everyone. Everyone and everything are related. This is *Mitakuye Oyasin* (pronounced "mih-TAHK-ooyay oh-YAH-seen"),[234] an all-encompassing prayer for all our relations."

"Thank you for sharing that with me. My heart is broken by the genocide that happened on Turtle Island. Sometimes I get overwhelmed, and I don't know what to do."

"Forgive yourself, and locate the center of all-inclusive compassion within," Basil asserted.

Forgiving myself had not occurred to me yet. I was not sure how to begin.

———

Later that day I sat next to the creek near my home. As the Water sang and tumbled over the rocks, red dragonflies and saucer-sized butterflies danced through the leaves overhead. I began to absorb

Basil's advice and found that I was paralyzed by fear of letting go of the past. How could I let go when racism, poverty, and environmental violence are hurting Indigenous and African-American communities? If I let go, would I be absolving myself of responsibility? How could I let go, with all these advantages still in my back pocket? Bitter tears overtook me. The creek murmured: how do you forgive the unforgivable?

Eventually, a fresh breeze swept through the canyon. It cleared my doubts away and revealed a place inside of me as tender as a leaf emerging in the springtime. The layers of debilitating shame, guilt, amnesia, orphanhood, ancestral avoidance, and self-delusion were subsiding. Something else was becoming tangible: a commitment to moving forward with joy and purpose.

———

The next day, a few women assembled in a community truth and reconciliation group. We had been sitting together in storytelling and friendship over several years, sharing our joys, sorrows, and dreams. We had wit(h)nessed each other's heartaches and enjoyed each other's cooking. I shared Basil's reflection on self-forgiveness.

One of our Diné grandma friends, Viki Blackgoat, comes from a community that resisted relocation during the so-called Navajo-Hopi land dispute. She has snowy white hair, kind eyes, and a steadfast, thoughtful presence. A talented sociologist, baker, seamstress, gardener, and interpersonal philanthropist, Viki's emotional intelligence is like a warm embrace. Viki looked at me pointedly and said, "There is nothing to forgive." Gesturing to the three white people in the room, she continued, "It was your ancestors who did those things, not you. All of you are thoughtful and careful about what you say and what you do. You are committed to this work along with all of us. You're in it up to your elbows just like we are."

Viki held my gaze until the tears in her eyes mirrored my own. Rather than push her words or her gaze away, I nodded my head and whispered, "Thank you."

I began experimenting with self-forgiveness. With my eyes closed, I found myself inside an old mine shaft, sitting in a cart with rusty wheels. At times, the rickety cart flew swiftly down the track. Other times I ran into rusted metal gates blocking further passage, bumps in the track that threatened to tip the cart over, or places where the cart's passage slowed to a squeaky crawl. Breathing slowly, I began to understand these obstacles as the *unforgivable* within.

Unforgivable was lurking in the shadows* of my personality, which has been marinated in systemic racism and settler privilege. Seeing the unforgivable in myself was new, but others had been able to see it for a long time. I recalled a few years before, when a Hopi grandmother spontaneously grabbed my hand and assured me out of the blue, "You are forgiven. Do you know that?" I awkwardly stuffed her remark down inside, unable to meet her eyes. Now I could see that withholding my own self-forgiveness made it harder for me to accept *her* forgiveness.

Previously unconscious fears were now visible: am I a multigenerational perpetrator, enthroned on a comfy seat at the top of the hierarchy? Am I a villain who benefits from capitalism and crimes against humanity? Am I a spiritual bypasser, casually adopting other cultures' practices to assuage my own guilt? Am I entitled and out of touch with reality? These fears are rooted in historic harm and current realities.

In his book *The Spiritual Journey of a Brave Heart*, Basil shares:

> By doing the sacred rituals in the physical or outer world, the shadow side can come to the light and be revealed. By doing this, we honor the darkness and make it a relative. And, by not suppressing it, we create balance for ourselves."[235]

---

* Swiss psychiatrist and psychoanalyst Carl Jung wrote about the concept of the shadow in his work. The shadow includes the parts of ourselves that we reject.

At last, I could see these shadows as the underbelly of American settler privilege, hidden in plain sight. Could I usher them into the light of day and invite them to dance? What would happen if I made my darkness a relative, instead of rejecting it? Thinking about these questions was like standing atop a volcano about to explode. I felt ready for the fire of transformation.

Why Apology and Forgiveness?

> Forgiveness is a life-affirming, conscious act of power, not weakness, because the forgiver holds and uses this power to free and heal all those involved, both victim and perpetrator, so both can become whole human beings again.[236]
> ~ Dr. Anita Sanchez ~
> (Nahua [Azteca and Toltec] Mexican-American Author)

Early in 2019, Basil asked me to support an upcoming Ceremony for Repentance and Forgiveness,[237] inspired by his grandma's teachings. The ceremony took place the following summer in northern New Mexico. For several months beforehand, I supported people in writing their prayers of apology and forgiveness that eventually became part of the ceremony. Like a midwife, I held hands, wiped tears, cleaned messes, gave hugs, and reminded people to breathe. During a birth, painful challenges can arise. Here are some of the challenges people shared with me as we prepared:

- Apology is useless. We just need reparations.
- What if people apologize and never make any real changes?
- How can I forgive when my people are still being oppressed?
- Forgiveness is a tool of assimilation.
- We don't deserve forgiveness.

Hearing these concerns taught me that apology and forgiveness can be used coercively. They can be used to "make up" superficially rather than heal deeply. The idea that someone "should" apologize or forgive can prohibit real accountability. The idea that forgiveness must be earned means that we sometimes withhold it as a form of punishment. These conversations taught me that many of us have been hurt by weaponized forms of apology and forgiveness.

I realized that I was midwifing another kind of apology and forgiveness, distinct from the superficial versions. I began calling them "radical apology" and "radical forgiveness." Taking responsibility and stopping harmful behavior are both critical to radical apology. Throughout my process of radical apology, I faced the ancestral past, engaged shame constructively, and peeled layers of self-delusion. This helped me begin to dismantle my racism and divest from whiteness. Over time, radical apology has built my capacity for making personal reparations to Black and Indigenous communities. Radical apology is a prayer, not a performance for other people. It involves trusting in the Divine and releasing attachment to any particular outcome. Being forgiven by other humans is not the objective of radical apology. In my experience, radical apology is its own form of healing.

Radical forgiveness seems to be baked into the Original Instructions of some traditional peoples.* Basil taught me that it is facilitated by ritual and prayer. Radical forgiveness requires strength. It does not condone abuse, nor enable abuse to continue. It is not about giving up power, forgetting what happened, or relinquishing accountability. It is a courageous commitment not to carry the pain anymore. It is an ongoing process, not a one-time achievement. I have seen radical forgiveness fine tune people into warriors. It enhances the power of their presence. It gives them the capacity to love all beings. And it makes them free.

Here, Basil shares his experience with radical forgiveness:

---

* I recommend:
  - His Holiness the Dalai Lama and Archbishop Desmond Tutu discuss this kind of forgiveness in the film *Mission: Joy—Finding Happiness in Troubled Times* (directed by Peggy Callahan and Louie Psihoyos).
  - Anita Sanchez's story of radical forgiveness in her book *The Four Sacred Gifts: Indigenous Wisdom for Modern Times.*

My first language is Lakota, and I think in Lakota. I was abused as a child in Catholic boarding school. As a paratrooper in the U.S. military, my regiment was assigned to an operation that resulted in carnage at a Chinese prison camp. For many years, these things haunted me. I could not forgive myself. I blamed and shamed the church and the military. I became addicted to drugs and alcohol. I lost many jobs, my family, and my self-esteem.

With divine intervention, after twenty-four years, I experienced shame as the guardian to the threshold of consciousness. Sitting in silence and prayer, I went into the shame and made it a relative.

When you forgive, even if it is unreciprocated, you are changing the Water everyone swims in. You are rearranging shame to a higher vibration. The shame doesn't disappear, but it loses its power. I am a divine human being, and my purpose is to serve the people.[238]

Observing Basil's radical forgiveness eventually gave me the courage to try it myself. One day, sitting on a sunny slope of *Dokoʼoʼosłííd*, I sensed the ancestors of this land. I offered Water to them and asked for their help. I reviewed the list of harms perpetrated by generations of white settlers, including my own ancestors. With rivers of healing tears pouring from my eyes, I addressed *my* ancestors: "I forgive you." The sacred mountain of kinship turned these simple words into a prayer that sang through my vocal cords.

After several hours, a change began taking shape in this liminal space. My internal walls of anger, bitterness, and debilitating shame were dissolving. The long lines of our family story were turning a corner. For the first time since learning about our family history, I felt the possibility of really belonging to this place. Years later, I recalled how my Diné friend Sunny Dooley had said that the DNA of the oppressors was turning back to make things right again. Now I knew how that *felt*.

My initiations into radical apology and forgiveness did not "let me off the hook." Instead, they deepened my commitment. I am not suggesting that any of us "should" engage in radical apology or radical forgiveness. I am saying that these forms of liberatory healing are available to anyone, anytime. (For guidance on creating your own radical apology or forgiveness ritual, please see the Appendices.)

Philanthropic Alchemy, v. 3.0: Melting the Ice

Philanthropy is commendable, but it must not cause the philanthropist to overlook the circumstances of economic injustice which make philanthropy necessary.[239]
~ MARTIN LUTHER KING JR. ~
(African-American Civil Rights Leader)

You may recall reading about Philanthropic Alchemy near the beginning of this book. It took several years of my own healing before I was ready to return to this topic. Near the end of these four years of contemplation, my relationships with money and philanthropy were changing. Even so, when I started writing the following portions of this book that focus on money and philanthropy, I easily became disoriented. My colonized mind reflexively tried to maintain control over appearances. For a while, I was agitated because I could not find the way out of my delusion. Finally, while walking in the icy forest near my home with metal spikes on my feet, the ice showed me what was true.

On an early spring day near Imbolc, an ancient Irish festival that honors the goddess *Bríg*, the ice was in a state of evolution. *Bríg's* association with smithcraft has led me to perceive her as a goddess of transformation. In some places the ice was still solid, while in others it was delicate, ready to splinter with a tap of my spikes. Indentations in the ice cradled pools of clear, chilly Water. Beside the trail there was still some snow. Shady portions of the trail were muddy, and the sunny spots were already dry. In other places, trickles of melting snow meandered their way downhill. The snowmelt would feed rivers and oceans when spring and summer came.

My second-year dream in which a desiccated goat leg and gold coins came out of the ATM had asked me to look at my relationships with money and philanthropy. Like this ice, I was in a state of transition. What was once frozen solid was beginning to melt. The layers of conditioning that had privileged *and* imperiled me were being transformed. Some layers were just beginning to thaw, and others had completely evaporated. Painfully, some are still frozen.

I was coming to viscerally understand that human beings made up this thing called money, and it has become a driving force behind the Dream of the Modern World. It has advanced human innovation, such as Eurocentric medicine, art, technology, and science. At the same time, it has reduced our capacity to maintain balanced relationships with each other and Mother Earth. Money tends to magnify our justifications for environmental plundering, oppression, greed, and abuse. For the last couple centuries, money has been enmeshed with various forms of capitalism that have created vast wealth for a few and poverty for many. Money is embedded with nuance, power, and potential. Whether we like it or not, almost all of us need to deal with money in one form or another. In my experience, it is easy to become addicted to money and the security it seems to guarantee.

———

Dysfunctional relationships with money shaped the institution of philanthropy. American institutional philanthropy originated in the early twentieth century when "the rise of industrialism...created a major wealth divide between the workers at the bottom and the so-called robber barons at the top."[240] Rather than improving working conditions and wages during their lifetimes, the men who reaped industrial profits gave away vast fortunes near the end of their lives. They funded libraries, universities, concert venues, medical schools, and art museums. They also passed wealth on to their descendants.

Their riches were derived from deep harm, including the underpaid and exploited labor of the working class. The robber barons used their fortunes to craft "benevolent" end-of-life legacies. These philanthropic gifts enabled their names to be featured prominently in the institutions they funded. This is why Carnegie, Rockefeller, Ford, and Getty are still household names.

In *Decolonizing Wealth*, Edgar Villanueva writes:

> The basis of traditional philanthropy is to preserve wealth and, all too often, that wealth is fundamentally money that's been twice stolen, once through the colonial-style exploitation of natural resources and cheap labor, and the second time through tax evasion.[241]

Not only has wealth been generated by theft, enslavement, and exploitation, but institutional philanthropy also keeps massive quantities of capital frozen. Private foundations are only required by law to give 5 percent of their assets annually, and part of this percentage can include foundations' expenses. Too often, philanthropic funds are invested in ways that oppose or even undermine the missions they purport to uphold. Investment in life-destroying industries perpetuates ever more wealth. This setup means that only a trickle of this capital flows toward life-sustaining endeavors.

Ironically, institutional philanthropy often positions itself as a savior to remedy the problems that are generated by wealth acquisition. In this echo chamber, we can sometimes perceive ourselves as being qualified to "fix" things. It can be easy to congratulate ourselves for being magnanimous souls. But inflated self-importance prevents philanthropists from becoming the good relatives who are needed now. Too often, we are holding back from the work of understanding these dynamics and leveraging our power toward changing them. What if we were to spend down the assets that allow us to participate in institutional philanthropy? What if we were to invest in solidarity and work toward returning the wealth and the lands from which the wealth was extracted? Who would we become?

These years of contemplation overhauled my relationship with money. I began prioritizing relationship, learning to trust, being more transparent, and sharing more generously. My process continues with giving back to the places and peoples whose existence and labor fuel the creation of wealth. It persists with showing me where I am still frozen and fearful of the thaw.

During my four years of contemplation, many layers of ice received the warmth of the sun, abrasion by stones, and the wear of footsteps. As more insights became visible, I developed a clearer understanding of institutional philanthropy than I had previously been able to see. After years of uncomfortable questions, another bubble of denial popped.

Today's institutional philanthropy is enabled by the racial wealth gap,* underpaid and stolen labor, and the abuse of Mother Earth. Institutional philanthropy is not our final destination, nor is it a place for philanthropists to get comfortable and congratulate ourselves on our generosity. There is much more work to do, to keep thawing and flowing.

The Vicious Cycle of Wealth

> The vicious cycle of poverty has been clearly articulated
> and is widely known. What is less obvious and goes
> almost completely unacknowledged is the vicious
> cycle of wealth. Open your compassion and include
> the wealthy. This is an important part of your life's
> work. Do not shut them out. They also are your work.†
> ~ MOTHER TERESA ~
> (Albanian-Indian Roman Catholic Nun)

---

* Please see:
  - "The Racial Wealth Gap: Understanding the Basis for Repair" (https://reparations4slavery.com/the-racial-wealth-gap-understanding-the-economic-basis-for-repair/).
  - "Justice," Episode 6 of *The 1619 Project* docuseries (https://1619education.org/builder/lesson/1619-project-docuseries-viewing-guide).

† Correspondence from The Soul of Money Institute, April 21, 2021. Read the story about this quote on pages 31–37 of *The Soul of Money*, by Lynne Twist.

Over time, I interacted with more circles of people who have proximity to wealth. I started becoming aware of nuances about how wealth can impact wealthy individuals and families.* While traversing this landscape, the following observations helped me navigate:

- Wealth accumulation relies on extraction and exploitation.
- Wealth accumulation hurts everyone.
- It's possible to stop this cycle.

Here, I've shared some insights that came from working with my observations.

You may already be familiar with the dynamics of wealth. Maybe, you are a wealthy person who is actively redistributing money toward racial healing. Perhaps you are a philanthropic or investment professional, wondering how you can influence your institution's practices. You may be a white working- or middle-class person, hoping to ensure economic opportunities for your children or grandchildren. Maybe finances are challenging for you. It could be that wealth feels distant from your reality.

Different life experiences tend to create divergent perceptions about wealthy people. Often, wealthy people are idealized and envied. Sometimes, they are blamed for all our social and environmental crises. Occasionally, I even hear them being labeled as "inhuman." I understand these reactions. Curiosity, envy, blame, and anger are normal responses to gross inequity. The pain of injustice can make it easy to resent wealthy people.

At the same time, I've seen how wealth can hurt people in ways that many of us can't imagine. Some actively choose to hoard and grow their wealth at the expense of Water and air, community, and future generations. Some are so overwhelmed by their wealth that

---

* Please see pages 113–20 of *Decolonizing Wealth: Indigenous Wisdom to Heal Divides and Restore Balance,* for Edgar's thoughts on how the colonizer virus harms colonizer-settlers and those with wealth.

they turn it over to corporate bank investment managers and forget about it. Others are tormented with shame when they discover that they were born as beneficiaries of inherited wealth.*

Some divest and give everything away, which can generate family conflict and division. Others work with their families to challenge long-standing narratives about wealth and entitlement. Some devote their lives to funding community and environmental well-being anonymously, without any recognition. Others enjoy public accolades for funding institutions that prominently feature their names. Often, several of these behaviors combine within one individual or family. Many wealthy people suffer from isolation, shame, self-loathing, perfectionism, exceptionalism, addiction, denial, fear, and other mental health issues. These wounds tend to thrive in isolation. Talking about them openly can unleash rage, end friendships, and create mistrust.

Interpersonal philanthropist Lyla June Johnston once shared her perspective that the current systems of wealth generation in the United States originate in millennia of European warfare. Capitalism, and the hoarding it relies upon,† emerged from violence, starvation, and the fear that we and our children will not have enough to survive another day.[242] With each generation caught in this hamster wheel, these fears and traumas replicate. Wealthy people are often impacted by this dysfunction. As I have personally wit(h)nessed and experienced, sometimes they feel frozen, wounded, and insecure about how to deal with the vicious cycle of wealth, as Mother Teresa described it.‡

---

* For people with inherited wealth, I suggest:
  - Resource Generation is a community of "young people…with inherited wealth and/or class privilege committed to the equitable distribution of wealth, land, and power." See: https://resourcegeneration.org/.
  - Morgan Curtis is an ancestors and money coach who works with people of all ages. She also co-facilitates "Ancestors and Money" cohorts. See: https://www.morganhcurtis.com/ancestors-money.
  - *Classified: How to Stop Hiding Your Privilege and Use it For Social Change*, by Karen Pittelman and Resource Generation, can be an empowering resource.

† I see today's hoarding of financial resources as pathological. It is different from the long-term food and seed storage that traditional societies have used throughout the world to ensure their survival in the coming years.

‡ For ideas on how elite white men can contribute to ending the vicious cycle of

As I shared earlier, I was raised in a middle-class family. When I was young, at times, our family relied on public assistance in order to eat. In my twenties, I married into upper-class privilege. It was a tremendous relief to stop worrying about paying my bills, and I loved being able to travel. Over time, I noticed that elevated class privilege gave me fabulous advantages but exacerbated my insecurities. For example, I often felt a confusing mixture of defensiveness and an impulse to hide.

Growing up, I'd developed an idealized yet conflicted perception of wealth. I learned to be both wary and envious of wealthy people. During my four years of contemplation, the mixed messages I'd absorbed in my family of origin rose to the surface of my awareness again. Another bubble of denial popped when I began to see how systemic wealth generation relies on extraction and exploitation. This was extremely challenging for me to accept because it contradicted my conditioning to idealize wealth. In their book *Beloved Economies*, co-authors Jess Rimington and Joanna L. Cea explain how the "loveless economy" prioritizes wealth accumulation without replenishing the sources from which wealth arises.

> Because the central tenet of the current extractive economy...is the more money, the better—no matter what, and at all costs—we tend to measure well-being only in terms of the accumulation of monetary wealth. We are told the more money we have, the better off we are.[243]

Over time, I started to realize that having more money does not necessarily equate to being "better off." To the contrary, systemic wealth accumulation hurts all people, as well as the Earth. This shift of perception increased my compassion.

Embracing discomfort, building diverse relationships, sharing power, and practicing self-forgiveness helped build my resilience.

---

wealth, I recommend *Rich White Men: What It Takes to Uproot the Old Boys' Club and Transform America*, by Garrett Neiman.

Rather than continuing to invest in individual and family security, wealthy people can choose *belonging* by becoming response-able[*] to Earth and all our relations. Imagine how we could change the Dream by doing the work to truly belong! In my experience, belonging requires actively redistributing resources for the well-being of all. Choosing belonging is not limited to wealthy people. Those of us with stable, middle-class incomes can also develop discernment about how much is enough and invest in solidarity across class and race.

———

Along the way, I've found some remedies for healing the vicious cycle of wealth. I refer to them as remedies because I experienced their capacity to heal, when lovingly applied to the root of the problem over time. I gained insight into these solutions when I accepted that in the United States, wealth is built on and extracted from stolen land. This is a foundational wound that land tax programs can help address. These platforms encourage paying voluntary contributions to funds administered by Indigenous Peoples. Some calculate your contribution based on your rent, mortgage, or business. They are accessible to people of diverse incomes, not only the wealthy. They shift colonial dynamics by supporting Indigenous Peoples in their roles as original caregivers.

The first time I heard about land tax, I felt a lump in my throat. I wanted to argue with the premise. This agitation was a signal—to *wait, feel,* and *listen.* After wading through my discomfort, I saw that the concept of land tax was challenging my sense of entitlement to land. No one had taught me this explicitly, but it was in the air I'd been breathing my entire life. As my resistance melted, I eventually saw that an economy built on stolen land requires land-based

———

[*] I learned the term "response-able" from a Jen Lemen Facebook post, May 30, 2020. I've used it here with her permission. See more about her work: https://www.thepathofdevotion.com/.

remediation. Here are some current land tax programs throughout the United States and Canada:

- Real Rent Duwamish (Seattle)
- Shuumi Land Tax (Bay Area)
- Honor Native Land Tax (New Mexico)
- Manna-Hatta Fund (New York)
- Ancestral Homelands Reciprocity Program (California)
- Lenapehoking Land Acknowledgment Honorarium (New Jersey/Delaware/Pennsylvania/New York)
- Nii'kinaaganaa Foundation (Canada)

These programs offer tangible ways to build solidarity with Indigenous communities and practice reciprocity. I regularly contribute to programs in Seattle, New York, New Mexico, and Canada. If there is not a land tax program where you live, I encourage you to support one (or more) elsewhere. Another possibility could be building relationships with the Indigenous community where you live and asking if they would like to co-create a land tax program.

The first time I heard the phrase "LandBack," irrational fear gripped my heart. Curiously, I slowed down and took some time to learn about the movement. As another bubble of denial popped, deep in my psyche, I noticed a paralyzing fear of losing access to land. In hindsight, my fear has twin origins. In part, it comes from ancestral memory of my people being dispossessed of their land in Europe. Also in part, it comes from knowing that my people later profited from a genocidal system that stole Indigenous land on Turtle Island. These fears are based in trauma and insecurity rather than *belonging*.

A 2020 Bioneers keynote address by Hupa, Yurok and Karuk professor and author Cutcha Risling Baldy[244] helped me move through my fears and eventually embrace LandBack. In her talk, she tells the story of Tulawat, an island off the coast of today's Northern California.

As she relates, the Wiyot people consider Tulawat the center of the world. It was the home of their World Renewal Ceremony, in which they danced for several days, praying for the health and well-being of all. In 1860, just after the completion of the annual ceremony, six white settlers paddled to Tulawat and massacred about 100 sleeping Wiyot people—mostly women, children, and grandparents. The island was taken from the tribe, and their World Renewal Ceremony was not practiced again for more than 150 years. In 2000, the Wiyot purchased 1.5 acres of their ancestral land. In 2014, they restored the World Renewal Ceremony for the first time since the massacre. The Eureka City Council returned forty acres of Tulawat to the Wiyot people in 2019,[245] a meaningful step toward truth, healing, and repair. Cutcha Risling Baldy shares:

> LandBack is the momentous dreaming, the centering of our shared reimagining. LandBack is about *our shared futures*. But it's also about putting the world back into balance.[246]

Today's LandBack movement is the current iteration of a process Indigenous Peoples initiated five centuries ago, when European colonizers first began arriving on this continent. LandBack is based on rematriation. Daisy Purdy,* a T'Salagi friend, educator, and organizer, shared her understanding of rematriation from the teachings of her Auntie. She describes it as "returning Mother Earth to herself and honoring Indigenous communities' agency as caregivers of the Earth."[247] This can take many different forms.[248]

For example, momentum is building to return federal lands, such as National Parks, to Indigenous management. This is a natural first step, because Indigenous Peoples have developed long-term scientific expertise in caring for their land. Land that was once held intergenerationally by settler families is being passed to Indigenous families rather than settler heirs.† Land that was once held by churches or other institutions is being returned to

---

* Daisy works with Honor Water (https://www.honorwater.org/). This organization is based on the ancestral principle of rematriation.
† I recommend Christine Sleeter's novel, *The Inheritance*.

Indigenous Nations and institutions. Some Indigenous communities,* such as the Ekvn-Yefolecv Maskoke ecovillage,[249] are returning to their ancestral lands and actively restoring ecosystems, language, and culture.

The Indigenous friends who are part of my life recognize that in many cases, settler and Indigenous lives are now deeply intertwined. I have not heard them describing LandBack as a form of retribution against white settlers. Remarkably, evicting us, deporting us, or exacting the kind of cruelty that our ancestors inflicted on their ancestors does not seem to be the goal. Rather, I hear their desire for white settlers to embody different ways of being. We can do this by building relationships, learning our own history, sharing power and resources, and relating with this land and her Peoples in ways that are reciprocal, balanced, and respectful. In my understanding, by asking us to support LandBack, Indigenous communities are asking us to become good relatives.†

———

Since moving through my initial entitlement and fear, the LandBack movement (including land tax and some of the other forms it can take) has offered me healing from the vicious cycle of wealth. Investing time, energy, and money in the movement has changed me in ways that are still unfolding. I perceive that rematriation has the capacity to transmute settler colonialism on Turtle Island.‡

---

* As I write, the Winnemem Wintu tribe of *Buliyum Puyuuk* (also known as Mount Shasta) is rematriating 1,080 acres of their ancestral land. See: https://docs.google.com/document/d/1rDjRLzoPJsWXCjj3haC3weI5siiZU2jxWBNwsoIpidE/edit.

† In my understanding, LandBack and rematriation are not meant to benefit only Indigenous Peoples. This is a movement to encompass and enhance the well-being of all communities and all life.

‡ Please see Anishinaabe/Ukrainian author Patty Krawec's explanation of LandBack on pages 130–43 of her book *Becoming Kin: An Indigenous Call to Unforgetting the Past and Reimagining Our Future.*

Philanthropic Alchemy, v 4.0: Joyful Reciprocity

We tell you to help us rebuild
our communities after you dropped
bombs on our roof tops.
We did not tell you that your help
was not for us.
We did not need you to rebuild
the walls of our homes.
You needed to rebuild
your beauty and honour.
Only when we build together
will we heal together.
These walls are not the destination.
They are the road to sisterhood.
The road to brotherhood.[250]
~ LYLA JUNE JOHNSTON ~
(Diné Artist, Scholar, and Community Organizer)

Gradually, I began understanding that the fasting ceremony was shared with me through *interpersonal* philanthropy. This particular philanthropic gift consisted of *cultural* wealth, offered with compassion and forgiveness. When I showed up as a spiritual orphan, cultural support was offered to me through the philanthropic values of "kindliness, humanity, benevolence, and love."[251] To my surprise, this transformed my white guilt into joyful reciprocity.

Being trusted with the most generous "grant" I could ever receive opened my heart and made me want to give back. Learning histories and building relationships helped me become accountable. I tended relationships with other-than-human relatives and honored the Indigenous ancestors of Turtle Island. Following the guidance of Lyla June Johnston, I asked Indigenous communities, "How (if at all) can I help?" How can I stand with you behind *your* needs, visions, resilience, expertise, and work? I was moved to prioritize these relationships and say yes as often as possible.

Indigenous communities do not need me to rebuild the walls of their homes. But I needed to rebuild my beauty and honor. *Building together* allows us to *heal together*. Building together makes brotherhood and sisterhood possible.

Forgiving the Unforgivable

> One of the problems that most afflicts this
> country is that white people don't know who
> they are or where they come from.[252]
> ~ JAMES BALDWIN ~
> (African-American Author and Activist)

A weathered, creaky rocking chair sits at the ancestor altar in my dining room. My father gifted the chair to my mother when I was born, and she nursed me there when I was a baby. As a young mother, I rocked my babies in the chair. Since my ancestral journey began in 2015, I've sat in the rocking chair while tending my ancestor altar. Most days, I honor them with fire, herbs, food, flowers, Water, and songs.

Working with this altar in 2018, my Earth-honoring ancestors were beginning to feel more present. To me, they seemed wise, loving, and kind. I perceived them as ancient, mythological archetypes. As my friend Clarissa had shared years before, the Old Ones can guide and look over us. With our consent and partnership, they are ready to help us, by supporting the work of the present time. In my life, they've made connections far more complex than anything I could orchestrate. In the long lines of our human lineages, we are the ones who now have a turn to be embodied in flesh and bone. Our presence, dreams, and visions are the next iteration of ancestral storylines becoming fulfilled.

For most of my first three years of contemplation, I was too disgusted, afraid, and angry to actively face our family legacy of enslavement. In 2018, the enslaving ancestors still seemed like hungry ghosts. I often thought of my paternal side as perpetrators. In hindsight, I've learned that this is a normal part of the process. But it is important not to get stuck there. Over time, with determination to keep trying, I tended my ancestor altar. Giving them my time, attention, and simple offerings, I asked the Old Ones to help me develop more courage and resilience.

Eventually, I was ready to ask the living generations of our family to look at our family legacy of enslavement together. In December of 2018, three generations of our family traveled to the Whitney Plantation Museum in Wallace, Louisiana. This museum is located on the site of a restored indigo, rice, and sugar plantation that was originally built in 1752. Over more than a century, hundreds of Africans were enslaved there. Today, the Whitney Plantation Museum is dedicated to public education about the institution of slavery. We chose this place because of its proximity to where several generations of our ancestors settled, beginning in the second half of the nineteenth century. At the entrance, we saw a sign that shared the aspirations and the paradox of the place:

> Every slave and every slave owner came to this place from different villages on different boats. Today we find ourselves all in the same boat awaiting another voyage.
>
> We must take the voyage together, regardless of the difficulty and the pain. Together we chart a course to a place where we can understand our part and find a cure for all evils brought here when the first boat visited our shore.[253]

I reflected on this sign for some time. Eventually, I realized that the word "slave" implies permanently altered personhood, dreams, and hopes. But *being enslaved* is an involuntary condition that is imposed by others. I find the metaphor of being in the same boat beautiful. But it also obscures the reality that Black lives are still being neglected and terrorized every day in America. Yes, we need to take a voyage together. Yet, we are not all in the same boat. Because we live in an unequitable society, some of us are clinging to driftwood while others are riding on yachts.

We spent an afternoon walking the land on which more than 300 enslaved people had lived, worked, and died. Our tour focused on those who grew sugarcane and processed it into refined sugar. As on other plantations, those who were enslaved at the

Whitney Plantation had been threatened and tortured to ensure they would work their lives away. Their grueling labor enriched the masters' family, generation after generation.

My hand ran across the wall of a tiny cabin that was home to up to twenty-four people at a time while the sugar was being processed. I touched the bricks in the hearth, where they must have cooked the vegetables they grew for themselves. We walked inside a rusty metal cage, where the enslaved people had been imprisoned, "fattened up," and washed with greasy Water to make their skin glisten prior to being sold. On seemingly endless memorials, we read the names of generations of people who had been enslaved.

Reading quotes from their stories of being stripped, tied up, beaten, raped, "bred," and having their children sold made me sick. I was freely walking on this land with three generations of my intact family. The cognitive dissonance was overwhelming. I followed the teachings I had received over the last few years. Breathing deeply into my heart, I made a prayer for all these people and their stories. I quietly laid an offering on the ground.

———

Next, we drove 190 miles to Sugartown, Louisiana, which looked to me like a tiny outpost in the middle of nowhere. The road to Sugartown took us through rice and crawfish fields, swamps and longleaf pine forest. Some of my paternal ancestors had settled here beginning seven generations ago. Their ancestors had immigrated from Scotland to North Carolina and Mississippi, starting in 1739. We passed a spot somewhere along the road where my blind great-great-grandmother's cabin had been. She was known as "Grandma in the Woods," and she lived there alone until her death. Next, we arrived at her daughter's house, where my grandfather was born. As a child, my father loved to visit his grandma and eat ice-cold Sugartown watermelons on the front porch of this house. The family-owned mercantile had once stood nearby, surrounded by multiple family dwellings. The Southern Baptist Church and cemetery were located across the street.

On the advice of interpersonal philanthropist Yeye Luisah Teish, I had collected and prepared some Mississippi River Water as an offering to the ancestors. Walking among their graves, I read the name "McFatter" engraved on many of the headstones. This was my birth surname that had surprised me on the wall of the church in Balquhidder, Scotland, six years before. My ancestors had made their way here from Scotland, Ireland, and France. Across their different cultures of origin, they had grown roots here together.

Kneeling on the ground before each grave with a Water offering, a rigid scar inside of me started to soften. I could sense their connection to this land, these tall pine trees, and these Waters. They had made community here even after the suffering among their forebears. My son laughingly handed me a pink camellia he picked from a bush in the graveyard. I smiled at his perfectly timed intuition.

Before we left the cemetery, I looked around. The earliest generation of white settlers here, and their parents and grandparents, had enslaved people in Mississippi. But where were the graves of the enslaved African ancestors? How had their family connections been passed down for their descendants to remember?* The sad answer reverberated in my cells. The graves of the enslaved were likely unknown and unmarked. Their families had been uprooted and divided because a dehumanizing system valued profit more than their lives. I placed an offering on the ground for those who were enslaved by our ancestors, with a promise to remember them.

In the coming days, we sat with our extended family. As I listened to their stories, I could sense the humanity of the family line I'd lumped together under the label of "perpetrator." After our trip, drawing on oral history, the family book of genealogy, and additional research, I pieced together some of our family stories:

When Mississippi seceded from the Union in 1861, my third-great-grandfather John McFatter was forty-six. He had

---

* To support African-American family research and be part of healing the wounds that are the legacy of slavery, visit the Our Black Ancestry website (https://ourblackancestry.com/).

a large family. But, as the story goes, he was called to join the Confederate Home Guard. Refusing to go, he called the Civil War a "rich man's war and a poor man's fight."[254] When the Mississippi Cavalry came to haul men off to the militia, John sent his son to warn several neighbors so they could escape. When John was later captured, one of the guards allowed him to flee the militia that night. The guard gave him a head start to run away through the woods with a shot fired above his head. He got away with a gunshot to his hat. To avoid capture, he hid in the woods. He and his wife signaled to each other with bird calls so she could bring him food. A few years later, in 1864, John's wife and four daughters died one after the other from April to November. This heartbreaking loss must have been one of the factors that led the family to relocate to Louisiana.

My Irish-Catholic third-great-grandfather Joseph Moore left home shortly after the Irish Potato Famine devastated his community in Westport, County Mayo. "To escape the wrath of an irate nobleman whose dog he had killed," he immigrated to America.[255] He later opened a store in a place called Westport (named after his hometown), in western Louisiana. It was close to the territory of the Louisiana Redbones, mixed-race people who fiercely guarded their land in the Cherry Winche Valley. The Redbones fought back against white settler encroachment. In 1881, Joseph Moore's store became the site of a race war. Joseph's fifteen-year-old son, my great-great-grandfather Mayo (named after the Irish county from which his father had emigrated), bolstered the men who were shooting at Redbones from inside the store. He reloaded their guns and served them liberal portions of alcoholic cherry bounce. But despite the white settlers' liquid courage, the Redbones eventually won the fight. Joseph's store was later burned to the ground. In the following years, the Redbones edged all remaining settlers out of their territory. I was happy to learn how the Redbones had prevailed.

———

Some people thought my great-great-uncle Claude was crazy. But he was also a skilled builder. He built mandolins and other musical instruments. He lived back in the woods somewhere. In his opinion, electric saws and nails introduced evil spirits into the wood, so he built his own cabin out of hand-sawed wood and wooden pegs. He also built a house of glass bottles. He thought that there were whales in the creek, and he built a giant wooden ark. But when his family members put pitch on the ark to see if it would float, he became enraged and broke it to pieces.

While gathering these ancestral stories, I reflected that story is a gift people have carried since the earliest times. These stories sparked my curiosity and helped me transcend judgment. I felt gratitude for my great-uncle Don and aunt Bobbie, whose meticulous research unflinchingly recorded our family's past. Although I didn't know them, their choice to include the family's land grants and the names of enslaved people in the book of genealogy opened a possibility for intergenerational truth-telling and healing.

As I began working with groups of white settlers in the coming years, I saw ancestral stories become catalysts to process the difficult feelings we sometimes carry in relation to our families. We can embrace our ancestors' stories to effectively move through our anger, guilt, and blame. Stories can also help us begin forming a clear vision for how we can contribute to reparations.

My family stories taught me about my ancestors' idiosyncrasies and struggles. I was amused to discover that I was more like them than I'd ever realized. For example, I inherited their tendencies to resist the status quo. Shifting my perception to see them as people in exile from beloved homelands, I could empathize with them. For the first time since learning that this branch of my family had enslaved people, I recognized them as more than just one-dimensional per-petrators. I saw them as ancestral beings with complex legacies that are still unfolding. In my family (and in many other white fami-lies) patriarchy tends to invisibilize women. The surviving stories were focused primarily on men. I wondered what treasures were hidden among the forgotten stories of my great-grandmothers and great-aunties. Even with these omissions, listening to stories among my extended family in Louisiana gave me a particular sense of be-longing that I had never experienced before.

My heart softened. I was learning to forgive the unforgivable.

Meeting John and Eliza

> i am not afraid
> of what i came here to do
> i'm made of stardust
> we are not afraid
> of what we're called now to do
> we're all made of god[256]
> ~ ADRIENNE MAREE BROWN ~
> (Black Author, Facilitator, and Doula)

A few days after we returned home from Louisiana, I awakened one morning with a song echoing in my ears. Since our trip, my ancestor altar had felt welcoming as a warm embrace. I sat in the rocking chair, lit a candle, and began singing the song that had come in my dream. As the reverberation of the song filled the room, I closed my eyes. I was surprised to see someone vividly standing before me.

It was John, one of the men whose names were listed on my ancestors' property ledger from the 1800s. Behind him, and slightly higher up, was Eliza, who was pregnant. Both John and Eliza ap-peared translucent and permeated with light. They looked at me intently. I noticed how the light sent messages back and forth be-tween us, dancing with all the colors of the rainbow.

I began communicating with John. At first, I felt an impulse to make excuses. But this time, my defenses quickly fell away and I spoke my truth: *I am sorry*. John took my hands in his. His hands and arms were covered in rough scar tissue. Seeing his scars brought a flood of healing tears through my eyes. My tears fell on our intertwined hands, and finally I looked back into his face. To my surprise, John said, "It hurt your people too. They lost their humanity."

After some time, John moved to the background and Eliza came forward, her rounded form glowing. The lines on her face and the shadows in her eyes conveyed the memory of her life-giving capacities being brutally exploited. As an ancestor, she had transcended the cruel conditions that were forced upon her in life. Now, exquisite light danced in and around her.

I've shared this experience to call attention to the sickness that dehumanized our African relations as "chattel." This sickness creates spiritual poverty that can last for generations among the descendants of the perpetrators. John and Eliza helped me begin recovering from the spiritual poverty I inherited.

———

I asked John and Eliza what was needed from our family now. To my amazement, I was given instructions for a ritual. They asked me to cook a feast and invite the three living generations of our family. We were to make artwork that would name all the people who had been enslaved by our ancestors. Using our intuition, we would celebrate the human qualities of the people who had been enslaved. We would share our reflections with each other at the feast. We were to place this artwork upon my ancestor altar with rosewater, candles, incense, song, and a plate of food. This offering would feed the ancestors for twenty-four hours. Finally, our artwork would be burned in a gesture of release.

I questioned John and Eliza: do I really need to invite all three generations? (My husband had gradually come to accept the ancestral communications I received. But I guessed that my children and parents would think this plan was nuts.) Their answer was definitive: "Yes, all three generations."

In my previous worldview, before I began these four years of contemplation, I would have considered the effort of enacting an "imaginary" ritual a waste of time. My perception was that ritual had no bearing on reality. I also would have doubted the sanity of anyone receiving such instructions. My years of contemplation changed the way I relate to visions, dreams, and ritual. When ancestors ask for attention from the living and we respond accordingly, alchemy becomes possible.

A week later, after receiving more instructions in my dreams—*be sure to remember the offering plate; make it plentiful and beautiful*—the day of the feast arrived. I prepared the altar and put a pot of black-eyed peas on the stove to cook. Just then, an intuitive white friend named Ana Sophia called to share her dream from the night before:

> *You are at a party with powerful and beautiful beings. The celebration is rippling out to the cosmos. A woman attends the party. She is so joyful that light pours out of her eyes.*

Ana Sophia did not know about my vision or the ritual I was preparing. But I received her dream as a confirmation. I cleaned the house and put on a colorful dress. When my family arrived, together we made the menu that had been prescribed: roast chicken; sweet potatoes mashed with butter, cinnamon, and tangerine; my grandmother's garlic cheese grits; collard greens; black-eyed peas with ham; sparkling cider; and Eliza's request of chocolate waffles with ice cream. When dinner was served, I prepared an abundant offering of these foods on my great-grandmother's china and placed it on the ancestor altar. I asked John and Eliza to guide us in becoming good relatives to Black communities.

We sat down at the table together and each member of our family shared the artwork they had made. In our handwriting, we had printed the names of the people our ancestors enslaved. Their names were encircled by ribbons of color and geometric patterns. Their children were represented by hearts in rainbow hues. We celebrated chains broken, shackles removed, and tender necks liberated from stifling collars. Our artwork depicted them as: beautiful, brother, healer, strong, ingenious, survivor, mother, artist, beloved ancestor, dancer, teacher, cherished friend, funny, intelligent, resourceful. We removed their names from the lists of property and embellished them with tiny yellow flowers and greenery. We celebrated the fact that they had always been full and complete human beings, even when they were enslaved.

Before we ate, my father, a quiet man with wavy silver hair, fair skin, and the blue eyes of our Celtic ancestors, offered a prayer:

"Lord, we are here today to remember the people our ancestors enslaved. We're sorry for all they suffered. Please forgive us for their pain. Amen."

My heart burst open with relief and tears flooded down my face. We were dissolving generations of constriction and melting the unnamed tension of "holding it together." My mother's blue eyes held tears as she watched me tenderly. The children wit(h)nessed this quietly, with *their* blue eyes wide open. After these many generations, we had finally come together as a family, to *name* those who had been rendered anonymous, *see* what had been made invisible, and *love* those who had been dehumanized. How could it be that a small, simple altar in the corner of the dining room had become a living portal to another dimension?*

John and Eliza's ritual became a balm for centuries of denial. It replaced my sense of frustrated guilt and immobilized shame with comfort and peace. It gave me the strength to develop and enact a personal reparations plan over the coming months and years.

Philanthropic Alchemy, v 5.0: Reparations—Repaying the Unpayable Debt

As a child, I was taught in school that slavery ended in 1865, thanks to the heroism of President Abraham Lincoln. After that, there was some unrest in the 1960s, and Martin Luther King Jr. was assassinated. Fortunately, slavery was now a relic of the past. I was taught

---

* My ancestor altar continues to sustain me with healing and insight.

that now, our country knows better, and every February is Black History Month. Like most white children who were indoctrinated with false history,* I accepted that I was innocent. I thought this history had nothing to do with me.

During my four years of contemplation, I began to understand that the institution of slavery was interwoven throughout every thread of this nation's original fabric. My eyes opened, and I saw: although it changed form, it never *really* ended. Even *if* our federal and state governments were to officially acknowledge the ongoing legacies of slavery and begin making formal reparations,† our nation would still carry an unpayable debt. Slavery inflicted a soul wound‡ that still aches within our national consciousness, whether we acknowledge it or not.

After seeing the names of enslaved people on my ancestors' lists of "property," I navigated the shadows of this unpayable debt. I learned how the institution of policing originated in the Antebellum South. Bands of armed men patrolled, chased down, and terrorized people who were trying to escape to freedom.[257] The unpayable debt was present in the torture and lynching of the Jim Crow South. It was

---

* I recommend:
- *Post Traumatic Slave Syndrome: America's Legacy of Enduring Injury and Healing*, by Joy DeGruy. This book discusses some of the horrors of the transatlantic slave trade, the lasting impacts of chattel slavery, the racial terror that continued for a century after Emancipation, and ongoing outcomes of these historic events within African-American communities.
- *The 1619 Project* docuseries (https://1619education.org/builder/lesson/1619 -project-docuseries-viewing-guide).

† The United Nations outlines five conditions that must be met for full reparations:
1. Cessation, assurances, and guarantees of non-repetition;
2. Restitution and repatriation;
3. Compensation;
4. Satisfaction;
5. Rehabilitation.

The Movement for Black Lives includes this and other important information in the paper "What Are Reparations?" See: https://m4bl.org/wp-content/uploads /2020/11/ defining-reparations.pdf.

‡ This is a term from the work of Apache/Tewa/Lakota psychologist Eduardo Duran, detailed in his book *Healing the Soul Wound: Trauma-Informed Counseling for Indigenous Communities*.

evident in the brutality perpetrated during the civil rights movement. Today, it is tangible in racial profiling and state-sanctioned murder of Black people by police. It is visible in the school-to-prison pipeline that criminalizes Black youth and incarcerates Black adults at a rate five times higher than white adults.[258] It is plain as day in the fact that Black people comprise 13 percent of the American population, but comprise 35 percent of those executed under the death penalty during the last four decades.[259]

The unpayable debt is obvious in the obscene wealth disparity between Black and white Americans. The median Black family owns only 12.7 percent of the wealth the median white family owns.[260] It is apparent in inequitable opportunities for housing* and healthcare, and predatory banking practices. It is unmistakable in maternal health disparities:† Black babies are twice as likely to die as white babies,‡ and Black mothers are three to four times more likely to die in childbirth than white mothers.[261] *The 1619 Project* docuseries explores the connection between these current maternal health statistics and the dehumanizing mentality that exploited Black women's bodies to produce more enslaved peoples.[262]

Since the founding of this nation, some white families have cultivated intergenerational wealth, security, and heroic legacies. Often, they have willfully ignored or actively imposed intergenerational traumatic stress, forced labor, relocation, and division among Black families. Today, many white families can enjoy political and institutional advantages. We don't need to worry about police killing our children in the streets with impunity. Systemic white dominance assures us that it is "normal" to live with ignorance and apathy about the terror and poverty impacting our Black relatives.

Sometimes, white family norms encourage compassion from the

---

* To imagine equitable access to housing, please listen to the "Home" episode of *The Light Ahead* podcast (https://www.belovedeconomies.org/about-the-light -ahead-podcast).

† To imagine how birthing people could be truly supported, please listen to the "Kayla's Village" episode of *The Light Ahead* podcast (https://www.belovedeconomies. org/about-the-light-ahead-podcast).

‡ I recommend contributing to Homeland Heart (https://www.homelandheart. com/) in support of their work to change these statistics.

sidelines, rather than addressing *our* problems with racism, amnesia, and denial. In white families, we are often taught decision-making processes that hardwire us to look out for ourselves first, reinforcing a belief that no one else will.[263] After years of discomfort and curiosity, a teaching dream about poisoning ants with white powder revealed these insidious patterns lurking in my own mind.

That dream illustrated how I've replicated these patterns, according to what I learned to prioritize a long time ago. In the dream, even after a heartfelt impulse to stop poisoning the ants arose, I returned to a habitual response. I was disheartened to see my patterns illustrated so clearly. My dream helped me begin the gut-wrenching work of turning the lens inward. *Feeling* the cognitive dissonance of White Peril motivated me to embrace the paradox of repaying the unpayable debt. For me, this means trying to reduce the harm from centuries of abuse that can never be undone.

The financial compensation owed to African Americans is at least in the trillions of dollars. But I have learned that reparations are only partially about money.[264] Reparations are also an intergenerational process of truth and healing. African-American author James Baldwin offers this guidance:

> White people in this country will have quite enough to do in learning how to accept and love themselves and each other, and when they have achieved this…the Negro problem will no longer exist, for it will no longer be needed.[265]

For several years after learning that my ancestors enslaved people, I was plagued with self-loathing. In despair over the collective harm we have caused, I had a hard time accepting and loving other white people as well. My impulse was to keep a low profile and hope that someone else would figure out how to make reparations, someday. John and Eliza's assignment helped me set down my heavy burden of denial and self-loathing. Their ritual taught me how to accept and love myself, my enslaving ancestors, and my living family enough to develop a personal reparations plan. In an astonishing paradox, those who were enslaved offered guidance that is delivering our freedom. In tandem with healing our own pain, we can do the work to become good relatives.

White people learning to accept and love ourselves and each other is not only an inside job. It is not something we can learn in a weekend workshop or a six-week certification program. In my experience, the self-love that facilitates true healing is not spiritual bypassing. Rather, it allows me to engage with complexity and embrace discomfort. It grows in community, through truth-telling and commitment to trusting, long-term relationships.

We can develop our self-love and acceptance through actions big and small. Here are a few examples:

- Advocating for H.R. 40, a bill to evaluate possibilities for reparations at the federal level
- Elevating the leadership of Black women and gender nonconforming people
- Establishing racial justice curricula in our children's schools
- Opening an account at a Black- or Indigenous-owned bank
- Supporting efforts to redirect funds away from excessive police budgets and toward community well-being
- Teaching our children to challenge racism
- Learning from films and books by BIPOC artists and scholars
- Advocating for student loan forgiveness
- Supporting IBPOC-owned businesses
- Protecting the sacred sites of Turtle Island
- Regularly contributing to land tax programs

I feel that those of us in proximity to wealth are ethically obligated to return resources. This can be done through reparative forms of investing* and banking.† I've included reparative philanthropy in my personal reparations plan as well.

Philanthropy reinforces systemic racism by largely ignoring

---

* I recommend investing in the regenerative economy with Chordata Capital (https://chordatacapital.com/) and RSF Social Finance (https://rsfsocialfinance.org/).
† I recommend One United Bank (https://www.oneunited.com/) and Native American Bank (https://nativeamericanbank.com/).

communities of Color. Only 0.04 percent of philanthropic dollars benefit Indigenous communities[266] and just 8 to 9 percent of foundation grants are directed to American communities of Color.[267] After learning these statistics, my husband and I began directing over 90 percent of our philanthropic budget to social and environmental work led by Black and Indigenous communities. This is a first step we are taking toward mutual healing.

There are countless opportunities to contribute to Black-led organizations. Some of the work I find most inspiring includes:

- Telling the truth of this nation's history
- Reforming the so-called criminal justice system
- Celebrating the beauty of the African diaspora
- Facilitating restorative justice, healing, and wellness programs
- Improving birth outcomes through policy and midwifery/doula care
- Guaranteeing income* to families experiencing poverty
- Empowering Black entrepreneurs
- Building Black political and institutional power
- Instituting zero-interest loans to Black farmers

For a few examples of Black-led organizations engaged in these types of work, please visit the resources page on my website, goodrelative.com, where you will find an up-to-date list. There are also infinite possibilities to contribute to Indigenous-led organizations. Some of the work I find most affirming includes:

- Protecting the world's Waters
- Defending sacred sites
- Supporting Indigenous food sovereignty
- Reclaiming language and culture
- Building Indigenous economic and political power
- Supporting Elders and youth

---

* Please see Aisha Nyandoro's TED Talk, "What Does Wealth Mean to You?" (https://www.ted.com/talks/aisha_nyandoro_what_does_wealth_mean_to_you).

- Healing boarding school trauma
- Rematriating land
- Offering humanitarian aid within Indigenous communities

For a few examples of Indigenous-led organizations engaged in these types of works, please visit the resources page of goodrelative.com, where you will find an up-to-date list.

As Edgar Villanueva shares in his book *Decolonizing Wealth*, philanthropy urgently needs to increase support work that is led by these communities. As part of our reparations plan, my husband and I have also committed to shifting imbalanced philanthropic power dynamics. Since the beginning of the colonial project on Turtle Island, power has been consolidated into the hands of a few. Once we chose to acknowledge our positionality within the bigger picture, we accepted our responsibility to return stolen power.

In the field of philanthropy, various forms of grantmaking are developing to return decision-making power to communities. The Fund for Global Human Rights defines participatory grantmaking* as follows:

> The practice of ceding grant-making power to affected community members and constituencies. In practice, it means placing affected communities at the center of grant-making by giving them the power to decide **who and what to fund**.[268]

One example in which I had first-hand experience was a participatory grantmaking circle in Mississippi. With collaboration between RSF Social Finance[269] and Springboard to Opportunities,[270] a community of Black-led organizations participated in a process of grantmaking in 2020. They allocated money without funder input and were compensated for their time and expertise. This process

---

* To learn more about participatory grantmaking in family philanthropy, please see the Share Fund's report, *Letting Go of Power, Centering Community* (https://thesharefund.org/resources/).

sparked cross-pollination within the community. For example, some of the participating organizations collaborated afterward to organize a food drive, combining their networks and resources to reach more people. The circle included organizations addressing food insecurity, voter suppression, education, public health, and building community wealth.

Flow Funding is a similar style of grantmaking in which donors share decision-making power. In this model, Flow Funders allocate resources according to their guidance and priorities. One example in which I have first-hand experience is Kindle Project's Indigenous Women's Flow Fund,[271] "an Indigenous-led grantmaking program that nourishes community-sourced initiatives that are actively transforming systems."[272] For three years, a cohort of five Indigenous Flow Funders from throughout the United States designed this program and made funding decisions. Supporting each other, the Flow Funders moved beyond colonial constructs to honor one of the traditional roles of women in their communities—as givers.

In a parallel process, a donor cohort worked together. Together, we discussed our challenges in relation to money. For example, some members of our cohort are program officers for institutions with mixed levels of readiness to share power, while others experience complex relational dynamics within their wealthy families. We shared ideas for expanding trust-based forms of philanthropy and supported each other as we unpacked our roles as donors. After its initial three years, Kindle Project's Indigenous Women Flow Fund continued for an additional four years, with more resources offered for redistribution.

For me, this project was fulfilling because we aspired to *move at the speed of trust*, with awareness that rebalancing entrenched power dynamics is a delicate process. It takes time and sustained effort. The two cohorts worked together independently for three years before we met each other online or came together in person. Rather than reporting, we focused on storytelling and relationships.

How we redistribute wealth matters. In my conversations with Oglala Lakota Elder Basil Brave Heart, he has reminded me that money can easily replicate colonial patterns within communities that have been impoverished. He recommended using money intentionally, to heal together.[273] In my experience, it is important to take the time to build relationships, share stories, and tend to our own wounds in tandem with redistributing money.

Some regranting funds and intermediaries return power to the communities from which it was taken. In the ones we support, Black, Indigenous, and People of Color leaders determine how grants will be made, according to their relationships with the communities they serve, or to which they belong. Some examples of BIPOC-led regranting funds* are Magnolia Mother's Trust, Seventh Generation Fund for Indigenous Peoples, Liberated Capital, NDN Collective, Na'ah Illahee Fund, Jubilee Justice, Colorado Plateau Foundation, and the Solidaire Network's Black Liberation Pooled Fund and Building the Fire Fund.

In our reparative grantmaking, communities are accountable only to themselves. My husband and I do not require reports from the organizations we support. As often as possible, we provide general operating support year after year, to build trust through long-term commitment. Within the above examples of participatory grantmaking, flow funding, and regranting, decision-makers work directly with grantees to design reporting requirements that are accessible, rather than cumbersome. In some of the examples I've encountered, reporting is based on qualitative, relational, and collaborative processes.

As I shared previously, the construct of whiteness has ensured

---

* I recommend visiting these websites, learning from them, and contributing:
  - Magnolia Mothers Trust (https://springboardto.org/magnolia-mothers-trust/)
  - Seventh Generation Fund for Indigenous Peoples (http://www.7genfund.org)
  - Liberated Capital (https://decolonizingwealth.com/liberated-capital/)
  - NDN Collective (https://ndncollective.org/)
  - Na'ah Illahee Fund (https://www.naahillahee.org/)
  - Jubilee Justice (https://www.jubileejustice.org/)
  - Colorado Plateau Foundation (https://coloradoplateaufoundation.org/)
  - Solidaire Network: Black Liberation Pooled Fund (https://solidairenetwork.org/grantmaking/black-liberation-pooled-fund/)
  - Solidaire Network: Building the Fire Fund (https://solidairenetwork.org/building-the-fire-fund/)

many advantages for white middle- and upper-class people. At the same time, the promises of whiteness remain unfulfilled for many poor and working-class whites. No matter where we fall on the class spectrum, White Peril keeps us disempowered and alienated from each other, stuck in divisive hierarchies. To redress this, we also return resources and power to organizations with white and/or multiracial leadership that are working across class and race. Some of the work I find most inspiring includes:

- Nourishing working poor and unsheltered people with food banks, community kitchens, and mobile care units
- Ensuring affordable housing for all
- Organizing for economic justice through multiracial, cross-class solidarity
- Ending white support for white supremacy

Bringing our reparations plan to life is energizing. It has helped transform my self-loathing into self-acceptance. For me, personal reparations are a tangible form of love, rather than a guilt-driven obligation. I love myself, my ancestors, Mother Earth, and all my relations. This love guides me to return resources. I ask my relatives to take their power and resources back, on outstretched palms, with an open heart.

Those who are not known descendants of colonizing or enslaving ancestors and those who have steady, middle-class incomes can also commit to personal reparations. Most of the philanthropic gifts in the United States come from individuals and households of modest income levels,[274] and these small gifts can add up to tremendous impact. For example, in 2022, individuals directed more than $319 billion toward charitable giving.[275] In my experience, giving is an empowering act, no matter the size of the gift. Contributions of every amount are capable of transforming apathy and amnesia. White people giving across class and race can disrupt systemic white supremacy, creating a culture of care, joy, and mutual liberation. This is one of many ways in which we can contribute to changing the Dream of the Modern World.

———

For years, my internal blockages kept me from engaging with reparations. I did not know how to acknowledge the magnitude of the unpayable debt. I was worried that my efforts would not be enough. I was afraid of giving up power and being exposed. If a blockage is coming up for you, I invite you to sit with it on the land, by the Water, and with your ancestors. Notice where the blockage resides in your body and how it feels. Greet the fear, listen to it, and make it a relative.[276] The fear does not need to define you, nor should it stop you from taking the first good step, and then the next. (The Appendices include a ritual to transform resistance and guidance on creating a personal reparations plan.)

Giveaway

We are showered every day with gifts, but they are not
meant for us to keep. Their life is in their movement, the
inhale and the exhale of our shared breath. Our work
and our joy is to pass along the gift and to trust that what
we put out into the universe will always come back.[277]
~ ROBIN WALL KIMMERER ~
(Potawatomi Scientist and Author)

In the spring of 2019, I opened my closet door with trepidation. Piles of skirts, sweaters, coats, jeans, shirts, scarves, purses, high heels, boots, and sandals stared back at me. Turning around was no easier. There, on the wall, was a rack filled with colorful necklaces and earrings. My heart hammered in my chest. It was time to gather things—*my favorite things*—so that I could put them in boxes and give them all away. Breathing purposefully, I returned to my task. I would simply put things in a pile and try to *think* about giving them away. That's how I would start.

As the days passed and I carefully went through my things, my resistance lessened and eventually dissolved. I began to understand why a giveaway ceremony concludes four years of the fasting ceremony I'd been part of. This would be a time to gratefully reflect on the last four years. I would prepare and serve a feast to the community that had hosted me, give away my favorite things, and offer prayers of gratitude for all the help I'd received.

In the days before the giveaway ceremony, I awoke predawn, overwhelmed by the countless forms of help I'd received. My parents had helped with our children. My in-laws had included me in the family's philanthropic work. My husband and children adapted to the uncomfortable versions of reality I presented to them. The ancestors gave assignments and the resources to work on them. Elders, friends, and mentors had invited me to sit beside them to listen, observe, and learn.

During the days that I fasted, supporters drank Water on my behalf, cooked meals, and washed dishes in camp. The Thunders had brought rain and hail to cool the hot, thirsty days. The Stars had immersed me in light and unconditional love. The Sun had arrived faithfully each morning to warm the chilly dawn. The Fire had been tended carefully around the clock for many days. The Earth had cradled me in her lap. Dreams had delivered teachings. Wild turkeys, snakes, rats, hummingbirds, spiders, ants, and butterflies had brought companionship.

As I prepared for the giveaway ceremony, I looked at my things in a way that was new to me. I asked each one: Do I love you? Or did I once love you? What do you represent? Can I open space to give you away and receive something unknown in return?

One by one, my beloved things formed neat stacks on the floor. With each new deposit, I could see the sea of generosity in which I'd been swimming. There was an antique coral necklace my husband gave me for an anniversary, a handmade dress from a Congolese friend, feather earrings gifted by Achuar women in the rainforest, and a red clutch purse from a white friend. There were silk and velvet scarves, handmade headpieces, and costumes I had made for dance performances. There were cherished aprons that my mother and son had given me. There were piles of books: literature from college and graduate school, photography books, and volumes of Indigenous, African-American, and European poems, stories, and history.

For two days before the giveaway feast, generous friends helped me chop and prepare green beans, cucumbers, limes, chicken, watermelon, tomatoes, mozzarella, grapes, cheese, bread, garlic, basil, zucchini, corn, onions, and strawberries. We laughed while we worked. Another group of friends arranged my favorite things with style and charm.

When the guests gathered, the prayers of gratitude began. The architecture of a vast, intelligent love became visible. This love had accompanied me during those days of fasting alone. It had also brought me through four years of contemplation with healing, insights, community, and more favorite things to give away than I knew I had.

We feasted, laughed, and told stories. After the ice cream, chocolate, and berries were served, the giveaway began. The guests selected their favorite skirts, sweaters, coats, jeans, shirts, scarves, purses, high heels, boots, sandals, necklaces, earrings, aprons, and books. One by one we hugged, laughing. My hands were empty; my heart was full of joy.

An' làmh a bheir, 's i a gheobh
(The hand that gives, receives)[278]
~ SCOTTISH GAELIC PROVERB ~

Ceremony for Repentance and Forgiveness

Like a snake eating its own tail, the end of my four years of contemplation was also a beginning. This teaching dream came to me in spring of 2019:

I am told to prepare a space for a woman to give birth. I must clear away all the things that are sharp and no longer needed. Many will gather. There will be a big drum and the people will dance. When the drumbeat starts, her womb will begin to open. The rhythm of the drum will support her labor.

This symbol is on the ground. It is a ceremonial circle for danc-ing. I am told to prepare the cake. The time has come for our celebration. It is our birthday, a day of new beginnings.

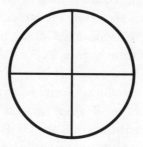

In 1938, eighty-one years before my dream, an Oglala Lakota grandmother named Lucy Paints Yellow Tyon began teaching her five-year-old grandson Basil to forgive the unforgivable. Basil's Grandma Lucy had never attended school and she did not know how to read or write. Like other oral traditions, her language and culture were saturated with sophisticated teachings. In the course of her everyday activities, she showed her grandson how to honor the sacred: Water, light, breath, and flowers.

Many decades later, when Basil was in his early eighties, Grandma Lucy appeared to him in a dream. She instructed him to change the name of the highest peak in the Black Hills. In the dream, she im-mersed him in a visceral experience of harvesting cherries, some-thing they'd done together when he was a child. She reminded him to embody *wokintunze*. In Basil's understanding, it was Grandma Lucy's forgiveness teaching that eventually led to the peak's name being changed.

Since 1896, the peak she referred to had been colonially called "Harney Peak," after General William Harney. In 1855, Harney com-manded the Blue Water Massacre of Lakota people in present-day Nebraska. Following his grandma's dream instructions, Basil collab-orated with descendants of Lakota Holy Man Nicholas Black Elk as well as Harney descendants. In 2016, the peak was renamed "Black Elk Peak" at the federal level.

The renaming of the peak brought long-forgotten ancestral con-nections to the surface. After Harney led the Blue Water massacre, he went on to become a senior officer to James Forsyth. The two men were stationed together for a time. In 1890, Colonel Forsyth gave the order that instigated the Wounded Knee massacre. At his command, the United States Seventh Cavalry used Hotchkiss Mountain Guns and other weapons to perpetrate the atrocity. Afterward, twenty soldiers were awarded Congressional Medals of Honor, though their conduct had been far from honorable. Forsyth was later promoted to general.

In the coming generations, several Forsyth and Hotchkiss descendants lived in silent anguish over what their ancestors had done. Beginning with the renaming of Black Elk Peak, Harney, Forsyth, and Hotchkiss descendants began finding each other through a series of synchronicities. They embarked on similar processes of grief, repair, and healing.

These encounters led two men to Basil in the fall of 2018. Brad Upton is General Forsyth's great-great-grandson, and Jeffrey Hotchkiss is related to Benjamin Hotchkiss, whose company manufactured the Mountain Gun in the late 1800s. With no expectation of forgiveness, Brad and Jeffrey shared their stories with Basil. They acknowledged their ancestors' actions, apologized, and asked how they could be of service. Their service took several forms in the following years, including advocating for the Remove the Stain Act in Congress, to rescind the twenty Congressional Medals of Honor. Brad and Jeffrey do not feel entitled to forgiveness by the Lakota people.[279] But they *are* committed to accountability, repair, and healing.

Lakota communities have endured incalculable suffering in the generations since Wounded Knee. Basil is related to ancestors who were killed that day, and he has lived near the site for most of his life. When Brad and Jeffrey contacted him, Basil remembered his grandma's instruction to forgive the soldiers who committed the massacre, as well as their ancestors and descendants. His own life experiences had also reinforced the healing power of *wokintunze*. Basil received Jeffrey and Brad as relatives. Embracing nonduality and the prayer of *Mitakuye Oyasin* (we are all related) Basil invited them to be part of a Ceremony of Repentance* and Forgiveness that would take place in New Mexico the following summer.[280]

A sacred energy in motion began turning in spirals, winding sideways like desert snakes, and rippling like ocean waves. From this auspicious beginning, the ceremony grew. In the coming months, several people diligently and humbly prepared all the logistics. The ceremony was not advertised, but everyone who heard about it and wished to participate was freely included. During the spring of 2019, Basil and I worked together to support people with their prayers. We invited each participant to make a bundle. They included written prayers and medicinal plants wrapped in cotton fabric and tied with cotton string.

When Basil first asked me to support the Ceremony for Repentance and Forgiveness, I thought we would be working with just a few people. But over several months, the ceremony magnetized hundreds throughout the world. When people called to discuss their prayer bundles, I often lit a candle, poured some Water, and sat in the rocking chair by my ancestor altar. In their stories, I heard generations of unspoken grief that mirrored my own. Often their stories carried such deep trauma and unexpected hope, they took my breath away. The process of writing this book had been showing me how to write my prayer. I made a bundle as well.

Some mailed their bundles to Basil and others mailed their bundles to me. I received them with care and placed them in a basket next to my ancestor altar. My altar now held stories of ancestors throughout the world, not just my own. At times, holding these prayers in my heart and my home was overwhelming. Basil taught me to work with my breath to make enough room for them.

Every day, often multiple times a day, Basil and I asked our ancestors and Mother Earth to help us. When the time came, I placed

---

* On page 186 of *Unsettling Truths: The Ongoing, Dehumanizing Legacy of the Doctrine of Discovery*, Mark Charles and Soong-Chan Rah write: "Repentance is not just sorrow and confession, it is the turning around of wrong behavior towards right and just action." This mirrors the understanding that Basil shared with me regarding *Repentance* in the name of the 2019 ceremony.

the bundles into a cloth bag and carried them on my lap to Pine Ridge, South Dakota. There, the bundles were presented to Basil's family and community. In a traditional Lakota ceremony, the ancestors gave their blessing for the Ceremony of Repentance and Forgiveness to take place.

A couple of weeks later, about 200 people came together on Pueblo and Apache land. Not everyone who had sent a bundle was able to join us physically. On a warm summer afternoon, shaded by monsoon rain clouds, those who were present sat in a circle, our feet resting together in the sandy desert soil. After Basil gave an opening prayer, I brought each bundle out of the bag and handed it to the person who'd made it.

Bundles in hand, we spoke about our process. Together we wit(h)nessed *how* our prayers had taken shape: by willingly walking into our grief, indignity, rage, and shame. Our prayers described violence that had been passed down through our families. They showed how unresolved family violence becomes systemic violence. They ended the silence that had maintained secrecy, complicity, and "safety" for generations. That afternoon, descendants of the enslaved *and* the enslaver, genocide perpetrators *and* victims, colonizer *and* colonized were united in kinship.

We had all been carrying heavy burdens. We were descendants of European settlers, as well as many other lineages. Some of our ancestors had stolen land, outlawed ceremonies, taken scalps for profit, kidnapped, raped, and brutalized people by burning homes and forcing people from their lands. Our relatives had invented plastic, profited from the pollution of the world's Waters, and invested in Big Oil to ensure our wealth at the expense of Life. Our religious institutions had abused and neglected children to death. We had killed human beings in wars that were manufactured to protect corporate interests. We had profited from cultural appropriation and hidden behind masks of whiteness to avoid accountability. A Nazi SS officer, an American president, General George Armstrong Custer, a CIA agent, and Spanish governors of the land called Texas were among our ancestors.

We were Indigenous Peoples: some of our ancestors had been

marched at gunpoint on the Navajo Long Walk. Our people had been intentionally infected with smallpox and punished for speaking their language. As young children, their long hair had been cut. We were descended from those who had been shamed for their reciprocal relationships with Mother Earth; those who had survived boarding schools and the Trail of Tears. We were African peoples: some of our ancestors had been forcibly separated from their families, kidnapped, brought here against their will, and robbed of their dignity and indigeneity. We were descended from those whose land was stolen and privatized for profit; those who were tortured, massacred, and executed in the name of "progress."

We were Two-Spirit* people who have suffered under artificial binaries. We were descended from a kidnapping victim of the empire of the Raj, from the only surviving family member of the Nazi Holocaust, from Palestinian refugees, from the enslaved. Among us were a survivor of the Mayan genocide in Guatemala, a survivor of war in eastern DRC, survivors of incest, and a descendant of those who were tortured and disappeared under Pinochet's regime in Chile.

These were only a few of the stories we carried. The enormity of our prayer was beyond comprehension.

———

Basil led the Ceremony for Repentance and Forgiveness the next day, on July 2, 2019. It began at sunrise on the fourth day of a Sundance ceremony. Sundance is an important part of the Lakota culture and is not for me to describe. But Basil asked me to share that the

---

* On pages 108–9 of her book *Becoming Kin: An Indigenous Call to Unforgetting the Past and Reimagining Our Future*, Anishinaabe/Ukrainian author Patty Krawec writes:

> Two-spirit emerged as a way to reclaim acceptance of people who do not fit neatly into a male-female binary and who are not exclusively attracted to what is thought of as the opposite gender. As with any broad term…it doesn't capture the diversity of attitudes regarding gender and sexuality in Native American tribes. Yet it is useful shorthand….

ceremony lasts four days, and it is a Divine Feminine prayer for the well-being of all life.[281]

The ceremonial circle was on the ground, as my recent dream had shown it would be. Four years before, this symbol appeared to me in a teaching dream at the beginning of my ancestral journey. I now recognized the symbol as being sacred to many Indigenous Turtle Island cultures. Sometimes it is referred to as a medicine wheel. I also recognized the symbol among those used by some of my Celtic and Nordic ancestors.

When we entered the circle to the rhythm of the big drum, multitudes of ancestors streamed to the center. They had been summoning us there for a long time. With the innocence of children and the brave hearts of warriors, we offered apology, asked forgiveness, and forgave the unforgivable. We dreamed repairs for our communities. We affirmed our shared humanity and called forth peace, equity, and joy for the future generations. It was upon us not only to grieve the harm done on Turtle Island, but to grieve cycles of violence sparked hundreds of generations before. It was upon us to honor the lands from which all our peoples originally came and re-member their Original Instructions. It was upon us to become good relatives.

A man named *Wakiyan* (meaning "sacred thunder and light beings" and pronounced "wah-KEE-yahn")[282] gave voice to a prayer that was mirrored by every heart. In the sky above, Thunder and Lightning answered his call. Together, we carried our bundles out of the circle and gathered around a sacred fire. Accompanied by the big drum and a song of gratitude, one by one, we offered our bundles to the fire. The fire transformed our prayers into smoke, and they dispersed to the cosmos. A gentle rain fell, cleansing us with the ancestors' tears. With our feet dancing on the damp sand, we embraced each other and wept with joy. The Divine Mother had given her blood, sweat and tears to open the way for us. She had pushed us through a dark tunnel into a different reality.

After the ceremony, we feasted. Several of us served birthday cake to the people. I shared my teaching dream about the symbol on the ground, the big drum, and people dancing. Together, we sang "Happy Birthday" and celebrated our rebirth, on this day of new beginnings.

PART THREE

The Fabric

Blessed be the longing that brought you here
And quickens your soul with wonder.[283]
~ JOHN O'DONOHUE ~
(Irish Poet, Catholic Priest, and Philosopher)

Rekindling Ancestral Memory

You may recall this dream that arrived just before I began my commitment to the fasting ceremony:

I am standing on top of an old stone tower. It looks like a medieval fortress in the Scottish countryside. Standing with me is a father figure, but not my own father. We look over the side of the tower together. I am horrified when he falls over the edge. In a panic, I run down the spiral staircase inside the fortress. Turn after turn, it feels like forever until I reach the bottom. Outside the fortress, I see this shape on the ground:

The man's body is nowhere to be seen. In the center of the circle, embers glow. Their presence conveys that his heart is still alive, even though he is no longer here physically. A part of him will continue living. His fire can be rekindled.

When this dream came in the summer of 2015, I was perplexed by it at first. A few years later, its meaning had become clear. The dream was an invitation to rekindle the embers of ancestral memory.

In Part Three, I've shared how this invitation has taken shape. As you read, please be assured that you can attune to your own ancestral memory. Asking your ancestors for guidance and listening to your dreams, intuition, and to nature can all open the door. Ancestral memory is present within and around each of us, all the time. I experience it as a deep knowing that I belong to people who once wove Earth-honoring stories, traditions, livelihoods, and ceremonies throughout every part of their lives. For me, sensations like security, affinity, calm, peace, and resonance can be indicators of this knowing. Rekindling ancestral memory is not a research project to approach with a linear mind, and there is no formula. But it can awaken over time as a mysterious gift from beyond the realms of typical perception.

To illustrate how ancestral memory feels to me, I'd like to share a story about my children. When they became overwhelmed as newborns, I'd place a small cotton blanket on the bed and wrap them up snugly inside. After carefully securing the blanket with a diaper pin, I would sit in the rocking chair, holding them firmly against my chest and humming. Sometimes, when they were agitated, upset, hungry, or tired, they would wail and squirm. But after being swaddled and rocked for a time, their little bodies would relax. Their breathing would slow down as they nursed or sucked on a pacifier. As their nervous systems settled, their eyelids would flutter, and they'd drop off to sleep. I remember feeling so grateful and relieved when this swaddling ritual brought my babies peace.

For me, rekindling ancestral memory is like having my wise, old ancestors wrap me in a swaddling blanket while rocking, humming, and holding me tight. This process has helped soothe the agitation, cognitive dissonance, and intense emotions of White Peril. It has allowed my cells to recalibrate to the reality of being loved, held, and cared for by multitudes of beings who lived here on Earth over thousands of generations.

Blueprints

The European diaspora is spread all throughout the world, searching the planet for something that lives inside.[284]
~ LYLA JUNE JOHNSTON ~
(Diné Artist, Scholar, and Community Organizer)

Many of the IBPOC relatives in my life have recommended that I learn about my ancestors and restore their memory. I heard one Elder say that this process could activate blueprints in my DNA. One commented that singing in my ancestral languages would heal my ancestors, and another taught me that Water holds ancestral memory. Several observed that learning about my people was helping me to become a better relative. In various ways, I also heard the call for European-descended settlers to create a new culture for ourselves.*

The supportive nature of these relationships gave me the encouragement to try. Soon, I discovered another paradox. For years, the prospect of trying to reweave the memory of my ancient people had seemed too daunting. I thought that I would need to spin the threads, prepare the loom, and painstakingly weave the fabric thread by thread. But finally, sensing its texture at my fingertips, I realized that the fabric had been there all along. These realities seem contradictory, but both are true at the same time. The spinning and weaving process I've shared in Part One and Part Two was needed to reveal the fabric that had always been there.

You may be wondering - why? Why would we try to revive the memory of ancestors who eventually invented the scourge of whiteness? For me, ancestral contempt and avoidance were unhealthy. They produced amnesia and made me susceptible to colonial delusion. I feel that it is important to forgive our ancestors, accept their complexity, and reweave their stories into fabric that is relevant for our present time. This process can offer healing for past, present, and future generations.

Rekindling my ancestral memory has helped me to identify with

---

* Gratitude to Clarissa Durán, Bill Edwards, Pat McCabe, Lyla June Johnston, Sunny Dooley, Alexis Bunten, Luisah Teish, Leny Strobel, Angela Angel, Rene Henery, Andy Dann, Darrell Marks, Basil Brave Heart, Ilarion Merculieff, Wendsler Nosie, Reyna Cárdenas Carrasco, Calvin Terrell, Kathy Sanchez, Dianna Sue WhiteDove Uqualla, Edgar Villanueva, Vhee, Mona Polacca, Brittíni Gray, Tara Trudell, Dan Isaac, and Brenda Salgado (among others) for reflecting this to me.

For ideas on how white people can develop new cultures for ourselves, please see "Whiteness without Supremacy," chap. 21 of *My Grandmother's Hands*, by Resmaa Menakem.

blueprints that are older and wiser than the traumas of our time. Eventually, this embodied knowing enabled me to bring a greater sense of wholeness to my relationships. It increased my capacity for making personal reparations from a grounded, centered, and joyful place rather than from orphanhood, guilt, and shame. Over time, ancestral memory can support a robust, sustainable practice of repaying the unpayable debt.

The best techniques I've found for rekindling ancestral memory are those I've already shared throughout this book. Regularly, I sat in the rocking chair before my ancestor altar. I asked my people for help as I unpacked the amnesia, denial, ignorance, entitlement, grief, shame, rage, insecurity, self-delusion, and despair of White Peril. With offerings of fire, Water, flowers, herbs, and food, I asked them to show me what I needed to see and to help me to re-member.

They facilitated a slow, subtle weaving process. If I hadn't been paying attention, I easily could have missed it. Patterns became visible after years of recording my dreams, honoring my moontime, and listening to my intuition. Spending time and making offerings on the land opened my capacity to listen. Allowing emotions to move through my body and voice helped me get unstuck. Some of the books, films, recordings, classes, and synchronicities I encountered in waking life let me know that I was on the right track.

The most important information I received came in the form of dreams. Before I knew anything about my ancestors, teaching dreams showed me Water, fire, cauldrons, trees, fairies, milk, cattle, thread, stone towers, snakes, horses, lions, dogs, caves, boars, deer, and elk within evocative storylines. Later, when I began learning about my ancestors' cultures, I noticed that these images were woven throughout their cosmologies in various ways.

In a particularly potent dream, I spent all night traversing the sacred mountain where I live. When the sun rose, Nordic ancestors joyfully welcomed me to join them in a celebratory gathering. In another, a group of ancient ancestors visited our home. They convened a circle around my altar, curiously investigating. They also stayed for dinner (but one grandma didn't care for the salad). In another example, for the first time, I became conscious of a recurring dream I've had since I was a child about an enchanted green dress and its connection to the Otherworld of the *Sìdh*. My dreams spoke to me in a whimsical dialect of symbols, pointing toward ancestral archetypes such as *Bríg* and the *Cailleach*. They allowed me to glimpse who my people might have been, long before they assimilated into whiteness.

In 2018, when I first began searching for the fabric of ancestral memory, what I perceived was so subtle that I sometimes wondered if I was making it up. As my process continued in the coming years, I found kinship among several white friends who are undertaking similar journeys.[*] The vulnerability of their processes resonated with mine. In various ways, I began supporting white relatives who are rekindling ancestral memory and making personal reparations to Black and Indigenous communities. For me, this is sacred work.

Reweaving ancestral memory makes me feel like a curious child following a trail of breadcrumbs through the forest. Following this trail over time, I experienced a visceral knowing that my people are with me. My ancestor altar increasingly became a place of quiet comfort, security, and resilience. My blood and bones felt more settled and secure.

Previously, I've shared some examples of rekindling ancestral memory, such as learning to sing Gaelic songs and re-creating ancestral rituals. In the following pages, I've shared a few more examples of experiences that have brought me healing and peace. I offer them in support of your journey.

Selkies

Water revealed my first glimpses of ancestral memory. *"Ionn Da"* (pronounced "yoon-DAH") is an old selkie song from the Hebridean Islands of Scotland that magnetized me when I first heard it.[†] Along the western coasts of Ireland and Scotland,

* Gratitude to Elyshia Holliday, Rebecca Roberts-Wolfe, Louise Dunlap, Erin Caitlin Sweeney, Reckoning & Remedy, Jamie Beachy, Sìne McKenna, Maija West, Rekindling Ancestral Memory Circles, and the Tending Ancestral Memory Circle.
† Gratitude to Madi Sato for sharing this song with me. Listen to Irish singer and songwriter Mary McLaughlin's recording of "Sealwoman/Yundah," on her album

selkies are shapeshifting seal spirits who can become human for a time and then return to seal form. Recalling our family's 2012 visit to the Hebrides, the seals who watched us from the shore, and the sense of belonging that I felt there, I practiced the song. I sang it to the ocean, the creek, and even to glasses of Water before drinking. Months later, I was delighted to read mythologist Sharon Blackie's story "The Selkie's New Skin," in her book *If Women Rose Rooted*.[285]

In the story, on a moonlit night, a selkie slips out of her sealskin and into her human form. Watching her secretly on the beach, a man becomes entranced by her beauty, which mirrors the beauty of the sea. He steals her sealskin off a rock, entrapping her in a human body. He asks her to be his wife and promises to return her skin in seven years' time. After marrying him, she gives birth to a daughter whom she loves. But over time, separated from her true nature, her vitality suffers.

Near death, she goes on a quest to find the Old Woman of the World, to ask for her help. After a challenging journey, the selkie returns to her original nature by grieving and singing an old lament. Blackie writes, "No one knows the language now, and nor is it a language that is usually written, but here are the words she sang:

> 'Ionn Da, ionn do
> Ionn Da, or-ar da.
> Hi-o-dan dao, hi-o-dan dao
> Hi-o-dan dao, od-ar de.'"[286]

When I first read this story, tears of joy came to my eyes. This was the same selkie song I'd been practicing for months, and Blackie's story vibrantly brought it to life in my consciousness. I was moved to realize that the story included several of the symbols from my dreams and waking experiences, such as a giant cauldron, a cave, a

---

Daughter of Lir.

cailleach, thread, the full moon, and the ocean. Much like my own story, Blackie's story includes a character who finds herself in an identity she didn't choose, but which she must navigate nonetheless. She takes a harrowing journey, approaches death, grieves, and surrenders parts of herself, in order to embody her true identity and return home.

Stories about selkies and other Water spirits have long been told in the lands now called Scotland and Ireland. New versions of these stories are still being told today. Even though my conscious mind had been unaware of the selkie archetype, I was surprised to find that my bones and blood re-membered. In the coming years, Sìne McKenna generously taught me the traditional Gaelic song "*Òran an Ròin*"* ("Song of the Seal"). I sang it at my altar to honor Water, selkies, and the sacred yearning to belong.

Other stories, songs, and films† about Water sprits of Celtic tradition also brought me comfort. They offered blueprints that helped me make peace with my identity as a ninth-generation white settler. Though I didn't choose this identity, it is still mine to navigate. I found that these ancestrally inspired stories could become maps to guide me home.

---

* I recommend the recording of "Òran an Ròin" by Scottish singer Julie Fowlis, from her album *alterum.*
† Here are some I love:
- Film: *The Secret of Roan Inish* (directed by John Sayles)
- Film: *Song of the Sea* (directed by Tomm Moore)
- Song: "Selkie-boy" from the album *The Lost Words: Spell Songs,* by the Spell Songs Collective
- Song: "*Oran na Maighdinn-Mhara*," recorded by Emma Leitch (https://www.youtube.com/watch?v=7oi6Lrbhriw&ab_channel=EmmaLeitch-Topic)
- Short Story: "The Water Horse" by Sharon Blackie, from her book *Foxfire, Wolfskin, and Other Stories of Shapeshifting Women*
- Poem: "Grey Seal," from *The Lost Spells,* by Robert MacFarlane and Jackie Morris
- Book: *The People of the Sea,* by David Thompson
- Book: *Secret of the Ron Mor Skerry,* by Rosalie K. Fry

Norns, Fates, and Völvas

When reading certain books, I can sometimes sense my ancestors whispering to me between the lines, wrapping me in a blanket, and rocking me gently. *Witches and Pagans: Women in European Folk Religion, 700–1100*, is one of the books that imparted these sensations. It was written by white independent feminist historian Max Dashú. For me, this book conveyed a felt sense of the worldviews my ancient people might have embraced.

For example, a thousand-year-old Norse poem names three divine maidens named *Urð* (Became), *Verðandi* (Becoming), and *Skuld* (Must Be). These beings, known as Norns, live underneath a world tree, where they "lay down the laws of Nature and shape the destinies of all beings, carving runes into the tree."[287] The Norns live near springs of fate, and they nourish the tree with Water from the springs. In their realm, time is nonlinear. It moves in conjunction with space, with curves, turns, and spirals.[288] In one example, the Norns use a golden thread to shape a child's destiny.[289]

Fate goddesses were important in other parts of Europe as well. They were often represented in sets of three, with different names and attributes in their respective places and cultures. Spinning and weaving the webs of destiny is a common theme among them.* In parts of western Europe, women made offerings to the Fates by setting tables with food and drink for them. The Fates were also honored as part of birth rituals.[290]

Learning about goddesses who were associated with a sacred tree, Water, nonlinear time, spinning, thread, weaving, destiny, and birth resonated with a blueprint that had been activated during my walks in the woods. There, I had heard instructions to organize this book in three sections relating to spinning, weaving, and fabric. While sleeping, I received teaching dreams about birth, and some of them are included in this book. My own intuitive listening felt more grounded when I sensed its congruence with some of the deities my ancient grandmothers honored.

---

* For a discussion on the importance of spinning in Nordic culture, please see page 142 of *The Nordic Animist Year*, by Rune Hjarnø Rasmussen.

I was enchanted when I read about a ceremony called *útiseta* (pro-nounced "OOT-ee-sehta")[291] that was once practiced in northern Europe. In this ceremony, a seeress known as a *völva* (pronounced "VEUL-va")[292] sat on the land alone, overnight. The purpose was to gain knowledge by listening in the open air. The *völva* held a sacred staff while sitting out and singing to the spirits of the land. Several of these staffs have been found in burials in Sweden, Norway, Denmark, and Ireland.[293]

Many of the staffs were designed to resemble distaffs, which are tools for spinning wool or flax. The distaff was a symbol of women's power in medieval Europe, often associated with magic.[294] In another ceremony called *seiðr* (pronounced "say-thr"),[295] sur-rounded by ceremonial chants, the *völva* entered an altered state of consciousness to share prophecy with her community.[296] When I learned about these two ceremonies, I was moved by the sense that my ancient Nordic maternal grandmothers had been guiding me. The fasting ceremony in which I'd taken part carries similarities to *útiseta* and *seiðr.**

In my experience, reweaving the fabric of ancestral memory includes grief as well as comfort. For me, it has been important to viscerally sense the painful events that impacted my ancestors. Spending time with *Witches and Pagans* helped me to access this experience. I found it particularly poignant to learn that the documentation of folk reli-gion was recorded by members of the all-male clergy. Dashú writes, "The priesthood invented penitential manuals to repress European paganism, internally colonizing the ethnic cultures there."[297] Church representatives scorned women's folk practices as well as reverence for nature. In one example, people who made offerings to stones,

---

* For a description of *Årsgang*, another Nordic ceremony that involved fasting, ancestral guidance, and vision-seeking, please see pages 135–36 of *The Nordic Animist Year*, by Rune Hjarnø Rasmussen.

springs, and trees were labeled "stupid" and "blind."[298] As Dashú points out, a thousand years later, the same dehumanizing tactics would be used to colonize the Indigenous Peoples of Turtle Island.

Throughout *Witches and Pagans*, I absorbed that some of the traditional European practices included sitting near and singing to the Waters; approaching plants with songs and asking their permission before cutting and uprooting them; purification with herbs; singing and chanting while spinning and weaving (which imbued cloth with blessings of protection); divination with birds and runes; dream interpretation; healing with herbs and fabric; knotting strings to "bind" illnesses and create talismans of protection; using charms to influence the weather, and making offerings.

I was developing a sense for how my ancestors had passed traditions from one generation to the next, through interrelated webs of family, community, and land. Their traditions were designed to protect entire communities' health, vitality, sustainability, and happiness. I could imagine how these interrupted and severed roots made their descendants susceptible to the construct of whiteness, centuries later.

As I rekindled these ancestral memories, more layers of my amnesia and denial dissolved. Just as Indigenous relatives had taught me to do, our European ancestors once made offerings to cultivate reciprocal relationships with the spirits of the land. Intuition, dream messages, and ancestral guidance were skills our ancestors fostered long ago. As I had heard in Indigenous spaces over the years, all peoples, including our ancient European ancestors, once followed Original Instructions. As much as possible, I've chosen to reclaim these skills, in honor of my ancestors who couldn't.

Keening

I also discovered that ancestral memory had been shaping my behavior. When I took a class with Irish singer and songwriter Mary McLaughlin[299] in 2021, she described surprisingly familiar grief rituals that were once integral to Irish culture. Various forms of keening were practiced in Irish communities for centuries until they were disparaged and disallowed by the Catholic Church in the 1600s and 1700s. However, in rural parts of Ireland and Scotland, remnants of these practices continued into the 1800s.[300]

One of the most important participants in the Irish keen was the lead mourner known as the *Bean Chaointe* (pronounced "ban-QUEEN-sha"). At the wake for a deceased person, the *Bean Chaointe* sang laments. Often depicted as being barefoot with loosened hair and torn clothes, she broke the rules for proper, everyday behavior to help the community navigate the unbearable chasm of loss. The *Bean Chaointe* led a group of women keeners called *Mná Chaointe* (pronounced "mraw-QUEEN-sha") who surrounded the corpse with clapping, hand movements, vocalizations, and rhythm.

Many believe the ritual the keening women performed originally had a spiritual function of helping the soul transition from one world to another. The keeners would sometimes sit on top of the coffin or walk beside it on its way to the graveyard. The keen would complete as the coffin was lowered into the ground. After the funeral, the family returned home with changed identities. The community could now adapt to loss.*

In Mary's class, I recognized that my ancestral journey had led me into my own process of keening before I knew anything about it. Learning that my ancestors had colonized and enslaved was like mourning a death. I had to allow my former self to die to integrate this knowledge. Ancestral grief frequently overtook me. It happened while wailing in the snowy forest, shedding healing tears into a bowl of Water, singing Gaelic laments at my ancestor altar, dancing rage out of my body, and drumming my remorse into resolve. My embodied ancestral grief became a conduit for transformation.

Coming from a family that has been assimilated into whiteness for many generations, I had a lot to grieve. White Peril has kept me segregated from communities of Color and Culture for most of my life. Settler ignorance and entitlement have dulled my capacity for

---

* Gratitude to Mary McLaughlin for sharing her interpretations of this custom, based on her scholarly research. Personal correspondence, December 2022.

right relations. Whiteness has led to ancestral neglect, including the erasure of our languages and stories. All of this has created a diminished sense of *belonging* during my lifetime. Reclaiming keening memory has helped me mourn the artificial identity of whiteness and begin the process of divesting from it. Keening has opened the possibility for a different identity and real belonging to emerge.

Symbols and Caves

Over several years, caves, lions, horses, dogs, boars, deer, and elk had appeared in my teaching dreams. Eventually, these breadcrumbs led me to ancient European archeological sites, where whispers of Indigenous European presence have been found. For example, some of the residents of what is today considered southeastern France started painting with natural pigments in the *Chauvet-Pont-d'Arc* cave some 36,000 years ago. Four hundred thirty-five images of animals are included in this cave,[301] as well as seventeen types of geometric signs.[302]

Gazing on film footage of these paintings, I could sense the lions stalking, the buffalo herds thundering across the land, and the horses' rippling manes. Many millennia after the paintings were made, the cave's artists still inspired a sense of wonder, reverence, and respect for the animals with whom they shared their lives. I was in awe when I recognized several of the animals from my teaching dreams in images of the walls of *Chauvet-Pont-d'Arc*[303] and other caves in Europe.

The generations who were in relationship with *Chauvet-Pont-d'Arc* spanned several thousand years. Artifacts in the cave include red ochre handprints, a cave bear altar with a child's footprints nearby,[304] and a reverent portrayal of a lioness and a bison merging with the lower body of a woman. In 2020, I began watching the film "Cave of Forgotten Dreams"[305] every year during winter solstice.* This is one of the ways that I honor the sacred darkness of this time,

---

* To learn about Nordic traditions around this time of year, please see *The Nordic Animist Year*, by Rune Hjarnø Rasmussen.

the darkness of caves, and the mysterious process of rekindling ancestral memory.

———

A dream of a French ancestor looking out at me from inside a cave eventually led me to *The First Signs*, by archaeologist Genevieve Von Petzinger. Her stories of studying European rock art ranging from 40,800 to 10,000 years old made me feel as though my cells were tingling. Accompanied by her narrative, I time traveled tens of thousands of years to glimpse the lives and art of these ancient ancestors. One story was particularly evocative.

A woman who lived 16,000 years ago in today's France has come to be known as *La Dame de St. Germain-la-Rivière*.[306] She lived during the Ice Age, when mile-high sheets of ice still covered the landscape. The people of her time likely lived in deep relationship with reindeer, bison, and wild horses. When she died at age twenty-five, her relatives found a burial place that was protected by a rock shelter and overlooking a river. They lovingly placed her in the fetal position and surrounded her with stone blades, deer antler daggers, seashells, and possibly food offerings.

Before covering her with earth, they anointed her with red ochre and left her with a necklace made of seventy-one polished deer teeth, many of which had been meticulously inscribed with geometric signs. With a great deal of intention, her people then built a tomb around her. Atop the tomb, they built a fire as a final part of her funerary rites. She rested undisturbed until 1934, when she was found by French archaeologists.

The rocky limestone region of her tomb is full of caves, many of which were occupied by Ice Age people. These caves hold a high concentration of cave art. And some of the symbols that had been engraved on the necklace of *La Dame de St. Germain-la-Rivière* exactly matched the symbols painted within the surrounding caves. Von Petzinger's suggestions about the significance of the symbols include that they may have been used as part of a storytelling or memory-keeping system.

Reading about the burial of *La Dame de St. Germain-la-Rivière* brought her world to life in my consciousness. No one knows how she died, why she was buried in such a unique way, or what the symbols on her necklace signify. But, guided by my dream of a French ancestor looking out at me from the doorway of a cave, I welcome her presence among the many ancestors whose imprints enrich my ancestral memory.

For countless generations, Indigenous Peoples have lived dreams of interrelation, and they still do today. Like other well-preserved ancient sites and burials, I feel that *La Dame de St. Germain-la-Rivière* offers a blueprint for European-descended peoples to sense our ancient peoples' interdependent relationships with their communities, land, animals, and symbols. She inspires me to weave similar connections in my own time and place.

The Ancestral Codes

My children sit together in the rocking chair by our ancestor altar. They hold a big book open across their laps. It is a family album.

Inside, color photos show our ancestors laughing, wearing silly hats, and having fun. My children are looking for a specific piece of information. Frustrated, they don't know exactly what they are looking for or how to find it among the photos.

I show them another section of the book. It contains endless pages of code. The answer we need is here. I will teach my children how to search the code and find answers.

This dream came in the spring of 2020. As I explored its message, I was reminded of the visit my nine-year-old daughter and I had made to the Achuar territory in Ecuador in 2012. Through the work of The Pachamama Alliance, I'd heard a mandate to "change the Dream of the Modern World" within one generation.[307] Over the years of writing this book, I have been listening, learning, and practicing changing the Dream.

For me, the changing Dream took shape on the inside first, in flutters and whispers. The changing Dream gradually transitioned outward, affecting my behaviors and relationships. I now perceive the longing to become a good relative as one of the components of our collective, changing Dream. I have come to understand the New Dream as one that emerges from ancient origins. We already carry it within our blood and bones. It is stored in our genetic codes. We have only to search earnestly for it to be revealed.

Over the last decade, my ancestors and I had traversed challenging terrain. With their help, I'd found the courage to face the past. This dream of my children allowed me to taste the first fruits of our labors. The ancestors who were once forgotten, wounded, and sinister are returning to balance. They came to us in color and sat on my children's laps in the family rocking chair. They are ready to partner with the present and future generations, to help us bring forth a New Dream for the Modern World. They are our future.

Farewell

The setting is a room with glass walls. There is a deep, dark pool of Water in the center. I am asked to help create a piece of art.

I'm tempted to play familiar roles, but those roles no longer fit. I'm not a good swimmer and I don't want to get into the pool.

I remember a black dress from a long time ago. The dress has long sleeves, a fitted waist, and a full skirt that falls to the ground. I begin frantically digging through a closet, tossing socks and an old umbrella over my shoulder. The black dress must be part of this creation.

Suddenly, I am submerged in the pool of Water. Floundering and gasping for air, I struggle not to drown. I'm not a good swimmer—how did I end up here? After struggling to the surface, I finally emerge, wearing the black dress. Antlers crown my head.

Taking a deep breath, I stand composed in the black dress. The antlers offer habitat for bees, flowers, and fruits. This piece of art is a joyful homecoming. The power of my people is with me.

I re-membered this teaching dream one quiet morning while I sat before my ancestor altar. It illustrated the assignments I was presented by this "already written" book. In service to our collective healing, I have offered my stories with the transparency of glass walls. Facing the shadows of colonialism has been like plunging into that pool of deep, dark Water. The long black dress summoned those my great-grandmothers might have worn on their journeys across the sea. The antlers and their flowering habitat recalled the antlered beings that once sustained our people. The piece of art I was asked to co-create eight years ago has finally come to life.

Many times I lamented: "What became of our songs, our plants, our rituals, our languages?" Now, sitting in our family rocking chair in the well-loved space of this altar, the ancestors respond by flickering the flame of the candle, dancing with the juniper smoke* twining in midair, whispering into my bowl of Water, and humming a tune through my vocal cords. Ancestral memory lives in our bones and blood. Nestled deeply among rocks, roots, worms, layers of soil, mycelial networks, and underground Waters, we are grounded. Nourished by sunlight, stars, rains, breezes, stories, and songs, we bloom.

With farewell blessings, here is a chant called *Sago an Snîjo*, from the album "Winter Folded Everything Inside a Shawl of Feathers,"

---

* To read more about the Scottish folk practices of purification with juniper, Water, and fire, please see: "Saining Not Smudging—Purification, Blessing, and Lustration in Scottish Folk Magic Practice" (https://cailleachs-herbarium.com/2019/02/saining-not-smudging-purification-and-lustration-in-scottish-folk-magic-practice/).

by musician and artist Carolyn Hillyer.[308] Like the other examples I've shared in Part Three, this collection of songs and stories has enriched my process of rekindling ancestral memory. It was created in the heart of a Neolithic-style roundhouse on a thousand-year-old farm in Dartmoor, England. This chant is written in a 4,000-year-old Bronze Age language that is in the process of being reconstructed. It is a parent of later Celtic languages:*

Kommano (We remember)
Nis Wertito (All that we have spun)
Nis Andeweg (All that we have woven)
Snateja Breto (Path of needle to the cloth)
Sago an Snîjo (The blanket and the braid)
Kommano (We remember)
Grendjo Soito (The magic of our bundles)
Saman Soito (The magic of our circles)
Nata Soito (The magic of our songs)
Kwakwo Witsu (All our wisdom)

---

* Please see the University of Wales Celtic Lexicon, which is a work in progress: https://www.wales.ac.uk/en/CentreforAdvancedWelshCelticStudies/ResearchProjects/CompletedProjects/TheCelticLanguagesandCulturalIdentity/CelticLexicon.aspx. Carolyn Hillyer brings this reconstructed language to life in the book *Her Bone Bundle / si knâmi grendyo*.

Closing Words

BY LYLA JUNE JOHNSTON, PhD

I BELIEVE the greatest trick to befall humankind is that we are separate, that we are at odds, that there isn't enough, that one must be above, that there is a below. In fact, there is no above, no below, no hierarchy—just One Great Circle.

This Circle is interdependent and miraculously woven of birth, trial, beauty, erudition, evolution, biological expression, and rebirth. It is the perfect and exquisite braiding of matter and spirit, in constant flux, all around us and within us, self-regulating, self-correcting, over the eons of time.

Our human breath is taken up by the plants and given back to us.

Collections of microbiota help us to digest, breathe, reproduce, walk, and be on this earthly plane—a tapestry that connects not only all Creation, but holds our individual bodies together like glue. If that wasn't enough, we are connected to the gravity of the moon, which so delicately perfects undulating sea levels, bringing life to tidal zones vaster than we could ever understand. We are connected to the miraculous tilt of the Earth, which gives rise to four seasons, seasons of bounty, seasons of hardship, seasons of breathtaking wonder. We are connected to the songs of our ancestors, the genetic codes of sacred life passed on through foremothers and forefathers. Our bodies are an exquisite union of organs, and blood, and flesh, and millions of tiny, essential processes that dance in synchrony each day for us to simply wake up, fix our coffee, and walk outside.

The whole thing is phenomenal. It is nearly unbelievable. It is infinitely complex, far beyond our ability to understand, yet the very reason for our being, seeing, hurting, and loving. This One Great Circle gives rise to the laughter of our children. It gives rise to every hair on the bear's massive coat. It gives rise even to my ability to communicate with you now. When we are in touch with this reality—the sheer beauty of creation—there is nothing left to do but stand in awe.

And yet, somehow, we are tricked out of this paradise. We succumb to angst and division. We are tricked into thinking that it makes any sense for one part of Creation to be more important than another. We are tricked into enslaving one another when we could be dancing together. We are tricked into cutting each other down when we could enjoy the ecstasy of rising together in synergy. The magic of the world must laugh at our antics. Who goes to a dinner party demanding to enslave other dinner guests? What a buzzkill. This place is a place for abundance, for party, for community, for joy, for kinship. Who trades all this in for the fleeting taste of domination? Only those who are tricked will do this.

We are not tricked easily, however. People must be severely and brutally tortured for a very long time before giving in. European groups, for example, had to first endure thousands of years of torture, disease, and warfare before they thought to attempt the conquest of faraway lands. My mother's people are the Diné/Navajo Nation. What Diné people call "Coyote" tricked Europeans into thinking there was not enough. But before they could be tricked, they had to first endure centuries of food insecurity. The pressure cooker of Europe simmered the souls of those ancestors for a very long time before Columbus was ever born. So much burning alive of so-called witches, rape of these same women, plagues, and war had to happen to bring them out of that state of love and awe. So many prolonged cycles of violence had to occur to slowly erode those long-standing pre-domination cultures that thrived all across Europe.

These cultures knew all about the One Great Circle and respected it deeply. We find figurines of women, which I believe represent the sanctity of the earth and the sanctity of the feminine, throughout Europe. One of the oldest was found in German soil and was radiocarbon dated to be 40,000 years old. I recently visited the caves in

France where they have paintings of bison, ibex, and horses (which look very similar to rock art in Turtle Island). These paintings are dated to be 17,000 years old! This is how long European ancestors molded the earth into the shape of a woman and honored the beauty of other beings on the sides of cave walls. This is who we are in our truest form, I believe, for those of us who are of European descent. It took millennia of war for these Earth-based, bio-egalitarian cultures to be slowly eroded, I believe, by Coyote spirit.

This is why my Native Elders say to have compassion and understanding for the colonizers who came here to Turtle Island, seemingly so bloodthirsty: because they themselves were run ragged by war and destruction and grief. So many of the war tactics we experience here as Indigenous Peoples were practiced and refined on the Indigenous cultures of Europe. Indeed, the Roman emperor Constantine was murdering Indigenous European people in the name of Christ a thousand years before conquistadors tried to do the same in the Caribbean. Roman soldiers relocated people from place to place via death march just as American soldiers would later do during the Trail of Tears and the Navajo Long Walk.

My point is that humans are not naturally harmful, war-faring beings. It takes a lot of trauma to fashion such a loving creature into a weapon. Our nature is awe. Our predisposition is generosity. Our propensity is towards love. It takes work and endurance on behalf of Coyote to play on our fears and weaknesses and break us down from understanding the One Great Circle that has *built-in* abundance, *built-in* beauty, *built-in* wonder, and *built-in* community.

I know this Great Circle is possible for us to feel and witness again. I know this because I have seen it with my own eyes. When I was fourteen, my mother's people celebrated my first menstrual cycle. They dropped everything for four days to enact the ceremony of the *Kiinaaldá* (pronounced "kee-nahl-DAH"), or the honoring of the birth of a new woman. During this ceremony, I was asked to make a circular cake of corn meal. It was about one foot deep, four feet in diameter, and was baked in an earth oven with a corn husk casing. It took a lot of work for me to grind enough corn throughout the four days to make such a cake. At the end of the four-day ceremony, I gave it all away. I was not allowed to have one bite. This was to engender within me a spirit of generosity. *My people wanted me to become a generous woman.* They say everything that happens during those four days will be a reflection of the rest of a woman's life.

There are similar Indigenous manhood ceremonies in which he hunts his first deer and must give it all away—can't have one bite. Indigenous cultures have thus institutionalized generosity itself (among other things). They have, over the millennia, found ways to endow children with characteristics that will nourish the spirits of the people and the community. Indeed, they are cultures of peace. They are cultures of harmony. They are cultures of what we call *Hozhó* (pronounced "Hoh-ZHOH"), or joy and beauty.

If my mother's people are capable of walking in this way, so is everyone else! We have no excuse to surrender to a false identity of selfishness and dysfunction. We must fight for a better culture. This is who we are as human beings, when our nature is supported and allowed to shine. This is the culture we come to after years of dabbling in hierarchy, only to find that peace was the best option all along. This is what happens when centuries of trial and error, mistakes and learning, are allowed to play out until we find our homeostasis. Indeed, Diné People have not always had harmony. We have many stories of floods, famine, war, destruction, and social disarray. But over time we learned. We self-corrected. We found our way home to peace. It is proof that we as humans are perfectly capable of community harmony.

My friends of the Haudenosaunee Indigenous Confederacy (from what is now sometimes called "New England") had so much war among them. They had so much war that a great prophet had to come to help them. His name was The Peacemaker. He helped them to craft the Great Law of Peace and some of the most sophisticated forms of community governance structures I know. Even today, they brag to me about how they can take any two people—*any two people*—and no matter how brutal of enemies they are, they can transform them into friends once again through a very specific ceremony/process. These are the social technologies they carry, borne from centuries of trial and error.

And so, here we are today. Children of war, children of atrocity, children of attempted genocide, children of all forms of discrimination, children of the buying and selling of beautiful, extraordinary human beings. Here we are thumbing around in the dark for a peace we have yet to see but feel somewhere deep inside our bones. Here we are, many Davids standing against many Goliaths, continuing like crazy people to work towards harmony and love, against what seem like impossible odds. I do not believe this work is futile, however. I believe every drop of effort we put into it will benefit our descendants. Every drop will be used by Creator to help us the way that He/She/It/They helped the Haudenosaunee.

Hilary and I, who have known each other quite a long time, are united in our belief that there is something beautiful to be made from these ashes. A belief that you can pulverize and alchemize the brick of pain, shame, and exhaustion into a foundation of healing, love, beauty, and solace. Make no mistake—it will take courage, it will take strength, it will take steadfastness, it will take accountability, it will take forgiveness. It will necessarily be the hardest thing we ever do. But did we come all the way to Earth to waste away in the illusion of our mediocrity? We are not weak. We are all so strong, and even stronger when we move as one.

With white skin and brown skin, Hilary and I have honored one another's lineages in powerful ways. We have searched the veins of our hearts like braille, looking for answers to heal a broken world. We have worked to metabolize the grief buried in our DNA into a balm for broken souls. We have attempted to model what it looks like to come back together again in amends, forgiveness, and beauty.

We have not seen the totality of our species' healing in our lifetime, and likely our children won't either. But we have had glimpses. Gorgeous, beautiful glimmers of what our culture can become on a broad scale. Hilary and I still believe that love, however simple, is the most important, potent, and worthwhile tool towards this future we seek. We believe this future is worth fighting for, every day of our lives. It is worth praying for, offering our vessels to, and surrendering our fates for.

In this journey, we know the ancestors are not asking us to be perfect, they are just asking us to try. Because when you cease to fear failure, and resolve to simply try, you open a small window for the ancestors. And from that small window they can weave miracles. Give the Creator an inch, and He/She/It/They can work a mile. But if we succumb to the temptation to take the easy road of surrender, we do not give harmony a chance to show its beautiful face. We do not give these so desperately needed truths a chance to live through us. So believe in yourself, dear soul, to do the work you came here to do. Weave your threads into the tapestry of the healing that is needed. Give it a try, and you will be pleased with what springs forth.

Now, I want to speak briefly on what I see as the mechanics of healing. I have come to believe that both colonizer and colonized, both enslaver and enslaved, have a role to play in the construction of harmony. The offender must of course apologize, not just with words but with actions. A verbal apology is hollow if we do not make the effort to alter the situation of harm. This process of amends and truth liberates the offender as much as it liberates the person they have harmed. It rescues them from denial and delivers them to truth. It saves them from mediocrity and brings them to deeper power. It alchemizes us from a problem to a solution.

On the other hand, we desperately need the harmed to play their role as well. This is the role of *forgiveness*. I'm sure it hurts many people to even read this. Why must we offer forgiveness to such atrocity? Doesn't the offender deserve as brutal of an experience as they dished out? Many of us may think forgiveness is for fools, and yet we can all remember a time when we wished we could be forgiven. Can you remember a time you made a terrible mistake and hid it from the world out of fear of punishment? Can you remember a time when you did something terrible and wished the world would give you one more chance? And if that forgiveness had come, how do you think you would have felt? What would be the sensation of a world offering you grace?

Within the mechanics of healing, each and every one of us has a role to play. We each have a puzzle piece to contribute to make the big picture whole. My controversial opinion is that in order to do so, we must ask the Universe for help in this process. The weight of accountability and the weight of forgiveness are massive things for most of us to lift. We need support from the forces around us to find the strength to do so. We must help each other and ask for help from the unseen to make it across the finish line. Such pains as ours are too big to take on alone.

I am going to challenge us to forget everything we've been taught about what is doable and not doable. I am going to invite us to be warriors who lean into battle and lean into that uncomfortable sensation. The sister of knowing we can do it is the remembrance of how challenging it will be. If we only push on doors that open easily, we will never know what lies behind those other mysterious doors. The ones that take months, years, and decades of pushing to finally open. Did we really come all the way here to take the easy road?

We all have these paint brushes and a full palette of color, yet we keep painting our canvas with colonial gray, again and again and again. If being a good relative is like poetry, then the colonial system has robbed us of our muse. It wants us to believe there is "no use" in trying. It wants us blind to our collective power to dream and build a different way of living.

I am here to push us to use some new colors. The exciting and terrifying colors of truth, love, and accountability. The colors of liberation. The colors of healing. I'm going to remind us all that there is so much power within us to not just dream a new vision, but paint it as well. To make it real for our children. Not only is it worth it, it's the only thing worth our time, energy, and presence.

So let us seek out the muse together again. Let us push for places we never thought were possible or die trying. In those moments where you lose hope, where you lose energy, let the smiles of your children push you onward. Let the beauty of creation remind you of all we are overjoyed and lucky to fight for. To become a good relative is to step back into the One Great Circle as a full participant in all its joys, challenges, privileges, and responsibilities. We were made for this. We were made for these times. To come into these bodies and play our unique roles and break the cycles of yesteryear. We are warriors for Creator. It is what we came to do.

APPENDICES

Historical Notes

ALTHOUGH I am not a historian, educating myself about certain aspects of history has been an important part of my healing journey. I've included some notes on the invention of whiteness and notes on the European witch-hunts here. These notes are not intended to be comprehensive histories. They simply include the insights I've found most valuable.

The Invention of Whiteness

> White supremacy is a project of psychic
> conditioning and toxic belonging.[309]
> ~ TEMA OKUN ~
> (White Anti-Racist Facilitator)

Writing this book required me to learn more about whiteness than I'd ever wanted to know. Increasingly confronted by how whiteness has shaped me, I often felt frustration and despair. Learning about some of its origins in European history[310] as well as how the identity of whiteness was later engineered in the United States built my resilience over time. As my bubbles of denial continued popping, this broader view helped me take my own whiteness less personally. Here, I've offered a brief overview of some sources that spoke to me. In the last few decades, many experts have studied the construct of whiteness. I encourage you to find resources that resonate with you.

Some of the sources that informed these notes are *An Indigenous Peoples History of the United States*, by historian

Roxanne Dunbar-Ortiz, *My Grandmother's Hands*, by trauma specialist Resmaa Menakem, *Dancing in the Streets*, by activist and journalist Barbara Ehrenreich, and the essay "Roots Deeper than Whiteness: Remembering Who We Are for the Well-Being of All,"[311] by political educator David Dean.*

These sources helped me to imagine a time before fair-skinned people were considered "white." They also illustrate how complex forces such as private property laws, land dispossession, capitalism, disruption of traditional cultures, institutional religion, and settler colonialism colluded, creating conditions that later gave rise to whiteness.

At one time, land known as "the commons" sustained subsistence farmers and small agrarian communities throughout Europe. Within the commons, communities shared space for farming, livestock, harvesting plants and firewood, festivals, and celebrations.[312] During the sixteenth and seventeenth centuries, in some places, the commons were enclosed and privatized. Many communities lost access to the land that had sustained them for generations. In England, the commons were enclosed for profitable industrial land use, such as large-scale pasturage to raise sheep for wool.[313] Enclosure of the commons generated wealth for the aristocracy, while impoverishing masses of peasants.[314]

Dunbar-Ortiz writes, "Privatization of land was accompanied by an ideological drive to paint the commoners who resisted as violent, stupid, and lazy."[315] With the emergence of capitalism, cultures that had long revolved around the merriment of seasonal festivals were now portrayed as backward and sinful.[316] Calvinist Protestant ministers condemned "idleness" and shamed traditional ways of life.[317] Beginning in the seventeenth century, people increasingly suffered from melancholy, as traditional sources of joy and cultural vitality were prohibited in various ways.[318]

---

* David Dean is a political educator and writer who supports white people's engagement in multiracial movement building with political clarity and emotional strength. His essay shares historical context for how his ancestors and other European settler and immigrant groups were displaced from their traditional ways of life and socialized to become "white" after their arrival to the land now known as the United States. Personal correspondence, August 2023.

Dean shares: despite active resistance and insurrection, more than a thousand English peasant communities were forced to abandon their villages. Dispossessed of land, they went to the cities, where the lucky ones got factory jobs processing wool. However, the destitute often had no option but illegal begging and homelessness. These crimes were punished with incarceration, mutilation, or death. In the early 1600s, corporate and government entities colluded to rid the cities of these impoverished people. The Virginia Company and the British government sent multitudes of indentured servants to the colony of Virginia. The conditions of their servitude were grueling, and many went unwillingly. Dunbar-Ortiz writes:

The traumatized souls thrown off the land, as well as their descendants, became the land-hungry settlers enticed to cross a vast ocean with the promise of land and attaining the status of gentry.[319]

After their long voyage to the colony of Virginia, European indentured servants toiled on Indigenous land now "owned" by elite European settler families. The Original Peoples of Turtle Island were being displaced to make room for capitalist agricultural production. In some cases, European indentured servants worked side by side with indentured and enslaved Africans as well as Indigenous Peoples. The three groups shared the same living conditions, built relationships, intermarried, and had families together. Over time, plantation elites saw their intermingling as a threat. Eventually, elites would employ a variety of tactics to generate division and curtail these cross-racial alliances.[320]

I learned about the next part of this history from the *Seeing White*[321] podcast, produced by the Center for Documentary Studies at Duke University. Episode Three, "Made in America," explores how whiteness developed in the early British colonies on Turtle Island and how its establishment shaped the United States.[322] Historians, authors, and professors Ibram Kendi and Nell Irvin Painter; professor, journalist, and organizer Chenjerai Kuamyika, and racial equity educators Suzanne Plihcik and Deena Hayes-Greene share how whiteness was conceived and written into law between 1640 and 1790.

An early example took place in the colony of Virginia in 1640. Three indentured servants who were living in similar circumstances ran away together. When they were caught, the Dutchman and Scotsman were punished with four additional years of servitude. But the African was punished with perpetual servitude. It was the first court ruling that enforced lifelong enslavement. This decision set a precedent for African and European peoples being treated differently under the law. Eventually, this ruling would enable wealthy, landowning men to expand their fortunes by exploiting the labor of enslaved peoples.

Bacon's Rebellion was an armed uprising of European indentured servants and free, enslaved, and indentured Africans. It took place between 1676 and 1677. According to Chenjerai Kumanyika, it was "a multiracial rebellion that showed the possibility of class solidarity across racial lines."[323] International civil rights expert, professor, and director of the UC Berkeley Othering and Belonging Institute john a. powell,[324] shares that Bacon's Rebellion was led by a white man, but it was later portrayed as a Black uprising. Blackness was being constructed as a violent, threatening identity.[325]

In the years following Bacon's Rebellion, racial categories were defined by law. In 1680, the Virginia House of Burgesses, the first legislative body in the colonies, debated about which men could be considered white. Two years later, in 1682, the Virginia House of Burgesses ruled that Black, Indigenous and mixed-race people were slaves, for all intents and purposes. At the same time, Virginia was giving fifty-acre land grants to European men. These racial categories ensured supremacy for some and subjugation for others. They began constructing a white middle class that would relate differently to the elite category above and the non-white category below.

Nine years later, in 1691, the House of Burgesses passed a law that wrote the word "white" into law for the first time. "White" described those who had access to full citizenship. Citizenship could be revoked from those who married outside their "race." But there were several loopholes built in. For example, elite white men could legally rape the women they enslaved and enslave their own mixed-race children. Ibram Kendi shares that under the laws of this era, white men could have sex with whomever they chose but white women and non-white men could not.[326]

In 1705, the Virginia House of Burgesses passed the "Virginia Slave Codes." Chenjerai Kumanyika shares how these codes "encouraged free white people to hunt down and capture escaped slaves."[327] In addition, reward systems incentivized free white people to pursue free Black people and turn them in. The Slave Codes allowed enslavers to torture and murder enslaved people with impunity. These "divide and conquer" policies ensured that white households, communities, and individuals would willingly enforce the new racial categories.

In 1790, the newly minted United States Congress passed the Naturalization Act, which wrote white identity into law. Only free white men had rights to citizenship, voting, civil rights, and due process. Only free white men could start businesses and sit on juries. Institutionalizing whiteness encouraged fair-complected poor people to abandon their cross-racial alliances. Professor john a. powell shares, "White identity was that middle stratum; identifying with the elites and controlling the non-whites."[328]

Assimilating into whiteness offered poor and working-class whites some minor material advantages to which Indigenous and African peoples did not have access. It kept them aspiring to elite status but rarely able to attain it. This imprint has persisted. Many poor white communities have been harshly excluded from the economic opportunities that middle- and upper-class white communities enjoy. David Dean writes:

> White identity was created as a tool to cement virtually all colonists of European origin…regardless of wealth, into a common superior racial category, creating solidarity along lines of race and reducing it along lines of class.[329]

Since 2009, the organization Showing Up for Racial Justice (SURJ) has been leading a movement to subvert the current iterations of this history. SURJ grows the leadership of poor and working-class people organizing for policy change, in support of racial and economic justice. The movement also brings people together across class and race to understand our mutual interest in ending white supremacy.[330]

The invention of whiteness came with costs, such as diminished cultural identity. Many communities abandoned their land-based identities, traditional foods, clothing, and customs in the process of assimilation into the "melting pot." Often, non-English families began speaking English exclusively and anglicized their names. Identification with the white ruling class became a point of pride.[331]

Despite these challenges, some Euro-American communities actively resisted hegemony and preserved their cultural characteristics. Some kept their languages and stories, marrying exclusively within their ethnic group for generations. For example, in certain parts of the country there are still Italian, eastern European, and Amish communities. On Dakota land, colonially called Minnesota, the American Swedish Institute currently offers linguistic and cultural programming to perpetuate Nordic identity.[332]

However, assimilation into whiteness was essential to the colonial American agenda. In the early 1900s, thirty million southern and eastern Europeans came to the United States. Thirty states passed laws that required their participation in "Americanization" programs. These patriotic classes incentivized immigrants to abandon their cultural identities and become white.[333] At the same time, Indigenous children were being forced into boarding schools intended to strip them of their cultural identities.

In the coming decades, as Professor john a. powell explains, assimilation to white identity rapidly increased after World War II. At this time, the United States invested in the creation of suburbs throughout the country. Many lower- and middle-class Euro-American families received subsidies and became homeowners. In the suburbs, Greek, Polish, Irish, Italian, and other Euro-American families often experienced deterioration of their diverse cultural identities. Within twenty years of moving to the suburbs, most simply considered themselves "white."[334]

Through discriminatory financial redlining policies, however, Black and other minority families were prohibited from buying homes in those same suburbs. Instead, they were relegated to urban housing projects. This resulted in housing becoming racially segregated throughout the United States between the 1930s to the 1960s.[335] Minority families were also denied bank loans and credit, which limited investment in and development of the communities where they already lived. Throughout the United States, many of us grew up in segregated neighborhoods, unaware that our entire country was intentionally being segregated. I learned to think of separate "white" and "Black" neighborhoods as unfortunate, but inevitable. In my life, segregation has limited my perception tremendously.

Whiteness manifests differently according to generation, gender, location, and socioeconomic class. In the eight years of writing this book, I began seeing how this history of whiteness has evolved in my family throughout the generations. By the time I was born in 1975, our whiteness was an unquestioned assumption. Our Scottish, Irish, English, and German roots were only a vague memory. Our Nordic, French, Basque, Ashkenazi, Hungarian, and Indigenous Turtle Island roots* had been completely erased.

When I first began seeing the impacts of whiteness, I was disgusted with my ancestors for "becoming" white. But over several years, as I learned more of their histories, I developed empathy for them. I've found it humbling to learn about the centuries of trauma, displacement, poverty, shame, and loss that led them to accept whiteness as a viable option. Today I am undergoing a process to re-member the languages, stories, songs, foods, and practices they left behind when they assimilated into whiteness.

---

* I learned about my Indigenous ancestry through DNA analysis. Claiming Indigenous ancestry as a white settler requires careful consideration. I have chosen to honor my Indigenous ancestors by mentioning them here, while focusing on repairing the legacies of settler colonialism and whiteness. I recommend *Native American DNA: Tribal Belonging and the False Promise of Genetic Science*, by Sisseton-Wahpeton professor Kim TallBear.

The European Witch-Hunts

The 2016 Ceremonies for Human Reunion sparked my interest in the circumstances surrounding the European "witch" hunts. In the following pages, I've shared the understandings I gathered seven years later, in 2023. I relied on *The European Witch-Hunt*, by Scottish historian Julian Goodare, and *The Oxford Handbook of Witchcraft*, edited by white American historian Brian P. Levack. These books focus on the economic, political, religious, social, and cultural conditions of the early modern era, from the sixteenth to the eighteenth centuries. The most severe European witch-hunts took place during this time. The highest numbers of executions were in the German-speaking lands of west-central Europe and in Scotland.[336]

During this era, the Sámi* people of northern Scandinavia were one of very few European tribal communities still practicing their pagan way of life.[†] Jewish and Muslim communities were tolerated, and sometimes hated and persecuted, on the margins of Christendom.[337] Goodare writes, "Christianity was basically an organized religion, defined and controlled by the intellectual and political elite, but it had won universal acceptance among the common folk."[338] For centuries, peasants had been inhabiting a "magical universe," weaving Christianity together with their earlier traditions.[339]

Though these were diverse cultures, many held similarities in common. In some places, plants, Waters, and landscape features were considered living beings with distinct personalities, and people reverently visited springs and wells.[340] Nature spirits, also known

---

* I recommend the music of Sámi musician Mari Boine.

† Sámi people are still here, and they are calling for a reckoning for the colonial policies that have impacted them. From the Swedish government's website (https://sweden.se/life/people/sami-in-sweden):

> The Sami have long been in contact with the nation states that were established on the land they called home. Through these encounters, the Sami have been forced to change their way of life. It's a history filled with abuses, violations, and racism.

In November 2021, the Swedish government announced that it was setting up a truth commission that will review the history of Sweden's policies toward the Sámi and the effect these policies have had on the Sámi people. The assignment runs until December 1, 2025.

as fairies (with different names, identities, and characteristics in their respective cultures), were tangibly present. Fairies lived in the Otherworld, but people also encountered them in nature. Fairies were often considered benevolent, but they were treated with respectful caution, because they could also create mischief and inflict harm.[341]

People were connected to their ancestral traditions. The status certain ancestors held in living memory could influence the status and well-being of their living descendants.[342] Experiences that would seem impossible to many of us today had been part of peoples' lives and stories for a long time. Individuals, and sometimes groups, reported shapeshifting into animal form, flying at night, interacting with angels, and visiting other worlds.[343] There was a widespread understanding that some people joined nocturnal processions with other-than-human entities.[344]

Most of the population lived in small villages, where they worked hard and depended on each other for survival. From one season to the next, conditions were uncertain, and the well-being of the people relied on favorable agricultural conditions to grow their crops. Because of their interdependence, villagers knew a lot about each other's strengths and weaknesses. When conflict erupted, everyone must have felt its impacts. Communities had reconciliation rituals that included gifts of food and drink.[345]

All the activities required for life, such as planting, harvesting, milking, food preparation, animal care, crafts, and building, were accompanied by practical magic to ensure greater likelihood of success.[346] Rituals of protection and blessing were carried out by common people as a regular part of life. Communities also identified certain magical practitioners as having special capacities, and these practitioners offered additional assistance, cures, and charms. Seasonal celebrations, dancing, and festivities were an important part of life.[347]

In the sixteenth century, the Reformation and Counter-Reformation galvanized hostility for this enchanted world. Competing Protestant and Catholic ideologies fostered a broad movement to enforce "correct religion"[348] among the people. Elites, including rulers, intellectuals, and landlords,[349] were living in different realities from the common people, yet they claimed increasing authority to manage and control the lives of peasants.[350] As folk beliefs were demonized, "magic" became a pejorative term. Increasingly, magic was seen as something to be feared.[351]

Complex factors combined during the European witch-hunts. One of these factors was an economic downturn in the sixteenth century.[352] Some communities' land was subdivided. Others were pushed off their land entirely. Increased population and failed harvests led to episodes of mass starvation.[353] At the same time, in the 1500s, rulers were consolidating state power with increased militarization.[354] Religious movements became politicized, and maintaining religious control grew into an important state objective. Goodare writes, "Rulers needed, more than ever, to prove that their states were godly."[355]

Between the 1520s and 1648, a series of religious wars took place in various parts of central and western Europe, with some southern and northern European states involved as well. Such pervasive war must have led to ideological pressures that lasted for generations. Fear, binary thinking, and the need to depict one's own nation as virtuous are some of the ways war can poison our minds. These patterns, in addition to labeling the "enemy" as inhuman and deserving of punishment, may have magnified the witch-hunting mentality.[356]

Patriarchy was another complex factor that led to 50,000 people being executed as witches during the early modern era, and another 50,000 officially labeled as witches.[357] Eighty percent of those executed were women.[358] Often, they were women over the age of forty,[359] those who were unmarried or widowed, and those of low socioeconomic status. Women who provided care for pregnant people, new mothers, children, and the sick or elderly could easily be blamed.[360] Those who were considered quarrelsome, sexually disobedient, and superstitious were targeted.[361] Healers were especially vulnerable to accusations that they were using their powers for evil.[362] Goodare writes,

> Early modern Europe was a patriarchal society, in which men
> wielded almost all the power—as husbands to subordinate
> wives, as fathers of deferential children, as masters of obedient

servants, as lords and kings of deferential subjects, as priests and pastors of anxious congregations. Men controlled all the courts which made decisions on crimes. Men preached all the sermons and wrote all the books. Men owned almost all the property and occupied almost all of the prestigious jobs.[363]

Patriarchy was the backdrop for the European nation-states' formation, and the witch-hunts were fueled by state power. Echoes of similar state power can be found in the Roman Empire, when "witches" were persecuted between 184 and 153 BCE. During these Roman hunts, women were executed for magically spreading disease. Some 1,500 years later, people were accused of witchcraft by their own neighbors, often sparked by jealous disputes within their communities.[364]

Conflict has always been (and continues to be) part of community life. During the fifteenth century, neighborly quarrels frequently included accusations of magic-induced harm. For example, in parts of today's Austria, Switzerland, Italy, Scandinavia, and Germany, historical records include allegations of curses, coercive love magic, milk theft, bewitched livestock, and harmful weather magic.* As Goodare explains, during the early modern era, magic was an accepted part of life. Peasant villages often had reconciliation rituals in place for reversing magical harm and restoring balance. These rituals encouraged tolerance and kept the peace.[365]

But during the early modern witch-hunts, an emergent concept turned allegations of magical harm much more deadly. The "demonic pact" was a widespread idea that women became witches by making a pact with the Devil, usually sealed with a sexual encounter.[366] Periodically, witch-hunting panics arose. During these panics, people who had long been suspect or marginalized in their communities increasingly became targets for trial and execution.

The circumstances witchcraft suspects faced while in custody were often deplorable. Some were kept in chains, without heat or

---

* For a discussion about harmful forms of magic, please see "Magic and Its Hazards in the Late Medieval West," by Richard Kieckhefer, pages 21–25 in *The Oxford Handbook of Witchcraft in Early Modern Europe and Colonial America.*

light, sitting in their excrement, surrounded by vermin, for months.[367] In some places, stripping and shaving women to search their bodies for the "Devil's mark" was standard procedure. Jailers sometimes sexually abused and raped prisoners.[368] These miserable conditions made suspects more likely to confess.

Torture was one of the strategies for eliciting confessions. In some cases, it was guided by procedural manuals such as the *Malleus Maleficarum*, which was first published in 1486 and was reprinted until 1669.[369] Torture usually produced confessions, but not always. Some committed suicide in prison to escape being tortured. Others endured multiple sessions of torture, resisting confession. In some cases, these brave souls were not exonerated, but banished.[370] Interrogators were looking for (and were usually able to extract) details of demonic pacts, including seduction by the Devil and intentional harm of people or animals. Some confessions included elements of folklore, personal experiences with nature spirits, and stories about weather magic.[371] Rather than being seen as expressions of peoples' cultural worldviews, these stories were interpreted as being demonic.[372] Witches were being portrayed as the "enemies of Christian society."[373] Sometimes, suspects were pressured to accuse others, including their own families and neighbors.

Some convicted witches were executed by hanging, drowning, or dismemberment. But the most common method of execution was burning. Witch burnings were public spectacles, with crowds of hundreds, thousands, or even tens of thousands in attendance. They were orchestrated to be theatrical. Confessions of the convicted witches would be read aloud, and preachers depicted witches' suffering as a cleansing and redemption. It took five or six hours of burning to reduce a human being to ashes, and there were no burials afterward. The so-called witches were erased.[374]

Witch-hunting was a labor– and resource-intense undertaking that involved many people. Judges, clerks, police, prosecutors, lawyers, juries, prisoners, torturers, "Devil's mark" inspectors, witnesses, victims, neighbors, executioners, tradespeople, friends, and family were all affected. Burning a witch required a tremendous amount of wood to be cut and transported, as well as specialized equipment to be made. Large crowds assembled to watch executions and hear the justifications for this "godly" project.[375]

———

Reading about these events centuries later, I realized: the involvement of so many people and the extensive use of resources meant that almost everyone must have been impacted in one way or another. Over generations, dehumanization, torture, and murder were cast as virtuous, necessary acts. I can still hear the echoes of this falsely justified terror in events taking place throughout the world.

My research about the witch-hunts helped me empathize with my ancestors who lived during this time. I grieved the loss of their enchanted worldviews, their magical techniques for blessing and protection, their relationships with the land, Waters, fairies, and spirits of nature. I lamented the centuries of war, famine, and poverty that hurt my people, as well as the shame they experienced. In my own religious upbringing, I could now perceive reverberations from the ideologies of this time. Learning this history helped me forgive the previous generations in my family, who had insisted on "correct" religion and compliance with patriarchal norms. It brought me liberation and peace.

Questions for Reflection

D EAR READER, the following pages are meant to support your healing. Please use the questions, prompts, practices, and resources that speak to you. I encourage you to feel these inquiries within your own heart. Express, enact, and ritualize them with your body and discuss them with your family and community.

Childhood

- As a child, what were you told about pilgrims, founding fathers, and pioneers?
- If you grew up in a primarily white neighborhood, what was your neighborhood like? What were the non-white neighborhoods around you like?
- How was your worldview shaped by your upbringing?
- What did you learn about money? Who taught you?

Family and Community

- What stories have been passed down in your family? How do you feel when you reflect on the stories today?
- Who are the interpersonal philanthropists in your life?
- What ancestral identities or places do you value?
- Have you ever discussed whiteness or colonization with your white friends and family?

Self

- Do you have any bubbles of denial?
- Have you ever received an important message from a dream?
- What paradoxes are you learning to live with?
- How do you connect with nature?
- Do you need to forgive yourself or someone else?

Colonization

- Throughout your life, what have you learned about colonization?
- How much do you know about your ancestors' presence on this continent? How much do you *want* to know?
- What kinds of personal reparations could you make?
- What does becoming a good relative mean to you?

Following these prompts, take a few minutes to quietly imagine. Consider doodling, moving your body, or making something to express your vision.

- If you come from a family who received land grants, enslaved people, or benefited from Manifest Destiny, imagine being transparent about it. How would that feel?
- Imagine millions of radical apologies, accompanied by millions of reparative actions. What could happen?
- Humans have been migrating throughout the world for millennia. During the last five centuries, the scale of plundering, annihilation, and hoarding has been uniquely devastating. Imagine humanity moving beyond this pattern.
- Listen to one or more episodes of *The Light Ahead* podcast.[376] Imagine economies that work for everyone.
- Imagine European-descended settlers creating new cultures for ourselves. What kinds of rituals, norms, and ideologies could we embrace?
- Imagine a New Dream for the Modern World. How does your Dream look and feel?

Practices to Accompany
Part One ~ Spinning the Thread

Learn about Whiteness

WHITENESS IS a socially constructed identity that was engineered to consolidate power among elite, landowning men. It often seems invisible or normal to those of us who are white. In my experience, *seeing* the construct of whiteness and learning about its history are some first steps toward divesting from it. I've found the storytelling aspects of these resources helpful:

- *Combined Destinies: Whites Sharing Grief About Racism,* edited by Ann Todd Jealous and Caroline T. Haskell
- *Waking Up White and Finding Myself in the Story of Race,* by Debby Irving
- *Whiteness is Not an Ancestor: Essays on Life and Lineage by White Women,* edited by Lisa Iversen
- *Ethnoautobiography: Stories and Practices for Unlearning Whiteness; Decolonization; Uncovering Ethnicities,* by Jürgen Kremer and R. Jackson-Paton
- *Living in Indigenous Sovereignty,* by Elizabeth Carlson-Manathara with Gladys Rowe
- The chapter "Forever Limited" in *Sand Talk: How Indigenous Thinking Can Save the World,* by Tyson Yunkaporta
- *Decolonial Dames of America,* by Morgan Curtis
- Four-part documentary miniseries *Exterminate All The Brutes,* directed and narrated by Raoul Peck

In addition, resources that focus on the historic creation of whiteness, how whiteness creates systemic harm, and on solidarity work to dismantle it have been valuable for me. Here are a few that I recommend:

- *Seeing White* podcast
- *My Grandmother's Hands: Racialized Trauma and the Pathway to Mending our Hearts and Bodies,* by Resmaa Menakem
- "Roots Deeper than Whiteness: Remembering Who We Are for the Wellbeing of All," by David Dean
- The (divorcing) White Supremacy Culture website
- Online classes with White Awake
- Materials and gatherings hosted by Showing Up for Racial Justice (SURJ)

Allow yourself to feel the impacts of whiteness. How has whiteness benefited you? How has White Peril prevented you from fully expressing your humanity? How will you divest from whiteness?

Water as a Sacred Power

Contemplate Water as a Sacred Power who imprints with our feelings, thoughts, intentions, and words. Each morning, pray with Water. Thank Water for her presence, bless her, and sing loving songs to her. Offer some Water to the land near your home or to a potted plant on your windowsill. Ask Water to restore your health and well-being before you drink. Bless yourself with Water. My understanding of these practices was informed by Tewa Women United.[377]

Whose Land Are You On?

If you do not yet know the names of the Indigenous Peoples on whose land you reside, refer to native-land.ca. This interactive website allows you to search by zip code, state, or city to learn whose land you inhabit. This information is not always complete, so do further research. Learn about the history of Indigenous Peoples where you ancestors settled, where you currently live, and throughout Turtle Island. Reading *An Indigenous Peoples' History of the United States* by Roxanne Dunbar-Ortiz is a good place to start. Support a land tax or LandBack program where you live or elsewhere.

Honor Grandmother Moon

If you physically experience moontime, contemplate your cycles as sacred. During your bleeding time, spend some time in solitude lying down on the ground. If you do not have access to a safe place outside, pray in the bathtub or sing to a bowl of Water. Listen, feel, rest, and reflect.

If you do not physically experience moontime, honor Grandmother Moon. Pay attention to the phases of the moon and notice how she influences you. Spend time outdoors under the moon and offer Water to her. Make an altar or some artwork to honor Grandmother Moon and/or moontime. Allow your intuition to guide you. My understanding of these practices was influenced by Pat McCabe[378] and Jewels Wingfield.[379]

Practices to Accompany
Part Two ~Weaving

Create an Ancestor Altar

HONORING ANCESTORS is important in traditional cultures throughout the world. Yeye Luisah Teish,[380] a Black Elder, high priestess of Yorùbá tradition, and expert in ancestor reverence suggests the following practice. First, learn about the ancestors of the land you inhabit. Find out which foods were important to them and gather some of these foods. If possible, collect Water from a local source. Make an offering of local foods and Water, speaking the names of the Indigenous Peoples of the unceded land on which you live. Gratefully acknowledge how your existence is enriched and enabled by the land. Repeat these offerings often.

Next, begin this universal practice to honor your own ancestors. Find a quiet place in your home where you can dedicate a space to them. Lay down a cloth, a candle, and a bowl of Water. If you have any rocks, plants, or Water from your ancestral lands, add them to the altar. If you do not have any, you may use rocks, plants, and Water from the land on which you live. Include fresh Water on your altar and offer the Water to the land after you work with your altar.

If there are herbs or incense that are part of your spiritual tradition or that would have been familiar to your ancestors, light them and use their smoke to purify the space. For those with western European ancestry, I recommend juniper, lavender, rosemary, thyme, or mugwort. It is best if you can grow and dry the plants yourself and/or harvest them using the principles of honorable harvest. In her book *Braiding Sweetgrass,* Potawatomi scientist Robin Wall Kimmerer shares these guidelines for honorable harvest:

- Know the ways of the ones who take care of you, so that you may take care of them.
- Introduce yourself. Be accountable as the one who comes asking for life.
- Never take the first. Never take the last.
- Take only what you need.
- Take only that which is given.
- Never take more than half. Leave some for others.
- Harvest in a way that minimizes harm.
- Use it respectfully. Never waste what you have taken.
- Share.
- Give thanks for what you have been given.
- Give a gift, in reciprocity for what you have taken.
- Sustain the ones who sustain you and the earth will last forever.[381]

Spend at least five minutes each day at your ancestor altar, and more if possible. Talk, sing, and listen to the ancestors. When grief comes, allow it to move all the way through you. Use rhythmic instruments like drums and rattles as well as crying, wailing, moaning, and screaming to transmute grief, anger, and shame. Stomp, dance, and roll on the floor. Ancestral tears can feel intense. Embrace them as a healing and cleansing gift.

As you go through this transformative process, remember to ask for help from friends, family, and the natural world. From Yeye Teish, I learned to hold a stone in my hand and ask the stone to help hold my grief. Place this stone in a bowl of natural salt to be purified. After the grief has passed, give the salt back to the land and rinse the stone with Water. Grief comes in cycles. Repeat as often as necessary.

Ask for the ancestors' help in becoming a good relative. Listen for their whispers in the stillness of your heart and in the mystery of your dreams.

Harvest Dreams

Record your dreams in a dedicated dream journal. Make a note of every dream, even if you only remember a word, image, or feeling. Over time, your dreams may become clearer, conveying important messages. You may see patterns, notice that your dreams are predicting future events, or receive visits from ancestral archetypes. If you have a powerful dream, be sure to say, "thank you." Share your dreams out loud with friends and family. Listen for how the dreams are teaching and guiding you collectively.

Dream with Water

Fill a bowl with Water. *Feel* your questions, intentions, and prayers in your heart. Hold the Water near your belly. Allow your intentions and prayers to communicate with the Water. Ask Water to show you what you need to see through dreams and intuition. Place the bowl under your bed and go to sleep. Pay attention to the dreams and insights that come to you over the next few days. Thank Water for helping you and offer the Water in your bowl outdoors with gratitude. This practice was inspired by teachings by Unangan Elder Ilarion "Kuuyux" Merculieff.[382]

Cultivate Reciprocal Relationships with Nature

Visit a tree, flower, stone, mountain, lake, creek, or ocean close to your home. Introduce yourself and ask permission to visit with this being. Make an offering of song, food, Water, or medicinal plants from your spiritual tradition. Return to this place often. Always come with a gift and willingness to listen. Mentors of diverse cultural backgrounds have shaped my understanding of this universal practice. Making offerings to other-than-human beings was once important within European cultures as well. In some places, it is still practiced.

For guidance on creating a non-appropriative, nature-based rite of passage, I recommend *Rites and Responsibilities: A Guide to Growing Up*, by Hungarian-descended anti-racist educator Darcy Ottey.

Seek Right Relations with Indigenous Communities

Learning directly from Indigenous Peoples can be a pathway to right relations. Indigenous-led organizations often host webinars that are open to people of all backgrounds. Here are a few examples:

- IINÁH Institute
- NDN Collective
- Lakota People's Law Project
- Liberated Capital

There are also Indigenous-produced podcasts that offer valuable perspectives. Here are a few examples:

- Bioneers *Indigeneity Conversations*
- *Nihizhí, Our Voices: An Indigenous Solutions Podcast*
- *All My Relations* Podcast

I suggest contributing to the organizations that teach you and amplifying their work within your networks.

In addition, research the work that is led by Indigenous relatives in your own community. If you are welcomed into their space, sit with the question, "How (if at all) can I help?" Listen carefully. Their responses may differ from your assumptions. Show up with humility and steadfastness. Come with a good heart and the awareness that there are cultural nuances you do not understand. Allow these relationships to develop slowly, at the speed of trust. If you make a mistake, acknowledge it, apologize, reflect, and learn from your mistake. Keep going and commit yourself to becoming a good relative over the long term.

Care about the Ongoing Impacts of Slavery

Those of us who were born into white identities are not able to fully understand the intergenerational trauma of slavery, nor the terror that continued long after Emancipation. We *can* intentionally do the work to build our awareness, empathy, and solidarity. The unacknowledged horror of slavery tends to numb our hearts. Stories, poems, personal narratives, and relational experiences have allowed me to feel again. I highly recommend the Experience Sankofa Project Living Museum[383] for a visceral experience of Black joy and resilience. In addition, the following books have been life-changing for me:

- *The Fire Next Time*, by James Baldwin
- *Beloved*, by Toni Morrison
- *Kindred*, by Octavia Butler
- *Between the World and Me*, by Ta-Nehisi Coates
- *Post Traumatic Slave Syndrome: America's Legacy of Enduring Injury and Healing*, by Joy DeGruy
- *Gather at the Table: The Healing Journey of a Daughter of Slavery and a Son of the Slave Trade*, by Thomas Norman DeWolf and Sharon Leslie Morgan
- *Nejma* and *Salt.*, by Nayyirah Waheed
- *Caste: The Origins of our Discontents*, by Isabelle Wilkerson
- *Emergent Strategy: Shaping Change, Changing Worlds*, by adrienne maree brown
- *The Little Book of Race and Restorative Justice: Black Lives, Healing, and US Social Transformation*, by Fania Davis

For me, it has been essential to learn how slavery fueled capitalism in the United States and how it laid the foundations for our economy. I recommend *The Half Has Never Been Told: Slavery and the Making of American Capitalism*, by Edward E. Baptist. It has also been important to understand that Indigenous women and children were enslaved and exploited by sex trafficking. Please see

The Other Slavery: The Uncovered Story of Indian Enslavement in America, by Andrés Resendéz.

Finally, I recommend doing the work to build respectful relationships with Black relatives. Know that there are some things you will never fully understand, but that you can *embody caring*. Come with an open heart, be a good listener, and move at the speed of trust. If you make a mistake, acknowledge it, apologize, reflect, and learn from the experience.

History of Immigration

All of us who are not Indigenous to Turtle Island are descended from those who came from other places. Some of our ancestors arrived here with institutional power and prestige, while others immigrated out of desperation. Tragically, many ancestors were brought here against their will, amidst deplorable conditions that lasted for generations.

For those in the European diaspora, learning about our peoples' immigration histories can offer a much fuller picture. If you find out where your people came from and when they immigrated, then you can research the circumstances that led to their migration. Giving historical context to our family stories can activate compassion for our ancestors, without condoning the harmful actions that some of them took. This guidance was shared by Kapampangan Elder Leny Strobel.[384]

Talking to our relatives and visiting family graves is one way to learn the family stories. Where did they settle and who did they unsettle? What did the family trajectory look like in the coming generations? Consider writing a story about your research and asking a white friend to wit(h)ness you as you share your story out loud. What legacies did you inherit from your people? Knowing who we are and where we came from is an important part of becoming a good relative.

To follow the guidance of a Euro-descended Elder, I recommend the book *Inherited Silence: Listening to the Land, Healing the*

Colonizer Mind, by Louise Dunlap. She shares about her lifelong relationship with stolen Wappo and Patwin land in Northern California that one of her ancestors purchased in the 1800s and passed down through the following generations. She compassionately shares about her ancestors and offers valuable reflections on relating with colonial family legacies.

Ancestral Apology and Forgiveness Ritual

Radical apology and forgiveness can be catalysts for our mutual healing and liberation. Here, Oglala Lakota Elder Basil Brave Heart shares a ritual anyone can use, based on universal principles.[385] Since the Ceremony for Repentance and Forgiveness in 2019, individuals and communities have been practicing variations of this ritual throughout the world.

In preparation for writing prayers of apology, Basil recommends singing and connecting with the natural elements, to align with unconditional love. Breathing slowly, go into your heart and feel what aspects of your ancestors' legacies need healing and repair. Allow the pain to exist. Know that resistance may come up, and that this is a normal part of the process. Take as much time as you need to write a sincere prayer of apology for any harms your ancestors perpetrated and the ways in which you've benefited from those harms. Radical apology is a commitment to end these patterns and learn different ways of navigating the world.

Do you need to forgive yourself, your ancestors, or an institution that perpetrated harm? Basil says, "Forgiveness is taking ownership of your shadow and willingly seeing what you don't want to see."[386] In your written prayer, you can ask for help with this process. How would it feel to let go of resentment, blame, and shame? Imagine *knowing* that you and your ancestors are already forgiven. Radical forgiveness is a promise not to carry the pain anymore.

When your written prayer is complete, consider it a sacred communication between you, your ancestors, and the Divine. These prayers should not be published, shared online, or read aloud to other people. However, Basil encourages us to do this ritual in community and share about *our process* with others, because it can be healing to wit(h)ness each other and know that we are not alone.

Wrap your written prayer in a piece of cotton fabric. You may include offerings such as lavender, thyme, rosemary, rose petals, juniper (or any healing plants that are part of your ancestral lineage or spiritual tradition). Tie the bundle with cotton string and place it on your ancestor altar. Notice whether any dreams or intuitive instructions come to you while the bundle sits on your altar. When the time is right, pray with some wood, set an intention to honor the element of fire, and light a sacred fire. Ask the fire to carry your prayers to the cosmos and reverently burn your bundle.

When the ritual is complete, you may feel tired. Drink lots of Water and make time to rest. Over time, you may notice synchronicities, dreams, and fresh inspiration. Blockages that once immobilized you may dissolve. These are evidence of sacred communication. After you complete one layer of apology and forgiveness, new layers may emerge. This ritual can be done as many times as necessary. Radical forgiveness and radical apology are long-term commitments that require repetition.

Ritual for Transforming Resistance

The following ritual was suggested by Yeye Luisah Teish for transforming resistance to LandBack, land tax, and reparations. It can also be practiced for healing ancestral avoidance, grief, guilt, shame, and anger.

On a full moon, write everything that you feel. All feelings are valid. Cry, rage, and vent if you need to. Only Grandmother Moon will see your paper, and she has been shining on all peoples since the beginning of time. After you have felt everything and written it all down, go outside with a fireproof container, some matches, and a bowl of Water. Speak to Grandmother Moon and to Water. Share all that you wish to release and transform, and anything that is heavy on your heart. Speak about your dreams for LandBack, land tax, and reparations, even if you do not know how to begin or are afraid to begin.

Burn your papers in the fireproof container. Allow the smoke to carry your feelings to the cosmos and the ancestors. When the papers are completely burned, wash your face and hands in the Water that has absorbed and reflects the light of the full moon. Offer the remaining Water to the land, with a prayer for the land and the ancestors.

The next day, collect the ashes when they are completely cool. Mix these ashes with soil in your garden or in a pot, and plant seeds that are well suited to your local environment. Before planting each seed, pray with it and ask it to bear the fruits of healing for the future generations. As you water the plants, speak loving words to them about your hopes and dreams for LandBack, land tax, reparations, and any ancestral healing you need. Harvest the plants and share them with your friends, family, and community using the principles of honorable harvest.[387]

Make a Personal Reparations Plan

Trying to reduce the harm of colonization and slavery is such an immense, multigenerational task that it can easily feel intimidating. Often, I hear white relatives say that they want to support reparations but don't know where to begin. Each of us can begin by making a personal reparations plan. These are living documents that help us clarify our intention and catalyze meaningful action. Begin by researching and joining online networks such as:

- Liberated Capital
- Coming to the Table
- Reparations 4 Slavery
- The Reparations Project
- The Truth Telling Project
- Reparations Summer

Learn what types of reparations are being called for. Pay attention to what sparks your interest and optimism.

Find out where your ancestors (or present-day family) settled and who they displaced. Consider how you currently benefit from an economy that was built with the labor of enslaved people, on stolen land. How do your talents, interests, time, and assets uniquely align with the needs of BIPOC communities and places? Plan what you will do and/or give today, within the coming month, six months, and twelve months. Putting your plan in writing is an important step. Revisit and revise your plan every year (or more often), visualizing the effects it could have over time. Share your reparations plan with your white friends and family. Support each other, be accountable, celebrate the steps you take, and build a culture of repair.

You may feel fear, resentment, grief, guilt, shame, blame, self-judgment, or anger on your journey of personal reparations. Even when you really want to begin, a part of you may resist by forgetting or becoming "too busy." You may feel overwhelmed and worry that reparations are an impossible ideal. You may feel impaired by rigid either/or thinking and "shoulds." These feelings are a normal part of the process. Allow them to move through you. The important thing is not to get stuck. Make an offering to the land and the ancestors. Ask for their help. Then return to the work.

While co-facilitating* circles of white settlers making their personal reparations plans, I've learned that unpacking our White Peril together can help our plans flow with ease and grace. When we courageously wit(h)ness our shadow material together in community, it loses its power over us. Over time, we can begin moving from a place of wholeness, sufficiency, and love in action. Our personal reparations plans can become beautiful expressions of our creativity and joy.† This orientation makes the process sustainable over the

---

* Gratitude to the Organization of Nature Evolutionaries (https://www.natureevolutionaries.com/), Elyshia Holliday (my friend and co-facilitator), and everyone who has been part of our circles.
† I love the song "Power of Kindness" by MaMuse, from the album *Prayers for Freedom*. For me, this song serves as a joyful reparations anthem.

long term. Here are a few examples of steps I've seen people incorporate into their reparations plans:

- Making recurring, automatic contributions to IBPOC-led organizations part of our monthly budget.
- Contributing to BIPOC-led projects in lieu of buying birthday or holiday presents for our white friends and family. Sharing why we are making this gift in their honor.
- Developing a "reparations menu" for a cooking workshop. Discussing reparations during the workshop. Returning some of the proceeds to a local Black-owned farm.
- Offering to prepare food or clean up after IBPOC community events.
- Financially supporting Black and Indigenous-produced journalism, podcasts, and comics.
- Gathering with white friends to work in an Indigenous Elder's garden. Spending a day preparing traditional foods with the guidance of the Indigenous community and sharing the feast together.

Breathe, relax, and allow reparative actions to flow from the authentic place inside of you that is longing to become a good relative. Take the first good step and then the next. Over time, your reparations plan may surprise you by rewriting you from the inside out.

Practices to Accompany
Part Three ~ The Fabric

Mythology, Archetypes, and Deities

I RECOMMEND reading folktales, mythologies, and archaeological accounts to learn about the deities, archetypes, animals, plants, storylines, or symbols that were important to your ancestors. Please see goodrelative.com for some of the films, books, and classes I've found particularly helpful.

As you read, take note of the sensations in your body. For me, feelings of comfort, curiosity, or sleepiness indicate that I've found something resonant. Sometimes this process can unleash grief for all that has been lost. Allow the grief to flow through you. When you sense your ancestral memory returning, thank your ancestors. Consider cooking a special meal, enacting a ritual, or creating some artwork to honor them.

Language and Songs

Many of us now write, speak, and sing exclusively in English. But we can begin coaxing ancestral memory back by learning bits and pieces of our ancestral languages. For example, Irish, Welsh, Breton, Cornish, Manx, and Scottish Gaelic are currently being reclaimed by the diaspora. Duolingo[388] offers Irish, Scottish Gaelic, and other European culturally endangered languages.

On my website[389] I've included some songs and chants that are available as recordings with phonetic lyrics. Learning this way has been particularly helpful for me. If you do not know where to start, I suggest choosing one song or a poem to learn. By practicing it for a few minutes every day, it will become part of you. One day, when you least expect it, the song or poem will start singing through you as you work in your garden, take care of your family, or cook a meal.

Relationships with Elders

The Dream of the Modern World tends to glorify youth and dismiss elderhood. We can change this pattern by actively seeking the wisdom of those whom our communities honor as Elders. Cultivate respectful relationships with Elders by bringing a gift, cooking a meal, or contributing to an organization that is dear to the person. If there are living Elders in your family, visit them and listen to their stories. Ask them to share memories of their grandparents. Be curious about how your family narratives have evolved over time. Re-member that you can help shape the family narratives during your lifetime.

If possible, spend time and make offerings on the land your ancestors have inhabited on Turtle Island *and* in Europe. I support organizations that are doing cultural and ecological restoration in my ancestral homelands, such as Brigit's Garden in Ireland[390] and Trees for Life: Rewilding the Scottish Highlands.[391]

Learning from people who carry songs, crafts, stories, dances, or recipes of your ancestral lines can be a powerful practice for re-kindling ancestral memory. As much as possible, learn the cultural context. Ask for permission to use the teachings and instructions on when and how to use them. Three of the people who have taught me are Sìne McKenna,[392] Mary McLaughlin,[393] and Jude Lally.[394]

Other Ways of Knowing

To attune with your ancestral blueprints, I recommend regularly tending an ancestor altar. Make offerings to your ancestors and ask them to help you. Rekindling ancestral memory is not a research project to approach with a linear mind. Rather, it's something that can reveal itself in whispers over time. Dreams, intuition, and synchronicities have been my most valuable teachers. Many of us have been trained to disregard these important sources of information. Reclaiming them can be an empowering act.

Pay attention to words, stories, symbols, and images that appear repeatedly in your daily experiences. One of my favorite forms of synchronicity is when an image or event appears in a dream and then shows up in waking life during the next few days. When you embrace other ways of knowing and express gratitude for them, you may experience them more often.

Glossary

ANCESTRAL AVOIDANCE—disinterest in and avoidance of one's own ancestry or family history. It can take the form of being overly identified with another culture, minimizing the importance of one's own ancestry, or distancing ourselves from our ancestral storylines. In my experience, pain and shame associated with the past can cause ancestral avoidance.

Ancestral Memory—the innate knowing of ancestral wisdom, carried in our blood and bones. Ancestral memory is nonlinear, intuitive, and can be experienced as a comforting feeling when we encounter language, symbols, dreams, songs, cultural teachings, or stories that are part of our ancestral blueprints.

BIPOC—a broadly accepted acronym* for "Black, Indigenous, and People of Color/Culture." These groups have been historically marginalized from decision-making due to racism and colorism, including conversations about their own community development. In this acronym, "B" is placed first to honor Black relatives. This emphasizes undoing anti-Black racism and working toward Black liberation.

In his work, Black therapist, trauma specialist, and best-selling author Resmaa Menakem uses the term "bodies of culture" to

---

* Using an acronym to identify people of tremendously diverse backgrounds, cultures, and experiences has limitations. We humans are constantly developing language in new ways. At the time of this book's publication, *BIPOC* is a widely accepted term. Over time, we may develop better language to express the richness and diversity of human identity in the context of evolving power dynamics.

describe all "human bodies not considered white."[395] Inspired by his insight, I embed "culture" in the BIPOC acronym to emphasize that racialized identity involves culture as well as skin color. Menakem posits that people of European descent must create a new culture of whiteness, devoid of supremacy.[396]

IBPOC, an alternate version of this acronym, is defined below. Both are used interchangeably throughout this book.

Colonization—Potawatomi scientist and author Robin Wall Kimmerer writes:

> Colonization is the process by which an invading people seeks to replace the original lifeways with their own, erasing the evidence of prior claims to place. Its tools are many: military and political power, assimilative education, economic pressure, ecological transformation, religion—and language.[397]

Colonization also includes resource extraction. From my perspective, colonization is caused by a spiritual sickness. Please see *Columbus and Other Cannibals*, by Powhatan-Renápe and Delaware-Lenápe descended author, Jack D. Forbes.

Cultural Appreciation—approaching another culture with respect and courtesy by observing patiently, waiting for an invitation, asking consent, and taking as much time as needed to learn from culture-bearers on their terms.[*] Cultural appreciation involves building relationships with its practitioners and contributing to the long-term well-being of the people and the culture.

Cultural Appropriation—the unauthorized taking of another culture's dance, dress, music, language, folklore, cuisine, traditional medicine, religious symbols, and practices, *especially* by those who represent a group in a more powerful social and political position.[†]

---

[*] Inspired by Indigeneity Program signage at the National Bioneers Conference, 2018.
[†] Ibid.

Cultural appropriation is particularly harmful when it involves taking elements of another culture out of context for personal or monetary gain.

Cultural Sampling˚ — seeking identity, healing, or self-expression from marginalized cultures, without reciprocity, relationship, or permission. It includes taking practices out of context and mixing them together, as well as skipping from one culture to another. In my experience, ancestral avoidance can lead to cultural sampling.

Decolonization — scholars Eve Tuck and K. Wayne Yang offer the following definition of decolonization: "Decolonization eliminates settler property rights and settler sovereignty. It requires the abolition of land as property and upholds the sovereignty of Native land and people."[398] For Tuck and Yang, focusing on decolonization of the mind perpetuates settler innocence. It renders decolonization as nothing more than a metaphor.

To focus on returning Indigenous land and life,[399] I use this term sparingly. I also acknowledge that my own healing process was facilitated by neurodecolonization, which is a term from the work of Michael Yellow Bird (see below).

Doctrine of Discovery — a legal framework based on three fifteenth-century papal bulls. Throughout the world, it has been (and continues to be) used to dispossess Indigenous Peoples of their land and lifeways. Please see *Pagans in the Promised Land: Decoding the Doctrine of Christian Discovery*, by scholar Stephen Newcomb and *The Land is Not Empty: Following Jesus in Dismantling the Doctrine of Discovery*, by Tewa-descended author Sarah Augustine.

Dream of the Modern World — in the 1990s, Achuar leaders shared this term with their partners in The Pachamama Alliance, accompanied by a mandate to "change the Dream of the Modern World."[400]

---

* Gratitude to Alexis Bunten for the term *cultural sampling*.

They identified the Dream of the Modern World as the root cause of our global environmental, social, and spiritual crises.[401]

Elders—I capitalize "Elders" as an honorific to describe people whose communities acknowledge them in this way. Elders' warmth, compassion, insight, knowledge, kindness, courage, wisdom, and humor serve the well-being of their communities, and even the world.

Healing Tears—crying can be a valuable way for white settlers to process our cognitive dissonance, shame, grief, and remorse. Healing tears are shed alone, with our white friends and family, or in the context of relational healing. They are not used to derail conversations about race. Nor are they used to manipulate, silence, or control.

IBPOC—an acronym* that refers to "Indigenous, Black, and People of Color/Culture." (See "BIPOC," above). I use "IBPOC" because the history of racialization and oppression on Turtle Island begins with Indigenous Peoples. Indigenous voices and experiences are still overwhelmingly marginalized and erased by settler culture. Placing the "I" first in this acronym honors Indigenous relatives past, present and future, and prioritizes Indigenous sovereignty.

In his work, Black therapist, trauma specialist, and best-selling author Resmaa Menakem uses the term "bodies of culture" to describe all "human bodies not considered white."[402] Inspired by his insight, I embed "culture" in the BIPOC acronym to emphasize that racialized identity involves culture as well as skin color. Menakem posits that people of European descent must create a new culture of whiteness, devoid of supremacy.[403]

---

* Using an acronym to identify people of tremendously diverse backgrounds, cultures, and experiences has limitations. We humans are constantly developing language in new ways. At the time of this book's publication, *IBPOC* is one accepted term. Over time, we may develop better language to express the richness and diversity of human identity in the context of evolving power dynamics.

Indigenous Peoples—the United Nations website describes Indigenous Peoples as follows:

> Indigenous Peoples are inheritors and practitioners of unique cultures and ways of relating to people and the environment. They have retained social, cultural, economic and political characteristics that are distinct from those of the dominant societies in which they live. Despite their cultural differences, Indigenous Peoples from around the world share common problems related to the protection of their rights as distinct peoples.
>
> Indigenous Peoples have sought recognition of their identities, way of life and their right to traditional lands, territories and natural resources for years, yet throughout history, their rights have always been violated. Indigenous Peoples today are arguably among the most disadvantaged and vulnerable groups of people in the world. The international community now recognizes that special measures are required to protect their rights and maintain their distinct cultures and way of life.[404]

Indigenous Worldviews—in my relationships with Indigenous Peoples, I have learned that among thousands of Indigenous groups and Nations, a single, pan-Indigenous worldview does not exist. Each is distinct in its worldview. Zuni traditional farmer and humanitarian Jim Enote shares:

> Within the spectrum of disparate Indigenous Peoples, there is a union of intrinsic Indigenous thinking. Especially in ancient times, before colonial contact, survival, contentment, and flourishing were never guaranteed. Consequently, many Indigenous Peoples maintain a connection to the cosmological process by observing and respecting nature's patterns and power, honoring previous generations, and prioritizing the

well-being of future generations. In modern times, Indigenous groups, rural or urban, vary in the depth and continuity of their worldviews. That does not make them any more or less spiritual because culture and worldviews for everyone will change over time.[405]

Interpersonal Philanthropy—relational generosity that doesn't rely on giving or receiving money. It connects people in kinship, through our shared humanity. I consider many of those who have taught me to be interpersonal philanthropists.

LandBack—the landback.org website, which is powered by NDN, offers the following definition:

> LANDBACK is a movement that has existed for genera-tions with a long legacy of organizing and sacrifice to get Indigenous Lands back into Indigenous hands. Currently, there are LandBack battles being fought all across Turtle Island, to the north and the South."[406]

LandBack is a decentralized movement that can take many dif-ferent forms. To learn more, please see the film *Lakota Nation vs. United States.*[407]

Manifest Destiny—a supremacist ideology with origins in fifteenth-century papal bulls and the Doctrine of Discovery. European settlers claimed a divine mandate to spread westward throughout Turtle Island, dispossessing Indigenous Peoples and cultivating the land. Please see *Unsettling Truths: The Ongoing, Dehumanizing Legacy of the Doctrine of Discovery*, by Mark Charles (Diné) and Soong-Chan Rah (Korean-American).

Neurodecolonization—a term from the work of Mandan, Hidatsa, and Arikara professor Michael Yellow Bird. He describes neuro-decolonization as being facilitated by mindfulness practice and meditation, sacred ceremony, and very uncomfortable life or death circumstances that increase neuroplasticity.[408] Please see his chapter, "Neurodecolonization: Using Mindfulness Practices to Delete the Neural Networks of Colonialism," in *For Indigenous Minds Only: A Decolonization Handbook.**

I see Neurodecolonization as part of the larger work of decolonization, which returns Indigenous land and life.[409]

Original Instructions—Anishinaabe, Cree, Métis, and Norwegian ecologist, writer, and professor Melissa K. Nelson writes:

> Original Instructions refer to the many diverse teachings, lessons, and ethics expressed in the origin stories and oral traditions of Indigenous Peoples. They are the literal and metaphorical instructions, passed on orally from generation to generation, for how to be a good human being living in reciprocal relation with all of our seen and unseen relatives. They are natural laws that, when ignored, have natural consequences."[410]

For perspectives on Original Instructions shared by over thirty Indigenous experts, please see *Original Instructions: Indigenous Teachings for a Sustainable Future*, edited by Melissa K. Nelson.[411]

Patriarchy—a historical development that is fueled by war and enforces male domination. Patriarchy colonizes women's bodies through governing rule, especially by controlling procreation. It has no single trajectory but is always correlated with economic exploitation and the accumulation of wealth. Patriarchal systems prioritize scarcity, competition, and linear time. Patriarchy is upheld by settler colonialism. People of all genders can work together to dismantle patriarchy. My understanding of patriarchy has been informed by Max Dashú's Suppressed History Archives.[412]

---

* This work is cited with the permission of Michael Yellow Bird. Personal correspondence, August 2022.

Philanthropic Alchemy—my process of unpacking internalized narratives about money, power, and philanthropy. This practice acknowledges that philanthropy takes place through both interpersonal and institutional lenses. Philanthropic Alchemy is steeped in mutual liberation, and it utilizes reparative frameworks. It seeks to correct power imbalances and envisions equitable economies that are based in relational interdependence.

Racial Capitalism—Black farmer and author Leah Penniman defines racial capitalism as, "The commodification of our people and the planet for economic gain."[413] Racial capitalism has been taking place for more than 500 years on Turtle Island. Confiscating Indigenous land and turning it over to white farmers to capitalize on that land is one example. Another example is exploiting the labor of enslaved people for profit to benefit white landowners. The commodification of the sacred mountain where I live is a current example of racial capitalism.

Radical Apology—uses naturally arising shame and remorse as catalysts. Radical apology is a sacred commitment to stop the harm, take responsibility, and begin our own healing. It opens the possibility for reparative action. It is not a performance, nor does it seek absolution from other people.

Radical Forgiveness—a commitment not to carry the pain anymore. Radical forgiveness liberates the forgiver. It does not condone abuse or suggest that harm should be forgotten. To learn more about the phenomenon that I call radical forgiveness, please see *The Book of Forgiving: The Fourfold Path for Healing Ourselves and Our World*, by Archbishop Desmond Tutu and Mpho Tutu, and *The Four Sacred Gifts: Indigenous Wisdom for Modern Times*, by Nahua (Azteca and Toltec) and Mexican-American author Anita Sanchez.

Rematriation—Daisy Purdy, a T'Salagi friend, educator, and organizer, shared her understanding of rematriation from the teachings of her Auntie. She describes it as "returning Mother Earth to herself and honoring Indigenous communities' agency as caregivers of the Earth."[414] Rematriation lies at the heart of the LandBack movement.

Re-Membering—the process of reuniting aspects of ourselves that have been dismembered by colonialism, racism, whiteness, and patriarchy. Please see Nayyirah Waheed's poem "the.remembering" in her book *Nejma*.

Reparations—The National Coalition of Blacks for Reparations in America (N'COBRA)[415] defines reparations as:

> A process of repairing, healing and restoring a people injured because of their group identity and in violation of their fundamental human rights by governments, corporations, institutions and families. Those groups that have been injured have the right to obtain from the government, corporation, institution or family responsible for the injuries that which they need to repair and heal themselves. In addition to being a demand for justice, it is a principle of international human rights law.[416]

In my *personal* commitment to reparations, I try to reduce the ongoing harm of genocidal acts such as land theft, settler colonialism, and slavery. I perceive reparations as a multigenerational process of spiritual, relational, and economic reckoning for horrific abuse that can never be forgotten.

Settler—using this identifier allows me to be transparent about the legacies of settler colonialism I inherited and from which I benefit. Paradoxically, in my experience, this term can also disrupt settler colonialism. For a nuanced discussion of "settler" and other identifiers, please see *Living in Indigenous Sovereignty*, by white Canadian settler and scholar Elizabeth Carlson-Manathara, with Swampy Cree scholar Gladys Rowe.

Settler Colonialism—when the descendants of colonizers continue to occupy the land in subsequent generations. Settler-colonial states use a variety of techniques to interpret colonial agendas as righteous and just, while violently displacing and erasing Indigenous Peoples. To learn more, please see *An Indigenous Peoples' History of the United States*, and *Not a "Nation of Immigrants": Settler Colonialism, White Supremacy, and a History of Erasure and Exclusion*, both by Roxanne Dunbar-Ortiz. People of all identities can work together to dismantle settler colonialism. For ideas, please see *Becoming Kin: An Indigenous Call to Unforgetting the Past and Reimagining Our Future*, by Anishinaabe/Ukrainian author Patty Krawec.

Spiritual Bypassing—a term developed by white psychotherapist John Welwood in the 1980s. He defined spiritual bypassing as using "spiritual ideas and practices to sidestep personal, emotional unfinished business."[417] Spiritual bypassing can be harmful when it allows individual feelings of positivity and detachment to override difficult, collective issues.

Turtle Island—a widely used Indigenous name for the land now called North America. It comes from the oral histories of Algonquian- and Iroquoian-speaking peoples.[418] To read a Turtle Island origin story, please see *Braiding Sweetgrass*, by Potawatomi scientist Robin Wall Kimmerer.

Underbelly—a term shared by Yeye Luisah Teish. In the underbelly, unexamined wounds of colonialism, imperialism, patriarchy, war, and racism fester. The underbelly enables ongoing denial, apathy, and resistance by hiding these realities from personal understanding as well as broad public discourse.

Whiteness—a socially constructed identity that was engineered to consolidate resources among elite, landowning men. To learn more about whiteness, please reference some of the many resources available on the topic or see my Historical Notes on the Invention of Whiteness in the Appendices.

White Peril—a term developed by Calvin Terrell,[419] a Black diversity, equity, and justice educator. Calvin defines White Peril as an outgrowth of historic trauma generated by violent historic eras perpetrated by Europeans, against Europeans. He shares:

> When identities are constructed around defending white dominance, and when humans called white are unwilling or unable to deconstruct these identities, this creates anxiety and fragility. Avoiding consideration of privilege leads to militarization. The souls of humans called white know that white supremacy is a lie. This lie creates dissonance, feeding a brokenhearted search for identity through materialism.[420]

I've used "White Peril" in this book to unpack the dangerous consequences of whiteness that I have personally experienced.

White Privilege—confers systemic financial, educational, social, and medical advantages upon white people. In societies characterized by racial discrimination, white privilege shapes reality in powerful ways. Privilege benefits white people differently, depending on class.

White Supremacy—Eriel Tchekwie Deranger (Dënesųłiné) and Carole Monture (Kanienkehá:ka)* define white supremacy as an ideological perspective. Over centuries, this ideology of dominance has idealized white bodies and minds. It consolidates resources and power within settler-colonial institutions and is reinforced by legal and economic systems. People of all identities can work together to dismantle white supremacy.

Wit(h)nessing—I first learned the term "wit(h)nessing" from Nigerian author Báyò Akómoláfé,[421] who uses the word to emphasize

---

* Eriel and Carole work with Indigenous Climate Action (https://www.indigenous climateaction.com/). They shared this definition at the 2023 National Bioneers Conference (https://bioneers.org/). I've used it here with their permission.

the relational quality of knowing and seeing. "Wit(h)nessing" originates in the work of artist, psychologist, and Freudian scholar Bracha
Ettinger.[422] I experience wit(h)nessing as an empathetic practice
that allows others' experiences to exist in my presence, without
subjecting them to my reactions. It is relational, compassionate,
and intuitive.

Bibliography

Books

Augustine, Sarah. *The Land Is Not Empty: Following Jesus in Dismantling the Doctrine of Discovery*. Harrisonburg, VA: Herald Press, 2021.

Baldwin, James. *The Fire Next Time*. New York: Vintage International, 1993.

Baptist, Edward E. *The Half Has Never Been Told: Slavery and the Making of American Capitalism*. New York: Basics Books, 2014.

Beauchamp, Elizabeth. *The Braes O' Balquhuidder: An Historical Guide to the District*. Glasgow, Scotland: Heatherbank Press, 1981.

Benedek, Emily. *The Wind Won't Know Me: A History of the Navajo-Hopi Dispute*. New York: Vintage Books, 1992.

Bennett, Margaret. *Scottish Customs from the Cradle to the Grave*. Edinburgh: Polygon, 1992.

Beresford-Kroeger, Diana. *To Speak for the Trees: My Life's Journey from Ancient Celtic Wisdom to a Healing Vision of the Forest*. Toronto: Random House Canada, 2019.

Black Elk and John G. Neihardt. *Black Elk Speaks*. Lincoln, NE: Bison Books, 2014.

Black Elk, Wallace, and William S. Lyon. *Black Elk: The Sacred Ways of a Lakota*. San Francisco: Harper & Row, 1990.

Blackhawk, Ned. *The Rediscovery of America: Native Peoples and the Unmaking of U.S. History*. New Haven, CT: Yale University Press, 2023.

Blackie, Sharon. *Foxfire, Wolfskin, and Other Stories of Shapeshifting Women*. Tewkesbury, UK: September Publishing, 2019.

———. *If Women Rose Rooted: The Journey to Authenticity and Belonging*. Tewkesbury, UK: September Publishing, 2016.

Brave Bird, Mary, and Richard Erdoes. *Lakota Woman*. New York: Harper Perennial, 1991.

Brave Heart, Basil. *The Spiritual Journey of a Brave Heart*. Self-published. 2011.

brown, adrienne maree. *Emergent Strategy: Shaping Change, Changing Worlds*. Chico, CA: AK Press, 2017.

Bruchac, Joseph. *Navajo Long Walk*. Illustrated by Shonto Begay. Washington, DC: National Geographic Society, 2002.

Butler, Octavia. *Kindred*. Boston: Beacon Press, 2003.

Calloway, Colin G. *White People, Indians, and Highlanders: Tribal Peoples and Colonial Encounters in Scotland and America*. New York: Oxford University Press, 2008.

Carlson-Manathara, Elizabeth, and Gladys Rowe, *Living in Indigenous Sovereignty*. Nova Scotia, Canada: Fernwood Publishing, 2021.

Carmichael, Alexander. *Carmina Gadelica: Hymns and Incantations Collected in the Highlands and Islands of Scotland*. 1900. Reprint, Edinburgh: Floris Books, 1992.

Charles, Mark, and Soong-Chan Rah. *Unsettling Truths: The Ongoing, Dehumanizing Legacy of the Doctrine of Discovery*. Downers Grove, IL: InterVarsity Press, 2019.

Coates, Ta-Nehisi. *Between the World and Me*. New York: Spiegel & Grau, 2015.

Colorado, Apela. *Woman Between the Worlds: A Call to Your Ancestral and Indigenous Wisdom*. Carlsbad, CA: Hay House, 2021.

Curtis, Morgan. *Decolonial Dames of America*, vol. II, no. 1. New York: The Constellation Project, 2023. www.morganhcurtis.com/decolonial-dames-of-america.

Dashú, Max. *Witches and Pagans: Women in European Folk Religion*. Richmond, CA: Veleda Press, 2016.

Davis, Fania. *The Little Book of Race and Restorative Justice: Black Lives, Healing, and US Social Transformation*. New York: Good Books, 2019.

DeGruy, Joy. *Post Traumatic Slave Syndrome: America's Legacy of Enduring Injury and Healing*. Portland, OR: Joy DeGruy Publications, 2017.

Denetdale, Jennifer. *The Long Walk: The Forced Navajo Exile*. New York: Chelsea House, 2007.

Devine, T. M. *The Scottish Clearances: A History of the Dispossessed*. New York: Penguin Random House, 2018.

DeWolf, Thomas Norman, and Sharon Leslie Morgan. *Gather at the Table: The Healing Journey of a Daughter of Slavery and a Son of the Slave Trade*. Boston: Beacon Press, 2012.

DiAngelo, Robin. *White Fragility: Why It's So Hard for White People to Talk about Racism*. Boston, MA: Beacon Press, 2018.

Donmoyer, Patrick J. *Hex Signs: Myth and Meaning in Pennsylvania Dutch Barn Stars*. Kutztown, PA: Pennsylvania German Cultural Heritage Center at Kutztown University of Pennsylvania, 2013.

———. *Powwowing in Pennsylvania: Healing, Cosmology, & Tradition in the Dutch Country*. Kutztown, PA: Pennsylvania German Cultural Heritage Center at Kutztown University of Pennsylvania, 2015.

Dunbar-Ortiz, Roxanne. *An Indigenous Peoples' History of the United States*. Boston, MA: Beacon Press, 2014.

———. *Not a Nation of Immigrants: Settler Colonialism, White Supremacy, and a History of Erasure and Exclusion*. Boston, MA: Beacon Press, 2021.

Dunlap, Louise. *Inherited Silence: Listening to the Land, Healing the Colonizer Mind*. New York: New Village Press, 2022.

Duran, Eduardo. *Healing the Soul Wound: Trauma-Informed Counseling for Indigenous Communities*. New York: Teachers College Press, 2019.

Ehrenreich, Barbara. *Dancing in the Streets: A History of Collective Joy*. New York, NY: Metropolitan Books, 2006.

Erdrich, Heid E., ed. *New Poets of Native Nations*. Minneapolis, MN: Graywolf Press, 2018.

Evans-Wentz, W. Y. *The Fairy Faith in Celtic Countries*. New Hyde Park, NY: University Books, 1966.

Flaherty, Jordan. *No More Heroes: Grassroots Challenges to the Savior Mentality*. Chico, CA: AK Press, 2016.

Forbes, Jack D. *Columbus and Other Cannibals*. New York: Seven Stories Press, 2008.

Foster, Sally M. *Picts, Gaels, and Scots*. London: BT Batsford, 2004.

Fry, Rosalie K. *Secret of the Ron Mor Skerry*. New York: New York Review of Books, 1957.

Gallagher, Thomas. *Paddy's Lament: Ireland 1846–1847: Prelude to Hatred*. New York: Houghton Mifflin Harcourt, 1982.

Goodare, Julian. *The European Witch-Hunt*. London and New York: Routledge Taylor & Francis Group, 2016.

Green, Miranda J. *Dictionary of Celtic Myth and Legend*. London: Thames & Hudson, 1992.

Greendeer, Danielle, Anthony Perry, and Alexis Bunten. *Keepunumuk: Weeâchumun's Thanksgiving Story*. Illustrated by Gary Meeches Sr. Watertown, MA: Charlesbridge, 2022.

Hausdoerffer, John, Brooke Parry Hecht, Melissa K. Nelson, and Katherine Kassouf Cummings, eds. *What Kind of Ancestor Do You Want to Be?* Chicago, IL: University of Chicago Press, 2021.

Heinrichs, Steve, ed. *Buffalo Shout, Salmon Cry: Conversations on Creation, Land Justice, and Life Together*. Harrisonburg, VA: Herald Press, 2013.

Hillyer, Carolyn. *Her Bone Bundle*. Dartmoor, UK: Braided River Books, 2020.

Hochschild, Adam. *King Leopold's Ghost*. Boston: Mariner Books, Houghton Mifflin Harcourt, 1999.

Horne, Gerald. *The Dawning of the Apocalypse: The Roots of Slavery, White Supremacy, Settler Colonialism, and Capitalism in the Long Sixteenth Century*. New York: Monthly Review Press, 2020.

Irving, Debby. *Waking Up White and Finding Myself in the Story of Race*. Cambridge, MA: Elephant Room Press, 2014.

Isenberg, Nancy. *White Trash: The Untold 400-Year History of Class in America*. New York: Viking, 2016.

Iversen, Lisa, ed. *Whiteness Is Not an Ancestor: Essays on Life and Lineage by White Women*. Bellingham, WA: Center for Ancestral Blueprints Publishing, 2020.

Jackson, Regina, and Saira Rao. *White Women: Everything You Already Know about Your Own Racism and How to Do Better*. New York: Penguin Random House, 2023.

Jarvie, Frances, and Gordon Jarvie. *Scotland's Vikings*. Edinburgh: National Museums Scotland, 2008.

Jealous, Ann Todd, and Caroline T. Haskell, eds. *Combined Destinies: Whites Sharing Grief about Racism*. Washington, DC: Potomac Books, 2013.

Jenkinson, Stephen. *Come of Age: The Case for Elderhood in a Time of Trouble*. New York: Penguin Random House, 2018.

Johnson, Broderick H., ed. *Navajo Stories of the Long Walk Period*. Illustrated by Raymond Johnson and Teddy Draper Jr. Tsaile, AZ: Navajo Community College Press, 1973.

Johnston, Lyla June, and Joy De Vito. *Lifting Hearts off the Ground: Declaring Indigenous Rights in Poetry*. Winnipeg, MB: Mennonite Church Canada, 2007.

Khan-Cullors, Patrisse, and asha bandele. *When They Call You a Terrorist: A Black Lives Matter Memoir*. New York: St. Martin's Griffin, 2017.

Kimmerer, Robin Wall. *Braiding Sweetgrass: Indigenous Wisdom, Scientific Knowledge, and the Teachings of Plants*. Minneapolis, MN: Milkweed Editions, 2013.

King, Martin Luther, Jr. *Strength to Love*. New York: Harper & Row, 1963.

Krawec, Patty. *Becoming Kin: An Indigenous Call to Unforgetting the Past and Reimagining Our Future*. Minneapolis, MN: Broadleaf Books, 2022.

Laing, Lloyd, and Jennifer Laing. *The Picts and the Scots*. Stroud, UK: Alan Sutton, 1993.

Land Acknowledgements: Historical Context and Contemporary Inquiries. Hudson, NY: Sequoia Samanvaya, n.d. https://www.sequoiasamanvaya.com/.

Levack, Brian P., ed. *The Oxford Handbook of Witchcraft in Early Modern Europe and Colonial America*. Oxford, UK: Oxford University Press, 2014.

Lushwala, Arkan. *The Time of the Black Jaguar: An Offering of Indigenous Wisdom for the Continuity of Life on Earth*. Ribera, NM: CreateScape, 2012.

MacFarlane, Robert. *The Lost Spells*. Illustrated by Jackie Morris. Toronto: Anansi, 2017.

MacLeod, Sharon Paice. *Celtic Myth and Religion: A Study of Traditional Belief, with Newly Translated Prayers, Poems, and Songs*. Jefferson, NC: MacFarland & Company Inc., 2012.

———. *The Divine Feminine in Ancient Europe: Goddesses, Sacred Women, and the Origins of Western Culture*. Jefferson, NC: MacFarland & Company Inc., 2014.

MacNair, Rachel M. *Perpetration-Induced Traumatic Stress: The Psychological Consequences of Killing*. London: Praeger, 2002.

Mails, Thomas E. *Fools Crow: Wisdom and Power*. Tulsa, OK: Council Oak Books, 1991.

Marshall, Joseph M., III. *The Day the World Ended at Little Bighorn: A Lakota History*. New York: Viking, 2007.

McIntosh, Alastair. *Soil and Soul: People Versus Corporate Power*. London: Aurum Press, 2002.

McFatter, Don, and Bobbie McFatter. *The McFatter Family Book*. Self-published, 1998.

Menakem, Resmaa. *My Grandmother's Hands: Racialized Trauma and the Pathway to Healing Our Minds and Bodies*. Las Vegas, NV: Central Recovery Press, 2017.

Merculieff, Ilarion. *Wisdom Keeper: One Man's Journey to Honor the Untold History of the Unangan People*. Berkeley, CA: North Atlantic Books, 2016.

Mitchell, Sherri. *Sacred Instructions: Indigenous Wisdom for Living Spirit-Based Change*. Berkeley, CA: North Atlantic Books, 2018.

Moffat, Alistair. *Before Scotland: The Story of Scotland Before History*. London: Thames & Hudson, 2005.

Monaghan, Patricia, and Michael McDermott, eds. *Brigit: Sun of Womanhood*. Las Vegas, NV: Goddess Ink, 2013.

Morales, Aurora Levins. *Medicine Stories: Essays for Radicals*. Durham, NC: Duke University Press, 2019.

Morrison, Toni. *Beloved.* New York: Penguin, 1987.

Mosionier, Beatrice. *In Search of April Raintree.* Winnipeg, MB: Portage & Main Press, 2008.

Narváez, Peter, ed. *New Fairylore Essays.* Lexington, KY: University Press of Kentucky, 1991.

Neiman, Garrett. *Rich White Men: What It Takes to Uproot the Old Boys' Club and Transform America.* New York: Legacy Lit, 2023.

Newcomb, Steven T. *Pagans in the Promised Land: Decoding the Doctrine of Christian Discovery.* Chicago, IL: Chicago Review Press, 2008.

Nies, Judith. *Unreal City: Las Vegas, Black Mesa, and the Fate of the West.* New York: Nation Books, 2014.

Nelson, Melissa K., ed. *Original Instructions: Indigenous Teachings for a Sustainable Future.* Rochester, VT: Bear & Company, 2008.

Nelson, S. D. *Crazy Horse and Custer: Born Enemies.* Illustrated by the author. New York: Abrams Books for Young Readers, 2021.

Nerburn, Kent. *Neither Wolf nor Dog: On Forgotten Roads with an Indian Elder.* Novato, CA: New World Library, 1994.

Newcomb, Steven. *Pagans in the Promised Land: Decoding the Doctrine of Christian Discovery.* Golden, CO: Fulcrum Publishing, 2008.

Newton, Michael. *Warriors of the Word: The World of the Scottish Highlanders.* Edinburgh: Birlinn, 2019.

Noble, Gordon, and Nicholas Evans. *The King in the North: The Pictish Realms of Fortriu and Ce.* Edinburgh: Birlinn, 2020.

Ó Crualaoich, Gearóid. *The Book of the Cailleach: Stories of the Wise-Woman Healer.* Cork, Ireland: Cork University Press, 2003.

O'Donohue, John. *To Bless the Space Between Us: A Book of Blessings.* New York: Convergent Books, 2008.

Oluo, Ijeoma. *So You Want to Talk about Race.* New York: Seal Press, 2018.

Ottey, Darcy. *Rites and Responsibilities: A Guide to Growing Up.* Big Pine, CA: Lost Borders Press, 2022.

Painter, Nell Irvin. *The History of White People.* New York: W. W. Norton, 2010.

Pittelman, Karen, and Resource Generation. *Classified: How to Stop Hiding Your Privilege and Use It for Social Change.* New York: Soft Skull Press, 2005.

Potter, David. *Constantine the Emperor.* New York: Oxford University Press, 2013.

Prechtel, Martín. *The Smell of Rain on Dust: Grief and Praise.* Berkeley, CA: North Atlantic Books, 2015.

Raffo, Susan. *Liberated to the Bone: Histories, Bodies, Futures.* Chico, CA: AK Press, 2022.

Rasmussen, Rune Hjarnø. *The Nordic Animist Year.* Denmark: Nordic Animism, 2019.

Resendéz, Andrés. *The Other Slavery: The Uncovered Story of Indian Enslavement in America.* Boston, MA: Houghton Mifflin Harcourt, 2016.

Rimington, Jess, and Joanna L. Cea. *Beloved Economies: Transforming How We Work.* Vancouver, BC: Page Two, 2022.

Sanchez, Anita. *The Four Sacred Gifts: Indigenous Wisdom for Modern Times.* New York: Enliven Books, 2017.

Schaefer, Carol. *Grandmothers Counsel the World: Women Elders Offer Their Vision for Our Planet*. Boston, MA: Trumpeter, 2006.

Sleeter, Christine. *The Inheritance*. Monterey, CA: Sleeter, 2018.

St. Pierre, Mark, and Tilda Long Soldier. *Walking in the Sacred Manner: Healers, Dreamers, and Pipe Carriers—Medicine Women of the Plains Indians*. New York: Simon & Schuster, 1995.

Stewart, Douglas. *MacTalla: Echoes of our Ancestral Past*. Canada: Hunter Rose, 1974.

Stokes, John, and Kanawahienton. *Thanksgiving Address: Greetings to the Natural World, Ohén:ton Karihwatéhkwen—Words Before All Else*. Illustrated by Kahionhes. Corrales, NM: Six Nations Indian Museum and the Tracking Project, 1993.

TallBear, Kim. *Native American DNA: Tribal Belonging and the False Promise of Genetic Science*. Minneapolis, MN: University of Minnesota Press, 2013.

Teish, Luisah. *Jambalaya: The Natural Woman's Book of Personal Charms and Practical Rituals*. San Francisco, CA: HarperCollins, 1985.

Thompson, David. *The People of the Sea*. London: Granada, 1980.

Treuer, David. *The Heartbeat of Wounded Knee: Native America from 1890 to the Present*. New York: Riverhead Books, 2019.

Tutu, Desmond, and Mpho Tutu. *The Book of Forgiving: The Fourfold Path for Healing Ourselves and Our World*. New York: HarperOne, 2014.

Twist, Lynne. *The Soul of Money: Reclaiming the Wealth of Our Inner Resources*. New York: W. W. Norton, 2006.

Villanueva, Edgar. *Decolonizing Wealth: Indigenous Wisdom to Heal Divides and Restore Balance*. Oakland, CA: Berrett-Koehler, 2018.

Von Petzinger, Genevieve. *The First Signs: Unlocking the Mysteries of the World's Oldest Symbols*. New York: Atria, 2017.

Waheed, Nayyirah. *Nejma*. Self-published, 2014.

———. *Salt*. Self-published, 2013.

Waziyatawin and Michael Yellow Bird, eds. *For Indigenous Minds Only: A Decolonization Handbook*. Santa Fe, NM: Center for Advanced Research Press, 2012.

Werner, Jürgen Kremer, and R. Jackson-Paton. *Ethnoautobiography: Stories and Practices for Unlearning Whiteness/Decolonization/Uncovering Ethnicities*. Sebastopol, CA: ReVision, 2014.

Wilkerson, Isabelle. *Caste: The Origins of Our Discontents*. New York: Random House, 2020.

Wolynn, Mark. *It Didn't Start with You: How Inherited Family Trauma Shapes Who We Are and How to End the Cycle*. New York: Penguin Books, 2017.

Woodham-Smith, Cecil. *The Great Hunger: Ireland 1845–1849*. New York: Penguin, 1991.

Younging, Gregory. *Elements of Indigenous Style: A Guide for Writing by and about Indigenous Peoples*. Edmonton, AB: Brush Education, 2018.

Yunkaporta, Tyson. *Sand Talk: How Indigenous Thinking Can Save the World*. New York: HarperOne, 2020.

Periodicals

Abourezk, Kevin. "Native American psychologists slam police tactics a year after Standing Rock." Indianz.com, October 30, 2017. https://www.indianz.com/News/2017/10/30/native-american-psychologists-slam-polic.asp.

Al Jazeera. "Vatican rejects 'Doctrine of Discovery' justifying colonialism." March 30, 2023. https://www.aljazeera.com/news/2023/3/30/vatican-rejects-doctrine-of-discovery-justifying-colonialism.

Alexie, Sherman. "The 'I' in BIPOC." *Persuasion*, June 2, 2023. https://www.persuasion.community/p/the-i-in-bipoc.

Amnesty International. "Justice Department Must Investigate Policing of Standing Rock Demonstrations" (press release). November 30, 2016. https://www.amnestyusa.org/press-releases/justice-department-must-investigate-policing-of-standing-rock-demonstrations/.

Animikii, "Building Trust before Truth: How Non-Indigenous Canadians Become Allies." February 22, 2019. https://www.animikii.com/news/building-trust-before-truth-how-non-indigenous-canadians-become-allies.

Armstrong, Megan. "From Lynching to Central Park Karen: How White Women Weaponize White Womanhood." *Hasting Women's Law Journal* 32, no. 1 (Winter 2021): 27–50. https://repository.uclawsf.edu/cgi/viewcontent.cgi?article=1449&context=hwlj.

Bioneers. "The Native American Prophecy of the Black Snake." 2016. https://bioneers.org/the-native-american-prophecy-of-the-black-snake/.

Blumberg, Jess. "A Brief History of the Salem Witch Trials." *Smithsonian Magazine*, October 24, 2022. https://www.smithsonianmag.com/history/a-brief-history-of-the-salem-witch-trials-175162489/.

Boscacci, Louise. "Wit(h)nessing." *Environmental Humanities* 10, no. 1 (2018): 343–47. https://read.dukeupress.edu/environmental-humanities/article/10/1/343/134705/Wit-h-nessing.

Brave Heart, Basil. Interview with Hilary Giovale. *Bioneers*, n.d. https://bioneers.org/conversation-with-oglala-lakota-elder-basil-brave-heart-part-1-zmbz2108/.

Brave Heart, Basil, and Hilary Giovale. "129 years after Wounded Knee, is forgiveness possible?" *Rapid City Journal*, January 17, 2020. https://rapidcityjournal.com/years-after-wounded-knee-is-forgiveness-possible/article_b6786b35-86fd-52fd-b863-0d24516ccb9b.html.

Brewer, Suzette. "They were taken from their families as children. Can that trauma be healed?" *National Geographic*, April 11, 2023. https://www.nationalgeographic.com/premium/article/native-americans-separated-families-children-feature.

Brown, Alleen. "Medics describe how police sprayed Standing Rock demonstrators with tear gas and water cannons." *The Intercept*, November 21, 2016. https://theintercept.com/2016/11/21/medics-describe-how-police-sprayed-standing-rock-demonstrators-with-tear-gas-and-water-cannons/.

Calvert, Brian. "The myth of American progress." *High Country News*, August 20, 2018. https://www.hcn.org/issues/50.14/editors-note-the-myth-of-american-progress.

Democracy Now! "Indigenous Activist Zip-Tied & Locked in Dog Kennel for 6 Hours for Protesting Dakota Access Pipeline." November 16, 2016. https://www.democracynow.org/2016/11/16/indigenous_activist_zip_tied_locked_in.

———. "Standing Rock Special: Unlicensed #DAPL Guards Attacked Water Protectors with Dogs & Pepper Spray." November 24, 2016. https://www.democracynow.org/2016/11/24/standing_rock_special_unlicensed_dapl_guards.

Giovale, Hilary. "Tribal Appropriations in Bellydance." *Gods&Radicals*, December 17, 2021. https://abeautifulresistance.org/site/2021/11/15/tribal-appropriations-in-bellydance.

Granillo, Gabriel. "80 years of Snowbowl: A history of the innovative and controversial ski resort." *Arizona Daily Sun*, February 22, 2018. https://azdailysun.com/flaglive/cover_story/80-years-of-snowbowl-a-history-of-the-innovative-and-controversial-ski-resort/article_c476a34c-20d5-55a3-86c8-25b00e3522fc.html.

History. "Manifest Destiny." November 15, 2019. https://www.history.com/topics/westward-expansion/manifest-destiny.

History. "This Day in History: Kit Carson begins his campaign against Native Americans," July 7, 2020. https://www.history.com/this-day-in-history/kit-carsons-campaign-against-the-indians.

Holmes, Kristen, and Gregory Wallace. "Biden Administration will not shut down Dakota Access Pipeline during environmental review, DOJ tells court." CNN, April 9, 2021. https://www.cnn.com/2021/04/09/politics/dakota-access-pipeline-biden-administration/index.html.

Katz, Brigit. "Early Briton Had Dark Skin and Light Eyes, DNA Analysis Shows." *Smithsonian Magazine*, February 7, 2018. https://www.smithsonianmag.com/smart-news/ancient-briton-had-dark-skin-and-light-eyes-dna-analysis-shows-180968097/.

Kaur, Harmeet. "Indigenous people across the US want their land back—and the movement is gaining momentum." CNN, November 26, 2020. https://www.cnn.com/2020/11/25/us/indigenous-people-reclaiming-their-lands-trnd/index.html.

Kimmerer, Robin Wall. "Corn Tastes Better on the Honor System." *Emergence Magazine*, n.d. https://emergencemagazine.org/feature/corn-tastes-better/, accessed December 20, 2023.

Klein, Christopher. "When America Despised the Irish: The 19th Century's Refugee Crisis." *History*, June 1, 2022. https://www.history.com/news/when-america-despised-the-irish-the-19th-centurys-refugee-crisis.

Knobel, Dale T. "Celtic Exodus: The Famine Irish, Ethnic Stereotypes, and the Cultivation of American Radical Nationalism." *Radharc* 2 (November 2001): 3–25.

Levin, Sam. "Dakota Access pipeline protests: UN group investigates human rights abuses." *The Guardian*, October 31, 2016. https://www.theguardian.com/us-news/2016/oct/31/dakota-access-pipeline-protest-investigation-human-rights-abuses.

MacInnes, John. "The Panegyric Code in Gaelic poetry." Cited by Ruth Lee Martin in "Paradise Imagined: Songs of Scots Gaelic Migrants in Australia, 1850–1940." *Humanities Research* 19, no. 2 (2013).

Matthews, Dylan. "The unbearable whiteness of American charities." *Vox*, July 1, 2019. https://www.vox.com/future-perfect/2019/7/1/18715513/philanthropy-people-of-color-racial-wealth-gap-edgar-villanueva.

McGivney, Annette. "Skiing on a sacred mountain: Indigenous Americans stand against a resort's expansion." *The Guardian*, June 21, 2022. https://www.theguardian.com/world/2022/jun/19/indigenous-native-american-ski-resort-sewage-water-arizona.

Native Knowledge 360°. "Treaties Still Matter: The Dakota Access Pipeline." National Museum of the American Indian, Smithsonian Institution, 2018. https://americanindian.si.edu/nk360/plains-treaties/dapl.

New York Times. "The Native American Boarding School System." August 30, 2023. https://www.nytimes.com/interactive/2023/08/30/us/native-american-boarding-schools.html.

Noble, Ross. "The Cultural Impact of the Scottish Clearances." BBC, February 17, 2011. https://www.bbc.co.uk/history/british/civil_war_revolution/scotland_clearances_01.shtml.

Penniman, Leah. "The Gift of Ecological Humility." *Yes!* magazine, Spring 2020. https://www.yesmagazine.org/issue/ecological-civilization/2021/02/16/afro-indigenous-land-practices.

Pew. "Racial Disparities Persist in Many U.S. Jails." May 16, 2023. https://www.pewtrusts.org/en/research-and-analysis/issue-briefs/2023/05/racial-disparities-persist-in-many-us-jails.

Pitrelli, Stefano, and Amanda Coletta. "Pope apologizes for 'deplorable conduct' of some Catholics in residential schools." *Washington Post*, April 1, 2022. https://www.washingtonpost.com/world/2022/04/01/canada-pope-francis-apologizes-residential-school/.

Pruitt, Sarah. "Broken Treaties with Native American Tribes: Timeline." *History*, July 12, 2023. https://www.history.com/news/native-american-broken-treaties.

Pullella, Phillip, and Tim Johnson. "Pope apologizes for 'deplorable evil' of Canadian Indigenous schools." Reuters, July 26, 2022. https://www.reuters.com/world/americas/pope-apologizes-canada-evil-residential-indigenous-schools-2022-07-25/.

Raab, Diana. "What Is Spiritual Bypassing?" *Psychology Today*, January 23, 2019. https://www.psychologytoday.com/us/blog/the-empowerment-diary/201901/what-is-spiritual-bypassing.

Scott, Kristy. "Twilight of the Gaels as ancient tongue falls silent." *The Guardian*, February 12, 2003. https://www.theguardian.com/uk/2003/feb/13/scotland.britishidentity.

Strickland, Patrick. "Life on the Pine Ridge Native American reservation." Al Jazeera, November 2, 2016. https://www.aljazeera.com/features/2016/11/2/life-on-the-pine-ridge-native-american-reservation.

The Week. "A brief history of billionaire philanthropists and the people who hate them." January 9, 2016. https://theweek.com/articles/597963/brief-history-billionaire-philanthropists-people-who-hate.

Torthman, Joshua. "The Origins of 'Privilege.'" *New Yorker*, May 12, 2014. https://www.newyorker.com/books/page-turner/the-origins-of-privilege.

Tuck, Eve, and K. Wayne Yang. "Decolonization Is Not a Metaphor." *Decolonization: Indigeneity, Education & Society* 1, no. 1 (2012): 1–40, https://clas.osu.edu/sites/clas.osu.edu/files/Tuck%20and%20Yang%202012%20Decolonization%20is%20not%20a%20metaphor.pdf.

Villarosa, Linda. "Why America's Black Mothers and Babies Are in a Life-or-Death Crisis." *New York Times Magazine*, April 11, 2018. https://www.nytimes.com/2018/04/11/magazine/black-mothers-babies-death-maternal-mortality.html.

Walker, Mark. "Tribes Want Medals Awarded for Wounded Knee Massacre Rescinded." *New York Times*, November 3, 2021. https://www.nytimes.com/2021/04/23/us/politics/tribes-medal-honor-wounded-knee.html.

Warfield, Zenobia Jeffries. "What Black America Is Owed." *Yes!* magazine, November 12, 2019. https://www.yesmagazine.org/issue/building-bridges/2019/11/12/the-collective-healing-that-is-owed/.

Wiseman, Andrew. "The Kilted Exciseman: Alexander Carmichael (1832–1912)." *History Scotland* 11, no. 1 (January/February 2011): 18–23.

Websites and Blogs

Akómoláfé, Báyò. "We Will Dance with Mountains." https://www.dancingwith-mountains.com/, accessed December 14, 2023.

———. "Welcome Traveller." 2022. https://bayoakomolafe.net/.

American Indian Movement. "Trail of Broken Treaties." 1972. https://cwis.org/wp-content/uploads/documents/premium/293wb10017.pdf.

American Swedish Institute. 2023. https://asimn.org/.

Ancestral Fire. 2023. https://ancestralfire.ca/.

Baldwin, James. "National Press Club speech." 1986. https://www.youtube.com/watch?v=7_1ZEYgtijk.

Bioneers. "Indigeneity Program." https://bioneers.org/indigeneity-program/, accessed December 22, 2023.

Bioneers. "Nina Talks Cultivating Women's Leadership." https://bioneers.org/nina-talks-cultivating-womens-leadership/, accessed December 14, 2023.

Brigit's Garden. https://brigitsgarden.ie/, accessed December 20, 2023.

Cailleach's Herbarium. "Saining Not Smudging—Purification, Blessing, and Lustration in Scottish Folk Magic Practice." 2022. https://cailleachs-herbarium.com/2019/02/saining-not-smudging-purification-and-lustration-in-scottish-folk-magic-practice/.

———. "Scottish Cultural Appropriation—Revisited" (blog posting). https://cailleachs-herbarium.com/2023/03/scottish-cultural-appropriation-revisited/, accessed December 21, 2023.

California Truth & Healing Council. https://tribalaffairs.ca.gov/cthc/, accessed December 22, 2023.

Carlisle Indian School Project. https://carlisleindianschoolproject.com/past/, accessed December 22, 2023.

Center for Support and Protection of Indian Religions and Indigenous Traditions. "Stop the Mankind Project's exploitation of Indigenous traditions." 2022. https://www.spiritprotection.org/.

Choctaw Indian Fair. https://www.choctawindianfair.com/, accessed December 22, 2023.

Choctaw Nation. "Choctaw and Irish History." https://www.choctawnation.com/about/history/irish-connection/, accessed December 26, 2023.

Chordata Capital. https://chordatacapital.com/, accessed December 21, 2023.

Coalition to Dismantle the Doctrine of Discovery. https://dismantlediscovery.org/, accessed December 26, 2023.

Collective Wisdoms. "Indigenous Peacekeeping from the Individual to the Collective, from Information to Knowledge to Wisdom." https://www.collectivewisdoms.org/, accessed December 21, 2023.

Colorado Plateau Foundation. https://coloradoplateaufoundation.org/, accessed December 26, 2023.

Cultural Survival. "Sacred Homelands Returned to Wiyot Tribe." July 16, 2004. https://www.culturalsurvival.org/news/sacred-homelands-returned-wiyot-tribe.

Curtis, Morgan. "Ancestors and Money: A 6-Month Coaching Cohort." https://www.morganhcurtis.com/ancestors-money, accessed December 26, 2023.

Dean, David. "Roots Deeper than Whiteness." *White Awake*. 2018. https://whiteawake.org/author/daviddean5/.

Ekvn-Yefolecv. "Pum ekvnv resyicet owēs: Returning to our homelands." 2021. https://www.ekvn-yefolecv.org/.

Findhorn Foundation. "Welcome to The Isle of Erraid." https://www.erraid.com/, accessed December 14, 2023.

Gaels Jam 2024. "Dé th' ann an Jam? | What's a Jam?" https://www.novascotiagaelsjam.org/d%C3%A9-th-ann-whats-a-jam, accessed December 26, 2023.

Gardner, Emma. http://www.emmagardner.com/store/c1/Featured_Products.html, accessed December 20, 2023.

Gather Victoria. "Rosemary Oat Bannock for Imbolc." https://gathervictoria.com/2018/01/15/rosemary-oat-bannock-for-imbolc/, accessed December 22, 2023.

Good Relative. "Recovering European Ancestral Memory." https://www.goodrelative.com/resources/project-two-6paba, accessed December 20, 2023.

Healing Roots: Community with Diversity. 2023. https://healingrootscommunity.com/.

Hero Women Rising. https://www.herowomenrising.org/, accessed December 22, 2023.

Hidden Glen Folk School. https://www.hiddenglenfolk.org/, accessed December 21, 2023.

Hillyer, Carolyn. *The Braided River*. https://thebraidedriver.co.uk/, accessed December 22, 2023.

Homeland Heart. https://www.homelandheart.com/, accessed December 26, 2023.

Honor Water. https://www.honorwater.org/, accessed December 26, 2023.

Humans of Chauvet-Pont d'Arc. "Aurignacian cave art." The Chauvet-Pont d'Arc Cave. 2023. https://archeologie.culture.gouv.fr/chauvet/en/aurignacian-cave-art.

Indigenous Climate Action, 2023. https://www.indigenousclimateaction.com/.

Inequality.org. "Racial Economic Inequality: Racial Wealth Divide." https://inequality.org/facts/racial-inequality/#racial-wealth-divide, accessed December 20, 2023.

JFK Library. "JFK Profile in Courage Award." https://www.jfklibrary.org/events-and-awards/profile-in-courage-award/award-recipients/covid-courage-2021/darrell-r-marks, accessed December 21, 2023.

Johnston, Lyla June. https://www.lylajune.com/, accessed December 21, 2023.

———. "Medicine Theory." https://lylajune.wixsite.com/medicinetheory, accessed December 22, 2023.

———. "The Vast and Beautiful World of Indigenous Europe." *White Awake* (blog). January 31, 2018. https://whiteawake.org/2018/01/31/the-vast-and-beautiful-world-of-indigenous-europe/.

Jubilee Justice. https://www.jubileejustice.org/, accessed December 26, 2023.

Jump Scale. "Alaska Native Resilience Circles." https://www.wejumpscale.com/resilience-circles) and Indigenous-led tourism.

Kabia, John. "Fund 101: Intro to Participatory Grant-Making." Fund for Global Human Rights. February 25, 2021. https://globalhumanrights.org/commentary/fund-101-intro-to-participatory-grant-making/.

Kap, Himko Kaps. "The Creator Has Been Heard" (blog posting). May 4, 2016. http://longmarchtorome.com/.

Kindle Project. "Kindle Project Indigenous Women's Flow Fund Storytelling Report, 2021–2022." https://kindleproject.org/wp-content/uploads/2022/07/2022-IWFF-Storytelling-Report.pdf, accessed December 20, 2023.

———. "Kindle Project Indigenous Women's Flow Fund." 2023. http://kindleproject.org/iwff/.

Kuilan, Antonio. "Remembering Hatuey and the Tainos" (blog posting). http://antoniokuilan.com/blog/malta-hatuey-taino-history/, accessed December 21, 2023.

Labyrinth Society. "Learn about Labyrinths." https://labyrinthsociety.org/about-labyrinths, accessed December 14, 2023.

Lally, Jude. *Path of the Ancestral Mothers.* https://www.pathoftheancestralmothers.com/, accessed December 22, 2023.

LANDBACK. https://landback.org/, accessed February 21, 2024

Lemen, Jen. "this is the path of devotion." https://www.thepathofdevotion.com/, accessed December 26, 2023.

Liberated Capital. "Money as Medicine, Wisdom as Healing." 2022. https://decolonizingwealth.com/liberated-capital/, accessed December 21, 2023.

Library of Congress. "Shadows of War" (classroom materials). https://www.loc.gov/classroom-materials/immigration/german/shadows-of-war/, accessed December 22, 2023.

Lost Valley Uggool. "Experience Ireland Naturally." 2021. https://www.thelostvalley.ie/.

Maine Wabanaki-State Child Welfare Truth & Reconciliation Commission. "Beyond the Mandate: Continuing the Conversation." 2015. https://d3n8a8pro7vhmx.cloudfront.net/mainewabanakireach/pages/17/attachments/original/1468974047/TRC-Report-Expanded_July2015.pdf?1468974047.

McCabe, Pat. "Woman Stands Shining (Pat McCabe)." 2018. https://www.patmccabe.net/.

McKenna, Sìne. https://ancestralfire.ca/, accessed December 21, 2023.

McLaughlin, Mary. https://www.marymclaughlin.com/, accessed December 21, 2023.

Menakem, Resmaa. "Bodies of Culture and Two Forms of Soul." *Embodied Anti-Racist Education* (blog). February 13, 2023. https://www.resmaa.com/somatic-learnings/bodies-of-culture-and-two-forms-of-soul.

———. "Resmaa: Teaching Embodied Anti-Racism." *Embodied Anti-Racism Education.* https://www.resmaa.com/, accessed December 14, 2023.

Movement for Black Lives. "What Are Reparations?" https://m4bl.org/wp-content/uploads/2020/11/defining-reparations.pdf, accessed December 22, 2023.

Mulhall, Daniel. "Blog by Ambassador Mulhall on Black '47: Ireland's Great Famine and its after-effects." Ireland Department of Foreign Affairs. December 3, 2018. https://www.dfa.ie/irish-embassy/usa/about-us/ambassador/ambassadors-blog/black47irelandsgreatfamineanditsafter-effects/.

Na'ah Illahee Fund. "Our name, na'ah illahee, is Mother Earth in Chinook Wawa." https://www.naahillahee.org/, accessed December 26, 2023.

NAACP. "Criminal Justice Fact Sheet." 2023. https://naacp.org/resources/criminal-justice-fact-sheet.

National Bioneers Conference. 2023. https://bioneers.org/.

National Coalition of Blacks for Reparations in America (N'COBRA), https://ncobra.org/, accessed December 20, 2023.

National Law Enforcement Officers Memorial Fund. "Slave Patrols: An Early Form of American Policing." 2023. https://nleomf.org/slave-patrols-an-early-form-of-american-policing/.

National Museum of Ireland. "Country Life: Turlough Park, Castlebar, Co Mayo." 2023. https://www.museum.ie/en-IE/Museums/Country-Life/.

National Native American Boarding School Healing Coalition. https://boardingschoolhealing.org/, accessed December 21, 2023.

National Philanthropic Trust. "Charitable Giving Statistics." 2023 https://www.nptrust.org/philanthropic-resources/charitable-giving-statistics/.

Native American Bank. https://nativeamericanbank.com/, accessed December 21, 2023.

Native Americans in Philanthropy. "Native Americans Are 2.9% of U.S. Population but Receive 0.4% of Philanthropic Dollars." November 17, 2020. https://native-philanthropy.org/blog/2020/11/17/native-americans-are-2-of-u-s-population-but-receive-0-4-of-philanthropic-dollars.

Native Wellness Institute. https://www.nativewellness.com/, accessed December 21, 2023.

Nature Evolutionaries. https://www.natureevolutionaries.com/, accessed December 20, 2023.

NDN Collective. "Dedicated to Building Indigenous Power." https://ndncollective.org/, accessed December 26, 2023.

Nicholas V, Pope. "The Bull Romanus Pontifex" (English trans.). January 8, 1455. http://caid.ca/Bull_Romanus_Pontifex_1455.pdf, accessed December 22, 2023.

Nobel Women's Initiative. "16 Days of Activism." 2023. https://nobelwomensinitiative.org/.

Northern Arizona University. "Sustainable Communities." https://nau.edu/sustain-able-communities/program/, accessed December 14, 2023.

Okun, Tema. "White Supremacy Culture—Still Here" (blog post). May 2021. https://drive.google.com/file/d/1XR_7M_9qa64zZoo_JyFVTAjmjVU-uSz8/view.

One United Bank. https://www.oneunited.com/, accessed December 21, 2023.

Online Etymological Dictionary. "philanthropy." https://www.etymonline.com/search?q=philanthropy, accessed December 19, 2023.

Our Black Ancestry. https://ourblackancestry.com/, accessed December 21, 2023.

———. "The People behind the Portal." 2023. https://ourblackancestry.com/about.php.

Pachamama Alliance. https://pachamama.org/, accessed December 20, 2023.

———. "Together, we are healing ourselves and the Earth." https://www.pachamama.org/, accessed December 14, 2023.

Path of the Ancestral Mothers. https://www.pathoftheancestralmothers.com/, accessed December 20, 2023.

Philanthropy Roundtable. "Who Gives Most to Charity?" 2023, https://www.philanthropyroundtable.org/resource/who-gives-most-to-charity/, accessed December 26, 2023.

powell, john a. "Othering and Belonging Institute." 2023. https://belonging.berkeley.edu/john-powell.

Reparations 4 Slavery. "The Racial Wealth Gap: Understanding the Basis for Repair." 2023. https://reparations4slavery.com/the-racial-wealth-gap-understanding-the-economic-basis-for-repair/.

———. "White Trauma / White Supremacy." https://reparations4slavery.com/white_trauma_white_supremacy/, accessed December 21, 2023.

Resource Generation. https://resourcegeneration.org/, accessed December 26, 2023.

Rigobon, Silvana. https://www.silvanarigobon.com/about, accessed December 14, 2023.

Robinson, Amanda. "Turtle Island," in *The Canadian Encyclopedia*. https://www.the-canadianencyclopedia.ca/en/article/turtle-island,accessed December 20, 2023.

RSF Social Finance. https://rsfsocialfinance.org/, accessed December 21, 2023.

Scene on Radio. "Made in America (*Seeing White*, Part 3) Transcript." 2017.www.sceneonradio.org/wp-content/uploads/2017/11/SeeingWhite_Part3Transcript.pdf.

Seventh Generation Fund for Indigenous Peoples. http://www.7genfund.org, accessed December 26, 2023.

Share Fund. "Resources." https://thesharefund.org/resources/, accessed December 26, 2023.

Smithsonian, National Museum of the American Indian. "Nation to Nation: Treaties between the United States and American Indian Nations." https://americanindian.si.edu/nationtonation/treaty-of-fort-harmar-with-the-six-nations.html, accessed December 21, 2023.

Solidaire Network. "Black Liberation Pooled Fund." https://solidairenetwork.org/grantmaking/black-liberation-pooled-fund/, accessed December 26, 2023.

———. "Building the Fire Fund." https://solidairenetwork.org/building-the-fire-fund/, accessed December 26, 2023.

Soul of Money. "Fundraising from the Heart." https://soulofmoney.org/fundrais
ing-heart/, accessed December 14, 2023.

Spearitwurx. 2022. https://www.spearitwurx.com/experience-sankofa-pro ject1.html.

Springboard to Opportunities. http://www.springboardto.org/, accessed December
20, 2023.

———. "Magnolia Mothers Trust." https://springboardto.org/magnolia-moth-
ers-trust/, accessed December 26, 2023.

Strobel, Tita Leny. https://www.lenystrobel.com/, accessed December 26, 2023.

Suppressed Histories Archives. "Restoring Women to Cultural Memory." https://
www.suppressedhistories.net/, accessed December 20, 2023.

SURJ. "Why Class Matters." https://surj.org/resources/why-class-matters/, accessed
December 20, 2023.

Sweden, Government of. "With a culture that remains strong, some 20,00 Sami
people live in Sweden." https://sweden.se/life/people/sami-in-sweden, accessed
December 26, 2023.

Teish, Yeye Luisah. http://www.yeyeluisahteish.com/, accessed December 21, 2023.

Terrell, Calvin. https://www.calvinterrell.com/, accessed December 20, 2023.

Tewa Women United. "Nurturing and celebrating the collective power of beloved
families, communities, and Nung Ochuu Quiyo (Earth Mother)." https://
tewawomenunited.org/, accessed December 20, 2023.

The 1619 Project (docuseries). Viewing guide. January 24, 2023. https://1619education.
org/builder/lesson/1619-project-docuseries-viewing-guide.

Trees for Life. https://treesforlife.org.uk/, accessed December 20, 2023.

UN Department of Economic and Social Affairs. "Indigenous Peoples at the United
Nations." https://www.un.org/development/desa/indigenouspeoples/about-us.
html, accessed December 20, 2023.

University of Wales. Celtic Lexicon (a work in progress). https://www.wales.ac.uk/en/
CentreforAdvancedWelshCelticStudies/ResearchProjects/CompletedProjects/
TheCelticLanguagesandCulturalIdentity/CelticLexicon.aspx, accessed December
21, 2023.

Upstander Project. "Doctrine of Discovery." 2023. https://upstanderproject.org/
learn/guides-and-resources/first-light/doctrine-of-discovery.

Wales, Government of. "The magic of the coracle." 2023. https://www.visitwales.
com/inspire-me/days-out/magic-coracle.

Whirlpool Scotland. "The Corryvreckan Whirlpool." 2023. https://whirlpool-scot-
land.co.uk/180-2/.

Whitney Plantation. 2023. https://www.whitneyplantation.org/.

WikiTree. "McFatter Name Study." https://www.wikitree.com/wiki/Space:McFatter_
Name_Study, accessed December 14, 2023.

Wingfield, Jewels. https://jewelswingfield.com/, accessed December 20, 2023.

Winnemem Wintu Tribe of Buliyum Puyuuk (Mount Shasta). https://docs.google.
com/document/d/1rDjRLzoPJsWXCjj3haC3weI5siiZU2jxWBNwsoIpidE/edit,
accessed December 21, 2023.

Wisdom Weavers of the World. https://www.wisdomweavers.world/, accessed
December 20, 2023.

Wolynn, Mark. "Inherited Family Trauma." Family Constellation Institute. 2023. https://markwolynn.com/.

Woodworth, Alice, and Joe Parker. "How to Be an Ally to Indigenous Peoples: A White Paper in the Spirit of a Red Paper." Arcata, CA: Seventh Generation Fund, 2017. https://static1.squarespace.com/static/5e02559d2a11646407b253a3/t/5f89aa2c0ccf92609a8be266/1602857519575/Allies7GenFundFinal11-2017-3.pdf, accessed December 21, 2023.

World Bank. "Indigenous Peoples." 2023. https://www.worldbank.org/en/topic/indigenouspeoples.

Ziibiwing Center of Anishinabe Culture & Lifeways. "American Indian Boarding Schools: An Exploration of Global Ethnic and Cultural Cleansing." http://www.sagchip.org/ziibiwing/planyourvisit/pdf/aibscurrguide.pdf, accessed December 22, 2023.

Film, Video, and Audio Sources

Baldy, Cutcha Risling. "Indigenous Voices for Decolonized Futures." 2020 Bioneers keynote speech. https://bioneers.org/cutcha-risling-baldy-indigenous-voices-de-colonized-futures-zstf2101/.

Brother Mikey. *Happiness* (music album). Apple Music. 2019.

Brown, Brené. "The Power of Vulnerability," TED Talk. 2010. https://www.ted.com/talks/brene_brown_the_power_of_vulnerability?language=en.

Callahan, Peggy, and Louie Psihoyos, dirs. *Mission: Joy—Finding Happiness in Troubled Times* (film). 2021. https://www.netflix.com/title/81658684.

Campanelli, Stephen S., dir. *Indian Horse* (film). 2017. https://www.indianhorse.ca/en/film.

Changing of the Gods (docuseries). Episode 6: "From Othering to Belonging: The Circle of Human Concern." Startracks Productions. 2022.

Edwards, Bill. "Voices of Support for Long March to Rome—Arizona, USA" (video). 2015. https://vimeo.com/148686345.

Fowlis, Julie. "Òran an Ròin." *alterum* (music album). Music Scotland. 2021.

Fresh Air. "A 'Forgotten History' of How the U.S. Government Segregated America." NPR. May 3, 2017. https://www.npr.org/2017/05 /03/526655831/a-forgotten-history-of-how-the-u-s-government-segregated-america.

Herzog, Werner, dir. *Cave of Forgotten Dreams* (film). 2010. https://www.imdb.com/title/tt1664894/.

Hillyer, Carolyn. "Sago an Snîjo." *Winter Folded Everything Inside a Shawl of Feathers* (music album). Seventh Wave Music. 2018. https://www.seventhwavemusic.co.uk/product/winter-folded-everything-inside-a-shawl-of-feathers/.

Jacobs, Michael. *The Wellbriety Journey to Forgiveness* (film). 2011. https://www.youtube.com/watch?v=RYU8CSxieaA.

Johnson, Lyla June. "3,000-Year-Old Solutions to Modern Problems." TEDx Talk. n.d. https://www.youtube.com/watch?v=eH5zJxQETl4.

Leitch, Emma. "Oran na Maighdinn-Mhara" (music video). https://www.youtube.com/watch?v=7oi6Lrbhriw&ab_channel=EmmaLeitch-Topic.

MaMuse. "Power of Kindness." *Prayers for Freedom* (music album). No label. 2018.

Mazo, Adam, and Bender-Cudlip, dirs. *Dawnland: A Documentary about Survival and Stolen Children* (film). 2018. https://upstanderproject.org/films/dawnland.

McLaughlin, Mary. "Sealwoman/Yundah." *Daughter of Lir* (music album). Rowan Records. 1999.

Menakem, Resmaa. "Notice the Rage; Notice the Silence." *On Being with Krista Tippett* (podcast). April 15, 2021. https://onbeing.org/programs/resmaa-menakem-notice-the-rage-notice-the-silence/.

Mirrors and Hammers. "Forgiveness Ceremony: Veterans Kneel at Standing Rock" (video). n.d. https://www.youtube.com/watch?v=OjotlPIlRqw.

Moore, Tomm, dir. *Song of the Sea* (film). 2014.

Mudd, Victoria, and Maria Florio. *Broken Rainbow* (film). 1985. https://www.youtube.com/watch?v=W5z8OgMfXXc.

Nyandoro, Aisha. "What Does Wealth Mean to You?" TED Talk. October 2023. https://www.ted.com/talks/aisha_nyandoro_what_does_wealth_mean_to_you.

Ó hEadhra, Brian. Òrain *Cèilidh Teaghlaich* (music album). Brechin All Records. 2011.

Peck, Raoul, dir. *Exterminate All the Brutes* (documentary miniseries). 2021. https://www.hbo.com/exterminate-all-the-brutes.

Rice, Rachael, Marybeth Bonfiglio, and Carmen Spagnola. "Confronting Whiteness." *The Numinous Podcast.* 2022. https://crspagnola.podbean.com/?s=confronting%20whiteness.

Sayles, John, dir. *The Secret of Roan Inish* (film). 1994.

Scene on Radio. *Seeing White* (podcast). 2017, https://www.sceneonradio.org/seeing-white/.

Schrei, Joshua. "For the Intuitives (Part 1)." *The Emerald* (podcast). 2023. https://www.buzzsprout.com/317042/14012159-for-the-intuitives-part-1.

Schrei, Joshua. "For the Intuitives (Part 2)." *The Emerald* (podcast). 2023. https://www.buzzsprout.com/317042/14225907-for-the-intuitives-part-2.Short Bull, Jesse, and Laura Tomaselli, dirs. *Lakota Nation vs. United States* (film). 2023. https://www.lakotanationvsus.movie/.

Spell Songs Collective. "Selkie-boy." *The Lost Words: Spell Songs* (music album). Quercus Records. 2019.

The 1619 Project (docuseries). January 24, 2023. https://1619education.org.

The Light Ahead (podcast). Beloved Economies. https://www.belovedeconomies.org/about-the-light-ahead-podcast.

Witch (podcast). BBC Radio 4. 2023. https://www.bbc.co.uk/programmes/moo1mc4p.

Endnotes

1. "Money as Medicine, Wisdom as Healing," Liberated Capital, 2022, https://decolonizingwealth.com/liberated-capital/ and "Land. Race. Money. Spirit." Jubilee Justice, 2024, https://www.jubileejustice.org/.

2. Tyson Yunkaporta, *Sand Talk: How Indigenous Thinking Can Save the World* (New York: HarperCollins, 2021), 36.

3. Sherman Alexie, "The 'I' in BIPOC," *Persuasion*, June 2, 2023, https://www.persuasion.community/p/the-i-in-bipoc.

4. Gregory Younging, *Elements of Indigenous Style: A Guide for Writing by and about Indigenous Peoples* (Edmonton, AB: Brush Education, 2018), 64–65.

5. Robin Wall Kimmerer, *Braiding Sweetgrass: Indigenous Wisdom, Scientific Knowledge, and the Teachings of Plants* (Minneapolis, MN: Milkweed Editions, 2013), 3–10.

6. Amanda Robinson, "Turtle Island," *Canadian Encyclopedia*, 2018, https://www.thecanadianencyclopedia.ca/en/article/turtle-island.

7. Jürgen Kremer Werner and R. Jackson-Paton, *Ethnoautobiography: Stories and Practices for Unlearning Whiteness/Decolonization/Uncovering Ethnicities* (Dubuque, IA: Kendell Hunt, 2018), 102.

8. "Indigenous Peoples," World Bank, 2023, https://www.worldbank.org/en/topic/indigenouspeoples.

9. Sharon Paice MacLeod, *The Divine Feminine in Ancient Europe: Goddesses, Sacred Women, and the Origins of Western Culture* (Jefferson, NC: McFarland, 2014), 176.

10. Resmaa Menakem, "Bodies of Culture and Two Forms of Soul," *Embodied Anti-Racist Education* (blog), February 13, 2023, https://www.resmaa.com/somatic-learnings/bodies-of-culture-and-two-forms-of-soul.

11. Robin DiAngelo, *White Fragility: Why It's So Hard for White People to Talk about Racism* (Boston, MA: Beacon Press, 2018), xv.

12. "Learn about Labyrinths," *Labyrinth Society*, https://labyrinthsociety.org/about-labyrinths, accessed December 14, 2023.

13. Edgar Villanueva, *Decolonizing Wealth: Indigenous Wisdom to Heal Divides and Restore Balance*, 2d ed. (New York: Penguin Random House, 2018), 34.

14. "Building Trust before Truth: How Non-Indigenous Canadians Become Allies," *Animikii*, February 22, 2019, https://www.animikii.com/news/building-trust-before-truth-how-non-indigenous-canadians-become-allies.

15. Resmaa Menakem, "Resmaa: Teaching Embodied Anti-Racism," *Embodied Anti-Racism Education*, https://www.resmaa.com/, accessed December 14, 2023.

16. Resmaa Menakem, *My Grandmother's Hands: Racialized Trauma and the Pathway to Healing our Minds and Bodies* (Las Vegas, NV: Central Recovery Press, 2017), 199–213.

17. Resmaa Menakem, "Notice the Rage; Notice the Silence," *On Being with Krista Tippett* (podcast), April 15, 2021, https://onbeing.org/programs/resmaa-menakem-notice-the-rage-notice-the-silence/.

18. adrienne maree brown, *Emergent Strategy: Shaping Change, Changing Worlds* (Chico, CA: AK Press, 2017), 55.

19. Nell Irvin Painter, *The History of White People* (New York: W. W. Norton, 2010), 15.

20. "Made in America (*Seeing White*, Part 3) Transcript," *Scene on Radio*, 2017, www.sceneonradio.org/wp-content/uploads/2017/11/SeeingWhite_Part3Transcript.pdf.

21. "Sustainable Communities," Northern Arizona University, https://nau.edu/sustainable-communities/program/, accessed December 14, 2023.

22. "Fundraising from the Heart," *Soul of Money*, https://soulofmoney.org/fundraising-heart/, accessed December 14, 2023.

23. "Together, we are healing ourselves and the Earth," Pachamama Alliance, https://www.pachamama.org/, accessed December 14, 2023.

24. Lynne Twist, *The Soul of Money: Reclaiming the Wealth of our Inner Resources* (New York: W. W. Norton, 2003), 174–83.

25. Ibid., 179–80.

26. Douglas Stewart, *MacTalla: echoes of our ancestral past: more Scottish-Canadian poems* (self-pub., Hunter Rose Company, 1974), preface.

27. "Welcome to The Isle of Erraid," Findhorn Foundation, https://www.erraid.com/, accessed December 14, 2023.

28. "McFatter Name Study," *WikiTree*, https://www.wikitree.com/wiki/Space:McF-atter_Name_Study, accessed December 14, 2023.

29. Thank you to Sìne McKenna for pronunciation support.

30. Michael Newton, *Warriors of the Word: The World of the Scottish Highlanders* (Edinburgh, UK: Origin Birlinn, 2019), 307–8.

31. John MacInnes, "The Panegyric Code in Gaelic poetry," cited by Ruth Lee Martin in "Paradise Imagined: Songs of Scots Gaelic Migrants in Australia, 1850–1940," *Humanities Research* 19, no. 2 (2013): 17.

32. Elizabeth Beauchamp, *The Braes O' Balquhuidder: An Historical Guide to the District* (Glasgow, UK: Heatherbank Press, 1981), 20.

33. Margaret Bennett, "Balquhidder Revisited," in *Good People: New Fairylore Essays*, ed. Peter Narváez (Lexington, KY: University Press of Kentucky, 1991), 94–115.

34. Gratitude to Michael Newton for pronunciation support, November 2022.

35. Sharon Paice MacLeod, *Celtic Myth and Religion: A Study of Traditional Belief, with Newly Translated Prayers, Poems, and Songs* (Jefferson, NC: MacFarland & Company Inc., 2012), 35.

36. Ibid., 34–35.
37. Personal correspondence with Sharon Paice MacLeod, January 2023.
38. MacLeod, *Celtic Myth and Religions*, 38.
39. "16 Days of Activism," Nobel Women's Initiative, 2023, https://nobelwomens -initiative.org/.
40. DiAngelo, *White Fragility*, 131–38.
41. Megan Armstrong, "From Lynching to Central Park Karen: How White Women Weaponize White Womanhood," *Hasting Women's Law Journal* 32, no. 1 (Winter 2021): 27–50, https://repository.uclawsf.edu/cgi/viewcontent. cgi?article=1449&context=hwlj.
42. Adam Hochschild, *King Leopold's Ghost* (Boston: Mariner Books, Houghton Mifflin Harcourt, 1999).
43. "Nina Talks Cultivating Women's Leadership," *Bioneers*, https://bioneers.org/ nina-talks-cultivating-womens-leadership/, accessed December 14, 2023.
44. "Nurturing and celebrating the collective power of beloved families, communities, and Nung Ochuu Quiyo (Earth Mother)," Tewa Women United, https://tewawomenunited.org/, accessed December 20, 2023.
45. MacLeod, *Celtic Myth and Religion*, 21.
46. Max Dashú, *Witches and Pagans: Women in European Folk Religion, 700–1100* (Richmond, CA: Veleda Press, 2016), 24–26.
47. Mark Charles and Soong-Chan Rah, *Unsettling Truths: The Ongoing, Dehumanizing Legacy of the Doctrine of Discovery* (Downers Grove, IL: InterVarsity Press, 2019), 154.
48. Brian Calvert, "The myth of American progress," *High Country News*, August 20, 2018, https://www.hcn.org/issues/50.14/editors-note-the-myth-of -american-progress.
49. Thank you to Lyla June Johnston for pronunciation support, October 2022.
50. Gratitude to Lyla June Johnston for pronunciation support, October 2022.
51. MacLeod, *Celtic Myth and Religions*, 1.
52. Hilary Giovale, "Tribal Appropriations in Bellydance," *Gods&Radicals*, December 17, 2021, https://abeautifulresistance.org/site/2021/11/15/tribal -appropriations-in-bellydance.
53. Personal correspondence with Alexis Bunten, August 2022.
54. Sherri Mitchell, *Sacred Instructions: Indigenous Wisdom for Living Spirit -Based Change* (New York: Penguin Random House, 2018), 215–25.
55. Mitchell, *Sacred Instructions*, 225–26.
56. Cultural privacy is a concept I learned from a Bioneers Indigeneity webinar (https://bioneers.org/indigeneity-program/) with Cara Romero (Chemehuevi) and Alexis Bunten (Aleut/Yup'ik). I've used it here with their permission.
57. MacLeod, *Celtic Myth and Religion*, 16.
58. Ibid., 32–33.
59. Ibid., 158.
60. MacLeod, *Celtic Myth and Religion*, 71.
61. Ibid., 32.

62. Sharon Blackie, *If Women Rose Rooted: The Journey to Authenticity and Belonging* (Tewkesbury, UK: September Publishing, 2016), 361.

63. Brigit Katz, "Early Briton Had Dark Skin and Light Eyes, DNA Analysis Shows," *Smithsonian Magazine*, February 7, 2018, https://www.smithsonianmag.com/smart-news/ancient-briton-had-dark-skin-and-light-eyes-dna-analysis-shows-180968097/.

64. Alistair Moffat, *Before Scotland: The Story of Scotland Before History* (London: Thames & Hudson, 2005), 153–55.

65. Miranda J. Green, *Dictionary of Celtic Myth and Legend* (London: Thames & Hudson, 1992), 223–24.

66. Rune Hjarnø Rasmussen, *The Nordic Animist Year* (Denmark: Nordic Animism, 2019), 87.

67. Ibid., 57.

68. Dashú, *Witches and Pagans*, 33–43.

69. Silvana Rigobon, https://www.silvanarigobon.com/about, accessed December 14, 2023.

70. Painting by Flagstaff artist Emma Gardner (http://www.emmagardner.com/store/c1/Featured_Products.html, accessed December 20, 2023).

71. Green, *Dictionary of Celtic Myth and Legend*, 194.

72. W. Y. Evans-Wentz, *The Fairy Faith in Celtic Countries* (New Hyde Park, NY: University Books, 1966), 313.

73. James Baldwin, National Press Club speech, 1986, https://www.youtube.com/watch?v=7_1ZEYgtijk.

74. Ta-Nehisi Coates, *Between the World and Me* (New York: Spiegel & Grau, 2015), 7.

75. Ibid., 143.

76. "The People behind the Portal," *Our Black Ancestry*, 2023, https://ourblackancestry.com/about.php.

77. Frances Jarvie and Gordon Jarvie, *Scotland's Vikings* (Edinburgh, UK: National Museums Scotland, 2008).

78. Charles and Rah, *Unsettling Truths*, 176.

79. Louise Dunlap, *Inherited Silence: Listening to the Land, Healing the Colonizer Mind* (New York: New Village Press, 2022), 205.

80. brown, *Emergent Strategy*, 109–10.

81. Julian Goodare, *The European Witch-Hunt* (London and New York: Routledge Taylor & Francis Group, 2016), 29.

82. Goodare, "Torture at Mellingen, 1577," in *The European Witch-Hunt*, 204.

83. Thomas Robisheaux, "The German Witch Trials," in *The Oxford Handbook of Witchcraft in Early Modern Europe and Colonial America*, ed. Brian P. Levack (Oxford, UK: Oxford University Press, 2014), 187.

84. Personal correspondence with Pat McCabe, April 2023.

85. Jude Lally, *Brigit: Sun of Womanhood*, ed. Patricia Monaghan and Michael McDermott (Las Vegas, NV: Goddess Ink, 2013), 14.

86. Moffat, *Before Scotland*, 80.

87. Ibid., 76–77.

88. Ibid., 77–79.

89. Personal correspondence with Sharon Paice MacLeod, January 2023.
90. Thanks to Max Dashú for pronunciation support. Personal conversation, August 2022.
91. Personal correspondence with Sharon Paice MacLeod, January 2023.
92. Gearóid Ó Crualaoich, *The Book of the Cailleach: Stories of the Wise-Woman Healer* (Cork, Ireland: Cork University Press, 2003), 100.
93. Ibid., 115.
94. MacLeod, *Celtic Myth and Religion*, 9–10.
95. Green, *Dictionary of Celtic Myth and Legend*, 50.
96. MacLeod, *Celtic Myth and Religion*, 51.
97. Ibid., 62.
98. Thanks to Jude Lally for pronunciation support.
99. MacLeod, *Celtic Myth and Religion*, 59.
100. Gratitude to Jude Lally for teaching me this ritual, and to Sìne McKenna for pronunciation support.
101. Thanks to Jude Lally for pronunciation support.
102. Aurora Levins Morales, *Medicine Stories: Essays for Radicals* (Durham, NC: Duke University Press, 2019), 102.
103. Gratitude to Lyla June Johnston for pronunciation support, October 2022.
104. Ibid.
105. Gabriel Granillo, "80 years of Snowbowl: A history of the innovative and controversial ski resort," *Arizona Daily Sun*, February 22, 2018, https://azdailysun.com/flaglive/cover_story/80-years-of-snowbowl-a-history-of-the-innovative-and-controversial-ski-resort/article_c476a34c-20d5-55a3-86c8-25b00e3522fc.html.
106. Annette McGivney, "Skiing on a sacred mountain: Indigenous Americans stand against a resort's expansion," *The Guardian*, June 21, 2022, https://www.theguardian.com/world/2022/jun/19/indigenous-native-american-ski-resort-sewage-water-arizona.
107. "This Day in History: Kit Carson begins his campaign against Native Americans," *History*, July 7, 2020, https://www.history.com/this-day-in-history/kit-carsons-campaign-against-the-indians.
108. Mitchell, *Sacred Instructions*, 225.
109. "Treaties Still Matter: The Dakota Access Pipeline," *Native Knowledge 360°*, National Museum of the American Indian, Smithsonian Institution, 2018, https://americanindian.si.edu/nk360/plains-treaties/dapl.
110. "The Native American Prophecy of the Black Snake," *Bioneers*, 2016, https://bioneers.org/the-native-american-prophecy-of-the-black-snake/.
111. Kevin Abourezk, "Native American psychologists slam police tactics a year after Standing Rock," Indianz.com, October 30, 2017, https://www.indianz.com/News/2017/10/30/native-american-psychologists-slam-polic.asp.
112. Alleen Brown, "Medics describe how police sprayed Standing Rock demonstrators with tear gas and water cannons," *The Intercept*, November 21, 2016, https://theintercept.com/2016/11/21/medics-describe-how-police-sprayed-standing-rock-demonstrators-with-tear-gas-and-water-cannons/.

113. "Indigenous Activist Zip-Tied & Locked in Dog Kennel for 6 Hours for Protesting Dakota Access Pipeline," *Democracy Now!*, November 16, 2016, https://www.democracynow.org/2016/11/16/indigenous_activist_zip_tied_locked_in.

114. Sam Levin, "Dakota Access pipeline protests: UN group investigates human rights abuses," *The Guardian*, October 31, 2016, https://www.theguardian.com/us-news/2016/oct/31/dakota-access-pipeline-protest-investigation-human-rights-abuses.

115. "Justice Department Must Investigate Policing of Standing Rock Demonstrations" (press release), Amnesty International, November 30, 2016, https://www.amnestyusa.org/press-releases/justice-department-must-investigate-policing-of-standing-rock-demonstrations/.

116. "Standing Rock Special: Unlicensed #DAPL Guards Attacked Water Protectors with Dogs & Pepper Spray," *Democracy Now!*, November 24, 2016, https://www.democracynow.org/2016/11/24/standing_rock_special_unlicensed_dapl_guards.

117. Kristen Holmes and Gregory Wallace, "Biden Administration will not shut down Dakota Access Pipeline during environmental review, DOJ tells court," CNN, April 9, 2021, https://www.cnn.com/2021/04/09/politics/dakota-access-pipeline-biden-administration/index.html.

118. Don McFatter and Bobbie McFatter, *The McFatter Family Book* (self-published, 1998).

119. Lloyd Laing and Jenny Laing, *The Picts and the Scots* (Stroud, UK: Alan Sutton Publishing, Ltd, 1993), 7.

120. Sally M. Foster, *Picts, Gaels, and Scots* (London: BT Batsford, 2004), 9.

121. Moffat, *Before Scotland*, 286, 314.

122. MacLeod, *Celtic Myth and Religion*, 40.

123. Moffat, *Before Scotland*, 17–18, 222, 288, 312–13.

124. Laing, *The Picts and the Scots*, 119.

125. Newton, *Warriors of the Word: The World of the Scottish Highlanders*, 11.

126. Gordon Noble and Nicholas Evans, *The King in the North: The Pictish Realms of Fortriu and Ce* (Edinburgh: Birlinn, 2020), 13.

127. Foster, *Picts, Gaels and Scots*, 104.

128. Newton, *Warriors of the Word: The World of the Scottish Highlanders*, 14.

129. Ibid., 15.

130. Ibid., 16.

131. Ibid.

132. Ibid.

133. Ibid.

134. Ibid., 13.

135. Laing, *The Picts and the Scots*, 6.

136. Moffat, *Before Scotland*, 335.

137. Noble and Evans, *The King in the North*, 10–11.

138. Foster, *Picts, Gaels, and Scots*, 109–10.

139. Carlson-Manathara and Rowe, *Living in Indigenous Sovereignty*, 44.

140. Menakem, *My Grandmother's Hands*, 62.

141. Cutcha Risling Baldy, "Indigenous Voices for Decolonized Futures," *Bioneers*, 2020, https://bioneers.org/cutcha-risling-baldy-indigenous-voices -decolonized-futures-zstf2101/.

142. Eve Tuck and K. Wayne Yang, "Decolonization Is Not a Metaphor," *Decolonization: Indigeneity, Education & Society* 1, no. 1 (2012): 1–40, https:// clas.osu.edu/sites/clas.osu.edu/files/Tuck%20and%20Yang%202012%20 Decolonization%20is%20not%20a%20metaphor.pdf.

143. Michael Yellow Bird, Somatic Archaeology Panel, Bioneers National Conference, October 2019.

144. Waziyatawin and Michael Yellow Bird, eds., *For Indigenous Minds Only: A Decolonization Handbook* (Santa Fe, NM: Center for Advanced Research Press, 2012), 64.

145. Steven T. Newcomb, *Pagans in the Promised Land: Decoding the Doctrine of Christian Discovery* (Chicago, IL: Chicago Review Press, 2008), 37–58.

146. *Wellbriety Journey to Forgiveness* (film), https://www.youtube.com/ watch?v=RYU8CSxieaA, accessed December 20, 2023.

147. "The Native American Boarding School System," *New York Times*, August 30, 2023, https://www.nytimes.com/interactive/2023/08/30/us/native -american-boarding-schools.html.

148. "The Native American Boarding School System."

149. Suzette Brewer, "They were taken from their families as children. Can that trauma be healed?" *National Geographic*, April 11, 2023, https://www. nationalgeographic.com/premium/article/native-americans-separated -families-children-feature.

150. "Confronting Whiteness" (a conversation with Rachael Rice, Marybeth Bonfiglio, and Carmen Spagnola), *The Numinous Podcast*, 2022, https:// crspagnola.podbean.com/?s=confronting%20whiteness.

151. Brené Brown, "The Power of Vulnerability," TED Talk, 2010, https://www. ted.com/talks/brene_brown_the_power_of_vulnerability?language=en.

152. "Beyond the Mandate: Continuing the Conversation," report of the Maine Wabanaki-State Child Welfare Truth & Reconciliation Commission, 2015, https://d3n8a8pro7vhmx.cloudfront.net/mainewabanakireach/pages/17/ attachments/original/1468974047/TRC-Report-Expanded_July2015. pdf?1468974047.

153. Ibid.

154. Brewer, "They were taken from their families as children. Can that trauma be healed?"

155. Raoul Peck, dir., *Exterminate All the Brutes* (documentary miniseries), 2021, https://www.hbo.com/exterminate-all-the-brutes.

156. Mark Wolynn, "Inherited Family Trauma," Family Constellation Institute, 2023, https://markwolynn.com/.

157. Mark Wolynn, *It Didn't Start with You: How Inherited Family Trauma Shapes Who We Are and How to End the Cycle* (New York: Penguin Books, 2017), 52.

158. Thomas Gallagher, *Paddy's Lament: Ireland 1846–1847: Prelude to Hatred* (New York: Houghton Mifflin Harcourt, 1982), 290.

159. Nature Evolutionaries, https://www.natureevolutionaries.com/, accessed December 20, 2023.

160. "Blog by Ambassador Mulhall on Black '47: Ireland's Great Famine and its after-effects," Ireland Department of Foreign Affairs, December 3, 2018, https://www.dfa.ie/irish-embassy/usa/about-us/ambassador/ambassadors-blog/black47irelandsgreatfamineanditsafter-effects/.

161. Roxanne Dunbar-Ortiz, *An Indigenous Peoples' History of the United States* (Boston: Beacon Press, 2018), 38.

162. Alastair McIntosh, *Soil and Soul: People Versus Corporate Power* (London: Aurum Press, 2002), 54.

163. Dunbar-Ortiz, *An Indigenous Peoples' History of the United States*, 38.

164. T. M. Devine, *The Scottish Clearances: A History of the Dispossessed* (New York: Penguin Random House, 2018), 66–67.

165. Dunbar-Ortiz, *An Indigenous Peoples' History of the United States*, 53.

166. Gallagher, *Paddy's Lament*, 148.

167. Dale T. Knobel, "Celtic Exodus: The Famine Irish, Ethnic Stereotypes, and the Cultivation of American Radical Nationalism," *Radharc* 2 (November 2001): 3–25.

168. Christopher Klein, "When America Despised the Irish: The 19th Century's Refugee Crisis," *History*, June 1, 2022, https://www.history.com/news/when-america-despised-the-irish-the-19th-centurys-refugee-crisis.

169. "Experience Ireland Naturally," Lost Valley Uggool, 2021, https://www.thelostvalley.ie/.

170. "Country Life: Turlough Park, Castlebar, Co Mayo," National Museum of Ireland, 2023, https://www.museum.ie/en-IE/Museums/Country-Life/.

171. Debby Irving, *Waking Up White and Finding Myself in the Story of Race* (Cambridge, MA: Elephant Room Press, 2014), 174.

172. Lyla June Johnston, Facebook post, 10/7/18, used here with her permission.

173. Werner and Jackson-Paton, *Ethnoautobiography*, 432.

174. Villanueva, *Decolonizing Wealth*, 113–27.

175. Ibid., 121.

176. Arkan Lushwala, *The Time of the Black Jaguar: An Offering of Indigenous Wisdom for the Continuity of Life on Earth* (Ribera, NM: CreateScape, 2012), 73–74.

177. Stewart, *MacTalla*, 123.

178. Kristy Scott, "Twilight of the Gaels as ancient tongue falls silent," *The Guardian*, February 12, 2003, https://www.theguardian.com/uk/2003/feb/13/scotland.britishidentity.

179. McIntosh, *Soil and Soul*, 56.

180. Newton, *Warriors of the Word*, 32–33.

181. Ibid., 33.

182. McIntosh, *Soil and Soul*, 57.

183. Ross Noble, "The Cultural Impact of the Scottish Clearances," *BBC*, February 17, 2011, https://www.bbc.co.uk/history/british/civil_war_revolution/scotland_clearances_01.shtml.

184. Devine, *The Scottish Clearances*, 142.

185. Ibid., 57.

186. Alexander Carmichael, *Carmina Gadelica: Hymns and Incantations Collected in the Highlands and Islands of Scotland* (Edinburgh: Floris Books, 1992).
187. Thanks to Sharon Paice MacLeod for pronunciation.
188. Personal correspondence with Michael Newton, November 2022.
189. Carmichael, *Carmina Gadelica*, vol. 1, p. 83: Kindling prayer/prayer of protection from Sìne McKenna's class materials.
190. Thanks to Sìne McKenna for pronunciation.
191. Margaret Bennett, *Scottish Customs From the Cradle to the Grave* (Edinburgh: Polygon, 1992); and MacLeod, *Celtic Myth and Religion*, 163–65.
192. Gratitude to Sharon Paice MacLeod for help with pronunciation.
193. Carmichael, *Carmina Gadelica*, vol. 3, p. 231: Morning prayer/prayer of protection from Sìne McKenna's class materials.
194. Gratitude to Sìne McKenna for help with pronunciation.
195. Carmichael, *Carmina Gadelica*, vol. 3, p. 231: "*A' Ghealach Ur*" ("New Moon Prayer") from Sìne McKenna's class materials.
196. Ibid., vol. 3, p. 317: "*A' Ghrian*" ("Sun Blessing") from Sìne McKenna's class materials.
197. Ibid., vol. 3, p. 282: "*Durachd*" ("Good Wish") from Sìne McKenna's class materials.
198. "*Chì mi na Mórbheanna*" ("Mist-Covered Mountains"), from Sìne McKenna's class materials: "written in 1856 by John Cameron (Iain Camshroin), a native of Ballachulish."
199. Ibid.
200. Ibid., vol. 3, p. 317: "*A' Ghrian*" ("Sun Blessing") from Sìne McKenna's class materials.
201. "*Gabhaim Molta Bríghde*" ("Praising Brigid"). Sìne McKenna's class materials share:
This is an Irish Gaelic song; the words were written in 1902, in London, England, by Tomás Ó Flannghaile. Known in English as Thomas Flannery, he was born in Ballinrobe, County Mayo, in 1846.
202. Ancestral voices *céilidh*, spring 2022. (See: Hidden Glen Folk School website: https://www.hiddenglenfolk.org/).
203. Stewart, *Mactalla*, 119.
204. MacLeod, *Celtic Myth and Religion*, 29.
205. John Stokes and Kanawahienton, *Thanksgiving Address: Greetings to the Natural World, Ohén:ton Karihwatéhkwen—Words Before All Else* (Corrales, NM: Six Nations Indian Museum and the Tracking Project, 1993).
206. Carol Schaefer, *Grandmothers Counsel the World: Women Elders Offer Their Vision for Our Planet* (Boston, MA: Trumpeter, 2006), 118.
207. Sarah Pruitt, "Broken Treaties with Native American Tribes: Timeline," *History*, July 12, 2023, https://www.history.com/news/native-american -broken-treaties.
208. Ned Blackhawk, *The Rediscovery of America: Native Peoples and the Unmaking of U.S. History* (New Haven, CT: Yale University Press, 2023), 202, 226, 335, 337, 339, 361.
209. Antonio Kuilan, "Remembering Hatuey and the Tainos" (blog posting), http://antoniokuilan.com/blog/malta-hatuey-taino-history/.

210. Sarah Augustine, *The Land Is Not Empty: Following Jesus in Dismantling the Doctrine of Discovery* (Harrisonburg, VA: Herald Press, 2021), 87.

211. Himko Kaps Kap, "The Creator Has Been Heard" (blog posting), May 4, 2016, http://longmarchtorome.com/.

212. Nicholas V, "The Bull *Romanus Pontifex*," January 8, 1455 (English trans.), http://caid.ca/Bull_Romanus_Pontifex_1455.pdf.

213. David Potter, *Constantine the Emperor* (New York: Oxford University Press, 2013), 2–3.

214. Mitchell, *Sacred Instructions*, 141–42.

215. Charles and Rah, *Unsettling Truths*, 20.

216. Mitchell, *Sacred Instructions*, 43–44.

217. Ibid., 44.

218. "Doctrine of Discovery," Upstander Project, 2023, https://upstanderproject.org/learn/guides-and-resources/first-light/doctrine-of-discovery.

219. Newcomb, *Pagans in the Promised Land*, 37–58.

220. "Manifest Destiny," *History*, November 15, 2019, https://www.history.com/topics/westward-expansion/manifest-destiny.

221. Mitchell, *Sacred Instructions*, 41.

222. Stefano Pitrelli and Amanda Coletta, "Pope apologizes for 'deplorable conduct' of some Catholics in residential schools," *Washington Post*, April 1, 2022, https://www.washingtonpost.com/world/2022/04/01/canada-pope-francis-apologizes-residential-school/.

223. Phillip Pullella and Tim Johnson, "Pope apologizes for 'deplorable evil' of Canadian Indigenous schools," Reuters, July 26, 2022, https://www.reuters.com/world/americas/pope-apologizes-canada-evil-residential-indigenous-schools-2022-07-25/.

224. "Vatican rejects 'Doctrine of Discovery' justifying colonialism," Al Jazeera, March 30, 2023, https://www.aljazeera.com/news/2023/3/30/vatican-rejects-doctrine-of-discovery-justifying-colonialism.

225. Personal conversation with Basil Brave Heart, February 2021.

226. Personal conversation with Basil Brave Heart, March 2023.

227. David Treuer, *The Heartbeat of Wounded Knee: Native America from 1890 to the Present* (New York: Riverhead Books, 2019), 3.

228. Personal conversation with Basil Brave Heart, August 2022.

229. Mark Walker, "Tribes Want Medals Awarded for Wounded Knee Massacre Rescinded," *New York Times*, November 3, 2021, https://www.nytimes.com/2021/04/23/us/politics/tribes-medal-honor-wounded-knee.html.

230. Patrick Strickland, "Life on the Pine Ridge Native American reservation," Al Jazeera, November 2, 2016, https://www.aljazeera.com/features/2016/11/2/life-on-the-pine-ridge-native-american-reservation.

231. Personal conversation with Basil Brave Heart, March 2023.

232. Ibid.

233. Melissa K. Nelson, ed., *Original Instructions: Indigenous Teachings for a Sustainable Future* (Rochester, VT: Bear & Company, 2008), 2–3.

234. Personal conversation with Basil Brave Heart, March 2023.

235. Basil Brave Heart, *The Spiritual Journey of a Brave Heart* (self-published), 32.
236. Anita Sanchez, *The Four Sacred Gifts: Indigenous Wisdom for Modern Times* (New York: Enliven Books, 2017), 55.
237. Basil Brave Heart and Hilary Giovale, "129 years after Wounded Knee, is forgiveness possible?" *Rapid City Journal*, January 17, 2020, https:// rapidcityjournal.com/years-after-wounded-knee-is-forgiveness-possible/ article_b6786b35-86fd-52fd-b863-0d24516ccb9b.html.
238. Personal conversation, March 2020.
239. Martin Luther King Jr., *Strength to Love* (New York: Harper & Row, 1963), 25.
240. "A brief history of billionaire philanthropists and the people who hate them," *The Week*, January 9, 2016, https://theweek.com/articles/597963/brief-history -billionaire-philanthropists-people-who-hate.
241. Villanueva, *Decolonizing Wealth*, 80.
242. In conversation with the Rekindling Ancestral Memory Circle, February 2022.
243. Jess Rimington, and Joanna L. Cea, *Beloved Economies: Transforming How We Work* (Vancouver, BC: Page Two, 2022), 27.
244. Baldy, "Indigenous Voices for Decolonized Futures."
245. "Sacred Homelands Returned to Wiyot Tribe," Cultural Survival, July 16, 2004, https://www.culturalsurvival.org/news/sacred-homelands-returned -wiyot-tribe.
246. Baldy, "Indigenous Voices for Decolonized Futures."
247. Personal conversation, July 2023.
248. Harmeet Kaur, "Indigenous people across the US want their land back—and the movement is gaining momentum," CNN, November 26, 2020, https:// www.cnn.com/2020/11/25/us/indigenous-people-reclaiming-their-lands -trnd/index.html.
249. "Pum ekvnv resyicet owēs: Returning to our homelands," Ekvn-Yefolecv, 2021, https://www.ekvn-yefolecv.org/.
250. Lyla June Johnston and Joy De Vito, *Lifting Hearts off the Ground: Declaring Indigenous Rights in Poetry* (Winnipeg, MB: Mennonite Church Canada, 2007), 40.
251. "philanthropy," *Online Etymological Dictionary*, https://www.etymonline. com/search?q=philanthropy, accessed December 19, 2023.
252. Baldwin, National Press Club speech.
253. Whitney Planation, 2023, https://www.whitneyplantation.org/.
254. McFatter and McFatter, *The McFatter Family Book*.
255. "The Westport Fight, Part Two," as told to Webster Talma Crawford by Frank Taylor, transcribed by Leora White, 2008. Author's papers, Flagstaff, AZ.
256. brown, *Emergent Strategy*, 127.
257. "Slave Patrols: An Early Form of American Policing," National Law Enforcement Officers Memorial Fund, 2023, https://nleomf.org/slave-patrols -an-early-form-of-american-policing/.
258. "Racial Disparities Persist in Many U.S. Jails," Pew, May 16, 2023, https:// www.pewtrusts.org/en/research-and-analysis/issue-briefs/2023/05/racial -disparities-persist-in-many-us-jails.

259. "Criminal Justice Fact Sheet," NAACP, 2023, https://naacp.org/resources/criminal-justice-fact-sheet.

260. "Racial Economic Inequality: Racial Wealth Divide," Inequality.org, https://inequality.org/facts/racial-inequality/#racial-wealth-divide, accessed December 20, 2023.

261. Linda Villarosa, "Why America's Black Mothers and Babies Are in a Life-or-Death Crisis," *New York Times Magazine*, April 11, 2018, https://www.nytimes.com/2018/04/11/magazine/black-mothers-babies-death-maternal-mortality.html.

262. *The 1619 Project* docuseries, Episode 2, "Race" (https://1619education.org/builder/lesson/1619-project-docuseries-viewing-guide).

263. Jen Lemen Facebook post, June 3, 2020.

264. Zenobia Jeffries Warfield, "What Black America Is Owed," *Yes!* magazine, November 12, 2019, https://www.yesmagazine.org/issue/building-bridges/2019/11/12/the-collective-healing-that-is-owed/.

265. James Baldwin, *The Fire Next Time* (New York: Vintage International, 1993), 22.

266. "Native Americans Are 2.9% of U.S. Population but Receive 0.4% of Philanthropic Dollars," Native Americans in Philanthropy, November 17, 2020, https://nativephilanthropy.org/blog/2020/11/17/native-americans-are-2-of-u-s-population-but-receive-0-4-of-philanthropic-dollars.

267. Dylan Matthews, "The unbearable whiteness of American charities," *Vox*, July 1, 2019, https://www.vox.com/future-perfect/2019/7/1/18715513/philanthropy-people-of-color-racial-wealth-gap-edgar-villanueva.

268. John Kabia, "Fund 101: Intro to Participatory Grant-Making," Fund for Global Human Rights, February 25, 2021, https://globalhumanrights.org/commentary/fund-101-intro-to-participatory-grant-making/.

269. "Goal: $5 million," RSF Social Finance, 2023, https://rsfsocialfinance.org/.

270. Springboard to Opportunities, http://www.springboardto.org/, accessed December 20, 2023.

271. "Kindle Project Indigenous Women's Flow Fund," Kindle Project, 2023, http://kindleproject.org/iwff/.

272. "Kindle Project Indigenous Women's Flow Fund Storytelling Report, 2021–2022," Kindle Project, https://kindleproject.org/wp-content/uploads/2022/07/2022-IWFF-Storytelling-Report.pdf, accessed December 20, 2023.

273. Personal conversations with Basil Brave Heart.

274. "Who Gives Most to Charity?" Philanthropy Roundtable, 2023, https://www.philanthropyroundtable.org/resource/who-gives-most-to-charity/.

275. "Charitable Giving Statistics," National Philanthropic Trust, 2023, https://www.nptrust.org/philanthropic-resources/charitable-giving-statistics/.

276. Brave Heart, *The Spiritual Journey of a Brave Heart*.

277. Kimmerer, *Braiding Sweetgrass*, 104.

278. "Dé th' ann an Jam? | What's a Jam?" Gaels Jam 2024, https://www.novascotiagaelsjam.org/d%C3%A9-th-ann-whats-a-jam.

279. Personal correspondence with Brad Upton and Jeffrey Hotchkiss, September 2022.

280. Brave Heart and Giovale, "129 years after Wounded Knee, is forgiveness possible?"

281. Personal conversation with Basil Brave Heart, August 2022.

282. Personal conversation with Basil Brave Heart, October 2020.

283. John O'Donohue, "For Longing," in *To Bless the Space Between Us: A Book of Blessings* (New York: Convergent Books, 2008).

284. Lyla June Johnston, "The Vast and Beautiful World of Indigenous Europe," *White Awake* (blog), January 31, 2018, https://whiteawake.org/2018/01/31/the -vast-and-beautiful-world-of-indigenous-europe/.

285. Blackie, *If Women Rose Rooted*, 71–80.

286. Ibid., 78.

287. Dashú, *Witches and Pagans*, 1.

288. Ibid., 1–2.

289. Ibid., 5.

290. Dashú, *Witches and Pagans*, 8–9.

291. Thanks to Linda Bowen Busklein for pronunciation support, September 2020.

292. Thanks to Max Dashú for pronunciation support, August 2022.

293. Dashú, *Witches and Pagans*, 103–12.

294. Ibid., 116.

295. Thanks to Max Dashú for pronunciation support, April 2023.

296. Dashú, *Witches and Pagans*, 114–15.

297. Dashú, *Witches and Pagans*, 90.

298. Ibid., 74–75.

299. Mary McLaughlin, https://www.marymclaughlin.com/, accessed December 20, 2023.

300. Bennet, *Scottish Customs from the Cradle to the Grave*, 173–262.

301. Humans of Chauvet-Pont d'Arc, "Aurignacian cave art," *The Chauvet-Pont d'Arc Cave*, 2023, https://archeologie.culture.gouv.fr/chauvet/en/aurignacian -cave-art.

302. Genevieve Von Petzinger, *The First Signs: Unlocking the Mysteries of the World's Oldest Symbols* (New York: Atria Books, 2017), 71.

303. Humans of Chauvet-Pont d'Arc, "Aurignacian cave art."

304. Apela Colorado, *Woman Between the Worlds: A Call to Your Ancestral and Indigenous Wisdom* (Carlsbad, CA: Hay House, 2021), 232.

305. Werner Herzog, dir., *Cave of Forgotten Dreams* (film), 2010, https://www. imdb.com/title/tt1664894/.

306. Von Petzinger, *The First Signs*, 191–205.

307. Twist, *The Soul of Money*, 174–83.

308. Carolyn Hillyer, "Sago an Snìjo," *Winter Folded Everything Inside a Shawl of Feathers* (music album), Seventh Wave Music, 2018, https://www. seventhwavemusic.co.uk/product/winter-folded-everything-inside-a-shawl -of-feathers/.

309. Tema Okun, "White Supremacy Culture—Still Here" (blog), https://drive. google.com/file/d/1XR_7M_9qa64zZ00_JyFVTAjmjVU-uSz8/view.

310. Gerald Horne, *The Dawning of the Apocalypse: The Roots of Slavery, White Supremacy, Settler Colonialism, and Capitalism in the Long Sixteenth Century* (New York: Monthly Review Press, 2020); and Nell Irvin Painter, *The History of White People*.

311. David Dean, "Roots Deeper than Whiteness," *White Awake*, 2018, https://whiteawake.org/author/daviddean5/.

312. Dunbar-Ortiz, *An Indigenous Peoples History of the United States*, 34.

313. Dean, "Roots Deeper than Whiteness."

314. Dunbar-Ortiz, *An Indigenous Peoples History of the United States*, 35.

315. Ibid.

316. Barbara Ehrenreich, *Dancing in the Streets: A History of Collective Joy* (New York, NY: Metropolitan Books, 2006), 100–101.

317. Dean, "Roots Deeper than Whiteness."

318. Ehrenreich, *Dancing in the Streets*, 129–53.

319. Dunbar-Ortiz, *An Indigenous Peoples History of the United States*, 36.

320. Dean, "Roots Deeper than Whiteness."

321. *Seeing White* (podcast), *Scene on Radio*, 2017, https://www.sceneonradio.org/seeing-white/.

322. "Made in America (*Seeing White*, Part 3)" (transcript), *Seeing White* (podcast), *Scene on Radio*, 2017, http://www.sceneonradio.org/wp-content/uploads/2017/11/SeeingWhite_Part3Transcript.pdf.

323. Ibid.

324. "john a. powell," Othering and Belonging Institute, 2023, https://belonging.berkeley.edu/john-powell.

325. "From Othering to Belonging: The Circle of Human Concern," Episode 6, *Changing of the Gods* (docuseries), Startracks Productions, 2022.

326. "Made in America (*Seeing White*, Part 3)" (transcript), *Seeing White*.

327. Ibid.

328. "From Othering to Belonging: The Circle of Human Concern," Episode 6, *Changing of the Gods*.

329. Dean, "Roots Deeper than Whiteness."

330. "Why Class Matters," SURJ, https://surj.org/resources/why-class-matters/, accessed December 20, 2023.

331. Dean, "Roots Deeper than Whiteness."

332. American Swedish Institute, 2023, https://asimn.org/.

333. Dean, "Roots Deeper than Whiteness."

334. "From Othering to Belonging: The Circle of Human Concern," Episode 6, *Changing of the Gods*.

335. "A 'Forgotten History' of How the U.S. Government Segregated America," *Fresh Air*, NPR, May 3, 2017, https://www.npr.org/2017/05/03/526655831/a-forgotten-history-of-how-the-u-s-government-segregated-america.

336. Goodare, *The European Witch-Hunt*, 29.

337. Ibid., 125.

338. Ibid., 126.

339. Edward Bever, citing Stephen Wilson in "Popular Witch Beliefs and Magical Practices," *The Oxford Handbook of Witchcraft in Early Modern Europe and Colonial America*, ed. Brian P. Levack (Oxford, UK: Oxford University Press, 2014), 51.

340. Goodare, *The European Witch-Hunt*, 122.

341. Ibid., 130.

342. Ibid., 132.

343. Ibid., 136–42.
344. Ibid., 148.
345. Ibid., 107–8.
346. Ibid., 285.
347. Ibid., 169–70.
348. Ibid., 20.
349. Ibid., 25.
350. Ibid., 22.
351. Ibid., 63.
352. Ibid., 8.
353. Ibid., 89.
354. Ibid., 156.
355. Ibid., 159.
356. Ibid., 171–73.
357. Ibid., 27.
358. Ibid., 267.
359. Thomas Robisheaux, "The German Witch Trials," *Oxford Handbook of Witchcraft in Early Modern Europe and Colonial America*, ed. Brian P. Levack (Oxford, UK: Oxford University Press, 2014), 191.
360. Ibid.
361. Goodare, *The European Witch-Hunt*, 311.
362. Bever, "Popular Witch Beliefs and Magical Practices," 62.
363. Goodare, *The European Witch-Hunt*, 269.
364. Bever, "Popular Witch Beliefs and Magical Practices," 53.
365. Goodare, *The European Witch-Hunt*, 107–13.
366. Ibid., 208.
367. Ibid., 205.
368. Ibid., 305.
369. Ibid., 48–49.
370. Ibid., 207.
371. Ibid., 208–9.
372. Richard Kieckhefer, "Magic and Its Hazards in the Late Medieval West," in *The Oxford Handbook of Witchcraft in Early Modern Europe and Colonial America*, 31.
373. Hans Peter Broedel, "Fifteenth-Century Witch Beliefs," in *The Oxford Handbook of Witchcraft in Early Modern Europe and Colonial America*, 43.
374. Goodare, *The European Witch-Hunt*, 217–19.
375. Ibid., 261–62.
376. *The Light Ahead* (podcast), Beloved Economics, 2022, https://www.belovedeconomies.org/about-the-light-ahead-podcast.
377. Tewa Women United, 2023, https://tewawomenunited.org/.
378. "Woman Stands Shining (Pat McCabe)" (personal website), 2018, https://www.patmccabe.net/.
379. Jewels Wingfield, https://jewelswingfield.com/, accessed December 20, 2023.
380. Yeye Luisah Teish, https://www.yeyeluisahteish.com/, accessed December 30, 2023.
381. Kimmerer, *Braiding Sweetgrass*, 183.

382. Wisdom Weavers of the World, https://www.wisdomweavers.world/, accessed December 20, 2023.
383. Spearitwurx, 2022, https://www.spearitwurx.com/experience-sankofa -project1.html.
384. Leny Strobel, https://www.lenystrobel.com/, accessed December 20, 2023.
385. Personal conversation, October 2021.
386. Personal conversation, May 2023.
387. Kimmerer, *Braiding Sweetgrass*, 183.
388. Duolingo, https://www.duolingo.com/, accessed December 20, 2023.
389. "Recovering European Ancestral Memory," Good Relative, https://www. goodrelative.com/resources/project-two-6paba, accessed December 20, 2023.
390. Brigit's Garden, https://brigitsgarden.ie/, accessed December 20, 2023.
391. Trees for Life, https://treesforlife.org.uk/, accessed December 20, 2023.
392. Ancestral Fire, 2023, https://ancestralfire.ca/.
393. Mary McLaughlin, https://www.marymclaughlin.com/, accessed December 20, 2023.
394. Path of the Ancestral Mothers, https://www.pathoftheancestralmothers. com/, accessed December 20, 2023.
395. Menakem, "Bodies of Culture and Two Forms of Soul."
396. Menakem, *My Grandmother's Hands*, 261–74.
397. Robin Wall Kimmerer, "Corn Tastes Better on the Honor System," *Emergence Magazine*, n.d., https://emergencemagazine.org/feature/corn -tastes-better/, accessed December 20, 2023.
398. Tuck and Yang, "Decolonization Is Not a Metaphor."
399. Baldy, "Indigenous Voices for Decolonized Futures."
400. Twist, *The Soul of Money*, 174–83.
401. Please see Pachamama Alliance's website (https://pachamama.org/, accessed December 20, 2023) to learn about the organization's ongoing work to change the Dream of the Modern World.
402. Menakem, "Bodies of Culture and Two Forms of Soul."
403. Menakem, *My Grandmother's Hands*, 261–74.
404. "Indigenous Peoples at the United Nations," UN Department of Economic and Social Affairs, https://www.un.org/development/desa/ indigenouspeoples/about-us.html, accessed December 20, 2023.
405. Personal correspondence with Jim Enote, October 2023.
406. LANDBACK, https://landback.org/, accessed February 21, 2024.
407. Short Bull and Tomaselli, *Lakota Nation vs. United States*.
408. Panel discussion with Michael Yellow Bird, 2019 Bioneers National Conference.
409. Baldy, "Indigenous Voices for Decolonized Futures."
410. Nelson, *Original Instructions*, 3.
411. Ibid., 17.
412. "Restoring Women to Cultural Memory," *Suppressed Histories Archives*, https://www.suppressedhistories.net/, accessed December 20, 2023.

413. Leah Penniman, "The Gift of Ecological Humility," *Yes!* magazine, Spring 2020, https://www.yesmagazine.org/issue/ecological-civilization/2021/02/16/afro-indigenous-land-practices.
414. Daisy Purdy (Honor Water), personal conversation, July 2023.
415. National Coalition of Blacks for Reparations in America (N'COBRA), https://ncobra.org/, accessed December 20, 2023.
416. "What Are Reparations?" Movement for Black Lives (M4BL), https://m4bl.org/wp-content/uploads/2020/11/defining-reparations.pdf, accessed December 20, 2023.
417. Diana Raab, "What Is Spiritual Bypassing?" *Psychology Today*, January 23, 2019, https://www.psychologytoday.com/us/blog/the-empowerment-diary/201901-/what-is-spiritual-bypassing.
418. Amanda Robinson, "Turtle Island," in *The Canadian Encyclopedia*, https://www.thecanadianencyclopedia.ca/en/article/turtle-island, accessed December 20, 2023.
419. Calvin Terrell, https://www.calvinterrell.com/, accessed December 20, 2023.
420. Personal conversation, June 2019.
421. Báyò Akómoláfé, "Welcome Traveller," 2022, https://bayoakomolafe.net/.
422. Louise Boscacci, "Wit(h)nessing," *Environmental Humanities* 10, no. 1 (2018): 343–47, https://read.dukeupress.edu/environmental-humanities/article/10/1/343-/134705/Wit-h-nessing.

Index

Acknowledgments

GRATITUDE TO all the lands, Waters, and other-than-human teachers who have held me. Ancestors, thank you for my life, and for the assignments you gave that are still unfolding.

I give thanks for my family. My parents, Deborah and Larry McFatter, have generously offered me a lifetime of love that gives me the strength to do this work. My brother Gavin has taught me to live fully. My grandparents, Jeanne and Eric Witherspoon and Geri and Milton McFatter, lovingly guided me during their lives and continue to do so as ancestors. Uncle Don and Aunt Bobbi's research made healing possible. Uncle Cam re-membered. Nona opened the door. The Giovale family embodies generosity. The vision, clarity, and compassion of our youth give me hope.

Many relatives have included, taught, and inspired me, planting seeds that grew into this book. My heartfelt gratitude goes to Yeye Teish, the Brave Heart family and their Pine Ridge community, Louise Dunlap, Leny Strobel, Isoke Femi, Jürgen Kremer, Báyò Akómoláfé, Brenda Salgado, Eve Annecke, Pat McCabe, Lyla June Johnston, Alexis Bunten, Arkan Lushwala, Marilyn Baeza, Edgar Villanueva, Ilarion Merculieff, Wally Brim, Apela Colorado, Helen Corbett, Harrison Caicedo Santibanez, Lorenzo Izquierdo Arroyo, Kumu Sabra Kauka, Lys Kruiper, Mona Polacca, Susanne Swibold, Tricia Walker, Zhaparkul Raimbekov, Anita Sanchez, Prajna Horn, Daniel Garcia, Sandra Lubarsky and Marc Ford, Miquel Vasquez, Viki Blackgoat, Neema Namadamu and Danny Walters, Cora Maxx-Phillips, Chris Jocks, Indigenous Circle of Flagstaff, Rose Toehe and Steve Darden, the Marks family, the Nosie family, Daisy Purdy, *Diné Bina'nitin Dóó O'hoo'aah*, the Achuar community of Kapawi, Andean communities of Ccototaki and San Clemente, Narcisa Mashienta, Lynne Twist, Sara Vetter, Auggie, Nina Simons, Rachel Bagby, Ana Sophia Demetrakopoulos, Konda Mason, Tracy Apple, Van Jones, Calvin Terrell, Mireille Muhigwa and Jean-Robert Mweze, Tony Skrelunas, the extended family of Andy Dann and Linda Clah, Amy Enoka Alston, Marie Gladue and Arvin Badonie, Katherine Smith, Clarissa Durán and family, Angela Angel, Sarah Eisner, Taij Kumarie Moteelall, Vernon Masayesva, Anita Poleahla, Reyna Cárdenas Carrasco and Alyosha Sándigo, Somana Tootsie, Morgan Curtis, Will Scott, Justine Epstein, Oona Coy, Elspeth Gilmore, Lotte Lieb Dula, Eleanor Hancock, David Dean, Kristin Mejia, Darcy Ottey, Annette McGivney, Visolela Namises, Sunny Dooley, Dinnawhan White, Ati Quigua, Sai Muktiswarimayi Kanniah, María Huenuñir, Ana Luisa Solis Gil, Dianna Sue WhiteDove Uqualla, Bucky Preston, Sìne McKenna, Tony Bond, Isha Braun, Jewels Wingfield, Michael Newton, Manari Kaji Ushigua Santi, Louise Benally, Jude Lally, Sharon Paice MacLeod, Max Dashú, Amanda Coslor, Mary McLaughlin, Timothy McLaughlin and Madi Sato, Mama Scrap's Family, Shaka Jamal, Tanya Henderson, Sarah Crowell, Toby Herzlich, Maija West, Megan White, Rulan Tangen, Robin DiAngelo, Dana Lanza, Cara Romero, Mizan Alkebulan-Abakah and Sizwe Andrews-Abakah, Ed Kabotie, Bill Edwards, Kathy Sanchez, Beverly Billie, the Ekvn-Yefolecv community, Shawn Mulford, Bacilio Zea Sanchez, Moran Henn, Andrea Hartley, Naima Penniman, Alixa García, Eliza Kenyon, Jim Enote, the Isaac family, Sharon Leslie Morgan, Thomas DeWolf, Stacey Jensen, Jess Rimington, Lise Weil, Teo Grossman, Marian and Susanna Moore, Wael Garas and Jamie Beachy, Sheena Brown, Vhee, the Decolonizing Wealth Healing Practitioners Collective, David Alexander, Eriel Tchekwie Deranger, Carole Monture, those who made bundles for the Ceremony of Repentance and Forgiveness, and the youth of Öomawki Peak. Thank you for being who you are.

Brilliant people served as readers for all or parts of the manuscript in its various phases, and I'm profoundly grateful. Thank you Lyla June Johnston, Yeye Luisah Teish, Basil Brave Heart, Rachel Bagby (who first suggested the title!), Calvin Terrell, Alexis Bunten,

Leny Strobel, Michael Yellow Bird, Max Dashú, Oona Coy, Connie Batten, Arianne Shaffer, Sadaf Rassoul Cameron, Kayla Leduc, Edgar Villanueva, Amber Starks, Konda Mason, Tia Oros Peters, Rebecca Roberts-Wolfe, Erin Caitlin Sweeney, Ilarion Merculieff, Marie Gladue, Viki Blackgoat, Darrell and Makaius Marks, Clarissa Durán, Aisha Nyandoro, Pat McCabe, Kathy Sanchez, Sunny Dooley, Margaret Wrinkle, Arkan Lushwala, Rose Toehe and Steve Darden, Rosalinda Namises, Dinnawhan White, Daisy Purdy, Elyshia Holliday, Jamie Beachy, Eliza Kenyon, Mary McLaughlin, Jen Lemen, Sharon Paice MacLeod, Michael Newton, Carolyn Hillyer, Shaka Jamal, Silvana Rigobon, Brad Upton, Jeffrey Hotchkiss, Ana Sophia Demetrakopoulos, Jewels Wingfield, Jude Lally, Sìne McKenna, Louise Dunlap, Madi Sato, Visolela Namises, Annette McGivney, Beatrice Woody, and Pete Giovale. Your perspectives have brought valuable nuances to this book. Any mistakes are my own.

Patricia Francisco's encouraging presence and astute suggestions helped me get out of the way. Thank you, Patricia, for offering the nudges and guidance I needed to coax this book into its final form.

Dede Cummings and Green Writers Press, thank you for believing in this book and for your support with bringing it into being. I deeply appreciate Rose Alexandre-Leach's nuanced editing and her kind, steadfast presence throughout the editing process. Becky Tsadik's copyediting, including her insights and attention to detail, were welcome gifts that improved the manuscript. I am profoundly grateful to Michael Fleming for his work on the bibliography, footnotes, and endnotes.

Thank you to the entire team at MindBuck Media, including Jessie Glenn, Emily Keough, Hannah Richards, and Deb Jayne, for your thorough, professional support and guidance. I'm delighted by the fruitful collaboration between illustrator Ashley Matelski and cover designer Bryn Kristi. I'm indebted to Melissa Ousley and Sarah Currin of Indigo Editing for their excellent proofreading, Johnna VanHoose Dinse for creating a thorough index, and Vinnie Kinsella for perfecting the design of these pages.

Gratitude to Elyshia Holliday and the Organization of Nature Evolutionaries for co-dreaming, co-facilitating, and hosting the

Rekindling Ancestral Memory Circles and Tending Ancestral Memory Circles. I honor all those who have joined us in making these circles possible. Each of you have helped me understand our work more deeply. Thank you for trusting us with your stories. Rebecca Roberts-Wolfe, Lathram Berry, and Lauren Valle, thank you for being dedicated partners and good friends in this work.

I appreciate the Liberated Capital community taking part in the "Good Relative" series. You've shown me how coming together to share our truths, stories, and struggles can begin transforming money into medicine. I give thanks for the many networks throughout the country who are waking up and joining forces to acknowledge the truths of our past, make personal and institutional reparations, and move toward healthy futures.

Brothers, sisters, and siblings who have walked beside me in friendship and prayer throughout the years, you are always in my heart.

Thank you to our Flagstaff community for keeping us afloat during the challenges of 2024, and to Rico the rescue dog (who rescued us).

With Pete's support, insight, kindness, steadfastness, and generosity, this journey of becoming a good relative is possible. I love you.

Credits

Poems by adrienne maree brown
reprinted with permission of the author.
Poem by Lyla June Johnston
reprinted with permission of the author.
Poems by Douglas Stewart
reprinted posthumously, with gratitude.
Excerpt from *Thanksgiving Address/Ohén:ton
Karihwatéhkwen* reprinted with permission
of Dave Fadden, Six Nations Iroquois Cultural Center.
"Sago an Snîjo" reprinted with permission
of the author, Carolyn Hillyer.
The author's friends and relations are named
with their permission.
Thank You All/Tapadh Leibh

About the Author

HILARY GIOVALE lives with her family next to a sacred mountain on Hopi, Havasupai, Diné, Hualapai, Apache, Yavapai, Paiute, and Pueblo land. She experiences the mountain as a loving grandmother, generous friend, and wise teacher. As a devoted reparationist, her work includes listening, writing, community organizing, facilitation, and philanthropy. Hilary is dedicated to divesting from whiteness and settler colonialism. She delights in wildflowers, stories, dark chocolate, starry nights, beeswax candles, Water, friendship, dancing, and walking in the woods with her dog, Rico.